Thinking Orthodox
in Modern Russia

Thinking Orthodox in Modern Russia

Culture, History, Context

Edited by
Patrick Lally Michelson
and
Judith Deutsch Kornblatt

The University of Wisconsin Press

Publication of this book has been made possible, in part, through support from Indiana University's Grant-in-Aid of Research & Creative Activity Program and from the Graduate School of the University of Wisconsin–Madison.

The University of Wisconsin Press
1930 Monroe Street, 3rd Floor
Madison, Wisconsin 53711-2059
uwpress.wisc.edu

3 Henrietta Street
London WC2E 8LU, England
eurospanbookstore.com

Copyright © 2014
The Board of Regents of the University of Wisconsin System
All rights reserved. No part of this publication may be reproduced, stored in a retrieval system, or transmitted, in any format or by any means, digital, electronic, mechanical, photocopying, recording, or otherwise, or conveyed via the Internet or a website without written permission of the University of Wisconsin Press, except in the case of brief quotations embedded in critical articles and reviews.

Library of Congress Cataloging-in-Publication Data

Thinking Orthodox in modern Russia : culture, history, context / edited by Patrick Lally Michelson and Judith Deutsch Kornblatt.
pages   cm
Includes bibliographical references and index.
ISBN 978-0-299-29894-4 (pbk. : alk. paper) — ISBN 978-0-299-29893-7 (e-book)
1. Russkaia pravoslavnaia tserkov'—Influence. 2. Religion and civil society—Russia—History. 3. Religion and civil society—Soviet Union—History. 4. Christianity and culture—Russia—History. 5. Christianity and culture—Soviet Union—History. 6. Russia—Church history. I. Michelson, Patrick Lally, editor of compilation. II. Kornblatt, Judith Deutsch, editor of compilation.
BR932.T47   2014
306.6′81947—dc23
2013027991

Dedicated to
OLIVER SMITH
IN MEMORIAM

Contents

Preface ix

Introduction 3
PATRICK LALLY MICHELSON *and*
JUDITH DEUTSCH KORNBLATT

PART I
THINKING ORTHODOX IN THE CHURCH

1 Orthodoxy and Enlightenment in Catherinian Russia:
   The Tsarevich Dimitrii Sermons of Metropolitan Platon 43
   ELISE KIMERLING WIRTSCHAFTER

2 Theology on the Ground: Dmitrii Bogoliubov, the
   Orthodox Anti-Sectarian Mission, and the Russian Soul 64
   HEATHER J. COLEMAN

3 Archbishop Nikon (Rozhdestvenskii) and Pavel Florenskii on
   Spiritual Experience, Theology, and the Name-Glorifiers Dispute 85
   SCOTT M. KENWORTHY

PART II
THINKING ORTHODOX IN THE ACADEMY

4 V. D. Kudriavtsev-Platonov and the Making of Russian
   Orthodox Theism 111
   SEAN GILLEN

5 The Struggle for the Sacred: Russian Orthodox Thinking
   about Miracles in a Modern Age   131
   VERA SHEVZOV

6 "The Light of the Truth": Russia's Two Enlightenments, with
   Reference to Pavel Florenskii   151
   RUTH COATES

PART III
THINKING ORTHODOX IN SOCIETY AND CULTURE

7 Written Confession and Religious Thought in Early
   Nineteenth-Century Russia   177
   NADIESZDA KIZENKO

8 Anagogical Exegesis: The Theological Roots of Russian
   Hermeneutics   196
   OLIVER SMITH

9 Kant and the Kingdom of Ends in Russian Religious Thought
   (Vladimir Solov'ev)   215
   RANDALL A. POOLE

10 Religious Thought and Russian Liberal Institutions:
   The Case of Pavel Novgorodtsev   235
   VANESSA RAMPTON

11 What Is Beauty? Pasternak's Adaptations of Russian
   Religious Thought   253
   MARTHA M. F. KELLY

   Afterword   275
   PAUL VALLIERE

   Contributors   285

   Index   289

Preface

The idea for this volume arose during a conversation between the two editors, one of whom was looking toward the end of her career, the other just beginning his. Both had wondered independently what had become—nearly two decades hence—of the ambition to found a new field of study within the American academy as stated in the landmark volume *Russian Religious Thought* (University of Wisconsin Press, 1996). From this fortuitous discussion grew a round-table discussion at the 2010 meeting of the Association for Slavic, East European, and Eurasian Studies (ASEEES), followed by an international symposium in the spring of 2011 in Madison, Wisconsin, and the draft of a volume of collected essays, all under the working title of *Rethinking Russian Religious Thought*. The success of those endeavors, now published under the title *Thinking Orthodox in Modern Russia: Culture, History, Context*, proves that the original volume's aspirations were indeed broadly achieved. Within the pages of the new volume, we discover a rich discussion about the diverse ways in which Russian Orthodoxy is studied by English-language scholars, many of whom acknowledge that their first exposure to the area came from a reading of *Russian Religious Thought*. That the contributors were trained in a variety of disciplines, from history to literature to philosophy to religious studies, testifies to the interdisciplinary nature of the field that was posited by the original volume. And that so many of the scholars who provide chapters are in the beginning of their careers points to a bright future for the study of the many ways in which one might "think Orthodox in modern Russia."

Together, the editors of this volume would like to thank the Alice D. Mortenson/Michael B. Petrovich Chair Fund, the Worldwide Universities Network (WUN), the George L. Mosse Program in History, the Association for the Study of Eastern Christian History and Culture (ASEC), the Wisconsin

Alumni Research Foundation (WARF), the Graduate School of the University of Wisconsin–Madison, and Indiana University for providing financial and institutional support. Judith Deutsch Kornblatt further acknowledges the scores of teachers and students without whom her long career would not have been possible. In particular, she would like to single out Professor Emeritus Richard Gustafson, with whom she edited the original volume of *Russian Religious Thought*. His teaching, his mentorship, his collegiality, and his friendship have meant the world to her. The late Robert Maguire stepped in as advisor for a dissertation on the Cossacks when Judith's attempt to study Russian religious thought during the Brezhnev era proved just about impossible, and ever maintained a faith in her return to the religious writing of the poet and philosopher Vladimir Solov'ev, along with a readiness to engage with her in spiritual debate. Robert Belknap, who served as advisor and reader along with Gustafson and Maguire, pushed Judith in new directions when, having learned of her interest in Russian Orthodoxy, he suggested she spend some time sitting in the courtyard of Saint John the Divine, near Columbia University, and contemplate the similarities and differences of the various Christian denominations. The late Father John Meyendorff welcomed her into classes at Saint Vladimir's Seminary outside of New York City, and introduced her to the history of Orthodoxy. At the same time, Paul Valliere helped launch Judith on her journey in the world of Orthodoxy, accompanied her on it all along the way, and kindly agreed to contribute his wisdom in the afterword of this volume. Thanks are also due to David Bethea, who mentored Judith within the hallowed walls of Van Hise Hall and only later in their intellectual collaboration came to see the joy of studying Russian religious thought. Equally important has been the career-long mentorship of Caryl Emerson, who never fails to see the value in any thought, no matter how inchoate. These individuals, along with all other colleagues, current and past, have helped shape Judith into the scholar she has become.

Although too numerous to name, Judith cannot fail to thank all the self-proclaimed members of the "Russian religious mafia" that gathered at national and international conferences to discuss the intricacies of a field that was only beginning in the United States. Thank you all for your role in the establishment of this endeavor. She would also like to thank the professionals at the University of Wisconsin Press, and especially Gwen Walker, who made the transition from graduate student to editor with amazing grace and intelligence. Patrick Michelson also traveled the road from (undergraduate) student to colleague in a way that can only gratify teachers everywhere. This volume would not exist if it were not for his vast intelligence, his wise judgment, and his good humor.

Neither he nor Judith, however, would have made it to this point without a phalanx of clear-sighted project assistants, especially those during the past two years: Nicholas Rampton, Tommy Tabatowski, Jose Vergara, Melissa Miller, and Lisa Woodson. Any errors that remain must have crept back in after their careful readings were completed.

Enormous thanks are owed to Susan Bernstein for her sensible counsel, clever repartee, informed intellect, and stress relief during countless walks, jogs, and bike rides. Similarly, Judith's psyche would not have remained intact without regular "whine" dates over wine with Jean Hennessey and David Danaher.

Finally, to the three closest individuals who have and will continue to support Judith on her next journeys in life: her dear husband, Marc, son, Jacob, and daughter, Louisa Kornblatt.

Patrick Lally Michelson's acknowledgements in many ways constitute a genealogy of this project. Many of the ideas and arguments made in the introduction, as well as the conception of the book itself, had their origin in graduate seminars that he took at the University of Wisconsin with Larry Dickey, Judith Kornblatt, and David McDonald, the last of whom was the first to provide financial support for this volume under the auspices of the Alice D. Mortenson/Michael B. Petrovich Chair Fund. It is to these three remarkable scholars that Patrick owes much of his academic career. Judith in particular deserves individual recognition, as it was her hard work, sustained enthusiasm, and diplomatic ways that helped to realize this book. Patrick also would like to thank Eric Carlsson, Fran Hirsch, and David Sorkin, who contributed in various ways to his education and, in conjunction with Ulrich Rosenhagen, participated as discussants in the volume's 2011 symposium. Scott Kenworthy and Nadia Kizenko greatly helped to promote this project, not least by their valuable contributions, along with Martha Kelly's, to a lively round-table discussion at the 2010 meeting of ASEEES. Several of the participants in *Thinking Orthodox in Modern Russia* were introduced to Patrick by Ruth Coates and Randall Poole, themselves contributors to this book. Randall also acted as a friendly foil to many of Patrick's historicist concerns, while Ruth and her family kindly opened their home to Patrick and his family during a summer holiday in England. Vera Shevzov has provided constant moral support for this project, as well as for Patrick's interest in recovering and contextualizing Russian Orthodox thought. If most of this project was imagined and developed at the University of Wisconsin, then a substantial portion of it was finalized at Indiana University's wonderful Department of Religious Studies, where scholarship and collegiality are equally valued. Special gratitude is reserved for Sean

M. J. Gillen, who early and often was Patrick's coconspirator in attempts to rethink Russian religious thought. Yet the greatest thanks that Patrick can give is to Peter and Martha. It is their laughter and love that matter most.

In conclusion, and on behalf of all of the contributors, the editors dedicate this volume to Oliver Smith, who lost his life among the treacherous cliffs of the Isle of Skye only days after submitting the final draft of his chapter. We are all the lesser for the loss of this excellent, vibrant scholar and friend. May his family find peace in his love for them.

Thinking Orthodox
in Modern Russia

Introduction

PATRICK LALLY MICHELSON *and*
JUDITH DEUTSCH KORNBLATT

It would be of little exaggeration to say that much of Russian discourse in the imperial and early émigré periods (circa 1721–1927) was informed by the lexicon, liturgy, and theology of Russian Orthodoxy. The Church's extensive educational system, whatever its many failings, trained thousands of clergy and hundreds of theologians who spoke to the faithful in various Russian Orthodox idioms that were then refracted in the conversations and cultural production of educated society (*obrazovannoe obshchestvo*). As members of that society began to engage contemporary European thought, they often did so from a self-consciously Orthodox perspective cultivated at home, learned at church, and articulated in Orthodox print culture. Differences between the Russian people (*narod*) and the peoples of Europe and Asia were frequently cast as spiritual distinctions between true believers (*pravoslavnye*) and apostates or pagans, especially during periods of military conflict, which in turn were often experienced through an Orthodox matrix of biblical narrative, Church history, and liturgical commemoration. Imperial decrees, like the Emancipation Manifesto of 1861, were invested with the "Grace of God," structured by the necessity of "Divine Providence," and guided by "Divine assistance." Sacraments of the Church, such as baptism and confession, generated specific notions of belonging among Orthodox believers and helped to shape their individual and collective psychologies. Orthodox liturgy, hesychastic piety, and monastic eldership (*starchestvo*) were imagined by some of Russia's most important authors, including N. V. Gogol' and F. M. Dostoevsky, to engender a type of religious disposition that could heal the fractured mind in an age thought to be marked by anomie. Even schemes for cultivating loyal, morally upright imperial citizens were commonly located in Scripture and writings of the Church Fathers. And many educated Russians turned to their faith as they sought to address a variety of problems specific to their historical experiences and consciousness, such as Russian backwardness and how to overcome it; educated society's cultural alienation from the *narod*; the antagonism between state and society, culminating in the revolutionary upheavals in 1905 and 1917; and the dilemma of demarcating inviolable spheres of personal and communal sanctity in a legal culture organized around the prerogatives of an interventionist, absolutist state. It is this Orthodox frame of reference, and the various thought-worlds generated by it, that contributors to this volume explore in the pages below. The result is the recovery of a history and culture that is deeply indebted to the tenets of Russian Orthodoxy.

The Orthodox Turn in Russian Religious Thought

One of the most significant historiographical developments to have occurred in the study of modern Russian history and culture since the collapse of the Soviet Union might just be the "religious turn." In the past ten to fifteen years, scholars have produced an impressive body of research that challenges many long-standing assumptions about the Russian Orthodox Church and the religious practices of its parishioners. English-language historians in particular have played an important role in demonstrating the dynamism and plasticity of Russia's dominant confession during the nineteenth and early twentieth centuries. No longer seen as some backward, exotic faith confined to formal ritual and inchoate mysticism, Russian Orthodoxy has been recovered for what it was: a multivalent, heterodox religion that, like its counterparts across the European Continent, helped to inform identity, modes of behavior, social and, later, political activism, even imagination and habitus. For their part, Russian-language scholars have performed a similar feat in the study of the Russian Orthodox Church. We now understand more fully why the Synodal Church (1721–1917), once portrayed as a static, monolithic body beholden to autocracy, was actually not a "handmaiden of the state" or an exclusively reactionary institution. It was populated by a host of distinct parties and vigorous personalities; shaped by an array of competing traditions and ideologies; driven by its own confessional concerns and institutional prerogatives; and marked by the same competing forces that make up any hierarchical organization dispersed across a vast cultural geography. With this newfound emphasis on context and contingency, it is almost impossible today to speak of Russian Orthodoxy in the singular. Rather, we are confronted by varieties of Russian Orthodoxy, a diversity of practice and institution shaped by time, place, culture, and personality that accurately reflects the historical reality of that confession.[1]

Nearly a decade before this shift toward the study of Russian Orthodoxy and its institutions, scholars of Russian literature and intellectual history began to focus their attention on another aspect of religion in modern Russia, namely the religious philosophy of the late nineteenth and early twentieth centuries. One of the earliest developments in this regard in post-Soviet, English-language scholarship was the international Conference on Russian Religious Thought hosted by the University of Wisconsin in 1993.[2] That event brought together more than thirty historians, Slavists, theologians, and philosophers to discuss the spiritual categories, philosophical systems, literary heritages, and cultural influences of V. S. Solov'ev, S. N. Bulgakov, N. F. Fedorov, S. L. Frank, and P. A. Florenskii. The principal result of that conference was the publication of *Russian Religious Thought*, coedited by Judith Kornblatt and Richard Gustafson, in 1996.[3] That volume, which in many ways constitutes the foundation of and impetus behind this collection of essays, broadly applied a textual hermeneutics to the study of religious ideas and thinkers. The intent of *Russian Religious Thought* and similar studies that followed was to analyze representative texts for an array of largely extra-historical purposes: to illuminate how Russian religious philosophy engaged and can still address epistemological and ontological questions; to familiarize non-specialists with the seemingly alien content of Russia's religious culture; to put Russian religious thinkers in cross-confessional dialogue with some of the leading theologians of Western Christendom, while simultaneously complicating the basic categories of Protestant and Catholic thought; to demonstrate the universality of Russian religious terminology in the philosophical quest to express the absolute; and to identify currents in Russian thought that might help construct a usable past for contemporary Russia.[4]

Despite this enthusiasm for Russian religious thought in the post-Soviet era, which has seen the publication of important monographs, articles, source collections, and English-language translations,[5] its impact on broader trends in the study of Russian history and culture has been minimal. This is especially true in regards to the turn in scholarship toward religious practice and institutions, which has almost entirely, and sometimes explicitly, disregarded Russian Orthodox theology, as well as the broader subject of Russian religious thought, as retrograde, elitist, or well-worn.[6] As such, our knowledge of how the theological tenets of Russian Orthodoxy informed the discursive patterns and ideological structures of Russian literary culture and intellectual history has not kept pace with advancements in studies about lived Orthodoxy or the Russian Church.[7]

One possible explanation for the historiographical disconnect between the religious turn and the study of religious thought is very likely methodological in nature. As noted above, the most common method used to examine Russian religious thought is one that privileges text over context as the principal lens through which to investigate the meaning of an utterance. This particular mode of analysis, which generally eschews chronology, elides paradox, and treats temporal sources as "atemporal resources,"[8] has long put the study of religious ideas at odds with historicist methods and goals.[9] In addition, scholars of Russian religious thought, with a few notable exceptions like Paul Valliere and L. E. Shaposhnikov,[10] have often examined their subject matter either in isolation from or in opposition to Russian Orthodox theology. In fact, lay religious thought is often conceptualized as a necessary and welcome "alternative" to the ecclesiastical thought of the Synodal Church, an alternative that is believed to have developed not only out of sociological, institutional, and cultural distinctions between laity and clergy but also out of the historical trajectory of the Church itself.[11] Even when churchmen like Archimandrite Feodor (Bukharev), Pavel Florenskii, or the later Sergei Bulgakov appear in the story, they are frequently chosen because their idiosyncratic and/or non-doctrinal statements about theology can be read as progressive or liberal solutions to the problem of Orthodox fundamentalism. Because of these differences in method, source base, and historiography, studies about Russian religious thought, lived Orthodoxy, and the Russian Church share little common ground other than their general innocence about Russian Orthodox theology.[12]

This volume bridges the historiographical and methodological gaps between the study of Russian religious thought and that of Russian Orthodoxy by examining those terms and concepts articulated by Orthodox laity and clergy who drew upon or reconfigured some aspect of their confession to address social, cultural, and political dilemmas specific to their time and place. In other words, *Thinking Orthodox in Modern Russia* understands context as a central factor in any attempt to understand and explicate the content of Russian religious thought, while still privileging thought as a valuable category through which to examine Russian history and culture. In addition, the volume's editors have expanded the conventional chronological framework of Russian religious thought, which is usually demarcated by the dates associated with what Nicolas Zernov called "the Russian religious renaissance" (circa 1880–1930),[13] so as to incorporate examples of Orthodox "thinking" from the late eighteenth and first half of the nineteenth century that both stand on their own as unique speech acts and help to inform the content and contours of religious thought at the fin de siècle.[14] Just as important, this volume broadens the definition of Russian religious thought to include what might best be called ecclesiastical Orthodox thought, a term that is meant to capture the institutional location, professional training, and confessional orientation of such religious thinkers. Religious thought in Russia was not just a secular or idiosyncratic Orthodox event that can be neatly separated from homiletic and theological articulations in the Church. The discursive boundary between lay religious thinkers and ecclesiastical Orthodox thinkers, who are sometimes referred to in this volume as Church intellectuals or Church intelligentsia, was porous, as partly evidenced by the public nature of such utterances in print journalism, published sermons, scholarship, and academic research projects.

The results of this shift toward contextual analysis, as well as the expansion of chronology and content, are manifold. This volume demonstrates that Russian religious thought was relevant to and mainly formulated in response to contemporary issues and problems. As such, it helps to place the study of Russian religious thought in conversation with some of the major themes in the study of religious practices and institutions in late imperial Russia, namely the vitality of religious consciousness in a supposedly secular age and the formation of government policy in a multiconfessional empire.[15] In addition, it opens new vistas for a reevaluation of Russian cultural production that can contribute to the growing interest in the ways in which Orthodox Christianity shaped Russian literature, literary criticism, cultural semiotics, and dissident discourse well into the Soviet and post-Soviet eras.[16] By broadening the category of Russian religious thought to include writings by clergy and professionally trained theologians, and by keeping those texts in their operative contexts, this volume also helps to situate the study of Russian religious thought in historiographical developments in European intellectual history, especially the move to study modern Protestant and Catholic theologians as public intellectuals deeply invested in the political, social, and cultural dilemmas of their day.[17] In turn, the volume's editors believe that ecclesiastical Orthodox thought has something to say to European intellectual history, as terms and concepts articulated by lay and ecclesiastical thinkers like Metropolitan Platon (Levshin) of Moscow, Archpriest F. A. Golubinskii, A. S. Khomiakov, Dostoevsky, Vladimir Solov'ev, N. A. Berdiaev, and Father Georges Florovsky traveled across national and confessional boundaries.

The recovery of these historical actors and the contexts in which they operated has been made easier by scholars who have situated Russian religious thought in a variety of professional associations, social networks, and publishing houses.[18] These studies help to delineate the areas of institutional overlap in which lay and ecclesiastical Orthodox thinkers interacted, exchanged ideas, and in some cases shared patrons. Concomitant with this growing body of scholarship is an increased interest among Russian scholars in the biographical, institutional, and social histories of the Church's four academies (Saint Petersburg, Moscow, Kiev, and Kazan') that illuminate not only how those schools operated at the administrative and curricular level, but also the various currents of thought within them, including moments of confluence between laity and clergy.[19] Considering these developments and the significant number of primary-source collections now being published in Russia, all of which have made the study of ecclesiastical Orthodox thought more accessible and meaningful to Russian speakers, the editors of and contributors to this volume think that it is long overdue to do the same for English-language audiences.

If the emphasis on context and contingency is somewhat exclusive in this volume, discipline is not. The various modes of scholarly interpretation represented here—literary criticism, intellectual, institutional, and cultural history, philosophy, and religious studies—are intentionally diverse, a fact that demonstrates not only the vitality of Russian Orthodox thought as a subject of academic analysis but also the underlying supposition of this volume that the tenets and lexicon of Russian Orthodoxy were (and still are) open to an array of historically situated interpretations. There was no single, authentic expression of ecclesiastical Orthodox thought, much less lay religious thought. Rather, there were highly contested, ever-changing choice fields available to those religious thinkers who innovatively deployed their faith to engage public opinion. Each philosophical or theological utterance in a Russian Orthodox idiom, including that made by a prelate, is understood in this volume as a unique interpretation of Orthodox Christianity that vied for but did not necessarily establish rhetorical or conceptual dominance, even if it was deemed canonical by the episcopate or, conversely, judged deviant from some normative standard.[20] In fact, this volume assumes that the very act of assigning doctrinal validity or heretical status to a religious utterance constitutes an area of analysis and investigation. Contestation, diversity, even cacophony were the order of the day in late imperial Russia, especially during the last several decades of the old regime (circa 1881–1917), as "religious rivalry" across the Church generated an array of highly contested questions about institutional authority and the type of Orthodox consciousness—monastic, episcopal, academic, parish—best suited to stimulate Russia's historical and cultural development.[21]

The Realities, Conventions, and Constructs of Russian Religious Thought

The tendency among scholars to isolate lay religious thought from ecclesiastical Orthodox thought, to treat the religious ideas in secular society and the intellectual currents in the Church as mutually exclusive, is grounded in a complex of historical, historiographical, and mythopoeic factors. At the historical level, the scholarly division between lay religious thought and ecclesiastical Orthodox thought reflects a concrete sociological reality in late imperial Russia. Lay religious thinkers often belonged to social estates (*sosloviia*), particularly the nobility, that culturally and ideologically distinguished them from their clerical counterparts, most of whom were reared in the clerical estate (*dukhovnoe soslovie*), a discrete grouping that over the course of the eighteenth and first half of the nineteenth century was almost entirely closed by social convention, separate educational institutions, legal restrictions, and, among parish priests, endogamy.[22] For nearly 150 years (circa 1721–1861), the noble and clerical estates were largely segregated from one another, a fact replicated in the different sources, symbols, and traditions that lay and ecclesiastical thinkers drew upon in their public utterances about Russian Orthodoxy. Even when sons of priests (*popovichi*) began to abandon the clerical profession in the last half of the nineteenth century for careers and endeavors outside the Church, including revolutionary activism, they brought with them values, mores, and identities formed at home and parish that separated them from their generational peers born into other estates.[23]

This segregation of lay religious thought from ecclesiastical Orthodox thought also reflects an actual historical contest that took place in public opinion as to who gave voice to authentic Christianity. The ruling episcopate claimed to possess normative authority over matters of faith and constantly exercised that authority to combat perceived deviations in doctrine, scriptural interpretation, liturgy, theology, and practice. As elements of educated society began to reconfigure the tenets of Orthodox Christianity in the post-Napoleonic era to accommodate advances in the natural, philosophical, and historical sciences, the Most Holy Governing Synod (commonly known as the Holy Synod) actively deployed its resources to differentiate what it considered to be correct expressions of faith from blasphemy, heresy, and falsehood. The list of lay religious thinkers who ran afoul of ecclesiastical censure in the late imperial period includes P. Ia. Chaadaev, Aleksei Khomiakov, Vladimir Solov'ev, and L. N. Tolstoy, that is, several of the figures who in the twentieth century would become the main protagonists in studies about Russian religious thought. In turn, it was lay religious thinkers who used their positions in journalism, voluntary associations, salon society, and higher education to level some of the harshest condemnations of the Synodal Church and Orthodoxy itself. The division between lay religious thought and ecclesiastical Orthodox thought in present-day scholarship, in other words, largely mirrors its institutional and ideological expression in history.

Yet historical factors alone cannot explain this partition. The divisions between lay religious thinkers and ecclesiastical Orthodox thinkers were not rigid or static, as evidenced by the biographies, intellectual trajectories, and posthumous legacies of Fedor Golubinskii, Feodor (Bukharev), N. P. Giliarov-Platonov, A. M. Ivantsov-Platonov, Metropolitan Antonii (Khrapovitskii), and Pavel Florenskii, just to name a few. Nor were institutional distinctions between the Russian Church and educated society fixed. By the end of the nineteenth century, for example, several theologians at the Moscow Spiritual Academy (Moskovskaia dukhovnaia akademiia) became active members of the Moscow Psychological Society (Moskovskoe psikhologicheskoe obshchestvo), a leading center of rational Christianity, religious philosophy, and liberation politics. There they presented papers, engaged Moscow's intellectual elite in conversation and debate, and published articles in the Society's quarterly journal, *Questions of Philosophy and Psychology* (*Voprosy filosofii i psikhologii*, 1889–1918).[24] The Church-sanctioned *Orthodox Review* (*Pravoslavnoe obozrenie*, 1860–91), whose editorial board was composed of priests, occasionally published works by both lay and ecclesiastical thinkers whose interpretations of doctrine, canon, Church history, and theology did not fully conform to that of the Holy Synod. This crossover is implicit in the 1814 charter (*ustav*) establishing the Church's system of higher education, which sought to ground the study of Orthodox Christianity and "evangelical truth" in methods of analysis and apology derived from moral philosophy, the history of philosophy, Platonic philosophy, and especially the philosophy of history.[25] The fact that K. P. Pobedonostsev, in his capacity as ober-procurator of the Holy Synod, was compelled in 1889 to enact a measure that required all essays written for a degree in theology to be reviewed to ensure doctrinal and canonical conformity suggests that Orthodox schools contained ideological and theological currents that were at odds with the Holy Synod. And the repeated need to censor religious utterances among members of the royal court, the ministerial government, and the Church itself, including a project to translate the Bible into the vernacular,[26] demonstrates that a neat division between ecclesiastical Orthodox thought and lay religious thought is in many cases historically inaccurate.

The persistence of this divide in scholarship, therefore, cannot be reduced solely to historical actuality. It also emulates a larger historiographical convention in English-language studies about modern Russian history that has long distinguished state from society. In this interpretative model, "civil society" (*grazhdanskoe obshchestvo*) is usually privileged as the medium through which liberal or progressive values might have been inculcated in late imperial Russia if not for the obscurantism of autocratic administration and the paradoxical motivations and results of state-sponsored modernization.[27] Translated into the Church-versus-society paradigm common to journalism and scholarship of the late nineteenth and early twentieth centuries, some religious element of the nascent Russian nation was imagined to be the agent of a more rational, creative, and/or democratic form of Christianity that, if it had been allowed to develop, would have liberated Russia's majority confession from the despotism of the Synodal Church. The anticipated result of this historiosophical advancement was the collective emancipation of Russian consciousness from spiritual subservience, cultural stasis, and political servility.[28] Revived in emigration by Nikolai Berdiaev and others to explain why the Church's "official theology" (*ofitsial'noe bogoslovie*) failed to prevent the atheistic catastrophe of October 1917,[29] coupled with the historical rise of reactionary politics within the clergy after the Revolution of 1905, this portrait of the Church as antagonist in Russia's struggle against autocracy helped to marginalize metropolitans, bishops, priests, theologians, and the Church's public apologists in post-1917 studies about Russian religious thought.[30]

The fact that much of this narrative was initially generated by the very same actors who either attacked the Orthodox Church as an impediment to Russia's historical development or became protagonists in the academic study of Russian religious thought reveals another important factor in the scholarly divide between lay religious thought and ecclesiastical Orthodox thought. It is not only historical and historiographical. The divide is also mythopoeic, in the sense that these binary, value-laden categories developed out of contemporaneous and retrospective stories that Russian thinkers, writers, and activists told about themselves as they struggled to actualize their ideas in social and political reality.[31] Many of these accounts originated in the 1840s and 1850s, as Slavophiles and Westernizers began their disparate critiques of the Synodal Church.[32] In his private correspondences and diary, for example, Ivan Kireevskii distinguished between a false Orthodoxy, which in his estimation was embodied in the Petrine system of ecclesiastical governance and the "scholastic" theology of the ruling episcopate, and an authentic Orthodoxy, which he and other Slavophiles variously located in the religiosity of the *narod*, devout elements of educated society, the hesychastic asceticism practiced at select Russian monasteries, and certain circles in academic theology.[33] The rigid distinction between educated society as the vanguard of Russia's historical advancement and the Church as a force of reaction and source of backwardness was articulated most notably by V. G. Belinskii and A. I. Herzen, who portrayed priests as "the embodiment of gluttony, avarice, servility, and shamelessness" and seminarians as "unhappy" adolescents "raised under the knout of monastic despotism, crammed with . . . rhetoric and theology."[34] Two of the many implications to be drawn from Belinskii's and Herzen's descriptions were that graduates of the Church's schools, excluding a few exceptional cases, could not produce "thought" on par with that of secular society, and that the center of religious creativity in late imperial Russia resided in extra-ecclesial groups, publications, and institutions.[35] Such unflattering depictions of clergy and especially seminarians were not uncommon in literary works of the day, finding expression in the comedies, poetry, short stories, and novels of D. I. Fonvizin, A. S. Pushkin, Gogol', Dostoevsky, and Lev Tolstoy,[36] that is, in texts that form the canon of Russian studies in North American and European universities.

Perhaps the two key historical moments in the privileging of lay religious thought over ecclesiastical Orthodox thought were the responses among members of educated society to the Holy Synod's decision in February 1901 to excommunicate Tolstoy from the Russian Church and its decision in April 1903 to shut down the Religious-Philosophical Meetings. Participants in and commentators about those events, like D. S. Merezhkovskii, Z. N. Gippius, Andrei Belyi, A. A. Blok, and other Silver Age writers or P. B. Struve, Sergei Bulgakov, Nikolai Berdiaev, and other members of Russia's so-called Liberation Movement, juxtaposed their "new religious consciousness" to the institutional heteronomy of the state-sponsored Church. Their memoirs, diaries, journalism, and narrative accounts commonly depicted clergy and theologians as "ambitious positive-moralists," "wild and wicked," "careerists," "uncultured," and "those who believe blindly, in an archaic, child-like way."[37] Similarly, the pursuit of free religious actualization in Russia (personified in part by the recently anathematized Tolstoy) was often contrasted with the religious obscurantism of Synodal power (embodied most commonly in the figure of Pobedonostsev).[38] Once the Silver Age and Liberation Movement became objects of memory, historical analysis, and literary criticism in the post-1917 and especially post-1945 eras, this binary construct was largely incorporated into scholarship about Russian thought and culture. In other words, the Church-versus-society paradigm that informs much of our present-day interpretation of Russian religious thought has been broadly determined by those historical actors who self-consciously participated in the autobiographical creation of lay religious thought as the salvational alternative to the supposedly corrupted thought of the Synodal Church. To begin to unravel the reifications embedded in this paradigm and, thus, understand the ways they have shaped the study of Russian religious thought, contributors to this volume have been encouraged to accept certain ideological and sociological divisions between lay religious thinkers and ecclesiastical Orthodox thinkers as historically actual, while complicating those very same distinctions as historiographical conventions and mythopoeic constructs.[39]

HISTORICAL REVIEW OF THE RUSSIAN CHURCH AND ORTHODOX THOUGHT

The origins of Christianity in what is present-day Russia likely date back to the ninth century when small groups of Eastern Slavs in the region of Kievan Rus' first began to practice Byzantine rites in the Slavonic language. This seminal, if opaque, moment in the history of Russian Orthodoxy was followed a century later by personal conversions of Kiev's ruling family (Princess Ol'ga, circa 945–57, Grand Prince Volodimer in 988) and mass conversions among the population at large. The adoption of Orthodox Christianity among the people of Rus' was coupled over the next several centuries by an array of events that shaped the early course of Russian Church history. By the mid-eleventh century, for example, the first monastic community was established in Kiev, which helped to lay the foundations for what would become a vibrant and varied monastic culture during the Muscovite and early Romanov eras.[40] The eleventh century also witnessed the rise of a distinct homiletic tradition in Rus', coupled with the writing of Russia's first Slavonic Bible, which helped to bring Christian terms and categories into the vernacular of literate society throughout Rus'.[41] The destruction of Kiev by Mongol invaders in 1240 eventually altered the site of ecclesiastical authority and religious culture in Rus' to the city of Moscow, where Orthodoxy began to take on new forms of expression that increasingly distinguished it from other churches in the Orthodox communion.[42] Russia's most important monastery, Trinity-Sergius Monastery (*lavra*), was founded a century later by Sergius of Radonezh, an event that helped to reconfigure Russian Orthodox practice, belief, and identity and that still shapes Russian Orthodox culture to this day.[43] Over the next several centuries the Russian Church began to exercise greater institutional autonomy within the confession. In 1448 the Russian episcopate elected its own metropolitan, an ecclesiastical event that reduced the authority of the Ecumenical Patriarch of Constantinople over the Russian Church. This extra-canonical decision was followed by another one in 1589, when the Russian episcopate established the Patriarchate of Moscow and All Rus', a decision that made the Russian Church autocephalous and, thus, on par with the churches of Constantinople, Alexandria, Antioch, and Jerusalem. The Church's first academy, the Kiev-Mohyla Collegium (the precursor to the Kiev Spiritual Academy) was founded in 1632 by Petro Mohyla. This important moment in the institutional history of Russian Orthodox thought and, more broadly, Russian intellectual and cultural history, was followed in the 1680s by the founding of the Slavonic-Greek-Latin Academy in Moscow (the precursor to the Moscow Spiritual Academy).[44] It was also in the mid- to late seventeenth century that the Russian Church was divided in schism over revisions in liturgy, ritual, and prayer books, a conflict that violently cleaved the Russian Orthodox Church between Old Believers and advocates of ecclesiastical renovation and episcopal authority for several generations.[45]

Around these central events in the life of Russia's pre-Petrine Church arose a variety of narratives that were to shape Orthodox discourse among educated Russians until at least the early eighteenth century and, in many cases, through the Soviet period. Russian Orthodoxy was rendered, for example, as a persecuted faith in passionate imitation of the Crucified Christ, as well as a victorious faith in glorious imitation of the Risen Christ. Sermons proclaimed that the conversion of the Russian lands to Christianity was the fulfillment of biblical prophecy and the culmination of ecclesiastical history. Paschal celebrations were commemorated as the rebirth of Rus' from pagan death to Christian life. Chronicle accounts were organized around the assumption that Russia's military successes and territorial expansion reflected providential favor, and that the vitality of the Russian Church determined the integrity of Russia's social order and political sovereignty. Such experiences and their interpretations also gave rise to the notion that Moscow constituted a New Jerusalem or perhaps a Third Rome, as well as the conviction that the Russian lands in their entirety were holy (*vsia zemlia Sviato-Russkaia*) or the apocalyptic battleground of the Antichrist. Just as significant for the formation of Russian religious thought in the modern era was the contest among clergy and laity over who gave voice to authentic Orthodoxy, as partly evidenced by conflicts surrounding the establishment and curriculum of religious schools, the content of apologetic literature, repeated efforts at local Church councils (*pomestnye sobory*) to regulate and standardize the faith, and the schism between Old Belief and the Patriarchal Church.[46]

One of the pivotal moments in the history of the modern Russian Church, and certainly the one that most fully informed the contours and content of religious thought examined in this volume, was the promulgation of the *Spiritual Regulation* (*Dukhovnyi reglament*) by Peter I in 1721. This law, which brought ecclesiastical administration under the purview of secular authority, generated a variety of results that became touchstones of Orthodox discourse throughout the late imperial period. Among other things, it abolished the Patriarchate, the office of which had remained vacant since the death of Patriarch Adrian in 1700, replacing it with the Holy Synod, an extra-conciliar, non-canonical body composed of prelates that governed the Church until 1917. It required priests to report seditious comments heard in confession to state agents, an obligation later cited by lay and clerical religious thinkers as evidence that the Synodal Church was fully compromised in its subordination to empire. A supplement to the *Spiritual Regulation* soon codified the prerogative of the emperor to intervene in ecclesiastical affairs through the office of the ober-procurator, the influence of which dramatically increased over the course of the nineteenth century, helping to make the Holy Synod and the Church it administered focal points of grievances among clergy and laity alike. The law also precipitated a series of legislative efforts to regulate and secularize monastic property for *raisons d'état*, which, as exemplified by Catherine II's edict (*ukaz*) of 1764, increasingly diminished the strength of the Church by shuttering many of its monasteries and placing the remaining ones under the financial administration of the state.[47]

State intervention in Church matters, however, was often mitigated by broader trends in Russian Orthodox culture, the distinct personalities of powerful and charismatic prelates, and the development of new currents of religious thought in the Church itself. Within two or three generations of the edict of 1764, for example, Russian monasticism experienced a significant resurgence in sheer numbers and popular influence.[48] This revival mainly had its origins in the person of Paisii Velichkovskii (1722–94), who institutionalized the practices of Hesychasm and eldership among Orthodox monasteries in Southeastern Europe and helped to disseminate the ascetic writings of the Church Fathers among the Eastern Slavs through the *Dobrotoliubie* (1793), a Slavonic translation of the *Philokalia* compendium (1782). It was Paisii's disciples who introduced these instructions and practices to Russian monasticism, innovations that were then made accessible to successive generations of laity and clergy by Serafim of Sarov (d. 1833), elders (*startsy*) at the Optina Hermitage (*Pustyn'*) (circa 1830–90), Feofan the Recluse's Russian-language translation of the *Dobrotoliubie* (1877), the character of Father Zosima in Dostoevsky's *Brothers Karamazov* (published serially in 1879-80), and a fictionalized account of a lay practitioner of the Jesus Prayer titled *The Way of a Pilgrim* (published as *Otkrovennye rasskazy strannika dukhovnomy svoemu ottsu* in 1884). By the early twentieth century, many Russian monasteries, especially those with elders, miracle-working icons, and/or relics of saints, had become centers of charismatic authority that competed with the Synodal Church for religious loyalty among the faithful.[49]

Peter I's abolition of the Patriarchate in 1721 and subsequent reforms in diocesan administration meant that the Metropolitanate of Moscow assumed the highest clerical position within the episcopate, a position whose influence in ecclesiastical affairs was commonly determined by the person of the metropolitan himself. This was certainly the case of Platon (Levshin), who used his tenure in that office (1775-87 as archbishop; 1787-1811 as metropolitan) to expand its authority at the expense of the Holy Synod and promote reforms in clerical education.[50] A similarly impressive metropolitan of Moscow, and one who had a similarly ambivalent relationship with the Holy Synod, was Filaret (Drozdov).[51] During his long tenure in that office (1821-67), Filaret helped to alter the trajectory of Russian Church history, most significantly through a variety of translation and scholarly projects, as well as through his own homilies, that sought to ground Russian Orthodoxy in Scripture and the writings of the Greek and Latin Fathers. It was these initiatives that broadly, if somewhat circuitously, shaped the discursive contours of Russian religious thought in both its lay and ecclesiastical expressions by rendering the entire canon of patristic writings and eventually the complete Bible in the Russian vernacular and by placing those texts in a scholarly apparatus of biography, exegesis, history, and theology accessible to educated society.

The principal sites of this biblical and patristic scholarship were the Church's advanced clerical schools in Saint Petersburg, Moscow, Kiev, and, later, Kazan', the modern iterations of which were largely structured by the reform charter of 1814 and subsequent reforms in curriculum and administration in 1869, 1884, and 1910-11. The centrality of these institutions to the intellectual histories of the Russian Church and educated society cannot be overestimated. It was in these academies, as well as in the Church's larger seminary network, that the varieties of ecclesiastical Orthodox thought were formulated and disseminated in lectures, scholarship, and journals like *Christian Reading* (1821-1917), *Works of the Holy Fathers in Russian Translation* (1843-65, 1871-72, 1880-91) and its *Supplements* (same dates), *Theological Herald* (1892-1918),

Orthodox Interlocutor (1855–1917), *Works of the Kiev Spiritual Academy* (1860–1917), and *Faith and Reason* (1884–1917).⁵² Metropolitans Platon and Filaret were intimately involved in the creation of these educational institutions. Platon was a leading proponent of transforming the Slavonic-Greek-Latin Academy, where he had been a student, instructor, and director, into the Moscow Spiritual Academy. Filaret helped to draft the first reform charter, served as rector of the Saint Petersburg Spiritual Academy from 1812 to 1819, during which time he helped to matriculate its first class, and later intervened in his capacity as metropolitan to promote special academic projects. Over the course of the nineteenth and early twentieth centuries, the four spiritual academies trained and employed thousands of future priests, monks, and theologians, several of whom, such as V. D. Kudriavtsev-Platonov, D. I. Bogoliubov, S. S. Glagolev, Antonii (Khrapovitskii), and Pavel Florenskii make an appearance in this volume. In addition to translation projects, the academies introduced new modes of analysis, such as the historical-critical method, the psychology of religion, and the philosophy of religion, to the study of Christian texts and history. They also helped to cast the tenets of Russian Orthodoxy in an idiom of scholarship that was partly intended to bridge the epistemological and ideological rifts between educated clergy and the intelligentsia. Similar to many of their monastic counterparts, several seminaries, academies, and even individual theologians became centers of religious authority that challenged the legitimacy of the Synodal Church and the prerogatives of the autocratic state itself.

The vitality of the modern Russian Church, which was partly expressed in the multiplicity of its constituent elements—episcopal, monastic, academic, parish—and partly undermined by those very same components, came under direct threat during the revolutionary upheaval of the early twentieth century.⁵³ The Church's historical involvement in sanctifying imperial authority, the autocracy's appropriation of Orthodoxy for statist goals, and the simple fact that the emperor, "as a Christian Sovereign," was designated in law as "guardian of Orthodoxy and decorum in the Holy Church" and "Head of the Church" meant that the Russian Church was often considered culpable for failures in imperial governance.⁵⁴ This culpability soon became a liability. The Russian Church was criticized after the fact for its support of Russia's disastrous war against Japan in 1904–5, a pattern that was to repeat itself during the course of the First World War as casualties mounted on the empire's western front. Even more detrimental to the Church's position and reputation in educated society was the fact that important members of the clergy publicly supported the regime's punitive policies following the Revolution of 1905. At this same time, the Church found its privileged position in the multiconfessional empire directly challenged by political events. Domestic unrest and popular pressure from revolutionary movements compelled the regime to grant toleration to religious minorities in April 1905 and establish "freedom of conscience" as one of the "inviolable foundations of civic freedom" in October 1905.[55] The convocation of the First State Duma in April 1906 opened the process of drafting and passing legislation about religious and ecclesiastical affairs to the hurly-burly of partisan politics and brought Orthodox churchmen into the arena of national politics, where several of them remained as elected representatives until the dissolution of the Fourth State Duma in October 1917. This politicization of Russian Orthodoxy exacerbated many of the long-standing fissures within the Church, as the popular politics of Orthodox identity were increasingly framed and fractured by radical ideologies ranging from revolutionary socialism to anti-Semitism.[56]

The upheaval of 1905 and a resulting shift in power in the Holy Synod eventually helped to realize one of the principal goals of those who long opposed the Petrine system of ecclesiastical governance, namely the convocation of a local Church council and the reestablishment of the Patriarchate. The initial step to this reform project was the Pre-Conciliar Commission (*Predsobornoe Prisutstvie*) of 1906. The Commission was composed of prelates, clergy, theologians, and laity, including Metropolitan Antonii (Vadkovskii) of Saint Petersburg and Ladoga, I. V. Popov, D. A. Khomiakov, F. D. Samarin, Prince E. N. Trubetskoi, E. E. Golubinskii, Archpriest P. Ia. Svetlov, A. A. Kareev, and Archpriest I. O. Koialovich, that is, the entire array of lay and ecclesiastical Orthodox thinkers who believed that the solution to Russia's spiritual crisis resided in the reordering of existing Church-state relations.[57] Due in part to concerns in the ministerial government that such reforms might reignite and institutionalize many of the same antagonisms that had precipitated the Revolution of 1905, as well as substantial resistance from within the Church itself, the opening of the All-Russian Church Council was delayed until August 1917. It was this body, which consisted of more than 560 clergy and laity meeting in three general sessions, that in November 1917 elected Tikhon (Bellavin) Patriarch of Moscow and All Russia, an election that brought the Synodal era of Russian Church history, if not the lingering contests and ideological discord within the Church, to an end.[58]

Yet the same political ruptures that ultimately helped to bring about comprehensive ecclesiastical reform and that were broadly embraced by clergy at all levels of the Church hierarchy, such as the abdication of Tsar Nicholas II and the establishment of the Provisional Government in March 1917,[59] soon generated a new set of challenges for the post-Synodal Church. The Bolshevik seizure of power in October 1917 and the Red Army's subsequent victory in the Russian Civil War (1918–20) meant that the reformed Church, which largely opposed the communist takeover, was confronted by a governmental authority and ascendant political ideology that was openly hostile to the country's dominant confession. Large numbers of Orthodox clergy fled the homeland with the retreating White Army, emigrating to Europe, East Asia, Australia, and North America, where they set up parallel institutions meant to preserve what they considered to be authentic Orthodox culture during the expected interregnum of Soviet rule.[60] Resistance in the Russian Church against state-sponsored campaigns to confiscate property and relics was met by imprisonment, trial, and execution, including that of Metropolitan Veniamin (Kazanskii) of Petrograd and Gdov and Archimandrite Sergii (Shein) in August 1922.[61] These punitive actions were soon institutionalized by a variety of Politburo directives and, more concretely, by the formation in 1925 of the League of the Militant Godless (Soiuz voinstvuiushchikh bezbozhnikov), the principal mission of which was to eradicate Orthodox belief and practice among the Russian people.[62] Ideological divisions among the clergy left unresolved by the Council of 1917–18 and exacerbated by the communist regime's burgeoning anti-religious campaigns soon precipitated what one scholar has called an "ecclesiastical civil war" in the Russian Church.[63] With the death of Patriarch Tikhon in 1925, the office of the Patriarchate was once again left vacant. Two years later, in June 1927, the *locum tenens* and members of the Provisional Patriarchal Holy Synod publicly declared that the Russian Orthodox Church would be "loyal" to Soviet authority, a declaration that was to remain in general effect until 1991.

Volume Structure and Contributors

As should by now be obvious, the study of Russian Orthodox thought is a multivalent, multidisciplinary, and often contradictory enterprise. The original volume of *Russian Religious Thought* sought to break through the commonplaces of our understanding of the modern Orthodox Russian religious world by offering new readings of major works from the several decades around the turn of the twentieth century. This new volume demonstrates the ways in which the field has developed and will continue to develop, particularly in its emphasis on context and its focus on various, sometimes competing intellectual currents within the Russian Church. The contributors all attempt, in their own ways, to bridge the gap between various definitions of Russian religious "thought," expanding beyond the religious philosophers covered in the first volume. As a whole, they prove that Orthodox churchmen, academic theologians, and lay Orthodox thinkers interacted with each other and the contexts around them much more frequently, and deeply, than has been previously acknowledged. The articles that follow examine a variety of genres of "religious" writing, from memoirs, diaries, letters, and fiction to journalism, philosophy, theology, and sermons. They move from the eighteenth to the twentieth century and back again, as they show how each new generation reinterpreted events and modes of religious activity or discourse from previous generations, as well as from its own time. Mere chronological order, therefore, would not be the most useful structure for this volume; it might give the erroneous impression of an inevitable, linear development toward some authentic or ideal expression of Russian religious thought. And the distinction between lived religion and religious thought that dominated scholarship over the past two decades would suggest incorrect assumptions about a non-existent distinction between the two categories. An artificial focus on "Western" philosophical influence versus indigenous "Russian" thought would also defeat the purpose of the volume to demonstrate the multiple and paradoxical influences always at play.

Ultimately, the editors have decided to group the contributions based on the main discursive realms from which the players write: the Church establishment (priests, bishops, metropolitans), the spiritual academies (instructors, both ordained and not, at the major educational institutions of the Church), and what we rather generically call "society and culture," meaning writings by individuals not specifically trained as professionals in either Church practice or theology. These categories, although real, are also constructs (as the term "culture" should clearly indicate), with permeable barriers, overlapping jurisdictions, and complex interactions. We know, for example, that Pavel Florenskii wrote his influential *The Pillar and Ground of the Truth* (*Stolp i utverzhdenie istiny*) while studying and teaching at the Moscow Spiritual Academy, and published it after being ordained a priest. Yet Florenskii was also an active member of modernist circles in secular society that included journalists, cultural critics, and experimental poets of the Silver Age. At the other end of his career, he continued to wear his cassock and explore radical ideas—in religion, science, and art—for several years after the establishment of Soviet authority. Furthermore, as will be explored several times in the coming articles, Religious-Philosophical Meetings, created and attended by those very modernist poets, writers, and philosophers who befriended Florenskii, turned out to be important venues for the interaction of clergy and political activists. The social, cultural, and institutional milieus of priests, academics, and lay writers, in other words, were far from discrete.

Thus, by structuring the volume around discursive writing zones, and placing contributions in one division or another, we do not intend to reify the distinctions, but rather to problematize them. Many of the articles would fit well in more than one section, and all three sections could be retitled. Not every essay in each section speaks directly to the other essays, although they complement each other and fill in blanks that might not otherwise be noticed. In essence, by grouping the articles and sections as we have, we intend to ask, rather than answer, questions about the framing of Russian religious thought and Orthodox "thinking" within distinct categories.

The first section of our volume—"Thinking Orthodox in the Church"—includes articles by Elise Kimerling Wirtschafter, Heather J. Coleman, and Scott M. Kenworthy on churchmen who speak clearly from the authority of the Church, including a metropolitan, a missionary, and an archbishop. Wirtschafter undertakes a revision of the long-standing view of the eighteenth-century Church as theologically stagnant. Instead, using the example of metropolitan of Moscow Platon (Levshin), she shows the post-Petrine Church to be a place of intellectual activity, both influenced by and influencing local and more broadly European culture. As the author demonstrates, Metropolitan Platon's sermons "effectively blended Enlightenment ideas into Orthodox religious teachings . . . , providing Christian answers to Enlightenment questions. In the process, he gave voice to a universalistic moral humanism consistent with Christian belief, absolutist monarchy, and social relationships based on patriarchy, hierarchy, and serfdom." In his sermons on the question of theodicy and the minor Russian saint, Tsarevich Dimitrii, Platon develops ideas of human responsibility that echo several concerns of the religious Enlightenment, while he instructs his flock about spiritual courage in an Orthodox setting. His interest, despite his theocentrism, is firmly based in ordinary human happiness. As Wirtschafter tells us, "the idea that every human life constituted a spiritual feat . . . , that every virtuous Christian performed spiritual feats, offered an explanation for the suffering of individuals." Platon, for Wirtschafter, contributed to the goals of the pan-European religious Enlightenment, and set the tone for an ecumenical and humanistic orientation in the Russian Church that continued well into the next century.

In the next contribution, Coleman moves the discussion up to the late nineteenth and early twentieth century, and down the ecclesiastic hierarchy from the metropolitan of Moscow to the journals, diaries, and memoirs of an "internal missionary": Dmitrii I. Bogoliubov. Trained at the Moscow Spiritual

Academy and sent to Tambov province to bring sectarians back to the fold, Bogoliubov began his mission with the belief that Orthodoxy was "essential, native, and inalienable for the Russian peasant." The encounter of this Church-based intellectual with "real life" in the village "forced him to rethink the broader cultural assumptions he had gleaned from his higher education," and instead of finding Bogoliubov's writings to be those of a neo-Slavophile and apologist for the Church, Coleman presents them as "a major site for the Church's engagement with modern society." It was not only the missionary's encounters with the clearly alienable souls of peasants, but also his interest in the intellectual, often secular, currents of his time that caused a "shift in his thinking toward an advocacy of freedom of conscience in Russia rooted in Orthodox ideas." Bogoliubov came to understand, and to relay in his many writings, that "the Russian soul was not Orthodox by nature but through historical development." He therefore "embarked on a new crusade of building a truly Orthodox nation based on the principle of fellowship [*sobornost'*]." As Coleman asserts, this missionary's quest was to defend freedom of conscience on Orthodox grounds and to demonstrate Orthodoxy's relevance in the modern age. As such, the project of this churchman, writing clearly from within the authority of the Church, did not differ significantly from that of other more secular intellectuals of the time.

Finally, Kenworthy's contribution to this section analyzes several commissioned reports to the Russian Holy Synod in 1913, and one in particular—submitted by Archbishop Nikon (Rozhdestvenskii)—concerning an early twentieth-century theological controversy about the nature of God between the Russian Orthodox Church and a group of Russian monks on Mount Athos: the proponents of *Imiaslavie*, or the Name-Glorifiers. These monks drew the condemnation of academy clerics, who believed only themselves to be responsible for articulating Church theology, and called the monks' assertion that "the name of God is God himself" to be counter to Church doctrine. In the course of his analysis, however, Kenworthy explodes the common view of a distinct antagonism between categories of mysticism and academic theology in Orthodox religious thought and practice. Although Nikon declared that "all dogmas, notwithstanding all their mystery and incomprehensibility to our mind, nonetheless never contradict the laws of our reason," he himself was not an academic theologian, and through his life was actually a major defender of monasticism and mysticism, never denying the importance of spiritual experience. In fact, "Nikon objected to *Imiaslavie* not out of a lack of understanding or sympathy for asceticism, but precisely because he believed that it would have a detrimental effect upon ascetical effort." Rather than a debate between rationalist academics and free-thinking mystics, Kenworthy demonstrates that the controversy lay in the question of who has the authority to speak for the Church. Archbishop Nikon, as both a theologian and a supporter of mysticism, in fact, spoke from many sides at once.

The second section—"Thinking Orthodox in the Academy"—looks specifically at the writings of instructors, professors, and theologians within the spiritual academies. The articles of two historians, Sean Gillen and Vera Shevzov, and one Slavist, Ruth Coates, demonstrate that the academies were spaces of much more fluid religious thought, both influenced by and uniquely differing from the secular and religious writings of Western Europe, than has previously been acknowledged. Gillen makes the claim, supported by the other authors in this section, that the intellectual culture of the four prerevolutionary spiritual academies in Russia has to date not been adequately studied. Gillen chooses to focus on one important academy instructor (important in part because of his influence on the Russian religious thinker, Vladimir Solov'ev): V. D. Kudriavtsev-Platonov. Kudriavtsev clearly read the secular press, and searched for "scientific" reasons for modern belief in Orthodoxy. The case of Kudriavtsev, and in particular his turn toward the discourse of theism, demonstrates for Gillen that this influential theologian was participating in a Europe-wide discourse. Theism, a "particular conception of God in which providential considerations in a transcendental sense and ethical considerations in an immanent sense were conjoined to form a theological anthropology—a theory of the self—that made moral perfection the purpose of human life," provided for Kudriavtsev a solution to questions of moral relativity that might be meaningful to contemporary debates about the stimulus to Russia's historical and cultural advancement, and helped him to "modernize religion without secularizing it."

Shevzov in her article also looks at the role of the academies in making "Orthodoxy relevant to the modern world," through the activity of a whole generation of instructors: Sergei Glagolev, Stefan Ostroumov, Ignatii (Brianchaninov), Ioann Orfanitskii, Evgraf Loviagin, Pavel Svetlov, Petr Smirnov, Andrei Predtechenskii, Nikolai Dobronravov, Feofan (Tuliakov), and Pavel Florenskii. These scholars in the nineteenth and early twentieth centuries "spoke to contemporary intellectual and philosophical challenges facing Orthodox Christians in a modernizing society" and "actively engaged in Western debates" (including those raised by Baruch Spinoza, David Hume, Immanuel Kant, George Wilhelm Friedrich Hegel, Johann Gottlieb Fichte, Herbert Spencer, William James, Hermann Samuel Reimarus, Ernest Renan, and Jean-Martin Charcot). Instead of focusing on one individual as do many of the other contributors, Shevzov is interested in a single contemporary discussion of the time: the meaning of miracles in relation to the "science" (*nauka*) of theology. While theologians gave credence to "sensibilities that they considered essential to an Orthodox worldview, and which, in modern times, remained otherwise bound to notions of superstition, ignorance, and deception," they also engaged in European debates about the topic. Shevzov shows that, unlike many of their Western counterparts, these "Orthodox thinkers focused on miracles as affirmations of the presence and agency of a personal God in the world in contrast to an impersonal metaphysical naturalism that denied the very possibility of a miracle." As the academic Predtechenskii asserted: "That which is higher than and external to nature is not necessarily opposed to it." He and his confreres in the academies accepted coexisting bodies of laws: the laws governing nature and those governing the phenomena of miracles. For them, miracles are not arbitrary displays of power but free, purposeful acts of God. "Orthodox defense of miracles . . . rested on beliefs in the reality of personal human agency as much as personal divine agency." In this way, Shevzov reminds us of the peculiarities of ecclesiastical Orthodox thought while recognizing that it exists in dialogue with the writings of other denominations and, indeed, non-denominational and so-called "scientific" thought.

Coates completes this section with a discussion of what she calls the "Orthodox Enlightenment" as an intellectual alternative to the values and aspirations of the English and German religious Enlightenments. These national and cultural distinctions between "enlightenments" are, of course, vexed, as recent scholars have demonstrated.[64] The case is even more so in the Russian context, where the Orthodox Church has long claimed to be the true beacon of light. In this article, Coates's central focus is on Pavel Florenskii, who, she argues, despite his formal appointment, wrote as an iconoclast in the academy. His initial education was at the Imperial Moscow University, a secular institution, and his own reading of Orthodoxy was quite idiosyncratic, as evidenced by the difficulty Florenskii had in getting his master's thesis in theology approved. In making her claim for a specifically "Orthodox Enlightenment," Coates looks, like Kenworthy in the previous section, at the hesychast interests of the Mount Athos monks involved in the *Imiaslavie* controversy, about whom Florenskii also wrote. Monastic elders (*startsy*) of the nineteenth century, who influenced such writers as Dostoevsky, and the theologically minded supporters of *Imiaslavie* in the twentieth found their inspiration in the *Philokalia*, reading those texts as "experiential rather than an intellectual philosophy." Coates turns to close textual readings of biblical, liturgical, philosophical, and other modernist texts to support her contention that there is a difference between the secular enlightenment (for which she uses the general Russian term for philosophy: *filosofiia*) and a Christian, more specifically Orthodox enlightenment (identified by the term *liubomudrie*, meaning—like "philo-sophy"—the "love" of "wisdom," but with native Russian linguistic roots). Her article therefore stands in some contrast to others that argue for integration, rather than separation of Russian religious or Orthodox thought from that of modern European philosophy. For Coates, it is significant that Florenskii wrote as someone who only recently returned to faith and acted as a "guide for outsiders, and an interpreter, attending to each discourse and translating each in terms of the other." Those outsiders, unlike a Church-trained audience largely addressed by the figures in the previous contributions, were already convinced of the truth of Western philosophical thought. Florenskii's "translation" served to bring them a spiritual truth, as well. Florenskii is also the first figure discussed in this volume not initially trained in the Church, and he therefore points the way toward the next section of this volume.

Our final section is the longest and the most diverse: "Thinking Orthodox in Society and Culture," in which our authors examine the works of lay writers who, in genres usually considered secular—literary criticism, philosophy, political discourse, novels—nonetheless adopted Orthodox categories of thought, metaphors, and imagery. Nadieszda Kizenko, Oliver Smith, Randall A. Poole, Vanessa Rampton, and Martha M. F. Kelly all take as their subjects figures not officially located "within" the Church, but who demonstrate the pervasiveness of Orthodox religious thought through Russian culture as a whole. The section begins with a contribution by Kizenko that illuminates how the theology of confession entered lay religious practice. The principal figure Kizenko examines, Natal'ia Fonvizina, is usually known for little more than being the wife of one of the Decembrists, that is, aristocrats, military officers, and litterateurs sent to Siberia for their aborted coup in December of 1825. Fonvizina, however, turns out to be a prolific writer on her own, with a rich story of "adultery, incest, and a chronic infatuation with men of the cloth." The tortured parishioner lays out this narrative in a new genre, a "written confession" conducted in letters between herself and her confessor. In the course of the correspondence back and forth, as Kizenko asserts, confessional texts "became a shared project" between the laity and clergy "that would form religious thought, religious practice, and Russian literature." Furthermore, written confessions provide "examples of how people absorbed Russian religious thought and transformed it into life-writing" that "both reflect and influence Russian religious thought," not to mention belles lettres of the nineteenth century. Indeed, in many ways we might read Fonvizina's letters as a cultural template of the complicated, sexually charged confessions of some of Dostoevsky's fictional characters.

Like Kizenko, Smith provides another example of the transmission of Orthodox categories into lay discourse, in his case of how an Orthodox method of interpretation helped to inform the secular genre of literary criticism in the nineteenth century. He returns us in his article to the writings of the eighteenth-century metropolitan Platon (Levshin) to "identify a common hermeneutic that passed from the academies to 'secular' literary criticism (wherein lay the first seeds of Russian philosophy)." In particular, Smith examines Platon and his followers, who "would later become known by two descriptors, the 'school of the learned monks' and 'school of believing reason,'" and their use of the interpretive tool called "anagogy," a hermeneutic method for the "bringing into correlation of the mystic and mystery . . . through ascent to God." According to Smith, Platon inherited his conviction about the autonomy of reason from the Enlightenment, but moved away from a naïve belief in reason to one that treated equally the spirit and the corporeal or, more accurately, insisted on their interaction. Having illuminated the content of Platon's Orthodox hermeneutics and identified several figures who later appropriate it, Smith points to the example of Vissarion Belinskii, arguably one of the most radical and secular thinkers of the 1840s, who exhibits "a relation to text and its interpretation that it would be no exaggeration to call a spiritual hermeneutics of a very Russian vintage."

Perhaps of all the articles in this volume, Poole's study of the Kantian roots of Solov'ev's philosophy adheres most closely to the tenor of the volume that first inspired this one: *Russian Religious Thought*. Poole demonstrates the influence of Kant, "whose moral religion or religion of pure reason laid the foundations of liberal theology," not only earlier on Platon—as Wirtschafter and Smith acknowledge—but on the late nineteenth-century philosopher Solov'ev as well. Poole asserts through an examination of direct, but often unattributed appropriations by Solov'ev that Kant's "kingdom of ends . . . was the model for Solov'ev's social ideal of 'free theocracy.'" For Poole, Solov'ev desired to "construct a synthesis of faith and reason," like many of the individuals examined in this volume, and took as his task "to justify and modernize religion, to show that it is reasonable." The picture painted of Solov'ev by Poole inevitably de-emphasizes the mystical and poetic aspects of Solov'ev's writing, not to mention his inconsistencies over time and genre, but it does help place him firmly in a European tradition that can broaden our understanding of the exchange between Russian and European religious philosophy, and the way in which such interactions might complicate the image of Russian thought among scholars of European intellectual history.

Rampton continues the historical and philosophical narrative where Poole leaves off, by contextualizing the writings of liberals after the turn of the twentieth century, themselves strongly influenced by Solov'ev, and asserts that they were "inspired by Kant's views on selfhood, but also by theological ideas on the divine element within individuals." By focusing especially on the Russian jurist and philosopher Pavel Novgorodtsev, Rampton asserts that the "idea of social commitment and desire to formulate a flexible answer to the most pressing problems of Russian society cut across different strands of the country's intellectual life, and blurred the categories and concerns of liberal and religious thinkers." For Novgorodtsev in particular, his "work can thus be approached as a vehicle to illuminate more broadly the place of religious concepts in the institutional settings normally associated with the development of liberalism in Russia." Furthermore, for Novgorodtsev and like-minded thinkers, "the liberation of Russia cannot be accomplished by politics alone, but rather depends on culture and creative (*sozidatel'nyi*) impulses that make the principles of freedom and equality immune to instrumentalization by politicians."

Finally, Kelly moves the chronology of the volume beyond the Russian Revolution of 1917 to show how the poet and author of *Doctor Zhivago*, Boris Pasternak, "leverages the achievements of Solov'ev and others to reclaim a place in the realist novel for beauty as he understands it." Pasternak accomplishes this feat in a literary polemic with Tolstoy, in which the twentieth-century Nobel Prize winner pits the nineteenth-century novelist and his followers against the person and legacy of a fictional turn-of-the-century religious philosopher who firmly believes that poets can save society. Kelly's analysis looks not only at the philosophical dialogues in Pasternak's famous novel, but at symbolic, poetic, and figurative means, as well. Although there are other excellent examples of close textual analysis in this volume, it is this contribution that most clearly demonstrates what a nuanced understanding of both Russian religious thought and of Orthodox practice can bring to literary and cultural studies. For Kelly, "Pasternak positions the poetic novel—belles lettres—as the genre by which religious traditions and religious-philosophical ideas might reach into and transform the world." In particular, she examines Mary Magdalene's figurative presence in the novel, showing how a complex invocation of "coverings" and ornaments, as well as Pasternak's "interest in the body and all that amplifies the flesh's beauty," brings the author back to the legacy of Russian religious thought in the prerevolutionary period. For Pasternak, as Solov'ev had insisted was true for Dostoevsky, "beauty"—physical beauty and poetry alike—"will save the world."[65]

A Note on Terms, Letters, Names, and Dates

As this introduction has already shown, it is impossible to discuss the questions this volume poses without stumbling over a number of philosophical and historical terms that raise particular problems in the Russian context. Perhaps the first vexing term to face readers is Orthodoxy itself. The Eastern Orthodox Church does not have sole claim to "true belief" (*orthos doxa*), just as the Catholic Church is not the only one alleging to be "universal" (*katholikos*). Eastern Christians, too, confess in their creed to believe in "one holy, catholic, apostolic church." Furthermore, within the Orthodox world the local churches, sometimes called "national" churches (Greek, Bulgarian, Georgian, Russian, etc.), serve their liturgy in the vernacular and have often developed unique customs and emphases unknown to their fellow religionists in other lands.

It is not only for geographic or cultural reasons, however, that we are inclined here to talk about the multiple dimensions of Orthodoxy, or even of "Orthodoxies." Indeed, a major purpose of this volume is to dispel assumptions about the monolithic nature of the Russian Church itself; the following articles present us with a multifaceted phenomenon that is not easily defined. In an effort to clarify terms, names, and conventions that might be new to some readers, or others that might seem familiar but take on a differently nuanced meaning in the Russian context, the editors offer the following comments.

Churches and Church Hierarchy

Readers more acquainted with the Western church(es) will find much that is recognizable in Orthodox ecclesiastical terminology, but also much that is different. First of all, it must be remembered that there is no pope in the Eastern Church, and, in actuality, no single church, but instead a communion of fourteen or fifteen separate, autocephalous churches, each headed by a patriarch or archbishop, as well as a variety of autonomous and self-governing churches. The Russian Orthodox Patriarchate is one of the "junior" patriarchates, following after the ancient, but now much smaller patriarchates of Constantinople, Alexandria, Antioch, and Jerusalem.

Ordained clergy are identified as metropolitans, bishops, deacons, monks, and priests. Clerics may be either "white," in which case they must marry before ordination in the priesthood, or "black." Only these latter "priest-monks" or hieromonks must remain celibate, with the senior among them called archimandrites. The Church also includes a large role for laypersons in the celebration of the mass and, as we will see for example in the articles below by Poole, Rampton, and Kelly, in the articulation of Russian Orthodox thought to the secular world. Kizenko goes so far as to refer to a "shared project" in the case of confession and confessional texts, as explained in her article below.

Patriarchs, metropolitans, bishops, and even priests bear their highest rank followed by first name, usually their chosen monastic name, with their surname in parentheses. Thus: Metropolitan Antonii (Khrapovitskii). To this is sometimes added the name of the diocese where the clergy member is assigned: Metropolitan Antonii (Khrapovitskii) of Kiev and Galicia or, perhaps, Antonii (Khrapovitskii), metropolitan of Kiev and Galicia. The articles below by Wirtschafter and Smith refer, for example, to metropolitan of Moscow Platon (Levshin).

True Belief, Reason, and Community

Although the Russian Orthodox Church did not undergo a Reformation as in the West, it did experience a major schism in the seventeenth century. In this case, the "protesting" group did not advocate a reformist agenda, but rather adherence to established practice and ritual. This group of schismatics, as we saw earlier in the introduction, is known as the "Old Believers." It is to that group, as well as other sectarians, that the internal missionary Bogoliubov, as described in Coleman's article, was sent to spread Orthodoxy.

As a number of chapters demonstrate, both lay and clerical writers knew about and felt the influence of the European Enlightenments in profound ways, but indeed have understood the meaning of that "light" in ways determined more by Russian history and experience—including the schism—than by that of France, Germany, or England. Indeed, the metaphor of light itself had always been a major trope within Orthodox liturgy, which no doubt had an effect on the ways in which enlightenment was understood in the Russian context. Similarly, the various terms for reason in Russian—*rassudok, ratsional'nost', razum*—each have a history and etymology that can make the interpretation of any discourse that employs them more multivalent than the translation into English might imply.

Another multivalent term used throughout this volume is derived from a root that means "collect" or "gather": the Russian *sobor*, its related adjective form, *sobornyi*, and perhaps most difficultly, the abstract noun *sobornost'*. *Sobor* means either a cathedral—where many people gather—or a council or synod, as in the

Seven Ecumenical Councils (*Vselenskie sobory*). Because of its relationship to the very common verb *sobirat'* (to collect), the adjective may easily be translated as "collective" or "collectivist." But because of its association with *sobor*, a better translation would usually be "communal" to denote the word's intended spiritual dimension. *Sobornost'*, something like "communal-ness," can sometimes mean fellowship, but, again, always with a spiritual or ecclesiastic connotation.[66]

Church Schools

Several of the articles that follow, especially those by Gillen, Coleman, and Shevzov, refer to the educational establishments where clergy and lay theologians received their training. Since the early nineteenth century, those learning institutions have been divided into schools, seminaries, and academies. These institutions bear the name of the diocese (*eparkhiia*) in which they were located, followed by the term *dukhovnyi*. This adjective derives from the root meaning spirit (*dukh*), and we have chosen in this volume to translate it somewhat literally as "spiritual," even though the adjective also denotes "clerical" and is related to the Russian word for clergy, *dukhovenstvo*. Thus: the Moscow Spiritual Academy or the Kiev Spiritual Academy. Note, however, that scholars—with excellent justification—have variously translated the names of these establishments, so readers might elsewhere encounter reference to ecclesiastical, theological, or clerical schools, seminaries, or academies. All refer to the same educational system.

Holidays and Saints

Holidays in the Eastern Orthodox Church correspond largely to those in the Roman Catholic calendar, although sometimes with a different emphasis, and occasionally with a different name. The Feast of the Assumption of the Theotokos (the Mother of God or *Bogoroditsa*), and also the large number of churches, cathedrals, and monasteries named after the feast, for example, is usually called the "Dormition" in Russian contexts. Note also that while Eastern Orthodoxy and Roman Catholicism share many saints, some of them are more central in one tradition or the other. Saint Augustine, for example, although revered in the Orthodox Church, did not play as central a role in the development of theology and doctrine in Orthodox Christianity as he did in Roman Catholicism. By contrast, a figure such as Gregory Palamas is relatively unknown in Catholic sources, but is crucial to our understanding of Hesychasm in the Russian Church, as described in the articles below by Shevzov, Smith, Kenworthy, and Coates.

DATES

Finally, we make note of the fact that, following the Bolshevik Revolution, the new Soviet government adopted the Gregorian calendar long in use in the West, abandoning the Julian calendar that was and continues to be used by many Orthodox Churches. In a decree signed by Lenin on January 24, 1918, the Julian dates of February 1–13 were dropped, bringing the official calendar in line with the dates celebrated in the West, but making printed dates from the previous era (called "old style" or OS), and dates of holidays celebrated by the Orthodox Church, up to thirteen days behind the "new style" (NS) dates. We adhere to a common practice in which OS is used for events that precede February 1, 1918, and NS is used for events that follow that date.

On a more mundane level, aiming at readability for audiences from multiple backgrounds, we have chosen to use the Library of Congress system for transliteration of Cyrillic with several modifications, including the elimination of rarely used diacritical marks. We have also chosen to efface the distinction between what were in prerevolutionary orthography and remain in modern Russian writing conventions very different letters, all here transliterated as e: ё (sometimes transliterated as ë, io, or yo), э (sometimes transliterated as é or eh), and ѣ (sometimes transliterated as ie).

Again for the sake of simplicity, we maintain a consistent transliteration system for proper names, except for those most likely to be known to an English-speaking audience. Thus: "Dostoevsky" instead of "Dostoevskii." Even this can be confusing, of course, since Solov'ev has been transliterated in various English-language publications as Solovyov, Soloviev, and Solov'ëv. Whenever possible we err toward clarity, rather than pedantic consistency.

NOTES

1. For a succinct review of this scholarship, see Paul W. Werth, "Lived Orthodoxy and Confessional Diversity: The Last Decade on Religion in Modern Russia," *Kritika: Explorations in Russian and Eurasian History* 12, no. 4 (Fall 2011): 849–65, esp. 849–56. The phrase "handmaiden of the state" belongs to Gregory L. Freeze, "Handmaiden of the State? The Orthodox Church in Imperial Russia Reconsidered," *Journal of Ecclesiastical History* 36 (1985): 82–102.

2. This turn toward the study of lay religious thought was not limited to scholars in the United States and Europe. For two examples, see V. N. Zhukov, *Russkaia religioznaia mysl' XIX–nachala XX veka* (Moscow: Institut molodezhi, 1992); L. E. Shaposhnikov, *Russkaia religioznaia filosofiia XIX–XX vekov* (Nizhnii Novgorod: Volgo-Viatskoe knizhnoe izd-vo, 1992).

3. Judith Deutsch Kornblatt and Richard F. Gustafson, eds., *Russian Religious Thought* (Madison: University of Wisconsin Press, 1996).

4. Kornblatt and Gustafson, *Russian Religious Thought*, 3-6. See also the introductory statements in Pavel Florenskii, *The Pillar and Ground of the Truth: An Essay in Orthodox Theodicy in Twelve Letters*, trans. Boris Jakim, intro. Richard F. Gustafson (Princeton, NJ: Princeton University Press, 1997); A. S. Khomiakov et al., *On Spiritual Unity: A Slavophile Reader*, trans. and ed. Boris Jakim and Robert Bird (Hudson, NY: Lindisfarne Books, 1998); *Freedom, Faith, and Dogma: Essays by V. S. Soloviev on Christianity and Judaism*, ed. and trans. Vladimir Wozniuk (Albany: State University of New York Press, 2008).

5. Catherine Evtuhov, *The Cross and the Sickle: Sergei Bulgakov and the Fate of Russian Religious Philosophy, 1890-1920* (Ithaca, NY: Cornell University Press, 1997); *Vzyskuiushchie grada: Khronika chastnoi zhizni russkikh religioznykh filosofov v pis'makh i dnevnikakh*, ed. and intro. V. I. Keidan (Moscow: Shkola Iazyki russkoi kul'tury, 1997); A. F. Losev, *Vladimir Solov'ev i ego vremia* (Moscow: Molodaia gvardiia, 2000); James P. Scanlan, *Dostoevsky the Thinker* (Ithaca, NY: Cornell University Press, 2002); Manon de Courten, *History, Sophia and the Russian Nation: A Reassessment of Vladimir Solov'ëv's Views on History and his Social Commitment* (New York: Peter Lang, 2004); Steven Cassedy, *Dostoevsky's Religion* (Stanford, CA: Stanford University Press, 2005); I. V. Vorontsova, *Russkaia religiozno-filosofskaia mysl' v nachale XX veka* (Moscow: PSTGU, 2008); Judith Deutsch Kornblatt, *Divine Sophia: The Wisdom Writings of Vladimir Solovyov*, trans. Boris Jakim, Kornblatt, Laury Magnus (Ithaca, NY: Cornell University Press, 2009); Avril Pyman, *Pavel Florensky: A Quiet Genius; The Extraordinary Life of Russia's Unknown Da Vinci* (New York: Continuum, 2010); Anna Lisa Crone, *Eros and Creativity in Russian Religious Renewal: The Philosophers and the Freudians* (Leiden: Brill, 2010); and the relevant articles in G. M. Hamburg and Randall A. Poole, *A History of Russian Philosophy 1830-1930: Faith, Reason, and the Defense of Human Dignity* (New York: Cambridge University Press, 2010).

6. For some important exceptions, see Vera Shevzov, *Russian Orthodoxy on the Eve of Revolution* (New York: Oxford University Press, 2004), esp. chap. 1; Jennifer Hedda, *His Kingdom Come: Orthodox Pastorship and Social Activism in Revolutionary Russia* (DeKalb: Northern Illinois University Press, 2008), esp. chap. 2.

7. For a lament about the inadequate state of our knowledge about Russian Orthodox theology, see Victoria Frede, *Doubt, Atheism, and the Nineteenth-Century Russian Intelligentsia* (Madison: University of Wisconsin Press, 2011), 217n23.

8. The phrase "atemporal resources" belongs to Charles Taylor, "Philosophy and Its History," in *Philosophy in History*, ed. Richard Rorty, J. B. Schneewind, and Quentin Skinner (New York: Cambridge University Press, 1984), 17.

9. For a corrective to the decontextualized tendency in the study of Russian religious thought, see Christopher Stroop, "Nationalist War Commentary as Russian Religious Thought: The Religious Intelligentsia's Politics of Providentialism," *Russian Review* 72 (January 2013): 94-115.

10. Paul Valliere, *Modern Russian Theology: Bukharev, Soloviev, Bulgakov; Orthodox Theology in a New Key* (Grand Rapids, MI: Eerdmans, 2000); L. E. Shaposhnikov, *Konservatizm, modernizm i novatorstvo v russkoi pravoslavnoi mysli XIX-XXI vekov* (St. Petersburg: Izdatel'stvo S.-Peterburgskogo universiteta, 2006). Other attempts to ground Russian lay religious thought in an Orthodox theological context belong to Patrick Lally Michelson, "'The First and Most Sacred Right': Religious Freedom and the Liberation of

the Russian Nation, 1825–1905" (PhD diss., University of Wisconsin, 2007), esp. chap. 1; Sean Michael James Gillen, "'A Foggy Youth': Faith, Reason, and Social Thought in the Young Vladimir Sergeevich Solov'ev, 1853–1881" (PhD diss., University of Wisconsin, 2012), esp. chap. 2.

11. Konrad Onasch, *Die alternative Orthodoxie: Utopie und Wirklichkeit im russischen Laienchristentum des 19. und 20. Jahrhunderts; 14 Essays* (Paderborn-Munich-Vienna-Zürich: Schöningh, 1993), chap. 1. Onasch's teleological explanations for the rise of alternative Orthodoxy are engaged and complicated in the next section of this introduction.

12. The failure among scholars of Russian religious thought to examine "the relationship and boundary" between lay religious thought and "Russian Orthodox thought" was noted by Vera Shevzov in her review of Kornblatt and Gustafson, eds., *Russian Religious Thought*. See *Russian Review* 57, no. 3 (July 1998): 475–76. Thomas N. Tentler has made a similar point about the failure among scholars of lived Orthodoxy to engage Russian Orthodox theology in "Epilogue: A View from the West," in *Orthodox Russia: Belief and Practice under the Tsars*, ed. Valerie A. Kivelson and Robert H. Greene (University Park: Pennsylvania State University Press, 2003), 263–64.

13. Nicolas Zernov, *The Russian Religious Renaissance of the Twentieth Century* (New York: Harper & Row, 1963).

14. The notion of speech act used here comes from Quentin Skinner, "Conventions and the Understanding of Speech Acts," *The Philosophical Quarterly* 20 (April 1970): 118–38.

15. Mark D. Steinberg and Heather J. Coleman, eds., *Sacred Stories: Religion and Spirituality in Modern Russia* (Bloomington: Indiana University Press, 2007); Paul W. Werth, *The Tsar's Foreign Faiths: Toleration and the Fate of Religious Freedom in Imperial Russia* (New York: Oxford University Press, 2014).

16. V. M. Zhivov, *Sviatost': Kratkii slovar' agiograficheskikh terminov* (Moscow: Gnozis, 1994); V. A. Kotel'nikov, ed., *Khristianstvo i russkaia literatura*, 6 vols. (St. Petersburg: "Nauka," 1994–2010); Victor Terras, "A Christian Revolution in Russian Literary Criticism," *Slavic and East European Journal* 46 (Winter 2002): 769–76; M. M. Dunaev, *Vera v gornile somnenii: Pravoslavie i russkaia literatura v XVII–XX vv.* (Moscow: Izdatel'skii Sovet Russkoi Pravoslavnoi Tserkvi, 2003); B. F. Egorov, *Ot Khomiakova do Lotmana* (Moscow: Iazyki slavianskoi kul'tury, 2003); E. M. Zastrozhnova, *"Malen'kii chelovek" v svete khristianskoi traditsii (ot Gogolia k Dostoevskomu)* (Moscow: TEIS, 2004); Philip Boobbyer, *Conscience, Dissent, and Reform in Soviet Russia* (London: Routledge, 2005); Leonard J. Stanton and James D. Hardy Jr., *Interpreting Nikolai Gogol within Russian Orthodoxy: A Neglected Influence on the First Great Russian Novelist* (Lewiston, NY: Edwin Mellen Press, 2006); Per-Arne Bodin, *Eternity and Time: Studies in Russian Literature and the Orthodox Tradition* (Stockholm: Acta Universitatis Stockholmiensis, 2007); V. A. Alekseev, ed., *S. A. Esenin i pravoslavie: Sbornik statei o tvorchestve S. A. Esenina* (Moscow: Izdatel'skii dom K edinstvu!, 2011); A. A. Pletneva and A. G. Kravetskii, eds., *Tserkovnoslavianskii iazyk: Akademicheskii uchebnik*, 5th ed. (Moscow: AST-PRESS, 2012); Iu. A. Kondrat'ev, *Pretsedentnye fenomeny russkoi pravoslavnoi kul'tury na materiale tekstov khudozhestvennoi literatury* (St. Petersburg: Renome, 2012).

17. Douglas J. Cremer, "Protestant Theology in Early Weimar Germany: Barth, Tillich, and Bultmann," *Journal of the History of Ideas* 56, no. 2 (April 1995): 289–307;

Rudy Koshar, "Where Is Karl Barth in Modern European History?," *Modern Intellectual History* 5, no. 2 (2008): 333–62; and the relevant articles in Leonard V. Kaplan and Rudy Koshar, eds., *The Weimar Moment: Liberalism, Political Theology, and Law* (Lanham, MD: Lexington Books, 2012). See also the Modern European Historiography Forum in *Church History* 75, no. 1 (March 2006).

18. M. A. Kolerov, *Ne mir, no mech: Russkaia religiozno-filosofskaia pechat' ot "Problem idealizma" do "Vekh"* (St. Petersburg: Izdatel'stvo Aleteiia, 1996), as well as many of the other works by Kolerov; Evgenii Gollerbakh, *K nezrimomu gradu: Religiozno-filosofskaia gruppa "Put'" (1910–1919) v poiskakh novoi russkoi identichnosti* (St. Petersburg: Izdatel'stvo Aleteiia, 2000); R. N. Kleimenova, *Obshchestvo liubitelei Rossiiskoi slovesnosti, 1811–1930* (Moscow: Academia, 2002); A. A. Ermichev, *Religiozno-filosofskoe obshchestvo v Peterburge (1907–1917): Khronika zasedanii* (St. Petersburg: Izd-vo S.-Peterburgskogo universiteta, 2007).

19. V. A. Tarasova, *Vysshaia dukhovnaia shkola v Rossii v kontse XIX–nachale XX veka: Istoriia imperatorskikh pravoslavnykh dukhovnykh akademii* (Moscow: Novyi khronograf, 2005); T. A. Bogdanova, "Iz akademicheskikh 'istorii': Zameshchanie kafedry tserkovnogo v Moskovskoi Dukhovnoi akademii v 1910 godu," *Vestnik tserkovnoi istorii*, no. 1 (2007): 31–77; N. Iu. Sukhova, *Vysshaia dukhovnaia shkola: Problemy i reformy, vtoraia polovina XIX veka* (Moscow: PSTGU, 2006); N. Iu. Sukhova, *Sistema nauchno-bogoslovskoi attestatsii v Rossii v XIX–nachale XX v.* (Moscow: PSTGU, 2009); N. K. Gavriushin, *Russkoe bogoslovie: Ocherki i portrety* (Nizhnii Novgorod: Tipografiia Rido, 2011).

20. The classic work of normative analysis belongs to Georges Florovsky, *Puti russkogo bogosloviia* (Paris, 1937), who sought to delineate those moments in the history of the Russian Church when Russian Orthodox theology deviated from or adhered to the proper "path" of its own internal development. Ironically, it is Florovsky's categorizations and criticisms of what he considered to be theological deviations in the Russian Church that helps us to recover the varieties and contested nature of Russian Orthodox thought in the imperial and early émigré periods.

21. Simon Dixon, "The Russian Orthodox Church in Imperial Russia 1721–1917," in *Eastern Christianity*, vol. 5 of *The Cambridge History of Christianity*, ed. Michael Angold (New York: Cambridge University Press, 2005), 325–47.

22. Gregory Freeze, "Russian Orthodoxy: Church, People and Politics," in *Imperial Russia*, ed. Dominic Lieven, vol. 2 of *The Cambridge History of Russia, 1689–1917* (New York: Cambridge University Press, 2006), 284–305, esp. 288–96.

23. Laurie Manchester, *Holy Fathers, Secular Sons: Clergy, Intelligentsia, and the Modern Self in Revolutionary Russia* (DeKalb: Northern Illinois University Press, 2008).

24. On the Moscow Psychological Society and *Questions of Philosophy and Psychology*, see the introductory essays by N. S. Plotnikov and M. A. Kolerov in *Problemy idealizma: Sbornik statei (1902)*, ed. P. I. Novgorodtsev (Moscow: Modest Kolerov i Tri Kvadrata, 2002), 5–60 and 61–224, respectively; Randall A. Poole, "Editor's Introduction," in *Problems of Idealism: Essays in Russian Social Philosophy*, trans. and ed. Poole (New Haven, CT: Yale University Press, 2003), esp. 3–51.

25. *Polnoe sobranie zakonov Rossiiskoi imperii s 1649 goda* (St. Petersburg: Pechatno v Tipografii II Otdeleniia Sobstvennoi Ego Imperatorskogo Velichestva Kantseliarii, 1830), 32:925–27 (hereafter *PSZ I*).

26. I. A. Chistovich, *Istoriia perevoda biblii na russkii iazyk*, 2nd ed. (St. Petersburg: Tipografiia M. M. Stasiulevicha, 1899); A. M. Skabichevskii, *Ocherki istorii russkoi tsernzury (1700–1863 g.)* (St. Petersburg: Izdanie F. Pavlenkova, 1892), chaps. 10 and 16; Stephen K. Batalden, *Russian Bible Wars: Modern Scriptural Translation and Cultural Authority* (Cambridge: Cambridge University Press, 2013).

27. For representative titles in this historiography, see Nicholas V. Riasanovsky, *A Parting of Ways: Government and the Educated Public in Russia, 1801–1855* (Cambridge: Clarendon Press, 1976); Marc Raeff, *Understanding Imperial Russia: State and Society in the Old Regime* (New York: Columbia University Press, 1984). For a critique of the state-versus-society paradigm and a review of scholarship that challenges it, see Martina Winkler, "Rulers and Ruled, 1700–1917," *Kritika: Explorations in Russian and Eurasian History* 12, no. 4 (Fall 2011): 789–806.

28. Much of this formulation was first articulated circa 1829–36 by Chaadaev in his condemnation of Orthodox Christianity as an "individualistic, volatile, and incomplete" religion that hindered Russia's historical development. See Raymond T. McNally, ed., "Chaadaev's Philosophical Letters and His Apologia of a Madman," *Forschungen zur osteuropäischen Geschichte* 11 (1966): 34–117. For an influential reading of certain currents in Orthodox asceticism and sectarianism as "liberal" alternatives to political and ecclesiastical despotism, see P. N. Miliukov, "Ocherki po istorii russkoi kul'tury," *Mir Bozhii*, March 1896, 96–97; Miliukov, *Russia and Its Crisis* (Chicago: University of Chicago Press, 1905), chap. 3; Miliukov, *Religion and the Church*, vol. 1 of *Outlines of Russian Culture*, ed. Michael Karpovich, trans. Valentine Ughet and Eleanor Davis (Philadelphia: University of Pennsylvania Press, 1942).

29. Nikolai Berdiaev, "O kharaktere russkoi religioznoi mysli XIX veka" and "Russkii dukhovnyi renessans nachala XX v. i zhurnal *Put'*," in *Tipy religioznoi mysli v Rossii*, vol. 3 of *Sobranie sochinenii* (Paris: YMCA Press, 1989), 11–49 and 684–708, esp. 695–702. Berdiaev had distinguished "official theology" from religious thought as early as 1912 in *Aleksei Stepanovich Khomiakov*. See *Sobranie sochinenii* (Paris: YMCA Press, 1997), 5:73–74, 82–83. A similar juxtaposition between "Christ's Church" and "official 'Orthodoxy'" informed Sergei Bulgakov's call in September 1905 to Christianize Russian politics. See Bulgakov, "An Urgent Task," in *A Revolution of the Spirit: Crisis of Value in Russia, 1890–1924*, ed. Bernice Glatzer Rosenthal and Martha Bohachevsky-Chomiak (New York: Fordham University Press, 1990), 140.

30. The privileging of some sort of progressive Orthodoxy over the Synodal Church's "official theology" has long been a commonplace in studies about Russian thought and consciousness. See, for example, Evgeny Lampert, "Nicholas Berdyaev," in *Modern Christian Revolutionaries*, ed. Donald Attwater (New York: Devin-Adair, 1947), 317; Andrzej Walicki, *A History of Russian Thought from the Enlightenment to Marxism* (Stanford, CA: Stanford University Press, 1979), 380; M. Iu. Smirnov, *Mifologiia i religiia v rossiiskom soznanii* (St. Petersburg: Izdatel'sko-torgovyi dom "Letnii sad," 2000), 92–99; L. D. Ezova, "Pereosmyslenie opyta russkoi dukhovnoi kul'tury parizhskim zhurnalom 'Put'," in *Rossiiskaia intelligentsiia na rodine i v zarubezh'e: Novye dokumenty i materialy; Sbornik statei*, ed. T. A. Parkhomenko (Moscow: Rossiiskii institut kul'turologii, 2001), 47–66, esp. 48, 53–54.

31. On the "mythopoeic method" and its effects on scholarly interpretation, see David Sorkin, "The Mendelssohn Myth and Its Model," *New German Critique*, no. 77 (Spring–Summer 1999): 7–28.

32. Patrick Lally Michelson, "Slavophile Religious Thought and the Dilemma of Russian Modernity, 1830–1860," *Modern Intellectual History* 7, no. 2 (2010): 239–67.

33. Letter to A. I. Koshelev (10 July 1851), in *Biografiia Aleksandra Ivanovicha Kosheleva*, vol. 2, ed. N. P. Koliupanov (Moscow: O. F. Koshelevoi, 1892), appendix, 101–3; Eberhard Müller, "Das Tagebuch Ivan Vasil'evič Kireevskijs, 1852–1854," *Jahrbücher für Geschichte Osteuropas* 14, no. 2 (1996): 167–94.

34. V. G. Belinsky, "Letter to Gogol," in *Selected Philosophical Works* (Moscow: Foreign Languages Publishing House, 1948), 506–7; A. I. Gertsen, *Sobranie sochinenii v tridtsati tomakh*, ed. V. P. Volgin (Moscow: Izd-vo Akademii Nauk SSSR, 1956), 8:106–9.

35. This sort of portrait of theological training in the Russian Church broadly informs Zernov, *The Russian Religious Renaissance*, esp. 45–50. For an early acknowledgement of the need to examine the Church's four academies as viable centers of religious thought, see Alexandre Koyré, *La philosophie et le problème national en Russie au début du XIXe siècle* (Paris, 1929), 197n100. The historiographical link among Herzen's depiction of seminarians, Zernov's appropriation of such a depiction, and Koyré's antidote belongs to Sean Gillen.

36. Here we have in mind characters like Kuteikin in Fonvizin's *Nedorosl'* (1782), the priest in Pushkin's "Skazka o pope i o rabotnike ego Balde" (1830; published in 1882), the seminary students in Gogol"s "Vii" (1835), Rakitin in Dostoevksy's *Brat'ia Karamazovy* (1879–80), and Father Sergius in Tolstoy's "Otets Sergii" (1898).

37. Zinaida Gippius, *Dnevniki*, ed. A. N. Nikoliukin (Moscow: NPK Intelvak, 1999), 1:125–26. It is important to note that Gippius did not label all churchmen that she encountered with pejorative terms. The general tone of her recollections about clergy who attended the Religious-Philosophical Meetings, however, is one of derision.

38. The contrast between the religiosities of Tolstoy and Pobedonostsev belongs to P. B. Struve, "Ot redaktora," *Osvobozhdenie*, no. 1 (1902): 2–3. Cf. Ak. [S. N. Bulgakov], "Pis'ma iz Rossii. II. Samoderzhavie i pravoslavie," *Osvobozhdenie*, no. 4 (1902): 59–60; no. 5 (1902): 72–73; no. 6 (1902): 86–87.

39. In this approach the editors are following a suggestion made to scholars of Russian Orthodox "belief and practice" that they should take "into account the stories Russians told about themselves, without being bound by them." See Laura Engelstein, "Old and New, High and Low: Straw Horsemen of Russian Orthodoxy," in Kivelson and Greene, *Orthodox Russia*, 32.

40. Fairy Von Lilienfeld, "The Spirituality of the Early Kievan Caves Monastery," in *Christianity and the Eastern Slavs*, ed. Boris Gasparov and Olga Raevsky-Hughes (Berkeley: University of California Press, 1993), 1:63–76; *The "Paterik" of the Kievan Caves Monastery*, trans. Muriel Heppell (Cambridge, MA: Distributed by Harvard University Press, for the Ukrainian Research Institute of Harvard University, 1989).

41. *Sermons and Rhetoric of Kievan Rus'*, trans. and intro. Simon Franklin (Cambridge, MA: Distributed by Harvard University Press, for the Ukrainian Research Institute of Harvard University, 1991); *The Edificatory Prose of Kievan Rus'*, trans. William R. Veder, intro. Veder and Anatolij A. Turilov (Cambridge, MA: Distributed by Harvard University Press, for the Ukrainian Research Institute of Harvard University, 1994).

42. Robert Crummey, *The Formation of Muscovy, 1304–1613* (New York: Longman, 1987), chap. 5.

43. Vladimir Tsurikov, *The Trinity-Sergius Lavra in Russian History and Culture* (Jordanville, NY: Holy Trinity Seminary Press, 2005); David Miller, *Saint Sergius of Radonzeh, His Trinity Monastery, and the Formation of the Russian Identity* (DeKalb: Northern Illinois University Press, 2010); Scott M. Kenworthy, *The Heart of Russia: Trinity-Sergius, Monasticism, and Society after 1825* (New York: Oxford University Press, 2010).

44. Omeljan Pritsak and Ihor Ševčenko, eds., *The Kiev Mohyla Academy* (Cambridge, MA: Ukrainian Research Institute, Harvard University Press, 1985); A. V. Panibrattsev, *Filosofiia v Moskovskoi Slavianskoi-greko-latinskoi akademii (pervaia chetvert' XVIII veka)* (Moscow: IFRAN, 1997); Panibrattsev, *Prosveshchenie razuma: Stanovlenie akademicheskoi nauki v Rossii* (St. Petersburg: Russkii Khristianskii Gumanitarnyi In-t., 2002).

45. Robert O. Crummey, *Old Believers in a Changing World* (DeKalb: Northern Illinois University Press, 2011).

46. Michael Cherniavsky, "'Holy Russia': A Study in the History of an Idea," *American Historical Review* 63, no. 3 (April 1958): 617–37; Robert Crummey, *The Old Believers and the World of Antichrist: The Vyg Community and the Russian State, 1694–1855* (Madison: University of Wisconsin Press, 1970); Omeljan Pritsak, "Kiev and All of Rus': The Fate of a Sacral Idea," *Harvard Ukrainian Studies* 10, nos. 3/4 (1986): 279–300; Franklin A. Sciacca, "In Imitation of Christ: Boris and Gleb and the Ritual Consecration of the Russian Lands," *Slavic Review* 49, no. 2 (Summer 1990): 253–60; Max Okenfuss, *The Rise and Fall of Latin Humanism in Early-Modern Russia: Pagan Authors, Ukrainians, and the Resiliency of Muscovy* (Leiden: Brill, 1995); Borys A. Gudziak, *Crisis and Reform: The Kyivan Metropolitanate, the Patriarchate of Constantinople, and the Genesis of the Union of Brest* (Cambridge, MA: Harvard University Press, 2001); Georg Michels, "Ruling Without Mercy: Seventeenth-Century Russian Bishops and Their Officials," *Kritika: Explorations in Russian and Eurasian History* 4, no. 3 (Summer 2003): 515–42; Michael S. Flier, "Till the End of Time: The Apocalypse in Russian Historical Experience Before 1500," in Kivelson and Greene, *Orthodox Russia*, 127–58; Brian P. Bennett, "Sign Languages: Divination and Providentialism in the 'Primary Chronicle' of Kievan Rus,'" *Slavonic and East European Review* 83, no. 3 (July 2005): 373–95; Stella Rock, "Russian Piety and Orthodox Culture 1380–1589," in Angold, *Eastern Christianity*, 253–75; Sergei Bogatyrev, "Reinventing the Russian Monarchy in the 1550s: Ivan the Terrible, the Dynasty, and the Church," *Slavonic and East European Review* 85, no. 2 (April 2007): 271–93; Isaiah Gruber, *Orthodox Russia in Crisis: Church and Nation in the Time of Troubles* (DeKalb: Northern Illinois University Press, 2012).

47. James Cracraft, *The Church Reform of Peter the Great* (Stanford, CA: Stanford University Press, 1971); Lindsey Hughes, *Russia in the Age of Peter the Great* (New Haven, CT: Yale University Press, 1998), 332–56; Isabel de Madariaga, *Russia in the Age of Catherine the Great* (New Haven, CT: Yale University Press, 1981), chap. 7.

48. For a case study of monasticism after the 1764 *ukaz*, see William Wagner, "The Transformation of Female Orthodox Monasticism in Nizhnii Novgorod Diocese, 1764–1929, in Comparative Perspective," *Journal of Modern History* 78, no. 4 (December 2006): 793–845.

49. Robert H. Greene, *Bodies Like Bright Stars: Saints and Relics in Orthodox Russia* (DeKalb: Northern Illinois University Press, 2009); Irina Paert, *Spiritual Elders: Charisma and Tradition in Russian Orthodoxy* (DeKalb: Northern Illinois University Press, 2010).

50. K. A. Papmehl, *Metropolitan Platon of Moscow (Petr Levshin, 1737-1812): The Enlightened Prelate, Scholar, and Educator* (Newtonville, MA: Oriental Research Partners, 1983); Elise Kimerling Wirtschafter, *Religion and Enlightenment in Catherinian Russia: The Teachings of Metropolitan Platon* (DeKalb: Northern Illinois University Press, 2013).

51. Vladimir Tsurikov, ed., *Philaret, Metropolitan of Moscow, 1782-1867: Perspectives on the Man, His Works, and His Times* (Jordanville, NY: Variable Press, 2003).

52. The Russian titles of these periodicals are *Khristianskoe chtenie, Tvoreniia sviatykh ottsev v russkom perevode, Pribavleniia k tvoreniiam sviatykh ottsev v russkom perevode, Bogoslovskii vestnik, Pravoslavnyi sobesednik, Trudy Kievskoi dukhovnoi akademii,* and *Vera i razum*. For a bibliography of Christian journals published in Russia between 1801 and 1917, see *Khristianskaia periodicheskaia pechat' na russkom iazyke, 1801-1917 gg.*, 3 vols., ed. A. N. Troitskii, comp. G. L. Andreev (New York: Norman Ross Publishing, 1998).

53. Another significant problem that helped to undermine the vitality of the Synodal Church was the endemic poverty and poor education of its parish priests, a problem that lasted well into the twentieth century. See Gregory L. Freeze, *The Parish Clergy in Nineteenth-Century Russia: Crisis, Reform, Counter-Reform* (Princeton, NJ: Princeton University Press, 1983).

54. *PSZ I* (25 January 1721), 6:316; ibid. (5 April 1797), 24:588. See also *Svod zakonov Rossiiskoi Imperii*, ed. I. D. Mordukhai-Boltovskii (St. Petersburg: Russkoe khizhnoe tovarishchestvo Deiatel', 1912), 1:1:5, for the way in which the emperor's place at the head of the Church was described in the Fundamental Laws of 1906. For a sense of how Orthodox images and tropes informed imperial authority, see Richard S. Wortman, *Scenarios of Power: Myth and Ceremony in Russian Monarchy from Peter the Great to the Abdication of Nicholas II* (Princeton, NJ: Princeton University Press, 2006), esp. chaps. 5 and 20; Andrew M. Verner, *The Crisis of Russian Autocracy: Nicholas II and the 1905 Revolution* (Princeton, NJ: Princeton University Press, 1990), chap. 3; Andrei Zorin, *Kormia dvuglavogo orla: Literatura i gosudarstvennaia ideologiia v Rossii v poslednei treti XVIII-pervoi treti XIX veka* (Moscow: Novoe literaturnoe obozrenie, 2001), chap. 10.

55. *Polnoe sobranie zakonov Rossiiskoi imperii: Sobranie tret'e* (hereafter *PSZ III*), 33 vols. (St. Petersburg: Gosudarstvennaia tipografiia, 1881-1913), 25:257-58, 754.

56. Gregory Freeze, "Church and Politics in Late Imperial Russia: Crisis and Radicalization of the Clergy," in *Russia under the Last Tsar: Opposition and Subversion, 1894-1917*, ed. Anna Geifman (Malden, MA: Blackwell, 1999), 269-97; Edward E. Roslof, *Red Priests: Renovationism, Russian Orthodoxy, and Revolution, 1905-1946* (Bloomington: Indiana University Press, 2002), chap. 1; Simon Dixon, "Archimandrite Mikhail (Semenov) and Russian Christian Socialism," *Historical Journal* 51, no. 3 (2008): 689-718; Dixon, "The 'Mad Monk' Iliodor in Tsaritsyn," *Slavonic and East European Review* 88, nos. 1/2 (January-April 2010): 377-415. For a sense of how this radicalism played out among lay religious thinkers, see Laura Engelstein, "The Old Slavophile Steed: Failed Nationalism and the Philosophers' Jewish Problem," in *Slavophile Empire: Imperial Russia's Illiberal Path* (Ithaca, NY: Cornell University Press, 2009), 192-232.

57. James W. Cunningham, *A Vanquished Hope: The Movement for Church Renewal in Russia, 1905-1906* (Crestwood, NY: St. Vladimir's Seminary Press, 1981); Georgii

Orekhanov, *Na puti k soboru: Tserkovnye reformy i pervaia russkaia revoliutsiia* (Moscow: Pravoslavnyi Sviato-Tikhonovskii Bogoslovskii Institut, 2002).

58. Catherine Evtuhov, "The Church in the Russian Revolution: Arguments for and against Restoring the Patriarchate at the Church Council of 1917–1918," *Slavic Review* 50, no. 3 (Autumn 1991): 497–511; George T. Kosar, "Russian Orthodoxy in Crisis and Revolution: The Church Council of 1917–1918 (PhD diss., Brandeis University, 2004); Shevzov, *Russian Orthodoxy*, 48–51.

59. P. V. Rogoznyi, *Tserkovnaia revoliutsiia 1917 goda: Vysshee dukhovenstvo Rossiiskoi Tserkvi v bor'be za vlast' v eparkhiiakh posle Fevral'skoi revoliutsii* (St. Petersburg: Liki Rossii, 2008); Hedda, *His Kingdom Come*, chap. 9.

60. Marc Raeff, *Russia Abroad: A Cultural History of the Russian Emigration, 1919–1939* (New York: Oxford University Press, 1990), chap. 6; A. A. Kostriukov, *Russkaia Zarubezhnaia Tserkov' v pervoi polovine 1920-kh godov: Organizatsiia tserkovnogo upravleniia v emigratsii* (Moscow: PSTGU, 2007); M. V. Shkarovskii, *Istoriia russkoi tserkovnoi emigratsii* (St. Petersburg: Aleteia, 2009).

61. Jonathan W. Daly, "'Storming the Last Citadel': The Bolshevik Assault on the Church, 1922," in *The Bolsheviks in Russian Society: The Revolution and the Civil Wars*, ed. Vladimir N. Brovkin (New Haven, CT: Yale University Press, 1997), 235–68; A. N. Kashevarov, *Pravoslavnaia Rossiiskaia Tserkov' i sovetskoe gosudarstvo (1917–1922)* (Moscow: Izdatel'stvo Krutitskogo podvor'ia Obshchestvo liubitelei tserkovnoi istorii, 2005).

62. N. N. Pokrovskii and S. G. Petrov, comps., *Politbiuro i tserkov': 1922–1925 gg.*, intro. Pokrovskii, 2 vols. (Moscow: ROSSPEN, 1997–98); Daniel Peris, *Storming the Heavens: The Soviet League of the Militant Godless* (Ithaca, NY: Cornell University Press, 1998).

63. Roslof, *Red Priests*, chaps. 2–3. See also Gregory Freeze, "Counter-Reformation in Russian Orthodoxy: Popular Response to Religious Innovation, 1922–1925," *Slavic Review* 54, no. 2 (Summer 1995): 305–39.

64. Here we have in mind the works of David Sorkin, Charles W. J. Withers, Roy Porter, Joachim Whaley, J. G. A. Pocock, Jonathan Sheehan, and Gertrude Himmelfarb, just to name a few.

65. Vladimir Solov'ev, "Krasota v prirode," in *Sobranie sochnenii V. S. Solov'eva*, ed. S. M. Solov'ev and E. L. Radlov, 2nd ed., 10 vols. (St. Petersburg: Prosveshchenie, 1911–14), 6:33. Reprinted with two additional volumes (Brussels: Zhizn' s Bogom, 1966–70). Solov'ev uses this phrase, which is spoken somewhat enigmatically in Dostoevsky's novel *The Idiot*, as an epigraph for his essay on beauty.

66. The inculcation of *sobornost'* and its derivations in Russian Orthodox discourse is largely, if somewhat circuitously, the responsibility of the early Slavophiles. See, for example, Shevzov, *Russian Orthodoxy*, 30–35. This terminology has even made its way into the history of Christian doctrine. See Jaroslav Pelikan, *Christian Doctrine and Modern Culture (since 1700)*, vol. 5 of *The Christian Tradition: A History of the Development of Doctrine* (Chicago: University of Chicago Press, 1989), chap. 6.

PART I

Thinking Orthodox in the Church

Chapter 1

Orthodoxy and Enlightenment in Catherinian Russia

The Tsarevich Dimitrii Sermons of Metropolitan Platon

ELISE KIMERLING WIRTSCHAFTER

The reforms of Tsar Peter I (ruled 1682/1689–1725) marked the onset not only of modern Russian history but also of the modern history of the Russian Church. Already in the late seventeenth century, and with greater intensity in the early eighteenth, Russia began to confront the challenge and allure of European civilization. Through a series of social, institutional, and cultural reforms, Peter and his supporters, including Church intellectuals such as Feofan (Prokopovich), embraced the fruits of European letters, arts, and sciences, and set Russia on a "Western" path to modernity.[1] In the cultural sphere, the Petrine reforms built upon earlier efforts, sometimes also led by churchmen, to assimilate the Latinist learning and technological advances of contemporary Europe. In addition, the reforms resolved outstanding political ambiguities by making clear the Church's administrative subordination to the monarch. Precisely because the Petrine reforms eliminated the patriarchate and flooded Russia with European cultural models, generations of historians tended to see the eighteenth-century Church as institutionally paralyzed, intellectually moribund, and spiritually sterile.[2]

Writing after the Bolshevik Revolution, Father Georges Florovsky associated the alleged spiritual malaise of the eighteenth-century Church with the scholastic erudition and "Protestant" orientation of leading Church intellectuals.[3] Echoing this judgment, twentieth-century scholarship showed only minimal interest in the sizeable corpus of eighteenth-century religious writings. Feofan

(Prokopovich) and the Petrine reforms invariably received their due, but most scholars took as their starting point the spiritual renaissance that began at the end of the eighteenth century. Represented by monastic renewal and the nineteenth-century flowering of theology (both lay and ecclesiastical), the new spirituality established meaningful barriers between sacred and profane culture while also bringing religious ideas into the mainstream of Russian literature and philosophy.

More than two decades ago historian Gregory L. Freeze suggested a counterpoint to the prevailing narrative of spiritual stagnation, when he questioned the notion of a Petrine ecclesiastical reform that had turned the eighteenth-century Church into the "handmaiden of the state." Recent scholarship endorses his assessment, and long-standing images of scholastic sterility have begun to erode. Indeed, just as Freeze finds in the changes of the Petrine era an innovative separation of the state from the Church, that, despite the monarch's role as head of the Church, preserved intact an ecclesiastical domain of Church governance and canon law, so too historians interested in the educated clergy who presided over the reformed Church recognize their significant contributions to the intellectual life of the eighteenth century.[4] By the eighteenth century, the strength of Russia's religious traditions, not their vulnerability in the face of European ideas, already represented an important aspect of cultural development.

Scholars who seek to understand the historical weight of the Russian Church—a weight that belies depictions of an institution unsuited for the conditions of modern European life—can begin by looking at the religious dimension of the Russian Enlightenment, an elite phenomenon that encompassed the court and educated service classes, including Church intellectuals from the monastic and urban clergy.[5] Among the cohort of eighteenth-century churchmen who can be viewed as religious enlighteners, metropolitan of Moscow Platon (Levshin, 1737–1812) stands out for his commitment to lay and ecclesiastical education, for the literary quality of his Russian writings (especially the sermons and catechisms), and for his desire to communicate with believers in a manner that addressed their everyday concerns.[6] At a time when the monarchy and educated classes began to make a distinctively Russian contribution to European culture, the homiletic sermons of Metropolitan Platon illustrated the vibrancy of eighteenth-century religious thought. Although historians rightly distinguish study of the Russian Enlightenment from study of Church teachings and devotional writings, recent scholarship suggests that both the glories of modern Russian culture and the strength of the modern Russian Church cannot be understood without reference to the synthesis of Orthodox teachings and Enlightenment ideas produced by the likes of Platon.[7]

One way to understand Metropolitan Platon's enlightened orientation is with reference to the pan-European religious Enlightenment that grew out of efforts to find a reasonable faith, neither excessively enthusiast nor rigidly doctrinaire, capable of sustaining belief in an age of ongoing scientific discoveries and new societal priorities.[8] Among Orthodox, Catholic, Protestant, and Jewish believers in Europe, religious Enlightenment(s) aimed to reconcile the new learning of the seventeenth and eighteenth centuries—the natural philosophy and mechanical arts derived from Cartesian, Baconian, and Newtonian science—with established authority and religious belief. Platon's contribution to this endeavor appeared in published sermons and devotional writings that echoed Europe's post-Westphalian interest in nonconfessional moral philosophy and that reproduced traditional Orthodox teachings in a contemporary Russian language.[9] Although Platon was neither a moral philosopher nor a nonconfessional thinker, he effectively blended Enlightenment ideas into Orthodox religious teachings.

Platon incorporated European Enlightenment into Russian Orthodoxy by providing Christian answers to Enlightenment questions. In the process, he gave voice to a universalistic moral humanism consistent with Christian belief, absolutist monarchy, and social relationships based on patriarchy, hierarchy, and serfdom.[10] Ironically, despite the criticism of Father Florovsky, it is precisely Platon's role as moral teacher—to monarchs, clergy, and the educated public—that makes him an interesting Enlightenment figure.[11] The churchmen who edited the metropolitan's sermons, rector of Moscow's Slavonic-Greek-Latin Academy Damaskin (Semenov-Rudnev) and prefect of the Academy Amvrosii (Serebrennikov), compared his literary talent and moral impact to that of John Tillotson, Jean Baptiste Massillon, and two students of Christian Wolff, August Friedrich Wilhelm Sack and Johann Joachim Spalding, who became renowned preachers in Prussia.[12] In Russia, and across the European continent, moral instruction permeated eighteenth-century education, literary culture, and religious thought.

The cultural accomplishments of Metropolitan Platon and many other eighteenth-century Russian intellectuals, both ecclesiastical and lay, are not widely appreciated in Enlightenment historiography. Depictions of the Russian Enlightenment as an offshoot of German *Aufklärung*, Wolffian philosophical rationalism, imported Freemasonry, and/or Pietist spirituality are, in so far as they go, illuminating and accurate. But they do not provide an adequate definition of the Russian Enlightenment. Contestation over the meaning of (the) Enlightenment is of course ongoing, and most present-day scholars prefer to think in terms of multiple Enlightenments with varied and eclectic sources.[13] Indeed, it is precisely because of (the) Enlightenment's social, intellectual, and institutional diversity that both the religious and radical Enlightenments appropriately carry the Enlightenment label.[14] Thus, while it is true that religious enlighteners tended to support the absolutist politico-religious order of the seventeenth and eighteenth centuries, they also promoted egalitarian Enlightenment ideals that to this day continue to generate social and political change.[15]

Through the reconciliation of modern knowledge with Christian teachings, religious enlighteners did much more than reformulate the synthesis of reason and faith achieved by ancient and medieval thinkers.[16] Attuned to the concerns of philosophical modernity, they produced innovation in the guise of tradition and in the process connected a world understood with reference to God and the promise of salvation to one in which human beings look to science and their own cognitive powers for immediate solutions to earthly problems.[17] In Russia, the teachings of religious enlighteners encouraged the Russian monarchy, Church, and educated classes to come to terms with European modernity within the framework of Orthodox Christian belief. The intellectual bridge provided by enlightened churchmen, Metropolitan Platon included, thus helps to explain how eighteenth-century educated Russians so readily assimilated and made their own the European cultural models that poured into Russia as a consequence of the Petrine reforms.

The Righteous Sufferer and the Cult of Tsarevich Dimitrii

Among the issues that in eighteenth-century Europe joined philosophical innovation to religious tradition, the theodicy question, the problem of innocent and righteous sufferers in a universe governed by divine providence, stands out for its painful and enduring resonance. Often described as the search for a rational or philosophical solution to the problem of evil in the world, the theodicy question assumed unprecedented urgency after the great Lisbon earthquake, tsunamis, and fire of 1755.[18] Although the Catholic Church may have justified the earthquake as divine punishment for sin, among growing numbers of secular thinkers, the tragedy showed that "God had ceased to be just and Nature to be beneficent."[19] Thus, when Voltaire addressed the theodicy question in the philosophical novel *Candide, or Optimism* (1759), he excoriated the likes of Alexander Pope and Gottfried Wilhelm Leibniz for their excessively rosy interpretations of the human condition.[20] Rejecting the idea that because God is omnipotent and good, his creation and all that happens in human history cannot be other than it is, Voltaire adopted the Spinozist vision of a clockmaker God, a God of nature, who had created the universe but did not directly manage human affairs. While Voltaire did not intend to undermine belief in the efficacy of divine providence or the rightness of God's creation, his intellectual opponents had ample reason to fear a slippery slope leading from Deist naturalism to materialism and unbelief.

For Metropolitan Platon, a firmly traditional Christian, the theodicy question did not intrude upon fundamental belief. Nor did Platon address the question with reference to the philosophical debates unfolding in Europe. The problem of the righteous sufferer remained the biblical problem of seemingly unjustified human suffering—a problem for which the idea of a clockmaker God could not provide a satisfactory solution. In the mind of Platon, the rationality of the universe was not at issue. Orthodox believers knew that Christ, the apostles, and numerous martyr saints had suffered painful torment and premature death, despite their goodness. The divine purpose behind their suffering could be explained in both biblical and theological terms. With respect to humble human innocents, by contrast, the suffering of the righteous could be more difficult to understand. Because the Enlightenment idea of progress assumed that through the use of reason and the pursuit of knowledge the human condition should and could be ameliorated, enlightened theologians and moderate enlighteners sought fresh answers to long-standing questions about the relationship between divine providence, human action, and earthly suffering.

Metropolitan Platon addressed not the philosophy but the reality of the righteous sufferer in sermons written between 1775 and 1804 to commemorate the feast day (May 15) of Tsarevich Dimitrii of Uglich.[21] A minor Russian saint, but one who enjoyed a popular following in the seventeenth and eighteenth centuries, Tsarevich Dimitrii was the son of Ivan IV (the Terrible, ruled 1533/1547–84) and his seventh (non-canonical) wife Mariia Nagaia. Dimitrii met his death in mysterious circumstances in 1591, and in 1606, during the period of civil war, social rebellion, and foreign occupation known as the Time of Troubles (1598–1613), Tsar Vasilii Shuiskii (ruled 1606–10) arranged for his canonization. Both the Romanov dynasty, established in 1613 at the end of the troubles, and the Russian Orthodox Church accepted Dimitrii as a martyr prince, murdered on the orders of Boris Godunov, the power-hungry brother-in-law of Ivan IV's successor, Fedor Ivanovich (ruled 1584–98). When Fedor died in 1598, Moscow's Daniilovich dynasty came to an end, and Godunov acceded to the throne, ruling until his sudden death in 1605. Godunov's reckless ambition, manipulation of Fedor, and suspicious crowning convinced generations of Russian observers that he had engineered Dimitrii's death. Modern historians question Godunov's culpability; however, the cult of Tsarevich Dimitrii continues to be celebrated. Represented as a Christ-like figure—an innocent child and legitimate heir who suffered a sacrificial death at the hands of evildoers—Dimitrii belongs to a Russian Orthodox tradition that glorifies nonresistance to evil and includes Russia's earliest indigenous saints, the murdered Kievan princes Boris and Gleb.[22]

Happiness and the Feat of Virtue

Metropolitan Platon's sermons commemorating Tsarevich Dimitrii affirmed the official history of the cult but also connected the saint's life to the concerns of eighteenth-century listeners.[23] Although Platon by no means equated the everyday trials of Christian believers with the spiritual feats (*podvigi*) of holy martyrs, he did take seriously the struggles of ordinary human beings. Writing at a time when Church intellectuals sought to encourage more cognitive forms of religious belief, Platon's interest in human happiness, also a key Enlightenment theme, helped to bridge the gap between mundane and holy lives.[24] Insisting that the attainment of happiness depends on virtuous living, even if virtue cannot be immediately rewarded, Platon appeared to rationalize the inequities of a Russian social order built upon human bondage, absolutist monarchy, and hierarchies of gender, age, and birth. Repeatedly in the Dimitrii sermons the preacher seems to say that people who suffer from poverty, disease, injustice, and abuse should not be regarded as unfortunate. If such people remain obedient to authority and fulfill God's commandments, they will be rewarded for their forbearance in the life to come. Modern critics of religion long have regarded this type of argument as a source of social passivity that prevents the oppressed and downtrodden from demanding the natural rights to which they are entitled as human beings. The critique is defensible, but it overlooks the Christian meaning of Platon's teachings and the religious beliefs of his audience. Apologist he may have been, but he was also a preacher who offered religious solutions to everyday human problems.

In the sermon from May 15, 1780, Platon considers why earthly happiness, even when clearly deserved, is not always evident. The preacher begins his sermon with the reminder that through the observance of Saint Dimitrii's feast day believers will be guided by God toward true philosophy (*liubomudrie*).[25]

Indeed, the "fate" (*sud'ba*) suffered by the martyr (*muchenik*) Dimitrii teaches us—Platon includes himself in the Christian flock receiving instruction—to bear the temptations (*iskusheniia*) sent by God and to fortify ourselves with the knowledge that a righteous person subjected to evil human action will receive divine "recompense and glorification."[26] Mortals are weak, Platon notes, and together with the promise of eternal blessings, they also hope for "a quiet life" here on earth. Indeed, when people see "nothing but disturbances and disasters," they find it difficult to take comfort in the promise of future joy. Understandably, they also want to spend their earthly lives "in tranquility and happiness." But, Platon insists, this is not always possible. In fact, the desire "never to be unhappy" can be the greatest obstacle to achieving "the feat of virtue."

To strengthen the message of happiness delayed, Platon quotes the Sermon on the Mount and the Book of Acts: 'For the gate is narrow and the road is hard that leads to life' (Matthew 7:14). Similarly, 'It is through many persecutions that we must enter the kingdom of God' (Acts 14:22).[27] Sacred history, the preacher continues, is filled with saintly individuals who passed through "fire and water," suffering insults and afflictions, before they found peace. For Platon, the important point is not that the righteous must endure suffering. He is convinced that their blessings will come, that God will not forget them. To his mind, the crucial point, proven by Holy Scripture and by biblical and historical experience, is that in this life only virtuous people can live in tranquility and happiness. Invoking Isaiah and the psalmist, Platon makes clear that there can be no joy among the ungodly: 'There are glad songs of victory in the / tents of the righteous' (Psalm 118 [117]:15). Only "good souls" can feel "true happiness," not only in the future life, but also here on earth.

At issue, it seems, is the meaning of happiness, a concept that could seem as slippery in the eighteenth century as it does today. Outside the Church, Russian literature equated happiness with good fortune and unhappiness with misfortune. Metropolitan Platon at times did the same. But secular thinkers also echoed Platon, and church teachings more generally, when they associated happiness with goodness, tranquility, and peace of mind. In eighteenth-century plays, for example, the happiness of virtuous characters is almost always represented by purity of conscience and the righting of social wrongs. Even the Russian version of *Hamlet*, as adapted in 1748 by Aleksandr P. Sumarokov, ends with rightful resolution.[28] Platon had knowledge of contemporary Russian literature, though his treatment of the human striving for happiness is actually more "realistic." Unable to write happy endings to fictional lives, he displays empathy and offers reasonable answers designed to comfort his Christian flock.

In the Dimitrii sermon of 1780, Metropolitan Platon considers how it might be possible to turn earth into heaven for righteous people. How, the preacher asks, can we ensure that the righteous at least feel "the beginning of eternal delights"? Platon's answer is traditional and unequivocal: "with the help of divine truth," people can overcome "deceptive human understandings." They can begin to see that human beings often find joy in what should make them sad and sorrow in what should make them happy. Over and over, Platon points out, we regard as misfortune what constitutes our well-being, and we regard as happiness what is in fact the source of our unhappiness or ruin.

Not surprisingly, Platon's assumptions about human happiness derive from biblical and theological teachings. They do not, therefore, make sense without reference to the belief in a divine truth that transcends and remains distinct from human or earthly life. Platon insists that what people see, or think they see, is not equivalent to divine truth. When virtuous people suffer, we consider them unhappy, even though divine truth confirms that such people are in reality tranquil and blessed. Similarly, when bad people spend their days in merriment, we envy their happiness, yet Holy Scripture teaches that there is no happiness for the impious. In other words, what we often consider to be happiness or unhappiness contradicts divine truth. Our human understandings lead us astray.

Platon's conclusion seems simple enough, but he does not end the sermon with formulaic statements about the inability of human beings to understand the ways of God. How is it possible, the preacher wants to know, to regard as happy someone who is slandered and persecuted? We naturally feel distressed, he continues, when good people, subjected to persecution and slander, lose everything, including even their lives. Yet we also regard as fortunate people who are burdened with difficult labors and sleepless nights in the service of society. The serviceman who faces danger and death in defense of the fatherland is recognized as fortunate, even though he suffers significant hardship. Platon's argumentation here is slightly garbled, but it conveys the confusion in the understanding of happiness that he wants to describe. Using the stark reality of death to make his point, Platon insists that what matters in all of this is not the form (*obraz*) death takes. The important thing is that we die by honorable means. The illness that precedes a person's death can be as difficult as a martyr's torment. Every life, the preacher implies, is a spiritual feat filled with pain and suffering.

The life of the Apostle Paul provides Platon with an unambiguous illustration of this teaching. People ask how an honorable person can be called happy, if he or she, like Paul, suffers endless misfortune and dies painfully. As Platon describes the issue, we are ready to weep for Paul, even though our perception of the apostle's situation is contradicted by his own judgment: 'I am now rejoicing in my sufferings for your sake' (Colossians 1:24). For Platon, the lesson of Paul's life is absolutely clear. True unhappiness is found only in corruption and debauchery, whereas happiness exists in a pure conscience. In other words, do not be deceived by outward appearances. "The path to true blessedness is crowded and vast, lamentable and cheerful, difficult and convenient." What is deplorable "in the opinion of the world" can be joyous when understood in an "enlightened" manner. If we follow the way of "the Prophet" (King David), "we can unite the hope of heavenly happiness with earthly tranquility." 'I shall walk at liberty / for I have sought your precepts' (Psalm 119 [118]:45). Acknowledging again the value of human life and the natural desire for happiness, Platon reminds his listeners that God created us not to suffer torment but to participate in his perfections. It is we who choose whether to preserve God's good intentions or turn them into our own unhappiness. Tsarevich Dimitrii suffered a violent death at the hands of evildoers, yet now he flourishes in heaven. Remembering this, we can feel reassured when confronted with "the struggle of this life" (*podvig zhizni seia*); we can find the capacity to hold fast in the face of external difficulties. If our spirit (*dukh*) is pure, we are blessed, and happiness is ours. The suggestion is that everyday struggles are akin to apostolic feats.

The connection between the human striving for happiness and the suffering of holy martyrs is again highlighted in the sermon of May 15, 1784, delivered in the Archangel Cathedral to commemorate Saint Dimitrii.[29] Here Platon begins by explaining why we should celebrate rather than bemoan the death of the tsarevich. Once again, "the wisdom of the world" leads us to question how God can rejoice at 'the death of his faithful ones' (Psalm 116:15 [115:5]). Once again, Platon's answer is simple: on earth the righteous are united with God by faith, whereas in death they are united with him in heaven for eternity. The promise of salvation is the highest reward for virtue, and the virtue that leads to salvation is the only life feat that really matters. Equated with eternal life, itself the purpose of creation, salvation is the essence of God's relationship to human beings.[30] Clearly, the promise of salvation satisfied the yearnings of Metropolitan Platon, a highly educated and spiritually mature Christian. But the preacher also understood that his listeners might need more tangible answers to the problem of human suffering.

To explain why the suffering of the righteous represents happiness, Platon draws a distinction between, on the one hand, the athletic and military feats celebrated in ancient Greece and Rome, and on the other hand, the spiritual feats celebrated by the Christian Church. Both physical and spiritual feats demand that the body be disciplined, but spiritual feats also require that heroes do battle with passion, vice, evil oppressors, and even the devil. Spiritual heroes and martyrs who suffered horrific physical torture attained true freedom and eternal life. Looking at their feats, it seems as if they did not live in their bodies. Indeed, they did not conquer cities or subdue enemies, but they defeated their own weaknesses. Military victors, by contrast, may have conquered vast territories, but their glory remains "empty," and the peoples they defeated curse them forever. Clearly, Tsarevich Dimitrii belongs to the ranks of the martyrs whose spiritual victories bring them eternal glory and recognition from God, with whom they are united. Deprived of the earthly kingdom that should have been his, Dimitrii entered the heavenly kingdom and is now the son of the heavenly Tsar. Given that the blessed rule with God in heaven, and given that God's kingdom is eternal, it is obvious that in the life of Dimitrii, evil has been put to shame and virtue glorified.

It would have seemed self-evident to eighteenth-century Christian believers that holy persons, including Christ, the apostles, saints such as Dimitrii, and numerous biblical heroes, received their just rewards in heaven. But what about the ordinary mortals who could not hope to perform the spiritual feats of glorified martyrs? Platon addresses this question in two ways. First, he treats every life, however humble, as a spiritual feat connecting human beings to Christ and the apostles. Second, he presents a conception of divine providence that explains the meaning of seemingly triumphant evil. In the sermon of May 15, 1786, Platon again reminds his listeners that although Tsarevich Dimitrii lost his earthly kingdom, God elevated him to the heavenly kingdom and crowned him with martyrdom, a crown adorned with faith, hope, and love.[31] Dimitrii's own blood stained his purple mantle, which now is "more brilliant than all the robes of earthly monarchs." In addition, God placed in Dimitrii's right hand a holy cross, the "symbol of victory over the devil and over all the intrigues and exertions of the world." Finally, Dimitrii's heavenly glory brings ongoing benefits to his subjects. Instead of promoting our temporal well-being, as Dimitrii would have done here on earth, the saint now acts to ensure our eternal well-being. If we can imitate the tsarevich's patience, we too will be able to remain on course in the spiritual feat that lies before us.

What is this spiritual feat that human beings are called upon to perform? Platon begins to answer the question by describing the difficulties of everyday life. Our life is a "constant war." We are surrounded by temptation and calumny, from without and from within ourselves. Citing Ephesians 6:13, which calls upon Christians, using God's weapons, to fight continually against evil, Platon highlights the need to "strengthen our spirit with Christian courage."[32] Once again the preacher turns to the distinction, drawn in numerous religious and literary sources, between physical and spiritual realities. Physical courage is not what is needed here. Physical courage often turns into evil, for it usually means that the strong oppress the weak. In the "feat of virtue" (*podvig dobrodeteli*), physical courage brings more harm than benefit. Indeed, when the righteous suffer bodily torture, physical courage is of no use to them. What they need is spiritual courage. The Apostle Paul bears witness to this truth. In his spiritual feat, Paul was both warrior and victor: 'but I punish my body and enslave it' (1 Corinthians 9:27). Paul suffered many trials and fought many battles against the entire world. Did he not then, Platon asks, need to satiate and strengthen his body rather than discipline and subject it? The apostle's own answer is no: 'Even though our outer nature is wasting away, our inner nature is being renewed day by day' (2 Corinthians 4:16). In other words, the weaker the body becomes, the more courageous is the spirit; consequently, for Christians spiritual courage is necessary and useful.

Having held up the example of the Apostle Paul, Platon addresses the needs of his listeners more directly. He points out that the temptations and slander hurled at them by enemies are directed not at the body, but at the spirit. Your enemy, Platon teaches, does not try to weaken your body or make it sick. Your enemy seeks to weaken your spirit and make you despondent; this is how he tries to prevent you from continuing "the feat of your virtue." Physical strength is meaningless in this situation. If your spirit does not waver, if it is supported by God, your enemies will be powerless. To sustain spiritual courage, two things are necessary. First, we must believe that there is no greater good on earth than honesty and "spiritual purity." Second, we must believe deep in our souls that true human happiness is found not on earth, but in heaven. Virtue and salvation—to a modern skeptic disturbed by human suffering, these answers surely beg the question. But Platon was not speaking to skeptics; he was speaking to fellow believers.

Divine providence, the preacher continues, gives to Christians two weapons, weapons that fortify your soul and ensure its victory. Evil people can deprive you of honor (*chest'*) and property, but they cannot take away your honesty (*chestnost'*).[33] In other words, although God allows what is insignificant and external to be taken from you, your enemies cannot deprive you of true blessedness. There is a purpose to the struggles you must endure. If you did not face opposition, you would not have the opportunity to show your courage. God enrolled you in his service as a "heavenly warrior," and the adversity he allows you to suffer is actually beneficial. God tests your courage in order to reveal to the world that you are not a weak warrior. He allows you to experience hardship—in Platon's mind, minor hardship—so that you can display "the greatest honor and glory." If this were not so, "our reason, our virtue, our faith would be either fruitless or their confluence would be hidden." All Christians are warriors in "the army of Christ." All are engaged in the spiritual feat of remaining firm in the faith and true to God's law, despite the hardships of everyday life. Invoking the image of Christian warriors, Platon identifies the trials and tribulations of his listeners with the spiritual feats of holy martyrs. No enemy, Platon concludes, can hold out against us when we are guided by the brave commanders, the holy martyrs, who head the army of Christ. We simply need to follow their lead, including that of Jesus Christ (*podvigopolozhnik*), who 'suffered for you, leaving you an example, so that you should follow in his steps' (1 Peter 2:21). The spiritual feats that bring salvation, Platon implies, are not limited to Christ, the apostles, or the saints of the Christian Church. They are the stuff of human hardship, the stuff of everyday life.

Did the promise of salvation and the example of holy martyrs represent an adequate solution to the Enlightenment's understanding of the theodicy question? As noted above, already in the eighteenth century, some philosophically minded intellectuals had rejected the Christian answer to human suffering. Yet for religious enlighteners such as Metropolitan Platon, Christian principle reigned supreme, and the goal of salvation continued to permeate all aspects of human existence. Salvation lay at the core of God's relationship to human beings. Salvation was the reason for the Church, for the divinely anointed monarch, and for Platon's own pastoral mission. But while salvation represented the overarching purpose of religious belief and practice, Platon also appreciated the difficulties of everyday life. The idea that every human life constituted a spiritual feat, that every virtuous Christian performed spiritual feats, offered an explanation for the suffering of individuals. Even so, another question arose. What was the purpose of human suffering in the broad sense? What did human suffering mean in a universe governed by a beneficent and benevolent God?

Divine Providence

Platon addressed the larger meaning of human suffering in discussions of divine providence. In the sermon of May 15, 1793, Platon acknowledges the doubts that can arise when human beings consider the demise of Tsarevich Dimitrii.[34] The preacher himself admits to feelings of uncertainty as he seeks to understand "God's providence and His wisdom." Platon lacks the psychological vocabulary of our own day, and he is not concerned with "why bad things happen to good people." Instead, he wants to know how it is that God invariably transforms human actions into his own eternal ends. The question leads Platon to thoughts of "the blessed Joseph," whose brothers intended to destroy him. But instead of being destroyed through their actions, Joseph became the ruler of Egypt. God thwarted the brothers' intentions and turned human evil into good. As Joseph himself states in Genesis 50:20, 'Even though you intended to do harm to me, God intended it for good.' A similar thing happened, Platon continues, when the Israelites rejected the savior who had been promised to them. Christ was sent 'to the lost sheep of the house of Israel' (Matthew 15:24) and not to anyone else. But because Israel denied Christ, God's wisdom established salvation for all peoples, not just for the house of Israel. Citing the Apostle Paul (Romans 11:11, 17), Platon points out that through the fall of the Jews, 'salvation has come to the Gentiles.' It is therefore clear that regardless of what human beings do or know, God does everything according to his divine will. Indeed, if human intentions and enterprises were successfully carried out, if divine providence did not transform them into God's design, the entire natural order would be overturned.

Platon applies this teaching to the life of Tsarevich Dimitrii, noting that evil human intentions sometimes appear victorious. Weak-minded people may look at Dimitrii's death and doubt the reality of divine justice. But having lost his earthly kingdom, the tsarevich attained martyrdom and rules in heaven. "Evil passion" wanted Dimitrii's name to be forgotten, but instead it brought him "blessed eternity." In other words, evildoers who try to overcome the divine order are doomed to failure. True, the fatherland suffered misfortune and destruction in the aftermath of the tsarevich's murder. But out of that unhappiness, divine providence brought the greatest happiness. Although Russia always had been celebrated among the nations, following the terrible misfortunes of the Time of Troubles, the empire achieved even greater glory and well-being. Without mentioning Poland directly, Platon compares "our neighboring country" to the house of Saul and Russia to the house of David: the house of 'David grew stronger and stronger, while the house of Saul became weaker and weaker' (2 Samuel 3:1).[35] Speaking in the era of the Polish partitions (circa 1772–95), which dismembered the Polish-Lithuanian state, and recalling the Polish intervention and occupation of Moscow during the troubles (circa 1598–1613), Platon concludes that both Poland and Israel got what they deserved, precisely because they tried to thwart God's plan. As stated in Exodus 20:5, God punishes 'children for the iniquity of parents, to the third and the fourth generation.'

Platon concludes the sermon by highlighting the lessons of the biblical stories he already has described. God governs all that happens in the world, and no one can change his intentions. Consequently, we must pursue all our endeavors with good intentions on the basis of God's "Holy Law." When we do this, our efforts will succeed, and our actions will achieve their good end. We may be thwarted for a time, but with good and right intentions, we cannot fail. If we seem to fail, it is either because our intentions are not pure, though we may think they are, or because God's judgment (*sud'ba*) is creating something better for us in this or the future life.[36] Simply put, evil deeds can never be successful against the will of God. They may appear successful for a time, but ultimately, divine wisdom will cover them with shame. Although God's truth may not be visible at every turn in every human situation, ultimately it will prevail. The divine order cannot be altered by human action. The divine order cannot be other than God intends it to be.

As the Dimitrii sermon of 1793 reveals, Platon's answer to the problem of the righteous sufferer rested upon two unchangeable principles. First, what human beings think they see, perceive, and experience is not equivalent to divine truth, which may not be visible to us. Second, God governs the universe, and all that happens must accord with his eternal design. When put together these principles "justify" human suffering. In Platon's homily, divine providence does not mean that every event in the world unfolds according to God's will, that every human action or experience is God-determined. Nor does it mean that the creator intervenes in everyday lives or even in the great exploits of heroes and martyrs. It does mean, however, that human intentions succeed only if they conform to God's design. God does not direct our mundane actions. To the contrary, Orthodox Christianity teaches that human beings possess free will, "the freedom to choose between good and evil," which "is one aspect of human nature created in God's image."[37] Divine providence is realized not by directly controlling human life, but by transforming human actions so that they serve God's eternal goals. Regardless of what may be visible at a given moment, these goals will prevail.

Conclusion

It is perhaps not difficult to understand why Metropolitan Platon's moralistic teachings appeared dated or "Protestant" to later generations of Russian religious thinkers. Father Georges Florovsky criticized Platon for "emotional moralistic humanism" and insufficient attention to correct doctrine and the sacramental meaning of Church life (*tserkovnost'*). For all Platon's piety, Florovsky opined, he was not sufficiently ecclesial (*tserkoven*), and his definition of the Church lacked precision.[38] Such modern characterizations of Platon suggest an antiquated and amateurish quaintness of no enduring cultural significance. This is not the place to evaluate Platon's religious legacy—clearly he was not a world-class theologian—but it should be noted that in present-day Russia historians and religious thinkers study the metropolitan's ideas, and there are even calls for his canonization.[39]

Among scholars of the eighteenth century, in Russia and abroad, Metropolitan Platon also is regarded as a serious intellectual who contributed to the goals of the pan-European religious Enlightenment. In aesthetically satisfying and accessible sermons, Platon absorbed and reworked Enlightenment ideas in a manner that kept Christian morality and Orthodox religious teachings meaningful and vibrant at a time when materialism, scientism, and atheism had begun to assume their modern forms.[40] At the turn of the nineteenth century, the metropolitan even tried his hand at writing history, an intellectual discipline widely recognized as a characteristic site of Enlightenment innovation.[41] *Short History of the Russian Church*, published in 1805 as a textbook for seminary students, reveals a capacity for historicist thinking grounded in source criticism and attention to empirical evidence.[42] In the introduction to the *History*, which relies on Old Russian chronicles, Muscovite narratives, and eighteenth-century historical publications, Platon expresses a "modern" Enlightenment understanding of the need to contextualize sources and reconcile conflicting "facts."[43]

Platon's religious teachings also suggest a historicist sensibility. In the Dimitrii sermon of 1775, the preacher draws a clear distinction between the scholarly investigation of historical events and the moral lessons to be learned from those events.[44] Speaking in the Kremlin's Archangel Cathedral before Empress Catherine II, Tsesarevich Paul, and Paul's first wife, Natal'ia Alekseevna, Platon describes the blessings that resulted from the death of Dimitrii and the troubles of the fatherland. Comparing Dimitrii's martyrdom and Russia's renewal to the spring greenery that covers the earth after a long winter, Platon does not pretend to provide a detailed explanation of the historical period in question. Without using the words historian or scholar, the preacher refers to persons who "devoted their time and talents to the investigation of the affairs, events, adventures, [and] consequences revealed in the course of governing states." "Our duty," Platon adds, "is spiritual and pastoral." It is to look at such events for the sole purpose of finding "appropriate moral teachings." When people see the happy successes of virtue, they will be aroused to honesty, and when they see "the futility of corrupt and evil intentions," they will understand that "vice is hateful and deserving of damnation." In Platon's mind, the moral lessons of history and Holy Scripture worked together.

Platon's moralistic approach to history echoed the religious Enlightenment of late seventeenth- and eighteenth-century Europe, the Christian humanism of the Renaissance, and the Christianized Platonic and Stoic thought of the Church fathers.[45] Stoicism, Christianity, humanism, and Enlightenment all emphasized righteous living and the moral development of the human person.[46] In Russia, the "rationalism" and "ecumenism" of Platon's humanistic orientation established an Enlightenment tone that resonated into the early nineteenth century. Only after the Napoleonic wars did the preacher's universalistic moral message begin to lose its salience in educated society.[47] Platon had his nineteenth-century admirers, though among elites accustomed to a liturgy that stressed immediate personal and collective experience of the divine, the religiously inspired romantic nationalism of the Slavophiles and the more mystical Orthodox spirituality of the hesychast revival became the iconic forms of Russian religious thought.[48] From the early nineteenth to the early twentieth century, religious thinkers focused on questions of "true Orthodoxy," the preservation of sacred space, interiorized spirituality, and Russian national distinctiveness—questions that did not directly concern Platon. Platon addressed a different set of problems, problems informed by the post-Petrine relationship between the Church and monarchy, particularly the emergence of the state and society as entities separate from the Church, and by Enlightenment ideals such as the dignity of the human person, the potential moral equality of all human beings, and the ability of people and governments, using God-given reason, to reform personal behavior and collective institutions. The humanistic expressions of empathy and the moderate tone of deliberation characteristic of Platon's sermons illustrate the churchman's non-doctrinaire mindset. Like religious enlighteners across Europe, Platon combined reason and faith in a way that effectively preserved God's relevance, even though the God-centered world had begun to crumble and human powers of cognition and transformation had reached unprecedented heights.[49]

NOTES

This chapter is based on material presented in Elise Kimerling Wirtschafter, *Religion and Enlightenment in Catherinian Russia: The Teachings of Metropolitan Platon* (DeKalb:

Northern Illinois University Press, 2013). Copyright 2013 by Northern Illinois University Press. Used by permission of the publisher.

1. James Cracraft, *The Petrine Revolution in Russian Architecture* (Chicago: University of Chicago Press, 1988); Cracraft, *The Petrine Revolution in Russian Imagery* (Chicago: University of Chicago Press, 1997); Cracraft, *The Petrine Revolution in Russian Culture* (Cambridge, MA: Harvard University Press, 2004).

2. For recent characterizations of the eighteenth-century Church as intellectually and spiritually moribund, see Raffaella Faggionato, *A Rosicrucian Utopia in Eighteenth-Century Russia: The Masonic Circle of N. I. Novikov*, trans. Michael Boyd and Brunello Lotti (Dordrecht: Springer, 2005); Irina Paert, *Spiritual Elders: Charisma and Tradition in Russian Orthodoxy* (DeKalb: Northern Illinois University Press, 2010).

3. Georges Florovsky, *Puti russkogo bogosloviia* (1937; repr., Minsk: Izdatel'stvo Belorusskogo Ekzarkharta, 2006).

4. Gregory L. Freeze, "Handmaiden of the State? The Church in Imperial Russia Reconsidered," *Journal of Ecclesiastical History* 36 (1985): 82–102. For recent recognition of the cultural significance of eighteenth-century Church intellectuals, see notes 7 and 39 below.

5. My understanding of Russia's religious Enlightenment is fully developed in Wirtschafter, *Religion and Enlightenment*. I also discuss various aspects of the vast Enlightenment question in "Thoughts on the Enlightenment and Enlightenment in Russia," *Journal of Modern Russian History and Historiography* 2 (2009): 1–26; "Religion and Enlightenment in Catherinian Russia: Father Platon at the Court of Catherine II," *The Slavonic and East European Review* 88, nos. 1–2 (2010): 180–203; *Russia's Age of Serfdom 1649–1861* (Malden, MA: Blackwell Publishing, 2008), 144–65; *The Play of Ideas in Russian Enlightenment Theater* (DeKalb: Northern Illinois University Press, 2003).

6. Recent scholarship also illuminates Platon's theological contribution. See the essay by Oliver Smith included in this volume and Pavel Khondzinskii, *Sviatitel' Filaret Moskovskii: Bogoslovskii sintez epokhi; Istoriko-bogoslovskoe issledovanie* (Moscow: PSTGU, 2010), 68–80.

7. The entire corpus of theological and devotional writings produced by eighteenth-century Church intellectuals deserves and has begun to attract greater attention from historians. See Joachim Klein, *Russkaia literatura v XVIII veke* (Moscow: Indrik, 2010); Gary Marker, *Imperial Saint: The Cult of St. Catherine and the Dawn of Female Rule in Russia* (DeKalb: Northern Illinois University Press, 2007); O. M. Goncharova, *Vlast' traditsii i "novaia Rossiia" v literaturnom soznanii vtoroi poloviny XVIII veka: Monografiia* (St. Petersburg: RKhGI, 2004); Olga Aleksandrovna Tsapina, "Iz istorii obshchestvenno-politicheskoi mysli Rossii epokhi prosveshcheniia: Protoierei P. A. Alekseev (1727–1801)" (Kand. diss., Moskovskii gosudarstvennyi universitet im. M. V. Lomonosova, 1998); Gregory L. Bruess, *Religion, Identity, and Empire: A Greek Archbishop in the Russia of Catherine the Great* (Boulder, CO: East European Monographs, 1997); Marcus C. Levitt, ed., *Early Modern Russian Writers, Late Seventeenth and Eighteenth Centuries*, vol. 150 of the *Dictionary of Literary Biography* (Detroit, MI: Gale Research, 1995); V. M. Zhivov, *Iazyk i kul'tura v Rossii XVIII veka* (Moscow: Shkola Iazyki russkoi kul'tury, 1996); Stephen K. Batalden, *Catherine II's Greek Prelate: Eugenios Voulgaris in Russia, 1771–1806* (Boulder, CO: East European Monographs, 1982); Lennart Kjellberg, *La langue de Gedeon Krinovskij, prédicateur russe du XVIII siècle* (Uppsala: Almqvist & Wiksells AB, 1957).

8. On the religious Enlightenment, see David Sorkin, *The Religious Enlightenment: Protestants, Jews, and Catholics from London to Vienna* (Princeton, NJ: Princeton University Press, 2008); Jonathan Sheehan, *The Enlightenment Bible: Translation, Scholarship, Culture* (Princeton, NJ: Princeton University Press, 2005); Joris Van Eijnatten, ed., *Preaching, Sermon and Cultural Change in the Long Eighteenth Century* (Leiden: Brill, 2009); James E. Bradley and Dale K. Van Kley, eds., *Religion and Politics in Enlightenment Europe* (Notre Dame, IN: University of Notre Dame Press, 2001).

9. On moral philosophy and the religious Enlightenment, see Steven Nadler, *Spinoza: A Life* (New York: Cambridge University Press, 1999), 290–92; J. B. Schneewind, *The Invention of Autonomy: A History of Modern Moral Philosophy* (New York: Cambridge University Press, 1998).

10. The sermons and other devotional writings are available in Platon (Levshin), *Pouchitel'nyia slova pri vysochaishem dvore e. i. v. . . . gosudaryni Ekateriny Alekseevny . . . i drugikh mestakh s 1763 goda po 1778 god skazyvannyia* . . . (hereafter *PS*), 20 vols. (Moscow: Senatskaia tipografiia, 1779–1806). Titles and publishers of individual volumes vary. The collection also can be accessed at the website of the Trinity-Sergius Monastery (*Lavra*): http://stsl.ru/lib/platon.

11. Florovsky characterizes Platon as a catechist and "enthusiast of enlightenment" who placed too much emphasis on moral instruction (*nravouchenie*) and emotional humanism and too little on faith (*vera*) and the sacramental meaning of the Church community (*tserkovnost'*). In interpreting Holy Scripture, Florovsky claims, Platon preferred to seek the literal meaning rather than the sacramental or mysterious meaning, which might not be present. Florovsky, *Puti*, 109–15. On Platon's role as moral teacher to monarchs, see Wirtschafter, "Religion and Enlightenment in Catherinian Russia," and Wirtschafter, "Christian Rulership in Enlightenment Russia: Father Platon at the Court of Catherine II," in *The Book of Royal Decrees and the Genesis of Russian Historial Consciousness*, ed. Gail Lenhoff and Ann M. Kleimola, UCLA Slavic Studies, New Series 7 (Columbus, OH: Slavica, 2011), 333–40. On the metropolitan's relations with students, see the essay by Sean Gillen in this volume.

12. Damaskin and Amvrosii edited the first nine volumes of Platon's collected sermons. On their role, see Evgenii (Bolkhovitinov), *Slovar' istoricheskii o byvshikh v Rossii pisateliakh dukhovnogo china Greko-Rossiiskoi Tserkvi* (Moscow: Russkii Dvor, 1995), 73. See also the introductory materials in vol. 1 of the *PS*.

13. For my contribution to this discussion, see Wirtschafter, *Religion and Enlightenment*.

14. On the Radical Enlightenment, see Jonathan Israel, *Enlightenment Contested: Philosophy, Modernity, and the Emancipation of Man, 1670–1752* (New York: Oxford University Press, 2006); Israel, "Enlightenment! Which Enlightenment?," *Journal of the History of Ideas* 67, no. 3 (July 2006): 523–45; Lynn Hunt, *Inventing Human Rights: A History* (New York: W. W. Norton, 2007).

15. For recent statements in this direction, see Tzvetan Todorov, *L'Esprit des Lumières* (Paris: Robert Laffont, 2006); James Swenson, "Critique, Progress, Autonomy," *Studies in Eighteenth-Century Culture* 36, no. 1 (2007): 1–11.

16. Josef Pieper, *Scholasticism: Personalities and Problems of Medieval Philosophy*, trans. Richard and Clara Winston (South Bend, IN: St. Augustine's Press, 2001).

17. For a theoretical statement of this dynamic, see Eric Hobsbawm, "Introduction: Inventing Tradition," in *The Invention of Tradition*, ed. Eric Hobsbawm and Terence

Ranger (Cambridge: Cambridge University Press, 1983), 1–14. According to historian Jonathan Israel, the principles of philosophical modernity, which can be equated with the Radical Enlightenment, include: (1) recognition of mathematical-historical reason as the sole criterion of truth, (2) rejection of all supernatural agency, magic, and divine providence (3) belief in the equality of all humankind, including racial and sexual equality, (4) belief in a secular, universalistic ethics, grounded in equality and concerned with equity, justice, and charity, (5) full religious toleration, freedom of conscience, and freedom of thought, (6) freedom of expression, political criticism, and the press, (7) acceptance of democratic republicanism as the most legitimate form of politics, and (8) personal liberty of life-style and sexual orientation. Israel, *Enlightenment Contested*, 866.

18. Luca Fonnesu, "The Problem of Theodicy," in *The Cambridge History of Eighteenth-Century Philosophy*, ed. Knud Haakonssen (Cambridge: Cambridge University Press, 2008), 2:749–78; Thomas Saine, *The Problem of Being Modern, or The German Pursuit of Enlightenment from Leibniz to the French Revolution* (Detroit, MI: Wayne State University Press, 1997), 87–119; Carl Becker, *The Heavenly City of the Eighteenth-Century Philosophers* (New Haven, CT: Yale University Press, 1932), 64–77. On the discussion in Russia, see Klein, *Russkaia literatura*, 127–31; E. Waegemans, "Literaturno-filosofskaia interpretatsiia lissabonskogo zemletriaseniia: Portugalo-franko-russkaia teoditseia," *XVIII vek* 22 (2002): 111–21.

19. Nicholas Shrady, *The Last Day: Wrath, Ruin, and Reason in the Great Lisbon Earthquake of 1755* (New York: Penguin Books, 2008), 207.

20. Voltaire, *Candide*, trans. and ed. Daniel Gordon (Boston and New York: Bedford/St. Martin's, 1999).

21. The sermons commemorating the feast day of St. Dimitrii of Uglich are published in Platon, *PS*, 3:33–40 (15 May 1775); 4:15–22 (15 May 1777); 4:358–65 (15 May 1779); 5:233–40 (15 May 1780); 10:131–39 (15 May 1781); 12:63–72 (15 May 1784); 13:78–83 (15 May 1786); 16:244–52 (15 May 1793); 18:206–12 (15 May 1797); 19:41–50 (15 May 1798); 19:217–23 (15 May 1800); 19:300–308 (15 May 1801); 20:28–34 (15 May 1803); 20:100–109 (15 May 1804).

22. A. M. Kleimola, "The Canonization of Tsarevich Dmitrii: A Kinship of Interests," *Russian History* 25, nos. 1–4 (1998): 107–17; Kleimola, "Romanovy i kul't Tsarevicha Dimitriia: Graficheskie refleksii," in *Religiia i tserkov' v kul'turno-istoricheskom razvitii russkogo severa: K 450-letiiu Prepodobnogo Trifona, viatskogo chudotvortsa*, ed. V. V. Nizov (Kirov: Viatskii gosudarstvennyi pedagogicheskii universitet, 1996), 1:228–34; A. M. Nikolaieff, "Boris Godunov and the Ouglich Tragedy," *Russian Review* 9, no. 4 (1950): 275–85; O. A. Tsapina, "K istorii izucheniia drevnostei moskovskogo kremlia vo 2-i polovine XVIII veka," in *Literatura i istoriia: Istoricheskii protsess v tvorcheskom soznanii russkikh pisatelei i myslitelei XVIII–XX vv.)*, vypusk 3, ed. Iu. B. Stennik (St. Petersburg: Nauka, 2001), 9–31; Chester S. L. Dunning, *Russia's First Civil War: The Time of Troubles and the Founding of the Romanov Dynasty* (University Park: Pennsylvania State University Press, 2001), 1–6, 245–60; A. P. Pavlov, "Fedor Ivanovich and Boris Godunov," in *From Early Rus' to 1689*, vol. 1 of *The Cambridge History of Russia*, ed. Maureen Perrie (Cambridge: Cambridge University Press, 2006), 264–85; Gail Lenhoff, *The Martyred Princes Boris and Gleb: A Socio-Cultural Study of the Cult and the Texts* (Columbus, OH: Slavica, 1989); Timothy Ware, *The Orthodox Church*, rev. ed. (New York: Penguin Books, 1997), 79–80.

23. The status of the Dimitrii cult remains uncertain. Platon clearly recognized the tsarevich as a martyr prince (*muchenik*), but according to Chester Dunning, the Church never accepted St. Dimitrii's vita because of its obvious political purpose. Platon (Levshin), *Kratkaia tserkovnaia rossiiskaia istoriia* (Moscow: Sinodal'naia tipografiia, 1805), 2:101-2, 187-88; Dunning, *Russia's First Civil War*, 244-60, 273, 313, 545n.

24. On cognitive Orthodoxy, see Gregory L. Freeze, "The Rechristianization of Russia: The Church and Popular Religion, 1750-1850," *Studia Slavica Finlandensia* 7 (1990): 101-36. On happiness, see Stephen Lessing Baehr, *The Paradise Myth in Eighteenth-Century Russia: Utopian Patterns in Early Secular Russian Literature and Culture* (Stanford, CA: Stanford University Press, 1991); Darrin M. McMahon, *Happiness: A History* (New York: Atlantic Monthly Press, 2006); Todorov, *L'Esprit*, 96-101.

25. Platon, *PS*, 5:233-40 (15 May 1780).

26. In Church Slavonic, *sud'ba* means judgment. See note 36 below.

27. Unless otherwise stated, the biblical passages cited in this essay appear in Platon's writings and are therefore set off by single quotation marks. In instances where Platon paraphrases or gives a partial biblical quote, and I provide the full passage, double quotation marks are used. For the preferred Orthodox translation of biblical passages, see the latest edition of *The Orthodox Study Bible* from the St. Athanasius Academy of Orthodox Theology (Nashville, TN: Thomas Nelson, 2008). The New Testament text is the New King James Version (Nashville, TN: Thomas Nelson, 1982), and the Old Testament text in the St. Athanasius Septuagint (St. Athanasius Academy of Orthodox Theology, 2008). In identifying the Psalms, I include the numbering found in the Septuagint (and used by Platon) in parentheses.

28. Wirtschafter, *The Play of Ideas*.

29. Platon, *PS*, 12:63-72 (15 May 1784).

30. Sergei M. Zarin, *Asketizm po pravoslavno-khristianskomu ucheniiu: Etikobogoslovskoe issledovanie* (1907; repr., Moscow: Palomnik, 1996), 6-10.

31. Platon, *PS*, 13:78-83 (15 May 1786).

32. The verse reads: "Therefore take up the whole armor of God, so that you may be able to withstand on that evil day, and having done everything, to stand firm."

33. For Platon honor and honesty are indistinguishable.

34. Platon, *PS*, 16:244-52 (15 May 1793).

35. 2 Kingdoms 3:1 in the Septuagint.

36. In Church Slavonic, *sud'by* refers to God's judgments, as in Psalm 36:6 (35:7): "your judgments are like the great deep." Platon uses the phrase "the Lord's judgments" (*sud'by Gospodni*) in a sermon of 13 November 1790 devoted to the feast day of St. John Chrysostom, another saint who though persecuted in earthly life is in death all the more glorified in heaven. Platon, *PS*, 15:695-703. My thanks to Ronald Vroon for identifying the biblical reference.

37. The human ability to reason and to choose freely reflects the divine image. Because human nature was created in the image of God, it is good, even if stained by sin. Through the grace of the Holy Spirit, the believer can be restored to the original uncorrupted state and reunited with God. *Orthodox Study Bible*, 1780, 1782, 1784. In Platon's sermons the attention to human free will is extensive and broad-based. For detailed discussion, see Wirtschafter, *Religion and Enlightenment*, esp. chap. 4.

38. Florovsky, *Puti*, 109-15.

39. A. I. Esiukov, *Filosofskie aspekty russkoi bogoslovskoi mysli (vtoraia polovina XVIII-nachalo XIX v.): Monografiia* (Arkhangel'sk: Pomorskii gosudarstvennyi universitet, 2003); Esiukov, *Chelovek i mir v pravoslavnoi prosvetitel'skoi mysle Rossii vtoroi poloviny XVIII veka: Istoriko-filosofskie ocherki* (Arkhangel'sk: Izdatel'stvo Pomorskogo gosudarstvennogo universiteta imeni M. V. Lomonosova, 1998); Iurii Valentinovich Kagarlitskii, "Ritoricheskie strategii v russkoi propovedi perekhodnogo perioda, 1700–1775" (Kand. diss., Rossiiskaia akademiia nauk, Moscow, 1999); P. V. Kalitin, *Uravnenie russkoi idei: Po-sviatootecheski novaia i original'naia sistema "mysli-postupka-sotsiuma" rossiiskikh uchenykh monakhov vtoroi poloviny XVIII-nachala XIX vekov* (Moscow: Editorial URSS, 2002); Zhivov, *Iazyk i kul'tura*; V. P. Zubov, *Russkie propovedniki: Ocherki po istorii russkoi propovedi* (Moscow: Editorial URSS, 2001). For recent scholarly studies and calls for Platon's canonization, see *Platonovskie chteniia: Sbornik materialov*, 8 vols. to date (Moscow: Perervinskaia dukhovnaia seminariia, 2005–11).

40. On Platon's literary eloquence, see Elise Kimerling Wirtschafter, "20 September 1765: Tsesarevich Paul's Eleventh Birthday and Father Platon's 'Sermon on Learning,'" in *Days from the Reigns of Eighteenth-Century Russian Rulers*, ed. Anthony Cross (Cambridge, 2007), 2:168–69; Anthony Cross, "8 August 1768: The Laying of the Foundation Stone of Rinaldi's St. Isaac's Cathedral," in Cross, *Days from the Reigns*, 2:176.

41. Dan Edelstein, *The Enlightenment: A Genealogy* (Chicago: University of Chicago Press, 2010), 19–23; J. G. A. Pocock, *The Enlightenments of Edward Gibbon, 1737–1764*, vol. 1 of *Barbarism and Religion* (Cambridge: Cambridge University Press, 1999).

42. Platon, *Kratkaia tserkovnaia rossiiskaia istoriia*.

43. Church fathers and medieval scholastic thinkers also distinguished theology from empirical and philosophical knowledge. Pieper, *Scholasticism*. The eighteenth-century publications cited by Platon include chronicles, the histories of Tatishchev and Shcherbatov, and Novikov's documentary collection, *Drevniaia Rossiiskaia Vivliofika*.

44. Platon, *PS*, 3:33–40 (15 May 1775).

45. Frederick Copleston, S. J., *Medieval Philosophy from Augustine to Duns Scotus*, vol. 2 of *A History of Philosophy* (New York: Doubleday, 1950), 1–39.

46. Alasdair A. MacDonald, Zweder R. W. M. von Martels, and Jan R. Veenstra, eds., *Christian Humanism: Essays in Honour of Arjo Vanderjagt* (Leiden: Brill, 2009).

47. The question of Platon's reception has not been fully studied for any period of Russian history. The divergence between religious and secular literature is documented in Zhivov, *Iazyk i kul'tura*.

48. Among Platon's admirers, see P. A. Beliaev, *Zhizn' Platona, mitropolita moskovskago s ego portretom* (1900; repr., Minneapolis, MN: AARDM Press, 1982); I. M. Snegirev, *Zhizn' Moskovskago Metropolita Platona*, 2 vols. (Moscow: Tipografiia Vedomostei Moskovskoi Gorodskoi Politsii, 1856).

49. Sheehan, *Enlightenment Bible*.

Chapter 2

Theology on the Ground

Dmitrii Bogoliubov, the Orthodox Anti-Sectarian Mission, and the Russian Soul

HEATHER J. COLEMAN

In the late nineteenth and early twentieth century, no one would have thought of the Russian Orthodox Church's "internal" mission as a site for "religious thought." Certainly, missionaries would seem by nature unlikely to be theologically adventurous types. This was particularly the case for members of the Church's internal mission, whose task was defined not so much in terms of expansion of the flock as of its preservation. The internal missionaries aimed to return to Orthodoxy those whom the Church had lost to Old Belief (the result of the Church schism of 1666–67) and various non-Orthodox faiths such as the Dukhobors, the Molokans, or the Baptists. This mission was highly controversial, both in Church circles and in broader Russian society, right up to 1917. It was identified with Konstantin Pobedonostsev, the famous reactionary and defender of the close unity of the state and its Orthodox Church, who exercised great influence as the ober-procurator of the Holy Synod and key advisor to Alexander III (ruled 1881–94) and, until his death in 1907, to his son, Nicholas II. Under his watch, religion became highly politicized and the Russian imperial state was mobilized to defend the legal prohibition against preaching non-Orthodox faiths or leaving the Orthodox Church.[1] The liberal press of the era recounted tales of missionaries enlisting the help of the police to force Old Believers and sectarians to debate them in public, and, in a few sensational cases, to remove the children of sectarians from their parents.[2] Criticism echoed inside the Church too. Metropolitan Evlogii (Georgievskii) remembered that, "in the dioceses, in Church circles, [the missionaries] were feared, but they were not loved nor were they trusted."[3] Yet, precisely because their mission was to their fellow Russians, to those souls that the Church considered to be canonically—indeed, naturally, essentially—its own, the internal missionaries confronted questions about the nature of the Russian soul and the role of the Church in Russian society.

Although scholars are paying increasing attention to the forms of internal missionary work in the Russian Empire, there has been very little study of the evangelists themselves, of their ideals and their understandings of their role in Russian state and society.[4] However, their mission was an important component of the increased attention to pastoral work within the late imperial Orthodox Church.[5] The internal mission reached out to peasants but also to the intelligentsia and its purview eventually extended beyond religious dissent to combating disbelief and socialism. It was thus a major site for the Church's engagement with modern society. And when we read the pages of the missionary press of the period, we discover a complicated picture of missionary work, one in which the missionaries were not so much confident instruments of the state as desperate to prove their utility to the government, not so much triumphant as anxiously searching for the best means to convert the Russian people, and not so much oblivious to the intellectual currents of their time as eager to engage and lend their voices to them.

The career and writings of Dmitrii I. Bogoliubov, who served as diocesan anti-sectarian missionary in Tambov, Khar'kov, and Saint Petersburg dioceses between 1894 and 1913, provide particularly fine insight into these features of missionary thinking. Recognized as a skillful and innovative evangelist "on the ground," Bogoliubov was also a prolific writer who sought to share his expertise and develop the internal mission into a full-fledged professional arm of the Church. Moreover, he took a great interest in the new religious thought of his day, attending talks at the Saint Petersburg Religious-Philosophical Society, for example, after he moved to the capital in 1903, and commenting on them in relation to the Orthodox Church's outreach to Russian society.

Bogoliubov's interventions in the political and religious debates of his day, especially his memoirs written between 1914 and 1917, provide insight into the middle-brow, practical engagement of the academy-educated professional missionary with the religious thought abroad in late imperial Russia. The motivation for this exchange lay in the conservative populism that dominated the clerical milieu of his youth.[6] Indeed, on the first page of his memoir, Bogoliubov recalled that, when he graduated from the Moscow Spiritual Academy in 1894, he had "burned with a religious-populist [*religiozno-narodnicheskoe*] mood. And I tried in every possible way to organize my life in order to be closer to the people—in order to see [the people's] true life, its joys and sorrow." "How could I," he wondered, "not yet encumbered with 'everyday worries,' be useful to my native Church, my native people, and the parish clergy in the battle against sects?"[7] Driven by this passion to serve, Bogoliubov had enlisted as a diocesan missionary in Tambov province, an area known for its large population of religious sectarians.[8] In a series of installments, Bogoliubov recounted for readers of *Missionary Digest* (*Missionerskii sbornik*) how his encounters with religious dissidents in the first year of his ministry had transformed his understanding of the village and his conception of mission. Bogoliubov's memoir serves as an example of the potential of missionaries' narratives of their work among sectarians for exploring a form of religious "going to the people" that arose from conservative nationalist views but was not limited by them.

The vast Orthodox periodical press where Bogoliubov's writings appeared developed rapidly from the 1860s and represents a valuable and still underutilized source not just for the intellectual and cultural history of the Orthodox Church, but also for major themes in late imperial Russian thought. New scholarship is demonstrating its value. For example, Vera Shevzov has used theological journals to explore ideas about theology, identity, and community, and William Wagner to describe thinking about the Christian woman's social role. Similarly, Laurie Manchester draws on priests' diaries, memoirs, and pastoral notes published in the Orthodox press to reveal the religious sources of Russian intelligentsia identity and thought.[9] *Missionary Digest*, in which Bogoliubov's autobiographical series appeared, was a well-regarded journal published by the Saint Vasilii Brotherhood of Riazan' diocese beginning in 1891. Major figures in the missionary movement from all over Russia wrote regularly for this journal, despite its provincial status.[10] *Missionary Digest* and the more prominent official organ of the internal mission, *Missionary Review* (*Missionerskoe obozrenie*), to which Bogoliubov was also a frequent contributor, are rich in materials for the study of religious dissidence and thinking within the Church about questions of conscience and culture, and about the relationships between Church and state and society.

This study is based on a broad sampling of Bogoliubov's extensive writings, focusing on his memoirs. Like all autobiographers, Bogoliubov searched the past for "essential times and patterns in [his life]," re-creating that life to some extent in the process.[11] The picture he paints of the village and his own background in his memoirs is governed by his primary goal of asserting the correctness of his own approach to evangelism at a time, as we will see, when he had lost his job precisely because of his methods and views. Moreover, like other missionaries' accounts of their work, Bogoliubov's writings had a strong didactic quality: a central point was to provide models of how to engage in religious disputes with followers of various non-Orthodox faiths. But as they explored how best to correct sectarians' "errors," they also became studies of the psychology of the religious dissident and the nature of the Russian soul. Through the story of his early mission, Bogoliubov made a series of arguments about the place of the Orthodox faith in Russian society, about the nature of the challenge presented by sectarianism, and about the best methods for meeting that challenge. His experiences, he concluded, had made him question the conservative nationalist vision of the inherently "God-bearing" (*narod-bogonosets*) character of the Russian people and to reject public debates with dissenters in favor of a long-term educational approach aimed at shoring up and expanding true Orthodoxy among the population at large.[12] Reading his memoirs together with his other writings on missions and on the encounter between the Church and Russian society, we can trace a shift in his thinking toward an advocacy of freedom of conscience in Russia rooted in Orthodox ideas, a view arrived at through his concrete experience of work with religious dissidents and shaped interpretively both by the Slavophile and conservative nationalist influences of his youth and by the ideas of leading figures of the fin-de-siècle Russian religious renaissance such as Vladimir Solov'ev, Sergei Bulgakov, and Nikolai Berdiaev.

The Russian Orthodox Church's Anti-Sectarian Mission

When Bogoliubov began his career in 1894, the anti-sectarian mission remained in its infancy. Proselytizing among the various non-Orthodox ethnic groups living under the scepter of the Russian tsar had gone hand in hand with imperial expansion since the sixteenth century; beginning in 1869, a semi-official lay association, the Imperial Orthodox Missionary Society, worked to support such missions. The internal mission, by contrast, served as the Orthodox Church's instrument against religious dissidence among the Russian-, Ukrainian-, and Belarusian-speaking populations that the Church considered naturally its own. Of course, missionary work in this sense had always been among the duties of the parish priest. The emergence of a more formal structure for the internal mission had its roots in the rising concern, from the 1820s onwards, that the schismatic Old Believers might actually be recruiting Orthodox parishioners to their fold.[13] Sustained Christian education and anti-schismatic programs developed haltingly. In 1828, at the time of the establishment of the first formal anti–Old Believer mission in Perm' diocese, the Synod issued a general set of instructions on missionary work with schismatics. Thereafter, missionary committees appeared in a few dioceses. Beginning in 1853, special missionary departments in some seminaries and spiritual academies began to train professional missionaries.[14] In 1886, the Synod gave all seminaries three years to establish such departments.[15] And in 1887 and 1891, the first two congresses of the internal mission took place in Moscow. As a result of the first of these, in 1888, the Synod published a new set of rules for internal mission, which addressed not only the challenge of the Old Believers but also that of the new evangelical sects that were emerging in the post-emancipation period.[16]

By the 1890s, the missionaries' arguments about the political significance of combating sectarianism began to resonate in the governmental sphere. Indeed, just before Bogoliubov embarked on his first missionary tour of Tambov in autumn 1894, the Council of Ministers had declared the new sect of shtundists (a catch-all term for Ukrainian and Russian Baptists and other evangelicals) to be very harmful and banned their meetings—one of the requests of the 1891 missionary congress. That same year the Holy Synod appointed Vasilii M. Skvortsov, a graduate of the Kiev Spiritual Academy, instructor at the Kiev Spiritual Seminary, anti-sectarian missionary, and secretary of the 1891 congress, as its first special advisor on non-Orthodox religious movements. In 1896, he would found the official journal of the internal mission, *Missionary Review*, in Kiev. In 1899, he moved to the capital, where he continued his work for the Synod and developed his publishing activity further. He served as the main organizer "from the Church side" of the Saint Petersburg Religious-Philosophical Meetings, which brought together representatives of the Church and the intelligentsia between 1901 and 1903, and the pages of *Missionary Review* increasingly addressed not just religious dissent but the broader religious, intellectual, social, and political issues of the day. In 1906, he founded a reactionary newspaper, *The Bell* (*Kolokol*), and became involved in various monarchist organizations.[17] Skvortsov would remain at the helm of *Missionary Review* right up to 1917. Celebrated in some circles, he was reviled in others for his reactionary politics and fierce advocacy of the responsibility of state institutions, including the police, to defend and preserve Orthodoxy.

In Search of the God-Bearing People: Academy Education, Missionary Encounters, and Rethinking Conservative Nationalism

When Bogoliubov set out on his first missionary trip in 1894, much of this was in the future. In his memoir, he presented himself as leaving the academy full of ambition but with no formal training in evangelism and no real preconception of what experiences lay ahead. He knew the Synod's instructions on missionary work and he had read various books on religious sectarianism and missions, but he had never actually tried out any of this knowledge on real dissenters. After filing the required itinerary with the local missionary brotherhood that oversaw his work, he headed out in a springless carriage across bumpy and muddy roads to meet them.

What did he hope to find? In short, to reconcile his book learning about the Russian people's Orthodox mission with the reality of religious dissent. As he recalled, "I was almost ill with worry about the question of how it was that in various corners of our motherland the Russian people, the God-bearing people, revealed a tendency toward sectarianism. Why were our holy, Orthodox beliefs not treasured everywhere, as before, by Russian people?"[18]

In the diaries on which he claims to base his account, Bogoliubov finds his young self struggling to make sense of his education at the academy. Perhaps reflecting educated society's renewed populist sense of the need to serve the people on the heels of the famine of 1891–92, Bogoliubov repeatedly used the term *narodnicheskoe* to describe his outlook in 1894, evoking the radical populist movement. However, like many people in the clerical milieu of his day, his populism was rooted in Slavophilism and the conservative nationalism of the *pochvenniki* or enthusiasts of the soil, such as Fedor Dostoevsky and Nikolai Danilevskii.[19] With some irony, he wrote of how, on his first trip to the village, "I felt myself to be a Slavophile among the people, the herald of profound and enlightened scholarly knowledge of Orthodox Christian truths. At the time, I imagined myself . . . literally as a 'walking Spiritual Academy' for priests."[20] What he would soon find out, was that he did not know much.

One of the central themes of Bogoliubov's account is the citified student's encounter with the village. Although Bogoliubov, like most of his fellow academy graduates, came from a rural clerical background—he was the son of a village psalmist from Samara province—his mission led him to see the countryside and its inhabitants in a new light. "I knew peasant and village life from my earliest childhood," he wrote, but now "I began to look at [the village] not with the eyes of a 'summer resident' [*dachnika*] and 'outsider,' but with the eyes of a Christian, himself experiencing the joys and sorrows of our village."[21] Bogoliubov's life as a missionary was one of mud, bumpy roads, bedbugs, food poisoning, endless cups of tea, and sore throats from long hours of talking in cramped, smoky peasant huts. It was also a journey into foreign territory, where local knowledge often trumped an academy diploma. He headed out with a map and an itinerary, only to discover that villages were called one thing on the map and another in the local dialect. He thought he had waited until the worst of the peasants' harvest work was over, yet found that they were still horribly busy in early October. As he discovered, "in work in sectarian parishes, by far not everything depends on the diligence and good will of the missionary. What are called 'conditions of life' carry a huge and sometimes decisive significance. And above all—the season of the year."[22] Time and again, he met peasants who seemed eager to discuss spiritual matters but told him that he should come back and spend the winter in their village, when they had time to chat.[23] And one of the central messages of his memoir was that all the book learning in the world could not replace getting to know the villagers as people.

On his missionary journeys, Bogoliubov was hosted by various village worthies, who provided an entrée for him into the local community. He relied on the local schoolteacher for advice and inside knowledge—and to lend him authority.[24] But most importantly, the man who had fancied himself a "pioneer among the clergy" learned that the missionary's most important ally was the local priest. Parish priests had usually not enjoyed the higher education of professional missionaries like him and they tended to fear them as inspectors. But what Bogoliubov discovered was that they were a fountain of local knowledge. Their reports "to the city," he insisted, were full of what they thought their superiors wanted to hear, but in person, priests were "exceptional experts on popular life." While they might lack knowledge and training, respecting them as friends and helpers could also arouse their excitement and motivation to improve their pastoral work.[25]

Now in fact most missionaries were themselves parish priests who took on additional leadership in this area. Moreover, the majority of diocesan missionaries, unlike Bogoliubov, were ordained clergymen. Still, as a group, the missionaries occupied an ambiguous position in the Church. The 1888 mission rules had envisioned a corps of diocesan missionaries composed of priests with spiritual academy or seminary diplomas, paid out of diocesan funds. They would be assisted by parish priests appointed as local missionaries and by enthusiastic and knowledgeable lay volunteers.[26] Indeed, three-quarters of the diocesan missionaries attending the 1897 Third All-Russian Missionary Congress in Kazan' were priests. However, a significant minority, including Bogoliubov (there representing Tambov diocese), consisted of laymen who had chosen missionary work as a full-time career. And unlike the overwhelming majority of parish priests, almost 40 percent of delegates—and every single non-ordained diocesan missionary like Bogoliubov—held higher degrees.[27]

What sort of intellectual world did Bogoliubov, "the walking Spiritual Academy," represent? Scholars have traditionally described the academies' isolation from the broader stream of Russian intellectual culture. After all, the clergy was a virtually closed estate in imperial Russia and the academies, overwhelmingly staffed and attended by priests' sons, perpetuated this social separation. On the academic side, historians have emphasized the destructive influence on academy life of Pobedonostsev's anti-intellectualism, his distaste for theology, and the 1884 counter-reforms he introduced to tighten discipline, reduce academic autonomy, and reorganize the curriculum to emphasize the training of students for ministry.[28] These measures reinforced the intellectual and social distance between academy theologians and philosophers and the secular intelligentsia.

There is much truth to the stereotype of two separate academic cultures, but it also rides roughshod over important commonalities and underestimates the engagement of the academies and their graduates in public intellectual life. For one thing, there were two schools of thought within the academies—one that supported a practical-pastoral model and another that aimed at a more scholarly approach to theology.[29] Far from being unique to the Russian setting, this simply reflects the inherent tension between the goals of scholarly and pastoral formation that existed in Western European seminaries as well.[30] The 1869 charter of the spiritual academies, which stressed autonomy for the institutions and a relatively specialized education for the students, tended toward the former. The 1884 charter, by contrast, favored the latter, emphasizing service to the state (and its Church) and purveying a broader but more superficial formation to the students.[31] More importantly from the point of view of people like Bogoliubov or Skvortsov, the program and ethos of the academies after the 1884 counter-reforms reflected a longer-term trend toward an increasingly this-worldly theology, one that emphasized the Christian duty to enter and Christianize the world—and by extension to engage the laity in order to transform its culture. The new program placed renewed importance on theological subjects in addition to increasing the number of required courses; both pastoral theology and homiletics became compulsory subjects for the first time in 1884, a fact that seems to have contributed to a flowering of original Russian pastoral theology in the late nineteenth century.[32] The policy of emphasizing pastoral training and encouraging students to find their calling as preachers yielded significant fruit in the form of students like Bogoliubov. Bogoliubov displays a commitment to engaging with society, an emphasis on self and social analysis through writing, and a broad but superficial acquaintance with key ideas in Russian intellectual life that were characteristics of his education at the academy.

Manchester argues that this this-worldly theology undergirded the conservative populism that was widespread in the clerical milieu by the second half of the nineteenth century.³³ Indeed, in his memoir, Bogoliubov turned desk-bound intellectuals into activists like himself, recalling his youthful ambition to influence the world around him, "inspired by the very same undying ideals with which our Slavophiles—Kireevskii, Khomiakov, I. S. Aksakov, and others—once burned in the battle for Orthodoxy."³⁴

The questions that engaged academy professors were also not so distant from the mainstream of Russian thought. Philosophers in the academies, in particular, had long been influential contributors to the broader discipline.³⁵ And, as Shevzov argues, spiritual academy theologians, philosophers, and historians explored essentially the same questions that preoccupied educated society at large: "If, for secular society, the current questions had to do with Russia's identity, originality, and future with respect to the West, for Orthodox academics the most pressing issues concerned the nature of Orthodoxy, its uniqueness (*samobytnost'*) and its relationship to the Christian West."³⁶

An important point of contact for these common questions lay in the shared interest within the Church and the intelligentsia at large in the problem of religious dissent.³⁷ Both groups regarded the issue as fundamentally related to culture—to what sectarianism revealed about the presence of rational and mystical tendencies and about collectivist and individualist values in Russian civilization.³⁸ But they disagreed on the significance of these elements and their place within that culture. One of the many points of contention between Church-based intellectuals and the "new religious thought" of fin-de-siècle Russia lay precisely in the idealization of religious dissent by Silver Age writers and philosophers.

The scholarly study of sectarianism based on written sources and ethnographic observation flourished in the spiritual academies of the 1880s and 1890s. Indeed, one of the pioneers of this field and a close associate of Pobedonostsev, Nikolai I. Subbotin, taught at the Moscow Spiritual Academy. Although study of Old Belief and sectarianism was not made compulsory for academy students until 1899, and Bogoliubov does not mention Subbotin, it is very likely that he had studied Old Belief, Subbotin's specialty, formally. However, Subbotin's approach was highly scholarly rather than practical in nature.³⁹ Textbooks with a more missiological emphasis were still in the future.

Bogoliubov's years at the academy, both inside and outside the classroom, had trained him to think about sectarianism in civilizational, religious, and cultural terms. But his initial encounters with the village forced him to rethink the broader cultural assumptions he had gleaned from his higher education. He had not understood, he realized, "the intense struggle that was taking place in the depths of the people around our religious beliefs." At the time, he was particularly enamored of the ideas of Nikolai Danilevskii. In his famous book, *Russia and Europe* (*Rossiia i Evropa*), Danilevskii had contrasted the materialist, corrupt, and factionalized Romano-Germanic civilization with the organic, Slavic-Orthodox culture of Russia, and predicted that the latter would one day come to dominate—or rather save—world civilization. Although written in 1869, the book enjoyed its greatest popularity in the late 1880s and early 1890s, and Bogoliubov recalled that he had uncritically "taken [it] as indisputable dogma for myself at the academy."[40] It is unlikely that Danilevskii formed part of the curriculum, but there would have been a substantial interest in such ideas in the nativist culture of the priests' sons who populated the academy.[41] Danilevskii's philosophy of civilizations, which argued for the autonomy of cultural-historical types and the impossibility of a universal human civilization, drew heavily on the variegated Slavophile tradition in its characterization of the Russian cultural-historical type.[42] Following Danilevskii, Bogoliubov remembered that he had expected that Orthodoxy would be essential, native, and inalienable for the Russian peasant. Moreover, according to Danilevskii, the historical specificity of the Russian people was the tendency to emphasize the collective over the personal or individual elements in life. Yet Bogoliubov found himself wondering how it was "that many Russian people were leaving their natural element and consciously and with conviction accepting a religious faith in the form of shtundism—the Baptist and Molokan faiths, where precisely personal, individual interests, [and] the personal, individual conscience are placed at the forefront, and where that which the Slavophiles call 'communal consciousness' [*sobornoe soznanie*] is devalued?"[43]

Echoing Dostoevsky's famous characterization, popular in conservative religious circles, of the Russian people's embodiment of true Christianity, Bogoliubov was initially inclined to explain dissent as a "clever 'alien intrigue'" perpetrated on the "childlike simplicity of the Russian God-bearing people." However, his own observations in the mission field and, especially, his conversations with priests and other members of the "village intelligentsia" revealed, instead, that "our people do not hold to the Church mystically or essentially."[44] Bogoliubov arrived in the countryside expecting to find such unity; he remembered being imbued with ideas about the national (*vsenarodnoe*) character of the Church and the liturgy at the academy. He had become a missionary precisely to protect the national nature of the Russian community. Yet, after a poorly attended service in a dilapidated church in a village with a large Baptist contingent, Bogoliubov had to admit that in that settlement, at least, "the existing Orthodox '*mir*' *manifestly* did not want to know about the Orthodox liturgy and church prayer meetings. This community appeared so indifferent to *its own* native Church, that it did not attend the service even *now*, if only in order to find out what *new* priest they had been sent to replace their *former* one."[45] The peasants turned out already to have been influenced by individualism and materialism.

On his way home from his first missionary trip, he sat in the third-class train compartment in order to chat with the common people. He asked his fellow travelers, mostly grain buyers and one village priest, about the condition of the peasantry. As they talked about economic problems and the market, about the peasants' untrustworthiness and lack of faith, Bogoliubov asked himself where the peasant envisioned by Dostoevsky and the Slavophiles had gone. He thought about how the "buyer" with whom he was chatting would never recognize the image of the Russian conveyed in Danilevskii's book: "he does not see in the Russian soul any special God-fearing quality or inclination to subjugate his mind to the collective [*sobornyi*] mind." He realized that "the Russian peasant—not the one out of books, not the Slavophile one, but the contemporary, living one with whom I have dealings, behaves not according to our theories and philosophical speculation but on the basis of the real considerations of life and *his* calculations."[46]

Confronted with the reality of the villagers, Bogoliubov began to interrogate Danilevskii's historical theories. On the one hand, his Christian faith led him to question broad cultural generalizations. He found himself troubled by the contradiction between a particularist view that assigned a special relationship between the Russian soul and Orthodoxy and the universalist teachings of Christ. "Was the Russian soul really *by nature* unlike the soul of, for instance, a German, an Englishman, or a Frenchman?" he asked himself. If there was indeed a special connection between the Russian soul and Orthodoxy, should it then not be sought in Russian history, in concrete reasons, motivations, and conditions? This spiritual reflection led him back to his history classes at the academy which, he now realized, had given him the tools to reevaluate Danilevskii. Suddenly, he thought of the essay he had written on the philosophy of history. He recalled how Nikolai I. Kareev, then a leading (and liberal) philosopher of history, had argued that it was a universal historical law that the individual personality and its environment or circumstances together drive the historical process. Was it really possible that the Russians had followed a different path?

Furthermore, his own Russian history professor at the academy, the celebrated Vasilii Kliuchevskii, had demonstrated the importance of material and tactical considerations in explaining the unification of the Russian lands or the Christianization of Rus'—thereby suggesting that Russia had a place in the universal patterns of the historical process.[47]

Once he had established that Russia did not have a special historical path, Bogoliubov reevaluated his missionary activity. He concluded that the appearance of the Baptists and other new sects reflected broader social, economic, and cultural changes in the village. If Russian traditions had their origins in the historical process rather than an innate, Russian, Orthodox soul, then the challenge was not to protect some essential Orthodoxy but to ensure the conditions of the faith's continued relevance and flourishing. "I said to myself," he remembered, "the Russian people, systematically moving in history from one condition to another, has arrived at the brink beyond which it is threatened by the danger of exchanging the communal [*sobornye*] principles in its life with personal, narrowly individual ones, of replacing the age-old Russian traditions of the *mir*, of the commune, with Protestant beliefs that are secluded in their isolation and alien to the beliefs of the Apostolic Church."[48] There was a historical process underway and knowing this meant that he could play a role in that historical evolution. His task was not to "win" in the theological debates with sectarians that were so central to missionary practice at the time, but to launch a long-term project of cultural, social, and economic work to both address change and preserve and strengthen important Orthodox values.[49]

For this was one of the central goals of Bogoliubov's writing project: to argue in favor of an approach to missions that focused as much, if not more, on those who remained within Orthodoxy as on those who abandoned it for the sects. As Eugene Clay has suggested, like churchmen elsewhere in Europe in the modern period, Russian missionaries sought to convey the rationalized Orthodoxy of the theological academy in a popular milieu that to them seemed heterodox and rife with superstition.[50] Ignorance was perceived to be the primary obstacle to correct faith and practice. In the early 1890s, missionary work centered around formal debates and discussions with dissenters on points of theology. The missionary's goal was to win these public debates and expose the sectarian leaders as self-willed, mistaken, and ignorant. Bogoliubov did not deny that theological discussion with sectarians was important: indeed, he met one inspiring priest in a parish with many sectarians who had energized his flock with a mass of activities, yet had not converted a single sectarian because he feared engaging them. Bogoliubov learned from his time there that success required both good parish work and active outreach to dissenters.[51] But he emphasized that these labors had as much to do with listening as with debating, with understanding the sectarians' perspective before countering it. Most importantly, his encounters with the Baptists, in particular the evidence of the sense of community and purpose that they seemed to engender, made him come to a crucial realization about missionary work: that "in the first instance [missionaries] needed to do the boring, unnoticed, samely work known as *Orthodox-Church education of the people* and forming among them lively and active missionary brotherhoods." At that time, he wrote, if a diocesan missionary had reported that he had spent his time working among the Orthodox rather than sectarians, he would have been disciplined. Yet this was precisely where the future of missionary work lay.[52] The obsession with theological disputes would not address the core of the problem. What was required was a holistic project aimed at restoring the communal basis of the parish.[53] In a sense, Bogoliubov had come to a remarkable view for his time: that nations were historical constructs rather than primordial essences needing to be awakened. He experienced this revelation as liberating as a missionary and embarked on a new crusade of building a truly Orthodox nation based on the principle of fellowship (*sobornost'*).[54]

Freedom of Conscience and the Nature of Missionary Work

As he moved from Tambov to Khar'kov to Saint Petersburg dioceses, Bogoliubov would develop and promote his vision of the renaissance of the parish as the central task of missionary work. He would also continue to work out what it meant to accept that the Russian soul was not Orthodox by nature but through historical development. As he did so, he struggled increasingly with the question of freedom of conscience and the connected issue of the relationship between the mission and the state, especially the police.

By the early twentieth century, freedom of conscience had become a burning topic in Russia. Perhaps surprisingly, a speech given at a diocesan missionary conference in Orel in September 1901 played a crucial role in bringing this debate into the open. To the amazement of delegates, the visiting dignitary Mikhail A. Stakhovich, marshal of the nobility of Orel province and member of the Beseda circle of reformers involved in the rural administrative assemblies (*zemstva*), asked to speak during the session on administrative and legal measures for dealing with religious crimes. He then proceeded, appealing to the heritage of the Slavophiles, to denounce the police approach and call for freedom of conscience. The speech was leaked to the local press and soon made a sensation nationally.⁵⁵ Indeed, Stakhovich's appeal would be the inspiration for Petr Struve's celebrated 1902 symposium, *Problems of Idealism*, where many key thinkers of the Russian Silver Age explored the philosophical foundations of liberalism.⁵⁶ Similarly, in April 1902, Stakhovich's speech served as the basis for two sessions about freedom of conscience at the Saint Petersburg Religious-Philosophical Meetings. It is worth remembering that these famous encounters between representatives of the "new religious consciousness" and churchmen were organized as a missionary endeavor by Skvortsov—in the political conditions of the time such semi-public discussion of religious questions could never have taken place without the sponsorship of the Church. Although these meetings are usually remembered as the site of the secular intelligentsia's return to religious questions in literature and philosophy, Skvortsov sought to use the sessions vigorously to assert the inherently Orthodox character of the Russian state and to defend the existing laws curtailing dissenting religious activity.⁵⁷

Bogoliubov, too, responded to Stakhovich's speech in the pages of *Missionary Review*. In early 1902, he quite conventionally rejected calls for freedom of conscience. Pointing to the "little developed" nature of the Russian common people, he argued that it would be a sin for educated society and the state not to protect them from "temptation"; the result of abandoning this responsibility, he warned, would be disorder that threatened social as well as religious authority.⁵⁸ But when, on Easter Day 1905, in the face of emerging revolution, Nicholas II decreed religious toleration in the Russian Empire, Bogoliubov stood out among missionaries for his joyous support of the new order. In the press and in his missionary reports, he celebrated the end of compunction in matters of faith as the dawn of a new era of mission through long-term cultural work. In the introduction to a collection of articles written between 1905 and 1908, Bogoliubov confessed that after 1905, he had changed his views on the relationship between the state and the religious consciences of its citizens: "There was a time when it seemed to us too that the battle with schism-sectarianism without police repression was inconceivable. Afterward we saw from experience that this routine legend could only be upheld by officials who feed at the table of the Orthodox mission, of the Church of God itself, for their own glory."⁵⁹

This realization launched Bogoliubov on a quest to defend freedom of conscience on Orthodox grounds and to demonstrate Orthodoxy's relevance in the modern age. Alongside his pastoral work, he threw himself into the religious intellectual life of the capital. He joined the Saint Petersburg Religious-Philosophical Society and his name appears in the minutes of several discussions.⁶⁰ He also began to write regularly about these issues and the ideas he encountered at Society meetings in reform-oriented Orthodox publications.[61] Although he could not agree with many of the religious views expressed by Silver Age writers such as D. S. Merezhkovskii or V. V. Rozanov, he regarded them as a wake-up call for those committed to building "an enlightened Christian public sphere [*obshchestvennost'*]."[62] In a lengthy article on the Church and contemporary life, Bogoliubov drew on his missionary experience to assert that there was no "organic affinity between the Russian soul and Orthodoxy"; this insight meant that there was also no necessary link between Orthodoxy and any particular political system, and that there was nothing un-Orthodox or foreign in citizens' efforts to transform Russia's political order.[63] As he struggled to work out his response to new political options such as Marxism or liberalism, to defend freedom of conscience on Orthodox grounds, or to explore the Church's place in a free society, Bogoliubov drew frequently on the writings of Slavophiles like Aleksei Khomiakov or Iurii Samarin, and even more on the new religious thought of Sergei Bulgakov and Vladimir Solov'ev that seemed to open up the possibility of a special Orthodox and Russian and modern path based on progress and individual freedom.[64]

Conclusion

Bogoliubov's memoir thus opens up the experiences of one of the new type of professional, lay missionary that was emerging just as questions of political freedom and national identity took on new importance in Russia. Bogoliubov wrote his account many years after his first missionary trips, and like all memoirs, it is shaped by what came next in his life. It is structured around convenient fictions—most importantly his alleged "discovery" of the countryside where he in fact grew up—but remains a useful document of how he understood his intellectual and religious evolution and the challenges of his form of "going to the people."

The kind of thoughtful, evolving, passionately spiritual encounter with sectarians and intelligentsia that Bogoliubov describes in his memoirs and other writings bears no resemblance to the public image of the rigid and aggressive anti-sectarian missionary of the 1890s and early twentieth century. Indeed, in some ways, Bogoliubov's perspective was not typical. By 1914, he was a controversial figure within the mission, widely admired but also regarded as a liberal and "soft" on dissent by his often right-wing colleagues. At the massive Fourth All-Russian Missionary Congress in Kiev in 1908, Bogoliubov had been the voice of the minority in favor of engaging with modern society and against a militant approach. He was henceforth shunned by his former colleagues at

Missionary Review, where he had been the top article contributor for many years, who attacked him as a "Kadet-lover" and sought to discredit both his politics and his theological knowledge.⁶⁵ In 1913, he lost his job as the Saint Petersburg diocesan missionary where, with the support of Metropolitan Antonii (Vadkovskii), he had worked precisely to develop his holistic approach to mission. Indeed, his successor Ivan G. Aivazov, appointed by the conservative new Metropolitan Vladimir (Bogoiavlenskii), had publicly attacked him for promoting sectarianism through the missionary brotherhood he had formed in the capital. According to Aivazov, Bogoliubov's methods did not recognize the need to launch an "offensive" against dissent.⁶⁶

Moreover, Bogoliubov's memoir differs in emphasis and level of interpretation from the numerous accounts that he and his colleagues wrote for missionary magazines to provide one another with ideas of how best to counter sectarianism.⁶⁷ His recollections have the reflective quality of hindsight, as he seeks to justify his approach to mission. But the story of his struggle to reconcile the Slavophile image of the Russian people with the realities of the village surely conveys an important reality of missionary work: the internal missionaries shared with their fellow educated Russians an obsession with defining the nature of the Russian soul.⁶⁸ Their accounts of their visits to the village were part of this process of defining Russianness and the range of spiritual and political options appropriate to the Russian people.

Bogoliubov was an activist, not an intellectual. He was interested in ideas that he found useful to his practical goal of successful missionary work. His understanding of the ideas he encountered could be eclectic and sketchy. In this he was typical of the missionaries. Indeed, although their personalities and views differed greatly, he was very similar in background and education to Skvortsov, the missionary leader whose name served as a shorthand for reactionary politics and a militant approach to mission. With her characteristic social and intellectual disdain, the poet Zinaida Gippius described Skvortsov, her partner in organizing the Religious-Philosophical Meetings, as "pushy, quite intelligent, but a coarse bumpkin," and mocked his aspiration to turn *Missionary Review* into a "real" journal.⁶⁹ She no doubt would have felt the same about Bogoliubov, both socially and intellectually. Yet his career of making sense of his theology degree on the ground, as an evangelist, illuminates the significance of the missionary milieu as a site for discussion about Orthodoxy in contemporary Russian life, the wider audience for the thought of the Russian religious renaissance, and the social impact that intelligentsia ideas could have beyond the salons of Petersburg or the desks of writers.

NOTES

1. A. Iu. Polunov, *Pod vlast'iu ober-prokurora: Gosudarstvo i tserkov' v epokhu Aleksandra III* (Moscow: AIRO-XX, 1996), chap. 4.

2. See, for example, *Russkiia vedomosti*, no. 221, 12 August 1897, 2; I. M. Gromoglasov, *Tretii Vserossiiskii missionerskii s"ezd (fakty i vpechatleniia)* (Sergiev Posad: 2 Tip. A. I. Snegirevoi, 1898), 3–8; M. I. Makarevskii and P. P. Dobromyslov, *3-ii Vserossiiskii missionerskii protivoraskol'nicheskii i protivosektantskii s"ezd v gorode Kazani* (Riazan': Tip. Bratstva Sv. Vasiliia, 1898), 143.

3. Evlogii Georgievskii, *Put' moei zhizni: Vospominaniia Mitropolita Evlogiia (Georgievskogo), izlozhennye po ego rasskazam T. Manukhinoi* (Moscow: Moskovskii rabochii, 1994), 187.

4. J. Eugene Clay, "Orthodox Missionaries and 'Orthodox Heretics' in Russia, 1886–1917," in *Of Religion and Empire: Missions, Conversion, and Tolerance in Tsarist Russia*, ed. Robert P. Geraci and Michael Khodarkovsky (Ithaca, NY: Cornell University Press, 2001), 38–69; Heather J. Coleman, "Defining Heresy: The Fourth Missionary Congress and the Problem of Cultural Power after 1905 in Russia," *Jahrbücher für Geschichte Osteuropas* 52, no. 1 (2004): 70–91; Daniel Beer, "The Medicalization of Religious Deviance in the Russian Orthodox Church (1880–1905)," *Kritika* 5, no. 3 (Summer 2004): 451–82; A. B. Efimov, *Ocherki po istorii missionerstva Russkoi Pravoslavnoi Tserkvi* (Moscow: PSTGU, 2007), 414–510.

5. See, for example, Gregory L. Freeze, "A Social Mission for Russian Orthodoxy: The Kazan Requiem of 1861 for the Peasants of Bezdna," in *Imperial Russia, 1700–1917: State, Society, Opposition*, ed. Ezra Mendelsohn and Marshall S. Shatz (DeKalb: Northern Illinois University Press, 1988), 113–35; Page Herrlinger, *Working Souls: Russian Orthodoxy and Factory Labor in St. Petersburg, 1881–1917* (Bloomington, IN: Slavica, 2007); Jennifer Hedda, *His Kingdom Come: Orthodox Pastorship and Social Activism in Revolutionary Russia* (DeKalb: Northern Illinois University Press, 2008).

6. Laurie Manchester, *Holy Fathers, Secular Sons: Clergy, Intelligentsia, and the Modern Self in Revolutionary Russia* (DeKalb: Northern Illinois University Press, 2008), 29.

7. D. Bogoliubov, "V bor'be s sektantstvom. (Iz zapisok eparkhial'nago missionera)," *Missionerskii sbornik*, no. 8 (1914): 572.

8. A. I. Klibanov, *History of Religious Sectarianism in Russia (1860s–1917)*, trans. Ethel Dunn (Oxford: Pergamon Press, 1982), 62.

9. Vera Shevzov, *Russian Orthodoxy on the Eve of Revolution* (New York: Oxford, 2004), chap. 1; Shevzov, "The Burdens of Tradition: Orthodox Constructions of the West in Russia (late XIX–early XX cc.)" (forthcoming); William G. Wagner, "'Orthodox Domesticity': Creating a Social Role for Women," in *Sacred Stories: Religion and Spirituality in Modern Russia*, ed. Mark D. Steinberg and Heather J. Coleman (Bloomington: Indiana University Press, 2007), 119–45; Manchester, *Holy Fathers, Secular Sons*.

10. Nikolai Ostroumov, "25-letie sluzheniia 'Missionerskago Sbornika' Pravoslavnoi tserkvi i missii. (Kratkii istoriko-literaturno-bibliograficheskii ocherk)," *Missionerskii sbornik*, nos. 1–2 (1916): i–lxi.

11. James Craig Holte, *The Conversion Experience in America: A Sourcebook on Religious Conversion Autobiography* (New York: Greenwood Press, 1992), xii.

12. Bogoliubov, "V bor'be," *Missionerskii sbornik*, nos. 10-12 (1917): 400-410; on Russia as a "God-bearing" nation, see James P. Scanlan, *Dostoevsky the Thinker* (Ithaca, NY: Cornell University Press, 2002), 12-13, chap. 6.

13. Gregory L. Freeze, "The Rechristianization of Russia: The Church and Popular Religion, 1750-1850," *Studia Slavica Finlandensia* 7 (1990): 107-8.

14. "Missionerstvo, sekty i raskol. (Khronika)," *Missionerskoe obozrenie*, nos. 7-8 (July-August 1896): 61-62.

15. *Vsepoddanneishii otchet ober-prokurora sviateishago Sinoda K. Pobedonostseva po vedomstvu Pravoslavnago ispovedaniia za 1887 god* (St. Petersburg: Sinodal'naia tipografiia, 1889), 195.

16. "Pravila ob ustroistve missii i o sposobe deistvii missionerov i pastyrei tserkvi po otnosheniiu k raskol'nikam i sektantam," *Tserkovnyia vedomosti*, no. 28 (9 July 1888): 175-82.

17. Vl. A. Maevskii, *Vnutrenniaia missiia i ee osnovopolozhnik* (Buenos Aires, 1954), 51-74, 87, 98-99, 220.

18. D. Bogoliubov, "V bor'be s sektantstvom. (Iz zapisok eparkhial'nago missionera)," *Missionerskii sbornik*, no. 8 (1914): 572.

19. Edward C. Thaden, *Conservative Nationalism in Nineteenth-Century Russia* (Seattle: University of Washington Press, 1964); V. Ia. Grosula, ed., *Russkii konservatizm XIX stoletiia* (Moscow: Progress-Traditsiia, 2000). The diaries Bogoliubov mentions were never published.

20. D. Bogoliubov, "V bor'be s sektantstvom," *Missionerskii sbornik*, nos. 3-4 (1916): 115. Another missionary recalled starting out with similar confidence that sectarianism would disappear when confronted with his theological knowledge acquired at the academy: Miss. D. Gratsianskii, "Skol'ko vy obratili?," *Missionerskoe obozrenie*, no. 5 (May 1904): 1143.

21. D. Bogoliubov, "V bor'be s sektantstvom," *Missionerskii sbornik*, no. 5 (1916): 288. On Bogoliubov's rural origins, see Sergii Matiushin, "Bogoliubov, Dmitrii Ivanovich," *Pravoslavnaia entsiklopediia* (Moscow, 2009), 5:457-58, http://www.pravenc.ru/text/149491.html.

22. D. Bogoliubov, "V bor'be s sektantstvom," *Missionerskii sbornik*, nos. 3-4 (1915): 199.

23. Ibid., no. 12 (1914): 911; no. 102 (1915): 55; nos. 7-8 (1915): 526.

24. Ibid., no. 5 (1916): 290; nos. 9-10 (1915): 670.

25. D. Bogoliubov, "V bor'be s sektantstvom," *Missionerskii sbornik*, no. 12 (1914): 908; no. 5 (1916): 290-91.

26. "Pravila ob ustroistvie," 175-76.

27. V. M. Skvortsov, *Deianiia 3-go Vserossiiskago missionerskago s"ezda v Kazani, po voprosam vnutrennei missii i raskolosektantstva*, 2nd ed. (Kiev: Tipografiia I. I. Chokolova, 1898), 43, 313-19.

28. Georges Florovsky, *Ways of Russian Theology*, part 2, vol. 6 of *The Collected Works of Georges Florovsky*, trans. Robert L. Nichols (Vaduz: Büchervertriebsanstalt, 1987), 193; N. Iu. Sukhova, *Vysshaia dukhovnaia shkola: Problemy i reformy, vtoraia polovina XIX veka* (Moscow: PSTGU, 2006), 420; on how the 1884 counter-reform of the spiritual academies paralleled that of the universities, see V. A. Tarasova, *Vysshaia dukhovnaia shkola v Rossii v kontse XIX–nachale XX veka* (Moscow: Novyi khronograf, 2005), 27-30, 34.

29. Tarasova, *Vysshaia dukhovnaia shkola*, 330–32; Hedda, *His Kingdom Come*, 38–51.

30. Hyacinthe Destivelle, *Les sciences théologiques en Russie: Réforme et renouveau des académies ecclésiastiques au début du XXe siècle* (Paris: Les éditions du Cerf, 2010), 825.

31. Ibid., 441–47.

32. Ibid., 744–49; Hedda, *His Kingdom Come*, 38–51, 63–72; Sukhova, *Vysshaia dukhovnaia shkola*, 424.

33. Manchester, *Holy Fathers, Secular Sons*, 29–30, 159–61.

34. Bogoliubov, "V bor'be," *Missionerskii sbornik*, no. 12 (1914): 908.

35. Sean Gillen, "V. D. Kudriavtsev-Platonov and the Making of Russian Orthodox Theism," in this volume; Destivelle, *Les sciences théologiques*, 488–89; V. V. Zenkovsky, *A History of Russian Philosophy*, trans. George L. Kline (London: Routledge and Kegan Paul, 1953), 1:103–4, chap. 10, 18.

36. Shevzov, "The Burdens of Tradition," 6.

37. Ronald Vroon, "The Old Belief and Sectarianism as Cultural Models in the Silver Age," in *Russian Culture in Modern Times*, vol. 2 of *Christianity and the Eastern Slavs*, California Slavic Studies 17, ed. Robert P. Hughes and Irina Paperno (Berkeley: University of California Press, 1994), 172–87; A. Etkind, *Khlyst: Sekty, literatura i revoliutsiia* (Moscow: Novoe literaturnoe obozrenie, 1998); Alexander Etkind, "Whirling with the Other: Russian Populism and Religious Sects," *Russian Review* 62, no. 4 (October 2003): 565–88; William J. Comer, "The Russian Religious Dissenters and the Literary Culture of the Symbolist Generation" (PhD diss., University of California, Berkeley, 1992); Patrick Lally Michelson, "'The First and Most Sacred Right': Religious Freedom and the Liberation of the Russian State, 1825–1905" (PhD diss., University of Wisconsin-Madison, 2007), chap. 3.

38. Heather J. Coleman, *Russian Baptists and Spiritual Revolution, 1905–1929* (Bloomington: Indiana University Press, 2005), 100–102.

39. See recollections of another missionary who studied with Subbotin: I. Polianskii, *Zapiski missionera Vologodskoi eparkhii: Vypusk I* (Moscow: Tipografiia E. Lissnera i Iu. Romana, 1890), 62; Sukhova, *Vysshaia dukhovnaia shkola*, 471.

40. Bogoliubov, "V bor'be," *Missionerskii sbornik*, no. 5 (1916): 293–94. Robert E. MacMaster, *Danilevsky: A Russian Totalitarian Philosopher* (Cambridge, MA: Harvard University Press, 1967), 293.

41. Manchester, *Holy Fathers, Secular Sons*, 29, 59–60.

42. Wayne Dowler, *Dostoevsky, Grigor'ev, and Native Soil Conservatism* (Toronto: University of Toronto Press, 1982), 167–68.

43. Bogoliubov, "V bor'be," *Missionerskii sbornik*, no. 5 (1916): 294. Bogoliubov refers to the central ecclesiological insight of the great Slavophile, Aleksei Khomiakov, who argued that *sobornost'* or fellowship of clergy and laity together formed the basis of church life. Although controversial and, indeed, implicitly critical of the hierarchical ecclesial model that governed Russian church life, by the late nineteenth century, as Vera Shevzov puts it, "the notion of *sobornost'* had taken on a life of its own." Shevzov, *Russian Orthodoxy*, 32–35.

44. Bogoliubov, "V bor'be," *Missionerskii sbornik*, no. 5 (1916): 295.

45. Ibid., nos. 7–8 (1915): 535–36.

46. Ibid., no. 5 (1916): 303–5.

47. Ibid., 296. Elsewhere, he remembered with particular fondness Kliuchevskii's famous lectures, while also criticizing the theology and philosophy professors for not engaging with the great thinkers of their own day such as Tolstoy, Nietzsche, or Marx: D. Bogoliubov, "O nashikh dukhovno-uchebnykh zavedeniiakh v sviazi s zaprosami sovremennosti," *Missionerskoe obozrenie*, no. 3 (March 1905): 652.

48. Bogoliubov, "V bor'be," *Missionerskii sbornik*, no. 5 (1916): 298.

49. Ibid., 293-98.

50. Clay, "Orthodox Missionaries," 41-42. See also: Hugh McLeod, *Religion and the People of Western Europe, 1789-1989*, 2nd ed. (Oxford: Oxford University Press, 1997), chap. 3 and 4; Kenneth Scott Latourette, *A History of the Expansion of Christianity* (Grand Rapids, MI: Zondervan Publishing House, 1970), 4:147-51.

51. Bogoliubov, "V bor'be," *Missionerskii sbornik*, no. 12 (1916): 773-87.

52. Ibid., no. 7-8 (1915): 526-27.

53. Ibid., no. 12 (1915): 940.

54. Scholars in Russia and across Europe were struggling with questions of the essence of the nation; Bogoliubov reveals no awareness of this debate in his memoir, however. See Francine Hirsch, *Empire of Nations: Ethnographic Knowledge and the Making of the Soviet Union* (Ithaca, NY: Cornell University Press, 2005), 24-45.

55. "Missionerskie eparkhial'nye s"ezdy v Orle i Novgorode," *Missionerskoe obozrenie*, no. 9 (1901): 490-95.

56. Randall A. Poole, "Editor's Introduction: Philosophy and Politics in the Russian Liberation Movement; The Moscow Psychological Society and Its Symposium, Problems of Idealism," in *Problems of Idealism: Essays in Russian Social Philosophy*, ed. and trans. Randall A. Poole (New Haven, CT: Yale University Press, 2003), 18-19.

57. S. M. Polovinkin, *Zapiski Peterburgskikh Religiozno-filosofskikh sobranii (1901-1903 gg.)* (Moscow: Respublika, 2005), 90-173, 497-99. For an example of the tendency to ignore the "Church" side, see Jutta Scherrer, "Les 'Sociétés philosophico-religieuses' et la quête idéologique de l'intelligentsia russe avant 1917," *Cahiers du monde russe et soviétique* 15, no. 3 (1974): 297-314.

58. D. Bogoliubov, "O svobode sovesti," *Missionerskoe obozrenie*, no. 4 (1902): 699-710.

59. D. I. Bogoliubov, *Religiozno-obshchestvennyia techeniia v sovremennoi russkoi zhizni i nasha pravoslavno-khristianskaia missiia* (St. Petersburg: Tipografiia I. V. Leont'eva, 1909), 4; Rossiiskii gosudarstvennyi istoricheskii arkhiv (RGIA), f. 796, op. 442, d. 2165, ll. 128-33.

60. A. A. Ermichev, *Religiozno-filosofskoe obshchestvo v Peterburge (1907-1917): Khronika zasedanii* (St. Petersburg: Izdatel'stvo Sankt-Peterburgskogo universiteta, 2007), 23, 24, 300.

61. For example, D. Bogoliubov, "Khristianstvo i sotsial-demokratiia," *Tserkovnyi golos*, no. 1 (8 January 1906): 18-20; D. Bogoliubov, "O 'veroispovednoi svobode' v Rossii," *Tserkovnyi golos*, no. 11 (17 March 1906): [page numbers illegible]; D. Bogoliubov, "K kharakteristike 'bezvremen'ia' perezhivaemago nashei pastyrsko-prikhodskoi missiei," *Prikhodskii sviashchennik*, no. 1 (8 January 1911): 6-8.

62. Bogoliubov, *Religiozno-obshchestvennyia*, 51.

63. Ibid., 210, 216, 219.

64. Ibid., 12, 157, 274. This search for a modern and Russian and free Orthodoxy can also be seen in Rampton's and Coates's chapters in the present volume.

65. Coleman, "Defining Heresy," 78, 85; Maevskii, *Vnutrenniaia missiia*, 102; N. Griniakin, "Skorbnyi trud missionera ili 'Pravoslavnyi protivosektantskii katekhizis' D. I. Bogoliubova," *Missionerskoe obozrenie*, no. 10 (October 1909): 1604–16.

66. Bogoliubov, "V bor'be," *Missionerskii sbornik*, no. 12 (1915): 933–40; no. 10–12 (1917): 408.

67. Among many examples, see D. I. Bogoliubov, *Ocherk sovremennogo Tambovskago sektantstva i ego bolee vidnykh predstavitelei. (Po lichnym nabliudeniiam)* (Tambov: Tipografiia Gubernskago pravleniia, 1897); D. Bogoliubov, "Moi pervyia besedy s sektantami," *Missionerskoe obozrenie*, no. 5 (May 1901): 698–710.

68. Frierson, *Peasant Icons*, 9.

69. Zinaida Gippius, *Zhivye litsa: Vospominaniia, Stikhotvoreniia*, vol. 6 of *Sobranie sochinenii* (Moscow: Russkaia kniga, 2002), 111.

Chapter 3

Archbishop Nikon (Rozhdestvenskii) and Pavel Florenskii on Spiritual Experience, Theology, and the Name-Glorifiers Dispute

SCOTT M. KENWORTHY

A favorite maxim for modern Orthodox theologians is the statement by Evagrius Ponticus that "[i]f you are a theologian, you will pray truly; if you pray truly, you will be a theologian."[1] This statement is frequently appealed to by such theologians to claim that Orthodox theology is rooted in direct personal experience of God, which they contrast to Western theology as primarily an academic and rational endeavor.[2] Just a century ago, however, a major controversy erupted in the Russian Orthodox Church that centered precisely on issues of how theology is to be articulated, who counts as a "theologian," and whether one must be a theologian to speak on matters of faith. This controversy was over the "name of God," and in the battle between the Church's Holy Synod and the Russian monks on Mount Athos, it apparently pitted "those who pray" against theologians. It was in the context of this debate, at least in part, that modern theologians began to construct Orthodox theology as mystical and experiential rather than academic and rational.

Since the collapse of the Soviet Union there has been a revival of interest in the Name-Glorifiers debate, but recent analysts have, on the whole, inherited the binary interpretations of the events that were shaped in the heat of the polemics at the time. A range of scholars and theologians view the dispute primarily as a conflict between the scholastic academic theology that dominated the prerevolutionary theological schools and mystical theology rooted in the Eastern Church Fathers.[3] Although such a way of characterizing the dispute might apply to some of the actors, it obscures much of what was in fact at stake. Archbishop Nikon (Rozhdestvenskii), one of the leading opponents of the Name-Glorifiers, was not a representative of Russian academic theology at all, but in fact had spent his life and career promoting the very same spiritual traditions that the Name-Glorifiers embraced. By focusing on Archbishop Nikon's critique of the Name-Glorifiers, and Florenskii's responses to Nikon, this essay seeks to uncover some of the complexities obscured by such binary interpretations. Moreover, contrary to the prevailing image among Western scholars of the monolithic nature of Russian Orthodoxy, an analysis of a theological dispute such as this one makes it clear that there were significant divergences and lively debate among leading proponents of Russian Orthodoxy on such basic questions as how to understand God, on the nature and role of religious experience, religious language and symbols, and even the philosophical presuppositions that lay behind their theologizing. Perhaps even more fundamental were differing views about religious authority and who was in a position to speak for the Church—and whether such authority was rooted in the Church's ordained hierarchy, belonged to those trained as theologians, or was to be found above all in those who had direct experience of spiritual things.

Background

Nineteenth-century Russia witnessed a remarkable revival of monasticism and in particular hesychast spirituality.[4] The revival of Hesychasm actually began on Mount Athos, the peninsula and monastic republic in Greece, at the end of the eighteenth century, and later flourished in Russia, whence it then flowed back to Athos. During the second half of the nineteenth century, the number of Russians on Athos skyrocketed, exceeding 5,000 by the turn of the twentieth century.[5] In 1907, former Athonite schemamonk Ilarion published a book on prayer and the spiritual life, *In the Caucasus Mountains* (*Na gorakh Kavkaza*), which immediately enjoyed great popularity among Russian monks on Athos. Criticism arose over the book's expression that "the name of God is God Himself," which sparked intense debate on Mount Athos between defenders and detractors of the book and even divided communities. By 1912, the debate spread to ecclesiastical periodicals in Russia. In May 1913, the Holy Synod of the Russian Orthodox Church condemned the Name-Glorifiers position. The schisms in the Athonite communities grew worse at the very moment that the political situation on Mount Athos was dramatically changing, and the Holy Synod and the Russian government felt compelled to restore peace and resolve the conflict. The Synod sent a delegation to Athos that included Archbishop

Nikon (Rozhdestvenskii), but its mission failed, and a month later the Russian government restored peace on Athos by force, as the Russian Navy removed over 800 monks from the Holy Mountain.[6]

Ilarion's *In the Caucasus Mountains* was on the theme of contemplative prayer, focusing particularly on the practice and meaning of the Jesus Prayer. Although much in the book was in keeping with Orthodox spiritual traditions, what was distinctive about it was its exclusive focus on the Jesus Prayer (above other prayers and practices) and also the assertion that the power of the prayer resided precisely in the name Jesus Christ itself, and that it was the name that transformed the person in prayer and brought about his mystical communion with Christ.[7] In order to defend the Name-Glorifiers' teaching against criticisms, the former hussar turned Athonite monk, Antonii Bulatovich, composed one of the key works in the debate, *Apology of Faith in the Name of God and in the Name of Jesus* (1913). In essence, the Name-Glorifiers' position was symbolized by the statement that "the Name of God is God Himself" (*Imia Bozhie est' Sam Bog*). Generally they understood this to mean that God is present in his name. The name is not identical to God, but neither can the divine name be separated from God himself.

The Greek theological school of Halki was the first to critically examine *Imiaslavie*, as the teaching of the Name-Glorifiers was known, and after their assessment the ecumenical patriarch of Constantinople condemned its teachings. The Russian monks refused to recant, however, so the Russian Holy Synod intervened. Three reports were commissioned and presented to the Synod in May 1913, and then the Synod issued its own declaration on the matter. Archbishop Antonii (Khrapovitskii) prepared the second report; he was a highly unusual bishop in that he came from an aristocratic background, and had distinguished himself by a brilliant if contentious career as both a theologian and a church leader. Archbishop Antonii was the leading instigator of the attack against the Name-Glorifiers, and his report was highly polemical, comparing the Name-Glorifiers with Russian sectarians instead of seriously engaging with them theologically. S. V. Troitskii, who prepared the third report, was a young theologian who was a specialist in canon law, not dogmatic theology; nevertheless, he gave serious, if critical, consideration to the Name-Glorifiers' position. Archbishop Sergii (Stragorodskii), future patriarch of the Russian Church and archnemesis of Antonii (Khrapovitskii) after the revolution, prepared the final declaration (epistle) of the Holy Synod; in 1913, Sergii was (together with Antonii) highly respected as among the most theologically sophisticated of the Russian bishops. The Synod's epistle, however, took a hard line against the

Name-Glorifiers, declaring it a "heresy" (which of the three only Antonii Khrapovitskii's report had done), banning the books by Ilarion and Bulatovich, and censuring the monks who refused to comply.[8] Archbishop Nikon (Rozhdestvenskii) and his report will be the focus of this article, because both his person and his argument (together with Florenskii's detailed responses that particular report) reveal the shortcomings of the prevailing binary interpretations.

The controversy, and its forceful resolution, received widespread coverage in both the secular and ecclesiastical press, mostly to the detriment of the Holy Synod and particularly Archbishop Nikon. The episode was covered in all the major newspapers, and even conservative ones—not to speak of liberal papers— harshly criticized the use of force in resolving the conflict; leading intellectuals of the day, such as Nikolai Berdiaev, expressed similar sentiments.[9] A circle of intellectual supporters of the Name-Glorifiers formed in Moscow in 1912–13 around Mikhail Novoselov that included Pavel Florenskii, Sergei Bulgakov, Vladimir Ern, and others.[10] Florenskii collaborated in ensuring the publication of Bulatovich's *Apology* and contributed to the preface, though, cautious as he was when it came to controversial topics, he did so anonymously. The preface to Bulatovich's *Apology* explicitly appealed to the distinction developed by Hesychast theologian Gregory Palamas (1296–1359) between the "Essence" and "Operations" or "Energies" of God, and also asserted that the name has a real connection to the thing named, and therefore has a reality, following a Platonic conception of ideas. These intellectuals asserted that the dispute represented a clash between "realism" and "nominalism"—using the categories of medieval Latin scholastic debates—which, for them, was the same as a clash between idealism and mysticism on the one hand and "rationalism," "positivism," and even "materialism" on the other.[11] After the publication of the Synod's three reports and the Synod's final epistle, Florenskii prepared a detailed commentary particularly on Nikon's report by pasting the pages of the reports on one side of a notebook and writing his responses on the facing pages. These commentaries were not apparently meant for publication, hence the visceral tone of his reactions to Nikon both personally as well as intellectually, and were first published only in 1995 in the journal *Nachala*. It is here, however, that Florenskii expanded in greater detail the ideas that were articulated in his only publication on the issue in 1913 (the preface to Bulatovich's *Apology*), and since their publication these commentaries have had a profound influence on shaping the way in which the *Imiaslavie* debate has been interpreted.[12] Florenskii's responses will be brought into conversation with Nikon's report in the analysis that follows.

Prevailing Binary Interpretations

The basic paradigm of interpreting the dispute as one between "mysticism" and "rationalism" has subsequently been filtered through the lens of Georges Florovsky's critique of prerevolutionary Russian theology as alienated from the Greek patristic tradition and instead subjected to a "Western captivity," together with the tendency of twentieth-century Orthodox theologians such as Vladimir Lossky and John Meyendorff to assert Orthodox theology as rooted in spiritual experience in contrast to rationalistic Western theology.[13] Ilarion Alfeev has produced the most exhaustive study of the Name-Glorifiers, which on the whole is very judicious and balanced. Nevertheless, he tends to oversimplify the conflict as a clash between rationalistic academic theology and mystical theology. This shapes his interpretation of the work of Nikon (Rozhdestvenskii) in particular. Alfeev interprets Nikon as arguing that the exposition of the teaching on the divinity of the name of God was the business of theology and not asceticism, and concludes that "such a positing of the question is very characteristic for academic theology at the turn of the nineteenth and twentieth centuries: mysticism and asceticism are the lot of simpletons and ignoramuses, and theology should be practiced by enlightened people who have no relationship either to asceticism or to mysticism."[14] Alfeev thus claims that, for Nikon, theology and spiritual life have nothing to do with one another, and that theology should entirely follow the laws of "common sense" (*zdravii razum*), reason, and logic.

Paul Ladouceur similarly views the conflict as one between academic theology, "to which belonged most of the Church hierarchy," and which was "characterized by a rational approach to theology inherited from Western scholasticism," on the one hand, and the mystical tradition that can be traced through Orthodox spirituality from the Desert Fathers to the "Philokalic revival" in the eighteenth and nineteenth centuries, on the other.[15] Dimitrii Leskin asserts that all of the Name-Glorifiers' opponents are "unified by a single general trait": the unwillingness to take the dogmatic dispute seriously, and the "academic" or "rationalistic" assessment of the mystical movement.[16] For him, the questions are all interconnected: *Imiaslavie*'s opponents were rationalists who denied not only the divinity of the divine names, but also the Palamite doctrine of the divinity of the energies of God. Consequently, they did not believe in the reality of communion between God and the human person in the act of prayer, but rather viewed all experiences during prayer as purely subjective; therefore they also denied the possibility of deification. Much of this interpretation was shaped by Florenskii; indeed, Leskin's analysis of Nikon's report to the Synod is quite clearly shaped by Florenskii's commentary, though without attribution.[17] In this line of argument, it is obviously the Name-Glorifiers that are taken to be on the side of authentic Orthodox tradition and therefore vindicated, by contrast with their Western-influenced rationalist opponents.[18]

Archbishop Nikon (Rozhdestvenskii)

Archbishop Nikon does not, however, fit neatly into these binary categories and defies the paradigm by which the debate continues to be interpreted. At one level he is the type of Russian hierarch that appears easy to stereotype: he was a member of both the Holy Synod and the State Senate and therefore a representative of the power of the Church and its alliance with the state.[19] He was ultraconservative or even reactionary on social and political issues; contemporaries characterized him as rigid, narrow-minded, intolerant, a severe "inquisitor." He was, however, a complex figure with a less than typical episcopal career; recent interpreters who have overlooked dimensions of his life and work have read into Nikon's arguments those of other critics of *Imiaslavie* and misunderstood much of what Nikon was attempting to argue. Contrary to Alfeev's claims, he was in fact a supporter of asceticism and mysticism rather than a disparager of it.

Born Nikolai Rozhdestvenskii in 1851, he was the son of a Moscow lower clergyman. After graduating first in his class from Moscow Spiritual Seminary, instead of pursuing the path of "educated monasticism" and going on to the Spiritual Academy, he chose to become a simple monk and entered the Trinity-Sergius Monastery (*Lavra*). In 1879, while still a novice, he began publication of one of the most influential popular periodical editions in Russia, *Trinity Leaflets* (*Troitskie listki*).[20] He was a very active leader during his monastic career at the Trinity Monastery, which included the establishment of the monastery's printing house. In 1902–3, he participated in an intense debate in ecclesiastical periodicals about the purpose of monasticism, defending the primacy of contemplative monasticism over those who sought to make monasteries more socially "useful" by transforming them into charitable institutions.[21] He was only ordained to the episcopate in 1904, at the age of fifty-three and after more than twenty-five years in the monastery, which was highly unusual for prerevolutionary Russian bishops, who typically followed a very different career trajectory that included study in a spiritual academy followed by teaching and administrative duties, but not actual monastic experience.[22] He became bishop of Vologda in 1906, a member of the State Council in 1907, and a member of the Holy Synod in 1912. Nikon retired from actively governing Vologda diocese in

1912 for reasons of health; in 1913 he was elevated to archbishop and from 1913 to 1916 served as chairman of the Holy Synod's Publishing Council. He retired from both the Synod and Senate in 1916 and died on December 30, 1918, at the Trinity-Sergius Monastery.[23]

By the time he was elevated to the episcopate in 1904, Nikon was widely regarded as the "defender of monasticism" and was highly respected in monastic circles as the foremost hierarch who had extensive personal experience of the monastic life. He organized and led the First All-Russian Congress of Monastics, held at the Trinity-Sergius Monastery in 1909, which discussed issues in the revitalization of monastic life based on contemplative prayer and spiritual eldership.[24] Nikon was not a representative of academic scholastic theology who had no sympathy for mystical, hesychastic spirituality; indeed, it was none other than Nikon who, in 1911, published the manuscript containing the continuation of the popularized treatise on the Jesus Prayer (first published in 1884), *The Way of a Pilgrim*.[25] Nikon was in fact a supporter and leading popularizer of the tradition of Serafim of Sarov, the Optina elders, and Feofan the Recluse. The root of his opposition to *Imiaslavie*, therefore, did not derive from rational academic theology (of which he was not a representative), nor from any lack of sympathy for asceticism, mysticism, and the practice of the Jesus Prayer, as Alfeev and others assume; rather, it must be sought elsewhere. Nikon's central arguments against *Imiaslavie*, together with Florenskii's responses, reveal the nuances of the debate. These arguments focused on the nature of religious authority, the role of reason in defining doctrine, differing theories of language, the relationship between spiritual experience and formal theology, the nature of spiritual experience, and the distinction between the essence and energies of God.

Archbishop Nikon's Report to the Holy Synod

In contrast to Antonii (Khrapovitskii)'s report to the Holy Synod, which mocked rather than engaged *Imiaslavie*, Nikon's report never accuses the Name-Glorifiers of heresy (he will only do this after encountering them on Athos in the summer of 1913), and attempts to engage *Imiaslavie* in a respectful and theologically serious way. Moreover, he is far from rejecting all aspects of *Imiaslavie*; rather, he specifically objects to the formula "the name of God is God Himself" and especially to their assertion that their teaching is a "dogma." Indeed, it was perhaps the very speed with which this handful of Athonite monks were willing to declare their own ideas as "dogma" that was most alarming to Nikon. In his report to the Synod, Nikon clearly prefers to think of the teaching on the name of God as neither a "heresy" nor as a "dogma," but something still under the Church's consideration, a "teaching" that "has not been precisely formulated by the Church in its expositions of the faith either positively or negatively."[26] He was cautious precisely because the Church had not declared a position one way or the other: "I am afraid to accept some sort of 'dogma,' not expressed clearly by the Church, not accepted by the fullness . . . of the Church, not [yet] formulated, so long as the Church itself has not clarified its relationship to it."[27] In short, Nikon was not declaring *Imiaslavie* to be a heresy, but he also rejected its formulation as a dogma, preferring instead a cautious approach that ultimately deferred to the judgment of the entire Church.

A key issue lying behind the debate was precisely who had the authority to speak for the Church. Nikon asserted that "the Church is infallible not in its separate members, but in its fullness."[28] Since the *Encyclical of the Eastern Patriarchs* in 1848 in response to papal claims, the Orthodox certainly had a notion that the "protector" or "preserver" of the purity of the faith was not just the hierarchy, but the "body of the Church," that is, the entirety of the people including the laity.[29] Nikon's language of "fullness of the Church" echoes these concepts. Yet who could speak as representative of this "fullness"? It was generally accepted that Church Councils, especially Ecumenical Councils, could do so: but what about in the absence of such Councils? This was perhaps why, in May 1913, Nikon still wanted to be cautious about declaring any teaching on the divine names "heresy" or "dogma." His position changed only after his encounter with the monks on Mount Athos; then he was quite willing to declare: "For the representatives of the Church, for the Church authorities—our Holy Synod and the Ecumenical Patriarch—there are no doubts whatsoever that this new teaching is a heresy."[30] Here he no longer speaks of a vague "fullness" of the Church, but rather the "representatives" of the Church who are clearly identifiable as the legitimate ecclesiastical authorities; even if their authority is not declared to be infallible, it is still to be obeyed.

Paradoxically, the Name-Glorifiers drew on the same general understanding of Church authority and its "infallibility" to declare that the Synod and the Ecumenical Patriarch did not speak for the whole Church; they claimed that true spiritual authority derived from their own direct personal experience of God, from which their teachings derived. Florenskii dismissed Nikon's arguments as one who was not a "legitimate" bishop (since he retired as bishop of Vologda, he no longer had a "flock"), was not an academically trained theologian, and (according to Florenskii) lacked spiritual experience. "With what does he undertake to teach and why should his voice be recognized as an oracle? And if the Synod . . . is constituted out of ten such Nikons, then why should . . . [it] be identified with the Truth Itself?"[31] He also took Nikon's comments about the "fullness of the Church" as if Nikon were asserting that the Synod had pretensions of infallibility, of being the "fullness of the Church," though it is not at all clear this is what Nikon intended.[32] Certainly, however, the Name-Glorifiers refused to recant their teaching because they did not regard the Russian Holy Synod as having the authority to speak for the "fullness of the Church," and precisely for that reason the issue continued to be debated, and still continues to be.

THE ROLE OF REASON IN THEOLOGY; PHILOSOPHY OF LANGUAGE

Nikon begins from the methodological basis that "all dogmas, notwithstanding all their mystery and incomprehensibility to our mind, nonetheless never contradict the laws of our reason. Incomprehensibility is not yet logical contradiction."[33] From this starting point, Nikon proceeded to present his own general understanding of language: the name is a conventional sign that is a mental conception about the object named, but which only exists subjectively in the mind and has no objective reality. It is virtually the same as the "equator" is for a geographer: an abstract idea that exists in and for human understanding, but does not have objective reality. If God is "the most real Being," then how can the "name"—which does not have any objective reality—"be" God?[34] Hence the Name-Glorifiers' claim that "the name of God is God" simply does not make sense.

Florenskii vehemently objected to Nikon's argument that dogmas should not contradict reason. Indeed, Florenskii's project in many important ways was precisely counter to rationalism, and he saw in Nikon's presentation everything he opposed.[35] According to Florenskii, "The characteristic feature of dogma is precisely in that it demands the *overcoming* of reason for faith in it. Where there is not contradiction to reason, there is *nothing* to believe. . . . That which 'does not contradict' is *not* dogma." When Nikon asserts that the formula "the Name of God is God" contradicts "common sense," Florenskii wonders "what would remain of any dogma" if one applied "Nikonian criteria" to them; "Virgin and Mother," bread that is actually the Body of Christ, and other core beliefs contradict "common sense." Nikon's line of argument brings one to "Tolstoyanism" according to Florenskii.[36] Indeed, Florenskii regarded Russian theology as dominated by "rationalism" and reacted to Nikon by projecting all of his criticisms of the seminary system onto him, often in quite visceral language.[37]

In addition to Nikon's assertion that dogmas must not contradict reason, Florenskii vigorously objected to Nikon's philosophy of language. It was perhaps on the very philosophy of language in the most basic sense—and indeed, the meaning of symbols in general—that the proponents and opponents of *Imiaslavie* were constructing irreconcilable arguments because they were working from completely different philosophical presuppositions, much like the debates between Realists and Nominalists in the medieval West. For Florenskii, the name has a real existence and an essential connection to ideas, which are also real (in the Platonic sense), and also an essential connection to the object named, whereas for Nikon the name was only a conventional symbol that existed in the human mind but had no reality and was not connected in any essential way with the object named.[38]

According to Florenskii, if praying the name of God can bring the one praying closer to God, then the name must exist as something that connects the two (the person praying and God); otherwise there would be no possibility of communion between them. Nikon is arguing that the name has no reality in and of itself, no essential connection to God, because he wants to avoid any magical connotation by which merely calling on the name of God places one in relationship to God. Florenskii counters that every time one calls on the name of God, one puts oneself "in ontological relationship to God"; but the key question is what kind of relationship, and that depends on how one calls upon God. In fact, he argues, the human mind has no way to think about God or approach God other than the name. Florenskii explicitly asserts that Nikon is approaching the whole matter, if unconsciously, from a "Kantian positivistic point of view," which he contrasts with the Platonic approach that he implicitly accepts.[39]

Spiritual Experience versus Academic Theology

Because the Name-Glorifiers' teaching was not logical, according to Nikon, they had to appeal to "mysticism" and "authorities" (*avtoritety*). In their appeal to mysticism, "they say that in doctrine about the spiritual life experience is more important than scholarship" (*nauka*). Nikon counters that "exposition of doctrine about the divinity of the names of God is the business of Orthodox theology, and not ascetics." However, rather than disparaging the role of spiritual experience, as Florenskii, Alfeev, and others claim, Nikon argues that "experience in the spiritual life is a great thing, and many theologians drew grace-filled help of God from it in understanding and articulating truths of the faith in their writings, but this is not given to every ascetic."[40] Nikon maintains that spiritual experience is important for theology, but that it is not enough; one also needs theological education, which of course most monks and ascetics in prerevolutionary Russia did not have since the majority came from the peasantry and had only a basic education.[41] Nikon also argued that the very spiritual writers to whom the Name-Glorifiers appealed as authorities "spoke with great audacity" of their spiritual experience but did not try to present that as "precisely expounded" dogmas; conveying one's experience admitted greater freedom of expression than formal doctrine allowed. Moreover, he claimed that "not one teacher of the Church dared to call his personal opinion a dogma, even if he found something in other Church writers that supported his opinion."[42] Thus, for Nikon, spiritual experience is important for theologians but does not automatically make every monk qualified to be a theologian. Moreover, it was permissible to express one's experience and opinions in personal terms, but an entirely different matter to articulate doctrine for the whole Church. In other words, Nikon's disagreement with the Name-Glorifiers was not with what they claimed they experienced, but with their attempt to make dogmatic assertions based on that experience.

Although the paradigm of "mysticism" versus "academic theology" has become so central in the interpretation of *Imiaslavie*, Florenskii's reaction to these passages in Nikon's report are also complex. Florenskii certainly interprets Nikon as valuing "scholarship" over "spiritual experience" and disdaining mysticism. However, his line of critique is not so much against Nikon's position, as against Nikon's person, by asserting that Nikon has neither spiritual experience nor theological training. Although theologians may lack spiritual experience, they can at least "boast" of their knowledge, "but Nikon is a monk, having promised to give himself to 'mysticism' which he hasn't fulfilled, and swaggers of scholarship, which he hasn't even sniffed. What impudence!"[43] In fact, however, Florenskii's position is hardly different from Nikon's. He asserts that spiritual experience and a spiritual life are necessary for "for the precise exposition of the faith," but it is also "desirable" or "even necessary" to have "philosophical development."[44] He regards intellectual preparation as well as spiritual experience as necessary for doing theology, which is not necessarily given to everyone who has spiritual experience alone. But for Florenskii, it also mattered what kind of intellectual preparation one had, and the Russian seminaries and academies, in his view, were inadequate. In short, neither for Nikon nor Florenskii is spiritual experience alone sufficient for articulating doctrine. Perhaps both would revise Evagrius's famous dictum like this: "if you are a theologian, you will pray truly, although not everyone who truly prays will be a theologian."

The Nature of Spiritual Experience

The importance of the names of God, for Nikon, is precisely in the realm of the "inner person," or "psychology," rather than in the realm of dogmatic theology.[45] Nikon discusses the Jesus Prayer and the process by which the mind is brought into the heart in a passage that is key to the debate because of what is understood to take place during prayer. Contemporary interpreters assert that Nikon (as other opponents of *Imiaslavie*) has only a psychological view of prayer, denying any divine action, and consequently negating the possibility of deification.[46] Nikon wrote:

> The practitioners of the Jesus prayer witness that "when the mind is enclosed in the heart," when all the spiritual being of a person becomes concentrated on thoughts of God, then thought, with the cooperation of the grace of God, stands reverently, as it were [*kak by*], before the invisibly present God.... Then the heart of the person is ignited by the grace of God that touches him and the very name of the Lord Jesus Christ becomes sweet to the one praying to hold in his mind, or better to say: in the heart.... This condition, experienced by the person in prayer, gives him the certainty that the Lord heeds his prayer and that the He, the merciful one, is *here*, near him.[47]

The human mind, Nikon continued, wants to embrace this presence of God, as it were, and searches for a "place" to locate this presence; when concentrated on the divine name, the person feels the "touch of grace in his heart," the presence of God. "And his thought takes hold of the most sweet name of God as if it were the garment of Christ, as if it were His most pure feet."[48] This experience happens so quickly that the person identifies the presence of God with the name.

Florenskii focuses on the repetition of the phrase "as if" (*kak by*) in the passage—"as if" standing before God, "as if" grasping the garment of Christ or his feet—and interprets these as meaning that, for Nikon, what is happening in prayer is purely subjective and the communion with God appears only "as if." His reading of the first sentence captures his interpretation of Nikon's understanding of prayer: "There, in these supposed synonymous expressions, is contained to the whole of Nikonism. Nikon interprets 'when the mind is enclosed in the heart' positivistically, in the form of a simple concentration of attention. The objective moment in cognition, that is the union of the cognizer with the cognized, for Nikon is completely missing."[49] These comments get at the very heart of the dispute: Florenskii maintains that if the "name" has only a subjective reality, a conventional symbol for the mind's cognition (like the equator for the geographer), then the experience of prayer is also a purely subjective one, and there is no real communion between God and the person praying. Although this critique may in fact apply to some of *Imiaslavie*'s opponents, such as Antonii (Khrapovitskii)—who evidently had little understanding of or sympathy for this kind of mystical approach—this is not what Nikon was arguing.[50] Florenskii unfairly pounces on Nikon's "as if" phrases—"'as if the feet'—means 'not the feet,' but the equator," in other words if the person in prayer does not literally touch God then there is no contact with God at all and the experience only exists in the person's mind.[51] But even those who believe in the reality of communion with God in mystical prayer surely do not actually believe that they are literally touching Christ's garment or feet, so that Nikon's "as if" in this case seems entirely appropriate; it is, after all, only an analogy.

Nikon repeatedly speaks of the heart being touched by grace: "When reverent thought turns to God, calling his most holy name, then the Lord in that very moment heeds the one in prayer, and more than that, He Himself gives prayer to the one praying." For sure, Nikon asserts that the person does not have direct experience of the divine essence, but rather what he calls a "certain divine power called grace." Nikon is not arguing that the experience of God in prayer is purely subjective, but rather that the one praying the Jesus Prayer focuses his entire being (and not just thoughts, as Florenskii reads him) on God by focusing on the name of Jesus Christ, and by focusing his being on Christ opens himself up to the grace of God (which he truly experiences), so that the practitioner concludes that the grace is inherent in, derives from, or is inseparable from the name, and it is only this latter aspect that Nikon wants to question. God is present to the one in such a state of prayer, just not automatically in the name. He is also arguing that God's grace appears to one in prayer not because of the name—as if mechanistically repeating the name itself would bring the power or presence of God—but because the person praying "pronounced it with sufficient reverence and faith, and also directing his heart to God."[52]

Even if Florenskii has exaggerated Nikon's position, there are clearly still important differences. Florenskii asserts that prayer itself is an action of synergy, although he does not use this term: if God "gives" prayer to the one praying (in Nikon's phrase), then Florenskii asserts that prayer is not just a human activity, but that it is both human and divine (*bozhestvenna*), that is, it is the energy of God that is operating from within the person praying. Florenskii objected to Nikon's emphasis on the inner condition of the person praying for the reception of grace. Rather, "we are as if surrounded by grace," but one can only receive it, the "window" is only opened up, when one calls upon God. (Here Florenskii himself uses the same "as if" language that he objects to so strongly in Nikon.) Calling upon the name of God automatically puts one in relation to God, but what effect it has upon the person depends upon his inner condition; if one calls upon the name of God in cursing or blaspheming, then one is calling upon himself judgment and condemnation. Any act of calling on the name of God is not simply "a physical or psychological process," but rather "an ontological process of union with the Divine energy, which cannot be ineffective and, consequently, either saves or singes."[53] In short, for Florenskii, either the power is in the name itself, in the prayer itself, or it depends upon our inner attitude, and in the latter case it is inevitably pure subjectivism and not real communion with God. But that is the way he construes it; Nikon can disagree with the notion that the power is inherent in the name without believing that prayer and contemplation are merely subjective processes.

Divine Names and Divine Energies

Both the Name-Glorifiers and contemporary interpreters have drawn parallels between the *Imiaslavie* controversy and that over Hesychasm in fourteenth-century Byzantium. At that time, critics of Hesychasm asserted that the experience of Hesychast mystics was not directly of God, for God was transcendent and unapproachable. Gregory Palamas gave theological defense to the Hesychasts: according to Palamas, the outpouring of God's energies, his actions toward creation, his grace toward creatures, was not the essence of God, which always remained absolutely transcendent and incomprehensible; nevertheless these energies of God were truly God and not something that belonged to the created order. Therefore Hesychast experiences of communion with God in contemplative prayer were truly experiences of God himself, though not of God's essence.[54] The distinction between the essence and operations (or energies) of God became central to the debate about *Imiaslavie* because the Name-Glorifiers identified the divine names with the operations of God and therefore claimed that their formula "the Name of God is God" was correct.

It must be noted, however, that the theology of Gregory Palamas had fallen into complete neglect in prerevolutionary Russia; the revival of hesychast spirituality in nineteenth-century Russia was not accompanied or informed by a revival of Palamite theology, which was virtually unknown either in monastic circles or among Russian theologians. Indeed, the first translation of the *Philokalia* into Slavonic by Paisii Velichkovskii at the end of the eighteenth century included no writings by Palamas. The nineteenth-century translation by Feofan the Recluse excluded Palamas's "One Hundred and Fifty Chapters," the most theological of the texts in the Greek *Philokalia*, precisely because they contained much that was "difficult to understand"; Feofan included only those texts that spoke directly to the practice of prayer rather than doctrine.[55] Moreover, S. V. Bulgakov's standard handbook for clergy included an inaccurate characterization of Hesychasm, which it listed in the category of heresies and schisms, although elsewhere in the same book he gives a positive, if also inaccurate, account for the Church's liturgical commemoration of Saint Gregory Palamas during Lent.[56] Although there was some treatment of Palamas's theological legacy, beginning with the work of Igumen Modest (Strel'bitskii) in 1860 and furthered by Bishop Porfirii (Uspenskii) some years later, these had virtually no impact on dogmatic theology in Russia.[57] It is quite clear from the *Imiaslavie* debates that Palamas's theology was not well known or understood; indeed the debates principally focused on the "Chapters against Barlaam and Akindynus" in the *Synodicon of Orthodoxy*, a text read liturgically on the Sunday of Orthodoxy (the first Sunday of Great Lent), rather than on any of the writings of Palamas himself.[58]

Given the general ignorance of Palamas's theology, therefore, it should not be surprising that the Synod's reports and final epistle were inconsistent and contradictory in the ways in which they grappled with the distinction between the essence and operations of God. Nikon likewise struggled to define his position. While Florenskii identifies the attributes of God with the operations of God, Nikon asserts that the attributes of God are only abstract mental conceptions about God whose essence transcends all such conceptualizations. Therefore, for Nikon, the divine names are conventional symbols for the divine attributes, which themselves are only abstract concepts, so that the names are twice removed from God himself.[59]

Much of the dispute revolved around the interpretation of the fifth anathema in the *Synodicon of Orthodoxy*, which rejects the teaching of those who declare that the term *theotis* (Godhead, divinity) applies only to the divine essence and not also to the divine operations. The debate centered especially on how to translate the term *theotis*: Bulatovich translated it as "God" (*Bog*), so that the divine operations are called "God."[60] Nikon, together with the other reports to the Synod and its final epistle, asserted that this was a mistranslation, that the operations of God are "divinity" (*Bozhestvo* or *Bozhestvennost'*), but not "God" (*Bog*) because the anathema refers to the divine operations as *theotis*, but not *theos*.[61] Nikon was ready to agree that the divine names are holy and "Divine as belonging to the one God," though evidently using the term "divine" in a broad sense as one would also speak of the "Divine Liturgy."[62] Nikon's central concern is to maintain the distinction, and avoid confusion, between the divine operations and God's essence. He equates the term "God" (*Bog*) with God's "Person" (*Lichnost'*), which he uses interchangeably with God's "Essence" (*Sushchestvo*). Therefore the divine operations or energies (Nikon uses both the terms *deistviia* and *energiia*) can be considered "divine" as belonging to or characteristic of God, but cannot be called "God" because that would blur the distinction with the divine essence. Thus he declares that "the power of God, called grace, is of course a manifestation of God's energy (*energiia*)—an energy uncreated, and on the contrary itself possessing creative power—nevertheless in no way can it be completely identified with the essence of God,"[63] just as our own activities are not identical to our person or essence but a manifestation of our characteristics. He uses the analogy of the sun and its rays; the sun's rays give heat and light, which are actions of the sun, but they are not identical to the sun itself. Arguing that one should not declare God's energies to be "God," he states: "not separating the 'activity' of God from God, we also do not identify them with God as with his Person when we speak about them."[64] In short, he is willing to define the energies as "divine" and as belonging to God, but asserts that it is incorrect to call them "God" because he equates this term with the divine essence.

Although Nikon is aware of the distinction between the essence and operations of God, he (like others in the debate) was only superficially familiar with the theology of Gregory Palamas and therefore was groping for language and concepts to articulate that the energies are divine and yet not the same as God's essence. The result is confused and contradictory. Much of the confusion, and a point of difference between Nikon and Florenskii, lay in the definition of the very word "God." Nikon opposed the claim that "the name of God is God Himself," because that would be tantamount to identifying the name with God's essence, which is unnameable.

Florenskii has a series of objections to Nikon's line of argumentation here. To begin with, he argues that the attributes are properties of God and not mere abstract concepts about God; because they are the way in which God manifests or reveals himself, they *are* God and the only way God can be known. Therefore the divine names are also names *of God* and not just this or that attribute, because each one ultimately points to the totality of God. Similarly, the names—as with images and all symbols—have a real connection to what they signify because without them we would have no way of knowing the signified at all; a true image gives "true cognition" of God.[65] He objects to the way in which Nikon speaks of God as Person, and particularly the way in which he uses "Person" and

"Essence" interchangeably. Rather, Florenskii asserts that God is not "Person" but "tri-person" (*trilichnost'*). He asserts emphatically that the Name-Glorifiers do not identify the name with the divine essence, that all the discussion is about the divine energies. Further, "God and the Divine Essence are not synonyms." We turn to God in prayer, not to the divine essence, which is unknowable.[66] According to Florenskii, divine manifestations "can be called God (*theotis*), that is, with the same term as the Divine Essence. . . . This is because *all* our terms in the strict sense of the word are related to the energy, not the essence," because the essence is only made known by or through the energies. He therefore accepted Bulatovich's translation of *theotis* as "God" as well as calling the divine energy "God," asserting that calling it "divinity" (*bozhestvennost'*) was inadequate because it was too imprecise.[67] For him the term "God" was inclusive of both the divine essence and the energies, in contrast to Nikon who equated it only with the divine essence. This point has continued in more recent debate, in which Alfeev and others assert that the opponents of *Imiaslavie* did not understand the theology of Palamas, which made no firm distinction between *theos* and *theotis*, and that it would be proper to term the divine energies "God."[68] It is worth noting, however, that Florenskii—like the other Name-Glorifiers and their opponents—nowhere cites the writings of Gregory Palamas directly when disputing the Synod's interpretation of the essence and energies of God.[69]

Conclusion

Nikon ends his report to the Synod on a note that was echoed both by the report of Antonii (Khrapovitskii) and the Holy Synod's epistle, namely that the real problem was less the actual teachings of Ilarion and Antonii Bulatovich, than the ways in which it could be understood by their more simple-minded followers. Nikon admits that Bulatovich does not identify the divine names with the divine essence. However, he is concerned that Bulatovich's followers will lose this distinction and, confusing the name of God with God's essence or person, will turn the name into a magical word or talisman that can have miraculous effects on its own, even used mechanistically.[70] In particular, Nikon feared that what lay behind the "new teaching" was a desire to find an "easier path to salvation": that one could simply repeat the prayer mechanically, "without the participation of the heart," and it would work to purify and transform the person and save him. By contrast, Nikon claimed that the "main thing is not in the sounds or the words of the prayer in themselves, not in this or some other name of God, but in a humble-repentant disposition of the heart, which attracts the grace of God,"[71] thereby echoing the works of other modern Hesychast writers.[72] In other words, Nikon objected to *Imiaslavie* not out of a lack of understanding or sympathy for asceticism, but precisely because he believed that it would have a detrimental effect upon ascetical effort.

Recent interpretations of the *Imiaslavie* controversy as a clash between mystical theology and rational academic theology are following an interpretation that was first shaped by partisans in the dispute, particularly Pavel Florenskii and other intellectual supporters of the Name-Glorifiers, and has been repeated rather uncritically. Archbishop Nikon (Rozhdestvenskii) was not a representative of academic theology; far from disparaging the Orthodox tradition of contemplative prayer, he had been one of its major defenders and popularizers. Although he did appeal to reason, "logic," and "common sense" in his argument—which left him open to Florenskii's criticisms and perhaps misinterpretations—Nikon was far from asserting that the experience of prayer was purely subjective or denying the reality of communion with God. Nikon's critique should not be dismissed as "rationalism" and "academic theology"; his line of argument in fact raised very important issues and indicates significant divergences in the way in which leading Orthodox thinkers understood fundamental issues. For both Nikon and Florenskii, the essence of God is totally unknowable and unnamable. For Nikon, the divine names are human symbols to indicate human conceptions about God (the divine attributes), and although they are to be venerated as representing God, God remains transcendent. However, this does not mean that there is no possibility of connection between God and creation: Nikon speaks of God's "power" or "actions," which he usually terms "grace," which *do* touch the person in prayer. What ultimately drove Nikon's interpretation, however, was the concern that calling the divine names "God" would mean the person praying only has to call on the Name and is automatically given the power of God, because he saw this as a spiritual short cut. Rather what mattered for him above all was not the names or words used in prayer but the inner disposition of the person praying and the ascetic struggle necessary for that.

Florenskii had a different set of concerns that was driven by his reaction against European philosophical traditions of rationalism, by his Neoplatonic philosophical presuppositions, and by his interest in symbols. For him, the attributes of God are identified with the operations of God, by which God manifests and reveals himself, and therefore they are real, in fact they are God and all humans can know of God. The divine names are real because without them we have no other way of knowing God, there is no other connection between the human mind and God. The divine names "are" God in the same way that one looks at a portrait of Peter and says "that is Peter," not that Peter is a picture, but we see Peter in the picture.⁷³ The Names give true "cognition" of God; in the deepest prayer there is communion of the "cognizer" and the "cognized," which is only made possible by the link that is the Name.

Far from the prevailing image of a monolithic Orthodoxy, a debate such as that over the name of God demonstrates that there were important differences among leading proponents of Orthodoxy and vigorous debate between them. However, the more significant of these differences are obscured if one simply dismisses the opponents of *Imiaslavie* as representatives of rationalist academic theology who had no sympathy for mysticism. On the contrary, Nikon's concerns were precisely to defend contemplative practice from the potentially harmful implications he saw in the Name-Glorifiers' teachings. Florenskii, by contrast, was in fact more concerned with abstract philosophical issues regarding epistemology and the meaning of symbols, and in this arena he was certainly a far more sophisticated thinker than Nikon. The tragedy of the episode was that neither side proved capable of listening to the other; the "conversation" broke down and degenerated into polemics that obscured, rather than clarified, the driving concerns and real points of disagreement.

NOTES

1. Robert E. Sinkewicz, *Evagrius of Pontus: The Greek Ascetic Corpus* (Oxford: Oxford University Press, 2006), 199.

2. See, for example, Timothy Ware, *The Orthodox Church* (London: Penguin, 1993), 206–7; Hilarion Alfeyev, *The Mystery of Faith: An Introduction to the Teaching and Spirituality of the Orthodox Church*, trans. Jessica Rose (London: Darton, Longman & Todd, 2002), xiii–xvii; Vladimir Lossky, *The Mystical Theology of the Eastern Church* (London: L. Clarke, 1957); John Meyendorff, *The Orthodox Church: Its Past and Its Role in the World Today* (New York: Pantheon Books, 1962), 190–97.

3. See Scott M. Kenworthy, "Debating the Theology of the Name in Post-Soviet Russia: Metropolitan Ilarion Alfeyev and Sergei Khoruzhii," in *Orthodox Paradoxes: Heterogeneities and Complexities in Contemporary Russian Orthodoxy*, ed. Katya Tolstaya (Leiden: Brill, forthcoming).

4. Scott M. Kenworthy, *The Heart of Russia: Trinity-Sergius, Monasticism, and Society after 1825* (Oxford: Oxford University Press, 2010); Irina Paert, *Spiritual Elders: Charisma and Tradition in Russian Orthodoxy* (DeKalb: Northern Illinois University Press, 2010).

5. Nicholas Fennell, *The Russians on Athos* (Oxford: Peter Lang, 2001).

6. Key collections of sources include E. S. Polishchuk, *Imiaslavie: Antologiia* (Moscow: Faktorial Press, 2002); Ilarion Alfeev, *Spory ob imeni Bozhiem: Arkhivnye dokumenty 1912–1938 godov* (St. Petersburg: Oleg Abyshko, 2007); A. M. Khitrov and O. L. Solomina, *Zabytye stranitsy russkogo imiaslaviia: Sbornik dokumentov i publikatsii po afonskim sobytiiam 1910–1913 gg. i dvizheniiu imiaslaviia v 1910–1918 gg.* (Moscow:

Palomnik, 2001); Antonii Bulatovich, *O pochitanii imeni bozhiia* (St. Petersburg: Aleteiia, 2013); S. N. Bulgakov, *Filosofiia imeni* (St. Petersburg: Nauka, 1998); and Sergius Bulgakov, *Icons; And, The Name of God*, trans. Boris Jakim (Grand Rapids, MI: Wm. B. Eerdmans, 2012). A. F. Losev, *Imia: Izbrannye raboty, perevody, besedy, issledovaniia, arkhivnye materialy* (St. Petersburg: Aleteiia, 1997); Konstantin Borshch, ed., *Imiaslavie: Sbornik bogoslovsko-publitsistecheskikh statei, dokumentov i kommentariev*, 3 vols. (Moscow, 2003–2005); and the journal *Nachala*, nos. 1–4 (1995) and nos. 1–4 (1998). See also A. Gorbunov, "Kratkaia istoriia imiaslavskikh sporov v Rossii nachala XX veka," *Tserkov' i vremia*, no. 12 (2000): 179–220; Loren Graham and Jean-Michel Kantor, *Naming Infinity: A True Story of Religious Mysticism and Mathematical Creativity* (Cambridge, MA: Harvard University Press, 2009); Helena Gourko, *Divine Onomatology: Naming God in Imyaslavie, Symbolism, and Deconstruction* (Saarbrucken: VDM Verlag, 2009); Zh. L. Okeanskaia, *Iazyk i kosmos: "Filosophiia imeni" ottsa Sergiia Bulgakova v kontekste poeticheskoi metafiziki kontsa novogo vremeni* (Moscow: BBI, 2008); Anna Reznichenko, *O smyslakh imen: Bulgakov, Losev, Florenskii, Frank, et dii minores* (Moscow: Regnum, 2012); Michael Hagemeister, "Imjaslavie—imjadejstvie: Namenmystik und Namensmagie in Russland (1900–1930)," in *Namen: Benennung, Verehrung, Wirkung; Positionen in der europäischen Moderne*, ed. Tatjana Petzer and Elke Dubbels (Berlin: Kadmos, 2009); Konstantinos Papoulides, *Hoi rosoi onomatolatrai tou Hagiou Orous* (Thessalonica: Institute for Balkan Studies, 1977).

7. Ilarion, *Na gorakh Kavkaza: Beseda dvukh startsev pustynnikov o vnutrennem edinenii s Gospodom nashikh serdets cherez molitvu Iisus Khristovu ili dukhovnaia deiatel'nost' sovremennykh pustynnikov* (1907; repr., St. Petersburg: Voskresenie, 1998). See G. M. Hamburg, "The Origins of 'Heresy' on Mount Athos: Ilarion's *Na Gorakh Kavkaza* (1907)," *Religion in Eastern Europe* 23, no. 2 (2003): 16–47.

8. Antonii (Khrapovitskii), "O novom lzheuchenii, obogotvoreiaiushchem imena, i ob 'Apologii' Antoniia Bulatovicha," *Pribavleniia k Tserkovnym vedomostiam*, no. 20 (1913): 869–82; S. V. Troitskii, "Afonskaia smuta," *Pribavleniia k Tserkovnym vedomostiam*, no. 20 (1913): 882–909; "Bozhieiu milostiiu, Sviateishii Pravitel'stvuiushchii Vserossiiskii Sinod vsechestnym bratiiam, vo inochestve podvizaiushchimsia," *Pribavleniia k Tserkovnym vedomostiam*, no. 20 (1913), reprinted in Polishchuk, *Imiaslavie*, 161–69.

9. For overview, see Ilarion Alfeev, *Sviashchennaia taina tserkvi: Vvedenie v istoriiu i problematiku imiaslavskikh sporov*, 2nd ed. (St. Petersburg: Olega Abyshko, 2007), 577–90.

10. See *Perepiska sviashchennika Pavla Aleksandrovicha Florenskogo i Mikhaila Aleksandrovicha Novoselova* (Tomsk: Volodei, 1998) for private exchanges between members of this circle.

11. See the preface "Ot redaktsii" to Bulatovich's *Apologiia very vo Imia Bozhie i vo Imia Iisus*, which has been reprinted in Polishchuk, *Imiaslavie*, 12–18; Pavel Florenskii, *Sochineniia v chetyrekh tomakh* (Moscow: Mysl', 1999), 3:1:287–94.

12. "Primechaniia sviashchennika Pavla Florenskogo k stat'e arkhiepiskopa Nikona 'Velikoe iskushenie okolo sviateishego Imeni Bozhiia,'" *Nachala*, nos. 1–4 (1995): 89–175, reprinted in Florenskii, *Sochineniia*, 3:1:299–344. Citations are from the latter edition.

13. Georges Florovsky, *Ways of Russian Theology*, part 1, trans. Robert L. Nichols (Belmont, MA: Nordland Publishing, 1979); for Florovsky as a lens through which

Imiaslavie is interpreted, see V. M. Lur'e, "Posleslovie," in *Zhizn' i trudy Sviatitelia Grigoriia Palamy: Vvedenie v izuchenie*, by John Meyendorff, ed. I. P. Medvedev and V. M. Lur'e, trans. G. N. Nachnikin (St. Petersburg: Vizantinorossika, 1997), 336–43.

14. Alfeev, *Sviashchennaia taina tserkvi*, 495.

15. See Paul Ladouceur, "The Name of God Conflict in Orthodox Theology," *St. Vladimir's Theological Quarterly* 56, no. 4 (2012): 415–36, esp. 431–33.

16. Dimitrii Leskin, *Spor ob imeni Bozhiem* (St. Petersburg: Aleteiia, 2004), 91.

17. Ibid., 114–23.

18. Of recent scholarly examinations, only Sergei Khoruzhii differs significantly from this line of interpretation, although he does so primarily by arguing the inconsistency between Florenskii and Palamas without reference to the Holy Synod's critique of *Imiaslavie*. S. S. Khoruzhii, "Imiaslavie i kul'tura serebrianogo veka: Fenomen Moskovskoi shkoly khristianskogo neoplatonizma," in his *Opyty iz Russkoi dukhovnoi traditsii* (Moscow: Parad, 2005), 287–308.

19. J. Eugene Clay, "Orthodox Missionaries and 'Orthodox Heretics' in Russia, 1886–1917," in *Of Religion and Empire: Missions, Conversion, and Tolerance in Tsarist Russia*, ed. Robert P. Geraci and Michael Khodarkovsky (Ithaca, NY: Cornell University Press, 2001), 65.

20. Kenworthy, *Heart of Russia*, 192–94.

21. See Scott M. Kenworthy, "To Save the World or to Renounce It: Modes of Moral Action in Russian Orthodoxy," in *Religion, Morality, and Community in Post-Soviet Societies*, ed. Mark Steinberg and Catherine Wanner (Bloomington: Indiana University Press, 2008); Kenworthy, *Heart of Russia*, 227–32.

22. Jan Plamper, "The Russian Orthodox Episcopate, 1721–1917: A Prosopography," *Journal of Social History* 34 (2000): 5–34.

23. Kenworthy, *Heart of Russia*, 132, 192–94, 263–66, 278–81.

24. Ibid., 232–38; Scott M. Kenworthy, "Pervyi Vserossiiskii s"ezd monashestvuiushchikh v 1909 g.," in *Troitse-Sergieva lavra v istorii, kul'ture i dukhovnoi zhizni Rossii: Materialy II Mezhdunarodnoi konferentsii, 4–6 oktiabria 2000 g.*, ed. T. N. Manushina and S. V. Nikolaeva (Sergiev Posad: Sergievo-Posadskii gos. muzei-zapovednik, 2002), 166–84.

25. Aleksei Pentkovsky, "Introduction," in *The Pilgrim's Tale* (New York: Paulist Press, 1999), 28. Florenskii was clearly aware of these aspects of Nikon's work and accused him of contradicting himself; see the article originally published anonymously, and later under Novoselov's name, though evidently penned by Florenskii: "Arkhiepiskop Nikon—rasprostranitel' 'eresi,'" in Florenskii, *Sochineniia*, 3:1:348–50 (and notes, 573–74).

26. Nikon (Rozhdestvenskii), "Velikoe iskushenie okolo sviateishego imeni Bozhiia i plody ego," *Pribavlenie k Tserkovnym vedomostiam*, no. 20 (1913): 853–69, reprinted in Polishchuk, *Imiaslavie*, 355–77, citation from latter edition, 356.

27. Ibid., 367.

28. Ibid., 361.

29. *Encyclical of the Eastern Patriarchs (1848), A Reply to the Epistle of Pope Pius IX*, "to the Easterns," can be found at http://www.fordham.edu/halsall/mod/1848orthodoxencyclical.asp.

30. From the preface to his Synodal report added when he reprinted the article later, in Polishchuk, *Imiaslavie*, 355.

31. Florenskii, "Primechaniia," 321.
32. Ibid., 324.
33. Nikon, "Velikoe iskushenie," 356.
34. Ibid., 357.
35. On Florenskii, see Avril Pyman, *Pavel Florensky: A Quiet Genius; The Tragic and Extraordinary Life of Russia's Unkown da Vinci* (New York: Continuum, 2010); Andronik (Trubachev), *Obo mne ne pechal'tes' . . . Zhizneopisanie sviashchennika Pavla Florenskogo* (Moscow: Sovet Russkoi Pravoslavnoi Tserkvi, 2007); Andronik (Trubachev), *Put' k Bogu: Lichnost', zhizn' i tvorchestvo sviashchennika Pavla Florenskogo* (Moscow: Gorodets, 2012–).
36. Florenskii, "Primechaniia," 300, 317.
37. See, for example, Florenskii, "Primechaniia," 311.
38. Ibid., 301–3, 319.
39. Ibid., 302, 304, 316.
40. Nikon, "Velikoe iskushenie," 359, 360.
41. Kenworthy, *Heart of Russia*, 117–39.
42. Nikon, "Velikoe iskushenie," 360.
43. Florenskii, "Primechaniia," 321.
44. Ibid.
45. Nikon, "Velikoe iskushenie," 365.
46. Alfeev, *Sviashchennaia taina tserkvi*, 478, 505–6; Leskin, *Spor*, 120–22.
47. Nikon, "Velikoe iskushenie," 361.
48. Ibid.
49. Florenskii, "Primechaniia," 325.
50. Compare the very different treatment of the same issue by Archbishop Antonii (Khrapovitskii), "O novom lzheuchenii," 870.
51. Florenskii, "Primechaniia," 326.
52. Nikon, "Velikoe iskushenie," 358–59.
53. Florenskii, "Primechaniia," 311.
54. John Meyendorff, *St. Gregory Palamas and Orthodox Spirituality* (Crestwood, NY: St. Vladimir's Seminary Press, 1974); Meyendorff, *A Study of Gregory Palamas* (London: Faith Press, 1974).
55. Sergey Nedelsky, "Palamas in Exile: The Academic Recovery of Monastic Tradition" (MTh thesis, St. Vladimir's Seminary, 2006), 18–23.
56. S. V. Bulgakov, *Nastol'naia kniga dlia sviashchenno-tserkovno sluzhitelei* (Kiev: Tip. Kievo-Pecherskoi Uspenskoi Lavry, 1913), 570–71, 1622.
57. Nedelsky, "Palamas in Exile," 25–28; Lur'e, "Posleslovie," 327–32.
58. Indeed, even Florenskii—who seems to have been interested in Palamas's theology—cites only secondary sources about Palamas in his major book. See *The Pillar and Ground of the Truth: An Essay in Orthodox Theodicy in Twelve Letters*, trans. Boris Jakim (Princeton, NJ: Princeton University Press, 1997), 468–69.
59. Nikon, "Velikoe iskushenie," 358.
60. Bulatovich, *Apologiia very*, 21.
61. Nikon, "Velikoe iskushenie," 363–64; for the epistle of the Synod, see Polishchuk, *Imiaslavie*, 163–64; Antonii (Khrapovitskii), "O novom lzheuchenii," 876; S. V. Troitskii, "Afonskaia smuta," 877–88.

62. Nikon, "Velikoe iskushenie," 364.
63. Ibid., 366.
64. Ibid., 370.
65. Florenskii, "Primechaniia," 308–15.
66. Ibid., 303, 312.
67. Ibid., 316, 331.
68. Alfeev, *Sviashchennaia taina tserkvi*, 522; Leskin, *Spor*, 92–94; Leskin explicitly accuses Nikon of "anti-Palamism," 119–20.
69. Florenskii, "Primechaniia," 331–33; see also his commentary on Troitskii's report, 345–47.
70. Nikon, "Velikoe iskushenie," 373–74.
71. Ibid., 376.
72. Kenworthy, *Heart of Russia*, 148–51.
73. Florenskii, "Primechaniia," 315.

PART II

Thinking Orthodox
in the Academy

Chapter 4

V. D. Kudriavtsev-Platonov and the Making of Russian Orthodox Theism

SEAN GILLEN

With the exception of Metropolitan Filaret (Drozdov) (1782–1867), perhaps no churchman's career shaped Russian Orthodox institutions and thought more than that of Viktor Dmitrievich Kudriavtsev-Platonov (1828–91) (hereafter Kudriavtsev). The son of a regimental priest, Viktor Dmitrievich led an itinerant early life. He was born in the province of Pskov and was educated in various seminaries and schools in the Russian Empire's western borderlands. It was not until entering the Moscow Spiritual Academy in 1848 that he found a permanent home.[1] Kudriavtsev soon became one of the Academy's leading students—he received a prestigious scholarship in memory of Metropolitan Platon that endowed him with his hyphenated last name—and eventually went on to head its department (*kafedra*) of philosophy from 1854 until his death in 1891.[2] At brief moments in 1875, 1876, and 1878, Kudriavtsev also acted as the Academy's interim rector. Outside the Academy, Kudriavtsev contributed to the 1869 statute that reformed spiritual academy curricula in order "to convey higher theological education in the spirit of Orthodoxy for enlightened service to the Church."[3] As a student, Kudriavtsev imbibed theology and enlightenment; as a teacher, he promoted them. In 1852, Kudriavtsev successfully defended his master's thesis, "On the Unity of the Human Race." In 1873, he defended his doctoral dissertation, "Religion: Its Essence and Provenance."[4] All of this work focused on philosophy, the history of religion, and theology. One alumnus of the Moscow Academy, in an attempt to synthesize Kudriavtsev's cumulative and lasting intellectual legacy to Russian Orthodoxy in general, and the spiritual academy in particular, called Kudriavtsev "the founder of Russian theism,"[5] that is, the founder of a particular way to talk about the characteristics of God. As we shall see, however, theism in the mind of Kudriavtsev was not just a doctrine about the nature of divinity. It was a theological answer to a historically specific question that in the mid- to late nineteenth century occupied a central place in debates about Russia's future: namely what role, if any, did religion play in Russia's advancement toward higher stages of moral and cultural existence.

Kudriavtsev's theism has important features that are both Russian and European. In his published work, Kudriavtsev connected theism to a number of sources that scholars regard as canonical.[6] The discourse of theism entered modern European thought through the writings of the Cambridge Platonist Ralph Cudworth (1617–88) in late seventeenth-century England and later philosophers and political theorists like David Hume (1711–76) and Jean-Jacques Rousseau (1712–78).[7] Above all, however, Kudriavtsev identified theism with the late eighteenth-century work of Immanuel Kant (1724–1804). Because of the overwhelming presence of Kant's work in his dissertation and published lecture notes, Kudriavtsev's intellectual career can be seen as a profound engagement with Kant.[8] Whatever the individual source, however, theism described a particular conception of God in which providential considerations in a transcendental sense and ethical considerations in an immanent sense were conjoined to form a theological anthropology—a theory of the self—that made moral perfection the purpose of human life. Kant developed an account of theism that was later codified by Protestant German philosophers and theologians. As Kant put it in *Religion within the Limits of Reason Alone* (1793) (hereafter *Religion*), the transcendent and the immanent were regarded "both together as active causes of a disposition adequate for a course of life well-pleasing to God."[9]

While Kudriavtsev committed himself to Kant's theistic program, he did so with at least two qualifications. Kudriavtsev recoiled from the secular and nihilistic implications of radically autonomous reason in order to present the Russian Orthodox Church as a custodian of the type of rational religious values that theism promoted. And he questioned Kant's ethically motivated separation of the history of mankind from the history of nature in order to show that human beings ought to strive toward the realization of values that were not part of physical nature. These two qualifications, I argue, make Kudriavtsev an ambivalent theist because while he strove for scientific and scholarly rigor in the study of religion, he understood theism's potential to dissolve the religion that he sought to preserve.

This essay describes and explains the structural ribbing of Kudriavtsev's account of theism in late imperial Russia. The aim is rather modest because Kudriavtsev never left a single account of theism; rather, he continued to refine and shape it according to intellectual and academic needs throughout his career. In doing so, this essay also aims to make several larger claims in the interest of rethinking Russian religious thought. First, it aims to complicate the standard account of Russian religious thought as fundamentally different from Catholicism or Protestantism by examining Kudriavtsev's appropriation and extension of theism. As Kudriavtsev well knew—like his younger contemporary A. E. Taylor (1869–1945)—theism was a "modern" philosophical justification of religion that was "discovered" and understood as a religious tradition only relatively recently.[10] By the nineteenth century, theism was a significant force in religious, social, and political discourse in the United States, France, and Germany.[11] Even John Stuart Mill devoted attention to theism late in his career.[12] In contrast to the standard account of Russian religious thought's sui generis and mystical nature, Kudriavtsev's promotion of theism places Kudriavtsev and Russian Orthodoxy within the context of intellectual developments across the European continent that promoted both religion and enlightenment—an intellectual movement that scholars of the late seventeenth and eighteenth century have called the "Religious Enlightenment." Second, because of Kudriavtsev's appropriation of a European religious discourse broadly tied to liberal Protestantism, this essay aims to enrich scholarship on the nature of Orthodox thought. Namely, how Orthodox is Orthodox thought if Church officials generously and professionally engaged with discourses from other Christian confessions? And third, this essay aims to suggest that religious discourses, Orthodox and otherwise, shaped the history of the intelligentsia just as much as German idealism, political economy, and natural science, a role that has until recently been underappreciated.[13]

An explanation of Kudriavtsev's conceptualization of theism in mid-nineteenth-century Russia requires an understanding of the "historicity of the questions and answers"—to borrow John Dunn's language—that Kudriavtsev thought he faced.[14] Why did Kudriavtsev think theism was relevant to Russian life during the era of the so-called "Great Reforms" and "Counter-Reforms" of the 1860s and 1870s? It may seem strange that anyone would be interested in moral questions during this period, which liberal activists in the late nineteenth and early twentieth century portrayed as an era of hope and optimism in the efficacy of scientifically based reform projects.[15] As modern scholarship has shown, however, the reforms undertaken in Alexander II's reign were perceived with great trepidation by nearly all estates of the realm.[16] On a general level, the very future of the Russian Empire was at stake. The government even tried to ban the word "progress" from official statements in order to mitigate the perception that the legislative reforms were radically transforming the economic, social, and political structure of the empire.[17] In the context of such radical structural reforms, broad swaths of Russian society agonized over the moral bases of the imperial order.

THE QUESTION IN EDUCATED SOCIETY: DID RELIGION HAVE A PLACE IN RUSSIA'S FUTURE?

The appearance of the so-called "new men" of the 1850s and 1860s increased and sharpened different visions of Russia's future that had been articulated by members of the intelligentsia late in Nicholas I's reign. Whatever his social and intellectual preferences, P. V. Annenkov (1813–87) captured the centrality of the future for these men when he described the break between the Westernizers and Slavophiles between 1845 and 1847. For the Westernizers and Slavophiles, according to Annenkov, socialism "opened up brilliant prospects on all sides and unfolded before their eyes a dazzling, fantastically illuminated vista to which there was no end in sight." The open-endedness of socialism promoted the articulation of "'visions' of the future structure of social life."[18] Among the competing visions of the empire's future, these men considered whether religion had played an essential and progressive role in the development of modern human culture, or whether it was an artifact to be overcome and left behind as humans gained more mastery of the world through natural science in an infinite and undetermined development of the human mind and culture. Leading intellectuals who defended religion as a source of circumscribed progress have been associated with individuals who articulated various iterations of Slavophilism, like Aleksei Khomiakov (1804-60), Ivan Kireevski (1806–56), Iurii Samarin (1819–76), and Ivan Aksakov (1823–86). Those who promoted the secularization of culture have been associated with the Westernizers of Alexander Herzen's (1812–70), Vissarion Belinskii's (1811–48), and Mikhail Bakunin's (1814–76) generation, or the "new men" in the 1850s and 1860s like Nikolai Chernyshevskii (1828–89), Nikolai Dobroliubov (1836–61), Dmitrii Pisarev (1840–68), and Petr Lavrov (1823–1900). Despite their specific and very public antipathies, all of these men were united in their fundamental concern for the nature of Russia's historical development, which they discussed in terms of *zakonomernnost'* (the law-governed nature of historical development).[19] As Herzen famously recalled in his memoirs, "Yes, we were opponents, but very strange ones. We had one love, and we, like Janus or the two-headed eagle, looked in opposite directions while our heart beat as one."[20] From either direction, neither group could see Russia's future clearly enough to reassure the other or themselves.

In the 1860s, Kudriavtsev confronted arguments for the secularization of culture that Petr Lavrov and Nikolai Chernyshevskii articulated in the 1850s. In their controversy over the methods and purposes for studying anthropology, these men portrayed religion as a regressive force in the course of human development and culture. Rather, the unending progress of human civilization would occur through the growth and perfection of secular, scientific disciplines.[21] While both agreed that religion—at least in its institutionalized form in the Russian Empire—was a mere fiction, neither agreed on what should guide the development of human culture. Indeed, both assumed that the development of culture was endless and undefined.

In the face of this open-ended and potentially frightening future, Kudriavtsev entered public life by defending religion's place in the modern world. He did so in an anonymous review of an encyclopedia that was greeted in print by a strange and resounding silence. As another anonymous reviewer for *The Contemporary* (*Sovremennik*) noted, almost no one talked about the *Encyclopedic Dictionary Composed by Russian Scholars and Writers* (1861).[22] However, this reviewer and Kudriavtsev acknowledged its appearance in critical terms. Both took issue with what they regarded as the epistemological naiveté of the *Encyclopedia*'s editor, who claimed the work's "aggregate of large, leading articles with minor, reference ones" provided readers with a "contemporary-scientific *factual* standpoint" on modern problems.[23] Since Pierre Bayle had organized his *Historical and Critical Dictionary* (1695–97) purely on the indeterminate principle of coordination and simple aggregation of materials, there had been a concerted effort from theologians to argue for the subordination of facts to a larger purpose.[24] Indeed, the very genre of encyclopedias raised a fundamental moral question—should the collection of facts be subordinated to a closed structure that expressed moral values, or an open-ended and eternal collection of facts that suggested an utter lack of moral purpose in the world?[25] *The Contemporary*'s reviewer based his criticism on the principle of utility. According to him, "any encyclopedic dictionary is a roiling sea, a boundless ocean in which the poor reader sails without a compass, 'without helm and sail'—not knowing where, to what side to set his course; and if he gives himself over to the course and path of the waves, then they will cast him where he would probably not at all want to go."[26] Kudriavtsev, by contrast, criticized the

Encyclopedia's organizational principle from a religious perspective. In his review, which was directed at Lavrov, Kudriavtsev argued that the main problem with the *Encyclopedic Dictionary* was its incompetent and superficial treatment of theological and philosophical themes. Such a shortcoming was lamentable since "an especially wide circle of readers, and, moreover, readers who are little acquainted with theological and philosophical sciences" would get what Kudriavtsev regarded as a false picture of vitally important subjects.[27] Moreover, it would contradict what Kudriavtsev and, ostensibly, the encyclopedia's editors regarded as the purpose of an encyclopedia: "The goal of an encyclopedic dictionary is not to put forward any of one's own, one-sided theories, but to communicate all the information that concerns known subjects. The reader looks to a dictionary not for the personal opinions of compilers of various, specialized articles . . . ; he looks to a dictionary for the dispassionate explication of opinions that had, or still have, actual significance in science."[28] Nevertheless, according to Kudriavtsev, the encyclopedia revealed "if not a completely negative" attitude "then at least an ambiguous light" on "Christian beliefs."[29]

In this early review, Kudriavtsev implicitly linked religion to the moral problem with which secular learned disciplines confronted Russia's future development. He was not the only one to appreciate this link. In an article that is better known for introducing the polemical term "nihilism" into Russian discourse, M. N. Katkov (1818–87) criticized a philosophical lexicon that had appeared in Kiev for containing nothing but "the most disturbing chaos of words, words, words" because it lacked a purpose.[30] However serious Katkov's criticism of liberal political economy may have been, his glib and aphoristic style indicates that he polemically simplified much more complex intellectual developments. Both Lavrov and Chernyshevskii were intensely interested in liberal political economy, anthropology, and religion; Lavrov even wrote a critical article on theism.[31] As scholars have come to appreciate, liberal political theory cannot deal with the future. It has a "depleting moral legacy" in which the open-ended pursuit of economic interests gradually leads to socially and politically destructive behavior.[32] Like liberalism, the anthropology of Herbert Spencer, Max Müller, and E. B. Tylor, which was founded on evolutionary social theory's vision of development from simple to ever more complex forms, threatened to undermine the preeminence of monotheistic religions as bearers of culture in the modern world.[33] Indeed, liberalism has difficulty accommodating larger ends outside immediate interests.[34] At this early stage in his career, Kudriavtsev had appreciated the problem that an undefined future posed. His subsequent career at the Moscow Spiritual Academy can be seen as an attempt to solve this problem by turning to the resources that theism provided. In doing so, Kudriavtsev was developing what Kant called philosophy's "chiliastic vision."[35] In clarifying this vision philosophically, Kudriavtsev turned to the history of the "development" (*razvitie*) of "religious consciousness."[36]

Kudriavtsev's Answer: Theism Accommodates Religion to the World

In this immediate ideological context, Kudriavtsev promoted theism as a resource to promote religion and morality in order to save the Russian Empire's future. According to the published version of Kudriavtsev's *Lectures in the Philosophy of Religion*, which he delivered at the Moscow Academy throughout the 1870s, he defined theism as a "religio-philosophical view" that constituted a significant part of "modern philosophy." As Kudriavtsev conceptualized theism, it occupied a middle position between the absolute extremes of moral autonomy and historical necessity, between pantheism and deism. It differed "from deism by the recognition of the unboundedness of the Divinity and, as a consequence of this, of the closest connection of It with the world; and from pantheism by the recognition of His personality [*lichnost'*] and distinctness from the world."[37] As Kudriavtsev instructed his audience, members of the Russian church had two guides for understanding God: F. H. Jacobi (1743–1819) or Immanuel Kant.[38] These giants of late eighteenth-century German culture offered contemporary Russian Orthodoxy a vision of morality that depended on a particular conception of God.

By conceptualizing theism as a modern, philosophical account of religion that maintained a middle position between deism and pantheism, Kudriavtsev was participating in a chronologically multilayered religious and philosophical endeavor that was a defining feature of the late seventeenth and eighteenth century's Religious Enlightenment and its nineteenth-century legacy in Europe.[39] The chronologically immediate context within which to appreciate Kudriavtsev's appropriation of theism to reform religion with philosophical science was German Protestant "Culture Protestantism." This movement sought to accommodate religion to the world without secularizing it. That was the main purpose for theism. Members of this philosophical-cultural movement traced the modern origins of this theistic project to Kant's later work, namely his *Critique of Judgment* (1790) and *Religion*. Kant's account of theism, mediated through its institutionalization in "Culture Protestantism," profoundly shaped Kudriavtsev's articulation of theism in his mature work at the Moscow Spiritual Academy.

That work consisted of a doctoral dissertation, lectures in theology, and textbook articles.

Kudriavtsev indicated the sources that shaped his understanding of theism in "Religion: Its Essence and Provenance" (1873). This dissertation was an important landmark in the development and institutionalization of theism at the Moscow Spiritual Academy. At Kudriavtsev's defense, no less than the Academy's rector, A. V. Gorskii (1812–75), called it a "strictly scientific" defense of religion.[40] As Kudriavtsev informed his small but influential audience, the "special science [*nauka*]" called the "philosophy of religion" was inaugurated with the "age of Kant." The main source for the new age was Immanuel Kant's *Religion*. That book, according to Kudriavtsev, called religious thinkers to give "a precise and correct conception of religion in general, its provenance and goal, and its normal demands and conditions in order to find in this conception a new confirmation of the necessity and truth of revealed religion."[41] Kudriavtsev called his extension of Kant's science "apologetics" (*osnovnoe bogoslovie*), which he advanced for both philosophical as well as apologetic and polemical reasons. Philosophically, the religious scholar ought to justify the "rational, philosophical substantiation and proof of those truths of religion that can be admitted to reason according to their content." Polemically, apologetics defended "the fundamental truths of Christianity from attacks against the Christian religion," which the apologist had to fight "with [the opponent's] own weapon—the weapon of philosophy and rational proofs."[42] For both ends, Kudriavtsev cited K. R. Hagenbach's (1801–74) influential *Encyklopädie und Methodologie der theologischen Wissenschaften* (1833–89).[43]

Kudriavtsev's invocation of Kant for philosophical purposes and Hagenbach for polemical purposes sheds light on the problems Kudriavtsev thought he was solving as well as the available solutions. Kudriavtsev's polemical interests derived from a German Protestant source. In the nineteenth century, Protestant theologians associated with "Culture Protestantism" standardized Kant's response. These theologians strove, in the words of its leading ideologue and pastor, Richard Rothe (1799–1867), for "the reconciliation of religion and culture."[44] Hagenbach's *Encyklopädie* was a foundation text in this German liberal Protestant movement. In that influential work, Hagenbach codified Kant's theism in a respectable, scientific format that became the cornerstone in the edifice of "Culture Protestantism."[45] In terms that Kudriavtsev echoed, Hagenbach framed the choice for modern theologians who wanted to treat theology "scientifically"— what Hagenbach called "Systematic Theology"—between "deistic," "pantheistic," or "theistic" philosophy. Hagenbach endorsed the latter programmatically and polemically: "*only the system of pure theism is applicable to Christian theology.*"[46] And he codified a genealogy of theism running from Colossians 2:8, through the early Church Fathers Irenaeus, Tertullian, and the Alexandrian Fathers, up to Kant, after whom "theology could no longer ignore the course of philosophy without debasing itself scientifically."[47] Like Rothe and Hagenbach, Kudriavtsev promoted theism in an institutional context that solved the philosophical and cultural problem of secularization, a move that might best be called "Culture Orthodoxy" to delineate its similarity to similar trends in contemporary Protestant thought.

Philosophically, Kant's late work offered Kudriavtsev resources for understanding the problem of, and developing an answer to, what scholars of Western religious history variously call the secularization or humanization of religious values or immanent and transcendent conceptions of God.[48] The fundamental problem that secularization posed for religion was whether man becomes the measure of God by evaluating the transcendent in terms of the immanent. The humanization of God and secularization of religious values threatened to undermine religion in general. From the perspective of religious orthodoxy, the relationship between the immanent and the transcendent was either/or. By contrast, proponents of "dipolar" theism conceptualized the relationship between the immanent and transcendent in both/and terms—the transcendent and immanent work together.[49] Theists thought they could humanize God and religious values without secularizing either. Kant's later work, which he articulated in response to the so-called "Pantheism Controversy" between Jacobi and Moses Mendelssohn (1729–86), first articulated a theistic response to Jacobi's criticism that all metaphysics inevitably secularized and humanized religion, which led to atheism and, ultimately, nihilism.[50] The "Pantheism Controversy" moved the issue of secularization to the forefront of the problems that theism and German idealism dealt with in the late eighteenth and early nineteenth century.[51] Kudriavtsev learned how to articulate questions and develop answers to the problem of secularization from Kant's later works on rational religion.

Indeed, Hagenbach's *Encyklopädie* provided Kudriavtsev with resources for dealing with the problem of secularization. In his dissertation, Kudriavtsev formulated the relationship between the immanent and the transcendent in terms almost identical to Kant's. As Kudriavtsev formulated this problem in his dissertation, there were three choices for a philosophical "representation" of a "supreme Being": (1) divinity "as completely separate from the world and man (transcendent in relation to the world)," (2) divinity "having an essential connection with the world by its very nature in view of its substantial identity with the world (immanent)," and (3) divinity "separated from the world in essence and nature, but acting and present in the world through its powers and perfections (transcendent and immanent together)."[52] Kudriavtsev called the first "representation" "deism," the second "pantheism," and the third "theism."[53]

Kudriavtsev promoted an apparently paradoxical account of a theistic God, who was both transcendent and immanent, because his education and professional activity testify to his commitment both to science and enlightenment as well as religion. As we have already seen, Kudriavtsev's student years were devoted to the study of philosophy, theology, and religion in its historical development. Early in his career, he was involved in the project to produce Russian translations of the early Church Fathers, many of whom were essential sources for theism.[54] Kudriavtsev synthesized this work in his dissertation, "Religion: Its Essence and Provenance," which culminated in a brief introduction of theism as the last stage of modern conceptions of religion.[55] Kudriavtsev had also participated in the construction of the post-1869 Moscow Spiritual Academy's scientific and enlightened curriculum. And as a professor in the 1870s, he proposed a course devoted to "the metaphysical doctrine of god [sic] and his relationship to the world with an explication of the fundamental principles of the philosophy of religion."[56] Kudriavtsev's scientific credentials were impeccable.

An answer to why Kudriavtsev thought theism formed an integral part of modern science and enlightenment can be found in his interest in the historical development of religion. As already noted, his dissertation traced religion from its origins to the present as a process of development. His *Lectures* were no different. They were organized as an overview of the development of the world's religions' conceptions of God: original religion, polytheism, paganism, deism, pantheism, and theism.[57] Such an interest in the historical development of religion toward more and more philosophical forms was a hallmark of the liberal Protestant scholarship that studied religions historically and contextually and ran from F. A. Wolf (1759–1824) to Hagenbach.[58] The concern of this scholarship, as we have seen, emphasized the connection between a proper conception of God and the moral perfection of humanity—a transcendent God and his creatures in an immanent realm. Moreover, the theological concerns of this scholarship imparted a closed structure to the movement of history because the narrative aimed at a final, moral end or *telos* of human existence. The foundation text in the nineteenth century for this sort of argument about history was Kant's *Religion*.[59] In the context of the open-ended and potentially immoral, and therefore frightening, futures imagined by Lavrov and Chernyshevskii, theism offered Kudriavtsev a resource for presenting religion as a source for humanity's moral uplift.

The way Kudriavtsev developed his theistic conception of religion was a model of rational religious scholarship that dealt with the problem of secularization. For Kudriavtsev, modern, theistic explanations of religion ought to accommodate religion to the world without secularizing it, or turning religion into a mere tool of any caste. Such a relationship was presented in a theistic narrative using what scholars have called the hermeneutic principle of accommodationism. This principle described a providential relationship between God and mankind in which God called to mankind in various ways throughout history to achieve his or her moral ends. The form and precise ends to which God called his creatures could change depending on the level of cultural or civilizational attainment achieved by particular peoples, but the ultimate end remained the moral improvement of humanity.[60] Crucially, too, the standard of morality and the origins of the call remained with a transcendent God. As Kant put it in *Religion*, humanity received "cooperation from above" in order to achieve moral ends.[61] Transcendent divinity remained the driving force behind mankind's acquisition of knowledge about God.

Russian Theism: Qualified Accommodation

Like nineteenth-century liberal Protestants, Kudriavtsev began his account of religion with history. Unusually, though, Kudriavtsev aimed his *Lectures* at the theory of original polytheism propounded by David Hume, G. W. F. Hegel (1770–1831), and J. G. Fichte (1762–1814). To do so, Kudriavtsev appealed to prehistory as a moment that could have witnessed original monotheism; it was impossible to tell because it preceded writing and other historical artifacts.[62] Because of this eccentric move, Kudriavtsev's history of religious development was the story of the recovery of a primordial unity. Following a French translation of Ralph Cudworth's *True Intellectual System*, Kudriavtsev located the moment of significant transformation from polytheism toward monotheism among the ancient Greeks and Romans, namely Plato, and the conception of "Providence" (*Promysl*).[63] However, the impetus for the change, according to Kudriavtsev, did not come from within the polytheistic religions of ancient Greece and Rome, but from without. Linking the transcendent and immanent together in his explanation, Kudriavtsev argued "this consciousness [of the imperfection of polytheism], which served as a transition to monotheism, arose not within polytheism, itself, but penetrated from without, partially as a consequence of the independent development of philosophical thought, but mainly because of the spread of the true, Revealed religion."[64] The main inheritance from the ancient philosophers, according to Kudriavtsev, were their "more sublime representations of the Gods" and their conception of "Providence," which he associated with Xenophanes (570–480 BCE) and Plato (428/27–348/47 BCE) and the Church Fathers.[65]

Modern scholars of Greek religion have identified the notion of *theoprepes*—what is "fitting" for God—as the central moment in the progressive nature of ancient Greek philosophical religion between Xenophanes of Colophon and Plato.[66] As Kudriavtsev knew, so, too, did the ancient Church Fathers and modern theists like Ralph Cudworth. Criticizing Homer and Hesiod for having "attributed to the gods all things that are shameful and a reproach among mankind," Xenophanes advised mankind "to praise God with decent stories and pure words."[67] Later, Plato developed this idea further when he coined the term "theology" as the "fitting" talk about the gods in contrast to Homer.[68] As Kudriavtsev himself noted, he endorsed the idea that speech about God should express "more sublime" ideals, and, like other thinkers, promoted this moment as a key event in the progressive development of religion.

If more and more "sublime" conceptions of God imparted a developmental shape to the history of religion, then there was a question of where the impetus for reform originated: God or mankind. Here, Plato, along with Holy Scripture, provided another important resource for theists to accommodate religion to the world without secularizing it. For a central feature of Plato's conception of God's relationship with the world was that morality originates outside individual human beings. For Plato, moral principles called to us from without to "connect up" with a divine plan.[69]

Kudriavtsev's conception of the process by which Providence communicated more and more sublime conceptions of deity to mankind rested on a special conception of the relationship between a providential God and mankind. Since at least the Cappadocian Fathers (circa fourth century), Christian theologians had formulated the theistic relationship between God and mankind as a "synergistic" relationship.[70] Based on a Platonized reading of Genesis 1:26, these men had argued that since mankind was created in the "image of God," all sentient creatures were enjoined to realize their moral "likeness to God" as far as humanly possible. The Church Fathers had fitted Plato's conception of a providential God who calls out to his or her creatures to achieve their moral selves into the story of the Bible. And modern theists described God in the same terms. Kant, for example, had described the relationship as "supernatural cooperation" or "cooperation from above."⁷¹ Following in the theistic tradition in which he self-consciously participated, Kudriavtsev also conceived of the relationship in synergistic terms when he described it as "an interrelation between God and man."⁷² God communicated high-minded moral principles to mankind, and it was mankind's destiny to realize these ideals as far as possible.

Communication between God and mankind in this synergistic relationship was made possible by the postulate of the existence of a "religious sense" (*religioznoe chuvstvo*). Based on his study of the comparative history of religion, Kudriavtsev regarded the religious sense as a natural need for the human mind given its presence in almost all epochs of human intellectual and religious history in three forms: polytheism, deism, and pantheism. As Kudriavtsev put it to his students and readers,

> Each of [these forms of religion], including several indubitable elements which satisfy the religious sense—otherwise they would not have persisted in the history of religion with such duration and established themselves with such insistence in the area of philosophical thinking—at the same time generally proved to be groundless before the court of more and more highly developed religious conscience and clearer philosophical thought.⁷³

Such a religious sense showed two things. First, that it was natural for human beings to have a religious sense. And second, that the religious sense has undergone development through time toward more and more perfect and fitting conceptions of God. Each of these epochs in the religious mind of mankind had its role to play in the development of a perfect conception of God, but ultimately they were mere moments in the development of the perfect conception. As Kant described the process, God showed human beings their higher selves, and human beings participated in their salvation by "the laying off of the old man and the putting on of the new."⁷⁴

Kudriavtsev did not uncritically accept Kant's rational account of religion, for he detected criticism of institutional religion in Kant's concept of the "invisible church" and a cynical attitude toward the supernatural in religion.⁷⁵ Following Jacobi, Kudriavtsev criticized Kant's grounding of morality in "moral feeling" or "practical reason" because it characterized the supernatural source of morality as a mere "supplement."⁷⁶ Scholars have noted Kant's paradoxical explanation of the supernatural in religion—either it is truly supernatural or it is a mere fiction that satisfies psychological needs.⁷⁷ Kudriavtsev's concern to modernize religion without secularizing it led him to appreciate Jacobi's insistence on the primacy of a transcendental God without giving up Kant's attempt to give scientific form to religious belief. Kudriavtsev invoked Jacobi at the end of his lectures: "If man is the image of the Creator, then it is natural that he contemplates in his prototype in the highest degree those characteristics which constitute the divine image of his nature [*bogopodobie ego prirody*]. Man, as Jacobi rightly notes, anthropomorphizes God precisely because God, in the process of creating, deomorphizes him [*Bog, sozdavaia cheloveka, deomorfiziroval ego*]."[78] Given his commitment and service to the institutional Russian Orthodox Church, Kudriavtsev relied on the institutional Church and its dogmas as a check against the expressivist tendencies of German idealism that Kant's metaphysics had brought into being.

Conclusion

Given the conventional historiography of Russian religious thought, with its emphasis on lay figures outside the Church's institutions or on idiosyncratic churchmen, it is surprising to see the development of rational religion, even a religious enlightenment, at the Moscow Spiritual Academy. Though religion might seem the least scientific subject to study, Kudriavtsev employed—like enlighteners in ancient Greece and nineteenth-century Europe—methods of philological and historical criticism as well as philosophical analysis in order to provide contemporary Orthodox Russians with "modern reasons to believe in myth and the marvelous."[79] In the context of the perceived decay and imperative to reform or revolutionize social and political life in post-emancipation Russia, Kudriavtsev's theistic account of religion provided a basis for making Orthodoxy relevant to new circumstances. Such an attitude and approach to the tenets of Russian Orthodoxy was eminently modern and scientific.

Kudriavtsev's articulation and dissemination of rational religion at the Moscow Spiritual Academy has broader implications for the study of Russian religious thought. Such a vision of Russian modernity contributes to a body of scholarship that examines the paradoxical nature of "nativist" Russian discourses articulated in Western categories of thought.[80] The inspiration for this work has been lay figures, who appropriated both Russian Orthodox and Western categories of thought in order to articulate their own vision of modernity.[81] This work, in turn, spilled over onto the social engagement of the Church and its effects on Russian society.[82] Much of this work, however, treats the Church and religion as a strange survival from the past that has continued to exist paradoxically in a modernity defined beforehand as secular. Kudriavtsev's career and European historiography complicate this notion of modernity. His career challenges us to reconsider our polemical conceptions of modernity against the complexity of the testimony of life from the past.

A conception of modernity that allows for the sacred and the secular to exist alongside each other as equals could also complicate our understanding of the fabled Russian intelligentsia. While there is a well-established tradition of treating Russia as a participant in European culture, it has tended to tell the story of the perversion of Western ideas in the Russian context.[83] More recently, scholars have treated Russian engagement with Western categories of thought without such a cultural value judgment.[84] Yet, like the new works on Russian Orthodoxy and religion in this volume and elsewhere, an examination of Kudriavtsev's career suggests that the relationship between the secular and the religious was more complicated than a mere paradox. For Kudriavtsev, Chernyshevskii, and Lavrov had much more in common over the issue of Russia's future than later generations of the so-called radical intelligentsia.[85] Whatever future these men of the 1860s and 1870s had imagined, it had little to do with Lenin and the Bolshevik Revolution that still shapes scholarship on the Russian intelligentsia. Indeed, even up to 1908 almost no one shared Lenin's vision of Russia's future.[86] By taking the clerical estate's institutions of higher learning as more than "mere" handmaidens of the state, however powerful such a vision of clerical life may have been as a rhetorical trope in the imperial period, we can enrich our understanding of the Russian Orthodox Church, its practices, its relationship to the government, society, and the empire.[87] Rethinking Russian religious thought could open up new vistas on Russia's futures past.[88]

NOTES

1. There is no modern biography of Kudriavtsev. The fullest is still I. N. Korsunskii, "Viktor Dmitrievich Kudriavtsev-Platonov," in *Sochineniia V. D. Kudriavtseva-Platonova*, 3 vols. (Sergiev Posad: Izdanie Bratstva Prepodobnogo Sergiia, 1892–94), 1:1:1–56, here 1–7. See also V. V. Zenkovsky, *A History of Russian Philosophy*, trans. George L. Kline (New York: Columbia University Press, 1953), 2:532–46.

2. Korsunskii, "Kudriavtsev-Platonov," 11; S. Kedrov, "Studenty-Platoniki v Akademii," in *U Troitsy v Akademii, 1814–1914: Iubileinyi sbornik* (Moscow: Tipografiia T-va I. D. Sytina, 1914), 224.

3. *Polnoe sobranie zakonov Rossiiskoi Imperii, Sobranie vtoroe* (hereafter *PSZ II*), 62 vols. (St. Petersburg: Tip. II Otdel. Sobstvennoi E. I. V. Kantseliarii, 1830–84), vol. 44, no. 47154, 545. For Kudriavtsev's role in writing and implementing this statute, see Korsunskii, "Kudriavtsev-Platonov," 46; Tsentral'nyi istoricheskii arkhiv Moskvy (TsIAM), f. 229 (Moscow Spiritual Academy), op. 3, d. 50, l. 26f; d. 66, ll. 64–64ob.

4. Korsunskii, "Kudriavtsev-Platonov," 13–14.

5. Kedrov, "Studenty-Platoniki v Akademii," 224. Kudriavtsev's teacher at the Academy, F. A. Golubinskii (1797–1854) is also sometimes referred to as the founder of Russian theism. See, for example, Korsunkii, "Kudriavtsev-Platonov," 7–14.

6. Kudriavtsev, "Iz chtenii po filosofii religii," in *Sochineniia*, 2:2:114–15n.

7. Ralph Cudworth, *The True Intellectual System of the Universe* (London: Printed for Richard Royston, 1678); David Hume, *The Natural History of Religion*, ed. E. H. Root (1757; repr., Stanford, CA: Stanford University Press, 1957), 41–48; Jean-Jacques Rousseau, "Rousseau juge de Jean Jacques," in *Oeuvres complètes*, ed. Bernard Gagnebin and Marcel Raymond (Paris: Gallimard, 1959), 1:968.

8. Kudriavtsev, "Religiia, ee suchnost' i proiskhozhdenie," in *Sochineniia*, 2:1:88–315, esp. 149–96; Kudriavtsev, "Iz chtenii," 2:2:104–347, 2:3:1–204. The lectures originally appeared serially in *Pravoslavnoe obozrenie* (*Orthodox Review*), 1879–89.

9. Immanuel Kant, *Religion within the Limits of Reason Alone*, trans. Theodore M. Greene and Hoyt H. Hudson (New York: Harper Torch Books, 1960), 162.

10. Kudriavtsev, "Teizm," in *Sochineniia*, 2:3:159; A. E. Taylor, "Theism," in *Encyclopedia of Religion and Ethics*, ed. James Hastings (New York: Charles Scribners' Sons, 1958), 12:281. Given the importance of "theism" to European religious and intellectual history, its absence in *Geschichtliche Grundbegriffe* is curious. This encyclopedia has only an 1810 reference to "political theism" by Friedrich Schlegel. See Otto Brunner, Werner Conze, and Reinhart Koselleck, eds., *Geschichtliche Grundbegriffe: Historisches Lexikon zur politisch-sozialen Sprache in Deutschland* (Stuttgart: E. Klett, 1982), 3:998.

11. James Turner, *Without God, Without Creed: The Origins of Unbelief in America* (Baltimore, MD: Johns Hopkins University Press, 1985), 146–50; Laurence Dickey, "Constant and Religion: 'Theism Descends from Heaven to Earth,'" in *The Cambridge Companion to Constant*, ed. Helena Rosenblatt (Cambridge: Cambridge University Press, 2009), 313–48.

12. John Stuart Mill, *Three Essays on Religion*, in *Essays on Ethics, Religion, and Society*, vol. 10 of *Collected Works of John Stuart Mill*, ed. J. M. Robson (Toronto: University of Toronto Press, 1969), 429–89.

13. Laurie Manchester, *Holy Fathers, Secular Sons: Clergy, Intelligentsia, and the Modern Self in Revolutionary Russia* (DeKalb: Northern Illinois University Press, 2008); Victoria Frede, *Doubt, Atheism, and the Nineteenth-Century Russian Intelligentsia* (Madison: University of Wisconsin Press, 2011).

14. John Dunn, *Political Obligation in Its Historical Context: Essays in Political Theory* (Cambridge: Cambridge University Press, 2012), 6.

15. A. K. Dzhivelegov, S. P. Mel'gunov, and V. I. Picheta, eds., *Velikaia reforma: Russkoe obshchestvo i krest'ianskii vopros*, 6 vols. (Moscow: Izdanie I. D. Sytina, 1911); G. A. Dzhanshiev, *Iz epokhi velikikh reform: Istoricheskii spravki* (Moscow: T-va tip. A. I. Mamontova, 1893).

16. Francis William Wcislo, *Reforming Rural Russia: State, Local Society, and National Politics, 1855–1914* (Princeton, NJ: Princeton University Press, 1990), 11–118; Dietrich Geyer, *Russian Imperialism: The Interaction of Domestic and Foreign Policy*, trans. Bruce Little (New Haven, CT: Yale University Press, 1987), 15–121; P. A. Zaionchkovskii, *Rossiiskoe samoderzhavie v kontse XIX stoletiia* (Moscow: Izd-vo Mysl', 1970), 217–33.

17. Geyer, *Russian Imperialism*, 19.

18. P. V. Annenkov, *The Extraordinary Decade: Literary Memoirs*, ed. Arthur P. Mendel and trans. Irwin R. Titunik (Ann Arbor: University of Michigan Press, 1968), 140.

19. The best introduction to the importance and ramifications of this concept is still N. L. Rubinshtein, *Russkaia istoriografiia* (Moscow: OGIZ Gospolitizdat, 1941).

20. Alexander Herzen, *My Past and Thoughts: The Memoirs of Alexander Herzen*, trans. Constance Garnett (Berkeley: University of California Press, 1982), 287.

21. N. G. Chernyshevskii, "Antropologicheskii printsip v filosofii," in *Polnoe sobranie sochinenii v piatnadtsati tomakh*, ed. V. Ia. Kirpotin et al. (Moscow: Khudozhestvennaia Literatura, 1939–1953 [1950]), 7:222–95, 1016–19, 1058–59; P. L. Lavrov, *Ocherki voprosov prakticheskoi filosofii* (St. Petersburg: Tip. I. I. Glazunova, 1860).

22. "Novye knigi," *Sovremennik* 88 (1861): 19.

23. A. A. Kraevskii, ed., *Entsiklopedicheskii slovar', sostavlennyi russkimi uchenymi i literatorami* (St. Petersburg, 1861), 1:iv.

24. Ernst Cassirer, *The Philosophy of the Enlightenment*, trans. Fritz C. A. Koelln and James P. Pettegrove (Princeton, NJ: Princeton University Press, 1951), 199–209.

25. Alasdair MacIntyre, *Three Rival Versions of Moral Enquiry: Encyclopedia, Genealogy, and Tradition, being the Gifford Lectures delivered in the University of Edinburgh in 1988* (Notre Dame, IN: University of Notre Dame Press, 1990), 8–23, 170–95.

26. Ibid., 26.

27. [V. D. Kudriavtsev-Platonov], "Entsiklopedicheskii slovar', sostavlennyi russkimi uchenymi i literatorami," *Pribavleniia k tvoreniiam sviatykh ottsov v russkom perevode*, chast' 22 (1863): 3:291–368 [first pagination], citation 291.

28. Ibid., 293–94.

29. Ibid., 295.

30. M. N. Katkov, "Starye bogi i novye bogi," *Russkii vestnik*, nos. 1–2 (1861): 899.

31. N. G. Chernyshevskii, "Ocherki iz politicheskoi ekonomii (po Milliu)," in Kirpotin et al., *Polnoe sobranie* (1949), 9:337–725; Chernyshevskii, *Iz avtobiografii, dnevnik, 1848–1853 gg.*, vol. 1 of *Literaturnoe nasledie*, ed. N. A. Alekseev, M. N. Chernyshevskii, S. N. Chernov (Moscow: Gosizdat, 1928); P. L. Lavrov, "Sovremennye Germanskie teisty," *Russkoe slovo* 1, no. 7 (1859): 141–212.

32. Fred Hirsch, *Social Limits to Growth* (Cambridge, MA: Harvard University Press, 1976), 115–51.

33. Kudriavtsev, "Iz Chetenii," 2:2:104–54. On evolutionary social theory, see J. W. Burrow, *Evolution and Society: A Study in Victorian Social Theory* (Cambridge: Cambridge University Press, 1966).

34. Quentin Skinner, "The Idea of Negative Liberty: Philosophical and Historical Perspectives," in *Philosophy in History: Essays on the Historiography of Philosophy*, ed. Richard Rorty, J. B. Schneewind, and Quentin Skinner (Cambridge: Cambridge University Press, 1984), 193–221.

35. Immanuel Kant, "Idea for a Universal History with a Cosmopolitan Intent," in *Perpetual Peace and Other Essays on Politics, History, and Morals*, ed. and trans. Ted Humphrey (Indianapolis, IN: Hackett Publishing Company, 1983), 36.

36. Kudriavtsev, "Teizm," in *Sochineniia*, 2:3:190.

37. Ibid., 159.

38. Ibid., 156–204. See also his textbook definition in Kudriavtsev, "Teizm: Uchenie o Promysle," in *Nachal'nye osnovaniia filosofii*, 3rd ed. (Sergiev Posad: Tip. A. I. Snegirevoi, 1893), 230–35.

39. David Jan Sorkin, *The Religious Enlightenment: Protestants, Jews, and Catholics from London to Vienna* (Princeton, NJ: Princeton University Press, 2008). J. G. A. Pocock

links religious enlightenment and theism in "Enthusiasm: The Antiself of Enlightenment," *Huntington Library Quarterly* 60, no. 1/2 (1997): 7–28, esp. 20.

40. TsIAM, f. 229, op. 3, d. 44, ll. 220b.–23.

41. Kudriavtsev, "Rech' na dispute, pred zashchitoiu dissertatsii na stepen' doktora bogosloviia: 'Religiia, ee sushchnost' i proiskhozhdenie,'" in *Sochineniia*, 2:1:88–89, 134, 168. The place of Kant in the spiritual academies is still poorly understood. See Alexandre Koyré, *La philosophie et le problème national en Russie au début du XIXe siècle* (1929; repr., Paris: Gallimard, 1976), 91–93.

42. Kudriavtsev, "Rech'," 2:1:81–84; Kudriavtsev, "Religiia," 2:1:91–92.

43. Kudriavtsev, "Rech'," 81n; Kudriavtsev, "Religiia," 90n.

44. Cited in F. W. Graf, "Kulturprotestantismus: Zur Begriffsgeschichte einer theologischen Chiffre," *Archive für Begriffsgeschichte* 28 (1984): 217. See also George Rupp, *Culture-Protestantism: German Liberal Theology at the Turn of the Twentieth Century* (Missoula, MT: Scholars Press for the American Academy of Religion, 1977).

45. Thomas Albert Howard, *Protestant Theology and the Making of the Modern German University* (New York: Oxford University Press, 2006), 303–23.

46. K. R. Hagenbach, *Encyklopädie und Methodologie der theologischen Wissenschaften* (Leipzig: Weidmann'sche Buchhandlung, 1833), 75, emphasis in original. On systematic theology, see 312–76.

47. Ibid., 66–68, quotation at 67.

48. Karl Löwith, *The Meaning of History* (Chicago: University of Chicago Press, 1949), 1–19; Eric Voegelin, *The New Science of Politics* (Chicago: University of Chicago Press, 1952), 119.

49. On dipolar theism, see Charles Hartshorne, *A Natural Theology for Our Time* (LaSalle, IL: Open Court Press, 1967), 126; Van Austin Harvey, *Handbook of Theological Terms* (New York: Macmillan, 1964), s. v. "theism."

50. Frederick Beiser, *The Fate of Reason: German Philosophy from Kant to Fichte* (Cambridge, MA: Harvard University Press, 1987), 44–91; John H. Zammito, *The Genesis of Kant's Critique of Judgment* (Chicago: University of Chicago Press, 1992), 6–7, 228–47; Michael Allen Gillespie, *Nihilism before Nietzsche* (Chicago: University of Chicago Press, 1995), 65–67.

51. John E. Toews, *Hegelianism: The Path toward Dialectical Humanism, 1805–1841* (Cambridge: Cambridge University Press, 1980); Warren Breckman, *Marx, the Young Hegelians, and the Origins of Radical Social Theory* (Cambridge: Cambridge University Press, 2001), esp. 20–27.

52. Kudriavtsev, "Religiia," 132–33.

53. Ibid., 133. See also Kudriavtsev, "Tezisy sochineniia: 'Religiia, ee sushchnost' i proiskhozhdenie,'" in *Sochineniia*, 2:1:318–19.

54. Patrick Lally Michelson, "'The First and Most Sacred Right': Religious Freedom and the Liberation of the Russian Nation, 1825–1905" (PhD diss., University of Wisconsin–Madison, 2007), 29–92; Korsunksii, "Kudriavtsev-Platonov," 28.

55. Kudriavstev, "Religiia," 279–80.

56. TsIAM, f. 229, op. 3, ed. khr. 51, l. 21.

57. Kudriavtsev, "Iz chtenii," 2:2:104–347, 2:3:1–204.

58. Anthony Grafton, *Defenders of the Text: The Traditions of Scholarship in an Age of Science, 1450–1800* (Cambridge, MA: Harvard University Press, 1991), 214–45.

59. Alasdair MacIntyre, *After Virtue: A Study in Moral Theory* (Notre Dame, IN: University of Notre Dame Press, 1984), 51–54.

60. Stephen D. Benin, *The Footprints of God: Divine Accommodation in Jewish and Christian Thought* (Albany: State University of New York Press, 1992); Amos Funkenstein, *Theology and the Scientific Imagination from the Middle Ages to the Seventeenth Century* (Princeton, NJ: Princeton University Press, 1986), 202–89.

61. Kant, *Religion*, 47.

62. Kudriavtsev, "Iz chtenii," 2:2:104–10.

63. Ibid., 113–14n. On "Providence," see also Kudriavtsev, "O Promysle," in *Sochineniia*, 2:1:35–79; Kudriavtsev, "Teizm; uchenie o Promysle," *Nachal'nye osnovaniia filosofii*, 3rd ed. (Moscow and Sergiev Posad: 2-aia Tip. A. I. Snegirevoi, 1893), 230–35.

64. Kudriavtsev, "Iz chtenii," 2:2:112.

65. Ibid., 114, 116–17.

66. Walter Burkert, *Greek Religion*, trans. John Raffan (Cambridge, MA: Harvard University Press, 1985), 305–37.

67. "Xenophanes of Colophon," in *Ancilla to the Pre-Socratic Philosophers*, ed. Kathleen Freeman (Cambridge, MA: Harvard University Press, 1948), 22, 20.

68. Plato, *The Republic*, trans. Allan Bloom (New York: Basic Books, 1968), 56 and 450n45.

69. Charles Taylor, "Plato's Self-Mastery," in *Sources of the Self: The Making of Modern Identity* (Cambridge, MA: Harvard University Press, 1989), 115–26, esp. 123.

70. Werner Jaeger, *Early Christianity and Greek Paideia* (Cambridge, MA: The Belknap Press of Harvard University Press, 1961), 88 and 141n5; Jaeger, *Two Rediscovered Works of Ancient Christian Literature: Gregory of Nyssa and Macarius* (Leiden: E. J. Brill, 1954), 85–98.

71. Kant, *Religion*, 40, 47. See also 150–51.

72. Kudriavtsev, "Iz chtenii," 2:3:199.

73. Ibid., 156.

74. Kant, *Religion*, 68. On this theme, see also Karl Jaspers, *The Origin and Goal of History*, trans. Michael Bullock (New Haven, CT: Yale University Press, 1953), 3–4.

75. Kant, *Religion*, 140, 166.

76. Kudriavtsev, "Religiia," 198–99.

77. Ernst Cassirer, *Kant's Life and Thought*, trans. James Haden (New Haven, CT: Yale University Press, 1983), 381–91, esp. 385.

78. Kudriavtsev, "Iz chtenii," 2:3:204.

79. Paul Veyne, "Social Diversity of Beliefs and Mental Balkanization," in *Did the Greeks Believe in Their Myths? An Essay on the Constitutive Imagination*, trans. Paula Wissing (Chicago: University of Chicago Press, 1988), 47.

80. Laura Engelstein, "Old and New, High and Low: Straw Horsemen of Russian Orthodoxy," in *Orthodox Russia: Belief and Practice under the Tsars*, ed. Valerie A. Kivelson and Robert H. Greene (University Park: Pennsylvania State University Press, 2003), 23–32.

81. Laura Engelstein, *Slavophile Empire: Imperial Russia's Illiberal Path* (Ithaca, NY: Cornell University Press, 2009); Patrick Lally Michelson, "Slavophile Religious Thought and the Dilemma of Russian Modernity, 1830–1860," *Modern Intellectual History* 7, no. 2 (2010): 239–67.

82. Nadieszda Kizenko, *A Prodigal Saint: Father John of Kronstadt and the Russian People* (University Park: Pennsylvania State University Press, 2000); Vera Shevzov, *Russian Orthodoxy on the Eve of Revolution* (New York: Oxford University Press, 2003); Manchester, *Holy Fathers*; Jennifer Hedda, *His Kingdom Come: Orthodox Pastorship and Social Activism in Revolutionary Russia* (DeKalb: Northern Illinois University Press, 2008).

83. Martin Malia, *Alexander Herzen and the Birth of Russian Socialism, 1812–1855* (Cambridge, MA: Harvard University Press, 1961).

84. Alexander M. Martin, *Romantics, Reformers, Reactionaries: Russian Conservative Thought and Politics in the Reign of Alexander I* (DeKalb: Northern Illinois University Press, 1997); John Randolph, *The House in the Garden: The Bakunin Family and the Romance of Russian Idealism* (Ithaca, NY: Cornell University Press, 2007); Andrei Zorin, *Kormia dvuglavnogo orla* (Moscow: Novoe Literaturnoe Obozrenie, 2001).

85. For an early and unsuccessful attempt to complicate the history of the intelligentsia, see Franco Venturi, *Roots of Revolution: A History of the Populist and Socialist Movements in Nineteenth-Century Russia*, trans. Francis Haskell (Chicago: University of Chicago Press, 1983). For the American editor's decision to give the English translation a teleological title contrary to Venturi's intention, see Franco Venturi, *Studies in Free Russia* (Chicago: University of Chicago Press, 1982), xi–xii, 216–87.

86. Ivanov-Razumnik, *Istoriia russkoi obshchestvennoi mysli: Individualizm i meshchanstvo v russkoi literature i zhizni XIX v.*, 2nd ed., 2 vols. (St. Petersburg: M. M. Stasiulevich, 1908).

87. Gregory L. Freeze, "Handmaiden of the State? The Orthodox Church in Imperial Russia Reconsidered," *Journal of Ecclesiastical History* 36, no. 1 (1985): 82–102, esp. 84.

88. Reinhart Koselleck, *Futures Past: On the Semantics of Historical Time*, trans. Keith Tribe (New York: Columbia University Press, 2004).

Chapter 5

The Struggle for the Sacred

Russian Orthodox Thinking about Miracles in a Modern Age

VERA SHEVZOV

In 1912, a group of parishioners from the church of Saint Nicholas in the Siberian diocese of Eniseisk embarked on a year-long campaign against local diocesan and central Church authorities in Saint Petersburg to prevent the removal of an icon of the Mother of God named "The Joy of All Who Sorrow" from their parish church. That year, a young peasant girl and her uncle had found this icon in a freshwater spring, where the two had stopped to drink. Many of the local faithful interpreted the finding of this icon as a sign of divine blessing during a particularly difficult period in the region's history. Because of drought and insect infestations, residents had been deprived of normal harvests for more than four years. Seeing the icon as a sign of hope, believers embraced its appearance as nothing less than a miracle.[1]

In the history of lived Orthodoxy in modern Russia since the time of Peter the Great, this case was in many ways routine. On the one hand, Orthodox believers—laymen and women and often parish clergy—made frequent reports of miracles, in which they identified certain icons with such words as "grace-filled light," "heavenly blessing," divine goodwill, and mercy. Insisting that their sentiments were based not on a "fleeting passion" but on a "solid and conscious conviction in the truth of [their] beliefs," believers often associated such signs with turning points in their personal or collective lives and sought them out as sources of joy and strength.[2] At the same time, diocesan and central Orthodox Church officials routinely attempted to neutralize the awe-inspiring character of certain events by insisting that such perceived "extraordinary" occurrences were, in fact, "ordinary." Guided by existing Church and civic legislation codified in the eighteenth century—whose purpose in large part was to clean up Orthodoxy's early modern image vis-à-vis its Western European Christian counterparts—nineteenth-century Church bureaucrats routinely initiated formal investigations into reported miracles in order to curtail "unfounded speculations" and to control the fate of the objects, sites, and, in cases of perceived healers, even people, that stirred believers' sacred sensibilities. Parish priests, in turn, often attempted to dispel grassroots claims about the miraculous, maintaining that such incidents involved little more than the "charlatanism of dishonest people."[3]

In the past two decades, scholars of Orthodox Christianity in modern Russia have turned primarily to such grassroots reports in order to determine Orthodox views on the phenomenon of miracles. Given that such exploration of the "theology of the streets" is conditioned in large part by available sources and the context from which these sources arose, scholars interested in Orthodox thinking about miracles have often been forced to consider Church institutional-related issues.[4] Having taken place on a local parish level and in the offices of consistory and Synodal officials, discussions about miracles in the "lived" context of nineteenth-century Russian Orthodoxy often digressed into statements and ideas concerning institutional authority, politics, power, and control. Notions concerning the workings of the "spirit" inherent in the phenomenon of miracles inserted a strong democratizing subtext into a hierarchically organized institutional world, often empowering the conventionally marginalized constituents within the faith community—especially common laymen and women. Consequently, debates regarding miracles often dovetailed with politically charged discussions concerning the relationship between clergy and laity, the source of authority within the community, especially episcopal authority, the relationship between local, diocesan, and national Church governance, and the image and role of laity in Church life.[5]

Furthermore, Church and civil legislation that guided nineteenth-century discussions about miracles were composed during the reign of Peter the Great, whose primary concerns led to the ill-defined project of freeing Orthodoxy from all that was "superfluous and not essential to salvation."[6] Inspired by a mixture of Counter-Reformation sentiments that sought to bring credibility to devotional practices in the face of corruption and Enlightenment rationalist sensibilities that tended to dismiss miracles as signs of ignorance, this legislation begged questions regarding the differences between "true" and "false" miracles and between superstition and religion. Tracing Orthodox thought on miracles based on these sources, consequently, has often left contemporary scholars of modern Orthodoxy attempting to define the parameters of "Orthodoxy" as well as of "popular" and "official" religious cultures in any particular period.[7] Finally, the persistent phenomenon of reported miracles in nineteenth- and early twentieth-century Russia has challenged scholars of Orthodoxy to question the conventional wisdom on modernity, progress, and secularization that foresaw an inevitable decline in religion.[8]

Orthodox thinking about miracles in late nineteenth- and early twentieth-century Russian Orthodoxy, however, was not limited to priests and peasants or to consistory and Synodal bureaucrats. The subject of miracles surfaced in other Orthodox quarters, namely among a group whose impact on modern Russian religious thought has yet to be fully appreciated: professors and graduates of Russia's leading theological academies. As the essay by Sean Gillen about V. D. Kudriavtsev-Platonov in this volume indicates, far from being "deaf to all practical demands of life" and, hence, removed from society and from matters of concern to Orthodox faithful at large, many of the graduates of Russia's Orthodox academies embarked during this period on a conscious mission to make Orthodoxy relevant in the modern world.[9] That relevance was being tested in Russian society wherever modernity seemed to find its most eloquent and persuasive expression: in the rise of science and the entrenchment of a world view grounded in positivism, in the idea of progress, and, for Orthodox Christians in particular, in the rise of critical historicism and Biblical interpretation, which challenged the relationship between faith and history.[10] In short, these thinkers sought to meet the philosophical challenges wherever doubt, materialism, and secularism seemed to dismiss the credibility of Orthodoxy as an all-encompassing world view suited to the demands of the times.

The subject of miracles was no minor matter in these endeavors. Academically trained Orthodox thinkers struggled to assert the viability of an Orthodox world view and the integrity of an Orthodox identity in an age where not only miracle-working icons and healings were considered hindrances to progress, but where the very foundational tenet of that world view—the resurrection of Jesus—was no longer tenable.[11] While some Christians in the West, namely German liberal Protestant theologians, actively embraced modernity and attempted, as one Orthodox academic theologian maintained, to celebrate the resurrection of Christ without believing in the resurrection, Orthodox theologians resisted the rift between faith and science or knowledge (*nauka*) that modernity had perpetuated.[12] Echoing the view of the apostle Paul in the first century, the priest and graduate of the Moscow Spiritual Academy, Stefan Ostroumov, reminded his readers, "if Christ was not resurrected . . . then the religious relationship to him of millions of those living today and in the past has been in vain and futile."[13]

Recognizing the centrality of the "fact" of the resurrection for the Orthodox world view, Russia's Orthodox academic theologians actively engaged in Western debates about the resurrection during this time period.[14] At the same time, some Orthodox academics also turned to the living nerve underlying belief in the resurrection—namely, the notion of miracle. Insofar as the resurrection was an event that was understood as "genuinely miraculous, as actually having occurred, and irrefutable," the resurrection begged the question of the very possibility of miracles—revelatory acts of God in nature, in the psychological nature of humans, and in the history of nations and peoples.[15] Aware of modern prejudices against miracles that came with the processes by which doubt and atheism were gradually becoming "speakable" among all segments of Russian society, many of Russia's Orthodox academic theologians considered it imperative to address the topic;[16] they sought to dispel reigning stereotypes that had contributed to making the miracle "the phantom of this age," more despised among certain segments of the population, as one priest noted, than religion as a whole.[17]

This essay offers an overview of the Orthodox exposition of the subject of miracles in the face of modern skepticism in late nineteenth- and early twentieth-century Russia. Unlike in modern Western thought where the topic of miracles immediately brings to mind such luminaries as John Toland, David Hume, Immanuel Kant, and Gotthold Ephraim Lessing, except for Feofan (Tuliakov), who authored the most comprehensive apologetic work on Orthodoxy and miracles in prerevolutionary Russia, no single thinker or group of Orthodox thinkers stood out for their work on miracles. Instead, Orthodox discourse on miracles dovetailed with authors' other academic interests—dogmatic theology, moral theology, history, or biblical scholarship. Focusing in particular on understandings of God and creation, nature and free will, as well as on the epistemic quality of miracles in the Orthodox world view, Orthodox thinkers expanded upon and problematized the discourse about miracles as it tended to surface in the lived context of local church life. In doing so, Russia's Orthodox academic thinkers offered theological, philosophical, and epistemological credence to sensibilities that they considered essential to an Orthodox world view, and which, in modern times, otherwise remained conflated with notions of superstition, ignorance, and deception.

The Thinkers and Their Sources

In his introductory lecture in a course on dogmatics at Moscow Spiritual Academy in 1914, professor of theology Sergei Glagolev reviewed briefly the history and purpose of the school, whose origins dated to the mid-seventeenth century, concluding that its ultimate purpose through the decades had been "the struggle for the sacred" (*bor'ba za sviatoe*). This was not a struggle primarily for churches, icons, or dogmas, he explained, but primarily against various world views that "attempt to empty our souls."[18] In large part, a similar sentiment motivated some other graduates from theological academies in the second half of the nineteenth and early twentieth century to write in defense of miracles. Far from being esoteric works aimed at other scholars, as had generally been the case regarding academic theological work prior to the mid-nineteenth century, these essays were existentially motivated and spoke to contemporary intellectual and philosophical challenges facing Orthodox Christians in a modernizing society.

The authors on whose work this essay is based enjoyed diverse vocations and fates. Often graduates of the Saint Petersburg, Moscow, or Kiev Spiritual Academies, the majority of the Orthodox thinkers who wrote about miracles at this time were born in the second half of the nineteenth century. They were raised in a society and a Church environment influenced by the reforms initiated during the reign of Emperor Alexander II (ruled 1855–81). Several writers, such as Grigorii D'iachenko (1850–1903), Ioann Orfanitskii (b. 1854) and Stefan Ostroumov (d. after 1918), were ordained to the priesthood and served in parishes after graduating from the academy.[19] Others, such as Evgraf Loviagin (1822–1909) and Sergei Glagolev (1865–1937), chose to retain their lay status and became professors at the Saint Petersburg and Moscow Spiritual Academies, or in the case of Pavel Svetlov (1861–1945), at Kiev University.[20] Petr Smirnov (d. 1906) and Andrei Predtechenskii (d. 1893) served as editors of prominent ecclesiastical journals, *Tserkovnye vedomosti* (*Church News*) and *Khristianskoe chtenie* (*Christian Reading*).[21] Two authors—Nikolai Dobronravov (d. 1937) and Feofan (Tuliakov) (1864–1937)—became bishops. At least five of the authors were arrested and executed for anti-Soviet activity following the 1917 Bolshevik Revolution.[22]

Some academically trained authors penned essays that were edifying descriptions of the Orthodox understanding of miracles and did not explicitly engage or draw upon any particular sources.[23] Most authors, however, actively engaged modern, Western attitudes toward miracles, inspired by such philosophical luminaries as Baruch Spinoza (1632–77), David Hume (1711–76), Immanuel

Kant (1724–1804), G. W. F. Hegel (1770–1831), I. H. Fichte (1797–1879), Herbert Spencer (1820–1903), and William James (1842–1910) in order to counter views and assumptions that were becoming increasingly more common in Russia. Occasionally, the ideas of less well-known Western theologians and philosophers, such as the German theologian Hermann Olshausen (1796–1839), the Anglican bishop Richard Trench (1807–86), the English mathematician and liberal theologian Bladen Powell (1796–1860), and the geologist and president of Amherst College Edward Hitchcock (1793–1864), also appeared.[24] Since miracles, including Jesus's miracles and resurrection, were also discussed in the context of modern biblical criticism and the resulting quest for the historical Jesus, Orthodox academic writers knew well the works of H. S. Reimarus (1694–1768), and the lives of Jesus by David Strauss (1808–74) and Ernest Renan (1823–92). Less frequently, authors tapped literature from the sciences, drawing on the work of geologists, physicists, physicians, and psychologists, including the work of French neurologist Jean-Martin Charcot (1825–93).

Orthodox academics also drew freely on a wide array of traditional Orthodox and more modern Russian religious sources for their explication of miracles. They drew on biblical texts, especially when engaging modern biblical scholarship on New Testament miracle stories or on the resurrection. In addition, modern Orthodox academics routinely cited patristic authors in their defense of miracles, but generally not more so than contemporary Western Christian authors whose views they shared, or, occasionally Russia's religious philosophers such as Vladimir Solov'ev, Sergei Trubetskoi, and Sergei Askol'dov. Sergei Glagolev's essay, "Miracle and Science," is particularly noteworthy since it did not draw on traditional sources. Instead, reflecting his conviction that truths of faith could be scientifically justified, his essay turned to logic and recent scientific discoveries in the realms of physics and thermodynamics to illustrate its points, thereby challenging common assumptions about the "mystical" quality of all Orthodox theology.[25]

The Orthodox defense of miracles before modern skeptics, however, did not suggest an uncritical approach to the subject matter. Indeed, when discussing miracles, authors routinely turned to the Gospel texts to show Christianity's own nuanced understanding of them. Authors shared the assessment of Bishop Ignatii (Brianchaninov) earlier in the century that in the Gospel texts "signs" and "wonders" were secondary to the proclamation of the teachings of Jesus, or the Word of God. A learned monk and spiritual writer who had received his education at the Military Engineering School in Saint Petersburg, Bishop Ignatii (1807–67) had provided what he considered a synthesis of patristic views on miracles. His series of three talks on the subject—first published in a collection of sermons in 1863 and then separately (and posthumously) in 1870—offered what might be seen as patristic justification for the guarded approach to miracles as described in the *Spiritual Regulation* and subsequent institutional policies.[26] Despite this tradition of restraint toward miracles, however, Russia's Orthodox thinkers did not believe that miracle stories were superfluous to the Gospel accounts or that they could be extracted from the texts without endangering the Gospels' integrity.[27]

While the authors' broad level of intellectual engagement with modern Western trends was in large part textually based, it also reflected their living contact with Western Europe and their own lived experience of Orthodoxy. Institutional reforms within Russia's theological academies in the mid-nineteenth century encouraged professors to travel abroad to further their academic work. As Nataliia Sukhova, a historian of Russia's theological academies has noted, such travel became a notable feature of academic life in Russia's theological schools beginning in the 1870s and was reflected in the scholarship that the academies' graduates produced.[28] Some academic theologians, such as Sergei Glagolev, who in 1900 was invited to be vice-president of the International Congress of the History of Religions, became internationally acclaimed figures.

Miracle and Agency

In a widely discussed essay on the resurrection of Jesus, academic theologian and professor of moral theology at Moscow Spiritual Academy Mikhail Tareev noted how, dogmatically speaking, the resurrection had often been reduced simply to "the miracle of miracles," which, in turn, served as proof of the divinity of Jesus and the foundation of the Christian faith. In his estimation, however, there was more to the resurrection than simply a display of divine power.[29] Similarly, Orthodox thinkers in the late nineteenth century did not look to miracles as arguments for the existence of a God. Many of the most ardent, modern European detractors of miracles believed no less in the existence of a higher power, a "Supreme Architect." Rather, Orthodox thinkers focused on miracles as affirmations of the presence and agency of a personal God in the world in contrast to an impersonal metaphysical naturalism that denied the very possibility of a miracle. In response to a world view that understood the physical world as governed exclusively by rational, eternally existing, self-sustaining laws, mechanically predictable once discovered and known, and independent of any "supernatural element," Orthodox thinkers insisted on a more personally interactive universe.[30]

Orthodox thinkers as a rule agreed with the modern view that the universe is guided by impersonal natural laws. They welcomed scientific investigation and maintained that people of faith should support such investigation since Christianity embraces what is "true."[31] Yet authors hesitated to embrace the manner in which those scientific laws were broadly understood and imagined at that time. According to Glagolev, humans were limited in their knowledge and simply did not know nature, including the human body, in enough depth to master its laws. Similarly, Andrei Predtechenskii, professor of history at Saint Petersburg Spiritual Academy, argued that, when pressed, many modern thinkers defined the "laws" of nature as little more than "the way things are."[32] Consequently, Orthodox thinkers did not agree with the modern argument that miracles were contrary to reason because they apparently presupposed either a suspension in or a violation of the natural order.[33]

Orthodox thinkers, like some of their Western Christian counterparts, saw no opposition between the laws of nature and the notion of a miracle. In their estimation, a given act might find its cause or impulse in a divine source but the resulting activity or action did not inevitably contradict or suspend the laws of nature. As Predtechenskii noted, "That which is higher than and external to nature is not necessarily opposed to it."[34] Similarly, he along with other Orthodox thinkers distinguished between the notions of augmenting and opposing powers. The phenomenon of a person returning to life after death did not, in his view, necessarily oppose nature. While such a phenomenon did not conform to the conventional laws or patterns of nature, it did not necessarily contradict them either. He maintained that no laws of nature necessarily precluded such a phenomenon from occurring, should nature be enabled to do so. "Nature may not possess enough power to return a person to life," he stated, "but such a [life-giving] power at the same time may not be opposed to nature."[35]

The graduate of Moscow Spiritual Academy Stefan Ostroumov expressed a similar idea when he maintained that even in day-to-day life laws of nature often serve as a foundation upon which others act in order to produce new results. Physicians, for instance, routinely reverse the processes of nature through medicine, but generally no one considers laws of nature in such instances to be disturbed or violated. Instead, humans routinely make use of laws of nature in order to overcome them by means of other laws. Laws of a higher order can use and interact with laws of a lower order without violating or destroying the latter.[36]

Orthodox thinkers, therefore, attempted to balance a teleological view of nature with a sui generis understanding of miracles for which no law of nature could ever account yet that were not contrary to nature as such. According to

Predtechenskii, it would be more scientifically accurate to acknowledge that the laws that scientists recognize as governing nature do not necessarily exhaust the body of all laws governing the physical world. He urged his readers to think in terms of coexisting bodies of laws: the laws governing nature and those governing the phenomena of miracles.[37] Perhaps, he mused, if humans were able more deeply to understand the physical world, they would be able to discover a link between circumstances demanding a miracle and the "event" of a miracle. Miracles, noted Grigorii D'iachenko, designated those unusual moments when the divine activity that is usually cloaked by the laws of nature "reveals itself" and "exposes a guiding hand."[38]

While the philosophes and their philosophical descendants opposed the notion of miracle on the grounds that it presupposed imperfection and flaws in God's creation, modern Orthodox thinkers embraced it for precisely those reasons. From the Orthodox perspective, however, these flaws were not inherent in God's work but the result of the exercise of human free will. Therefore, it is not God's work that miracles "fix," in their estimation, but the work of free creatures. The Orthodox defense of miracles, consequently, was linked to a defense of both divine and human agency.

According to Orthodox authors, miracles were not arbitrary displays of divine power but free, purposeful acts of God.[39] God acted in the world, according to Orthodox academic thinkers, because God chose to do so. His acts had an aim and a moral purpose. Miracles were acts of divine love and mercy whose purpose or meaning, Glagolev insisted, could be identified in two contexts: in critical historical periods when miracles usually signaled a new phase in human development or in cases where humans, exercising their free will, created circumstances that needed to be set aright.[40] Other thinkers maintained that miracles facilitated the development of human mind and will.[41] According to the graduate of Moscow Spiritual Academy Petr Smirnov, the moral aspect was so significant in defining a miracle that even "ordinary" phenomena or events—entirely explainable by the laws governing nature—might be deemed miraculous given the power of their perceived meaning and their edifying quality.[42] The essential purpose of miracles in any case, according to the graduate of Moscow Spiritual Academy and priest Ioann Orfanitskii, was the renewal or restoration of creation, whose fate was continually being challenged by the misuse of human free will.[43]

Orthodox defense of miracles, consequently, rested on beliefs in the reality of personal human agency as much as personal divine agency. According to Glagolev, despite all of the psychological, physical, and circumstantial constrictions placed on humans, in the Orthodox world view they nonetheless retain freedom of will and creativity that can direct existing forces of nature. Since the consequences of their actions can be and often are detrimental to society and nature, and since often these consequences lie beyond the scope of human ability to control or reverse them, God, in the Orthodox world view, can choose to respond through miracles. Miracles, in this understanding, can block evil or "redirect evil to positive outcomes" in nature, in personal lives, and in entire societies.[44]

Indeed, the bishop of Kronstadt, Feofan, author of the most comprehensive Orthodox study of the phenomenon of miracles, insisted that "the reality of human free will is logically linked with the reality of Divine Providence in peoples' lives."[45] Affirming the reality of human freedom yet recognizing human limitation, Bishop Feofan agreed that humans have the capacity to act in ways that do not conform to goals of salvation. For this reason, miracles were indeed "natural" and "necessary" in the Orthodox world view since they enabled humans individually and collectively to stay "on course" with respect to the economy of salvation, while insuring the integrity of human freedom and the free path of personal self-determination.[46] In contrast to modern enlightened rationalists and Deists who denied miracles and revelatory acts of God in the name of freedom of spirit and independence of thought, Orthodox thinkers argued that those who embrace the notion of divine revelation "know that they do not lose freedom but discover it."[47]

Miracle and Sight

While Orthodox thinkers maintained that the reality of miracles was dependent on the existence of a God that was both wholly transcendent and wholly immanent, faith in that God was not necessary for miracles to occur. God was not bound by unbelief or lack of faith. As the prolific writer, bishop of Kostroma, and graduate of Moscow Spiritual Academy Vissarion (Nechaev) noted, "Miracles take place entirely by the grace of God," a grace that not even all believers enjoyed.[48] Examining the miracles of Jesus as reported in the Gospel texts, the graduate of Moscow Spiritual Academy and professor of theology at the University of Kiev Pavel Svetlov noted that people who were healed by Jesus were not always people of faith.[49] Faith, however, did matter in the process of *identifying* a phenomenon or event as miraculous. The miraculous, in this sense, lay in the eye and spiritual disposition of the beholder.[50] Miracle was to a large extent a matter of perception.[51]

The notions of discernment and perception were intrinsic to Orthodox discourse about miracles, although the tenor of that discussion depended to a large extent on the faith orientation of a given audience. As indicated in the 1912 case regarding believers from the church of Saint Nicholas in the Siberian diocese of Eniseisk at the outset of this essay, many church officials were exceptionally cautious when it came to the proclamation of miracles among Orthodox believers, often marginalizing the significance of such supposed "signs" with regard to salvation. In his essay, "Thoughts about Miracles," the priest Stefan Ostroumov acknowledged, along with his modern detractors, that not every event or phenomenon that might initially appear miraculous to believers truly is so.[52] Similarly, Sergei Glagolev admitted that historically Christians had often deemed occurrences miraculous that, in fact, were not. Sight, in the Orthodox understanding, was a subtle notion. Authors noted that the lack of its proper cultivation and conditioning among believers often precluded the quality of vision necessary to discern genuine miracles. Consequently, while academic theologians wholeheartedly defended the reality of miracles in the face of modern philosophical skepticism, they also drew on an Orthodox intellectual and spiritual heritage that was nuanced when it came to the proclamation and recognition of miracles.

Perhaps the most detailed consideration of this complex heritage belonged to the bishop and well-known spiritual guide Ignatii (Brianchaninov), who in the mid-nineteenth century articulated what might be deemed a modern Orthodox apology for skepticism. Drawing on a detailed reading of New Testament texts, along with writings of such Eastern Christian luminaries as Macarius of Egypt, Ephrem the Syrian, and John Chrysostom, Bishop Ignatii distinguished between sight conditioned by "a mind that is set on the flesh" (*plotskoe mudrovanie*) and sight enlightened by spiritual reason (*dukhovnyi razum*).[53] A "mind set on the flesh," in his view, reflected a false consciousness of life, guided as it was by a sense of self-sufficiency and self-importance.[54] It oriented itself primarily to the human condition and to worldly concerns. Such a mindset was little moved by longer-term moral or spiritual considerations.[55] Since the body was the barometer of life in this world view, those guided by a "mind set on the flesh" usually considered bodily illness as a calamity and healing a marker of unqualified well-being. Ironically, although those conditioned by such a mindset usually had little sense of the holy or an awareness of the divine, in Ignatii's estimation they nevertheless were among those who most desired and sought signs and miracles. Such people, in his view, tended to understand miracles in terms of demonstrations of power and were captivated by the performative aspect of what might appear to them as miraculous. According to Ignatii, their search for signs and miracles often resulted only in mishap and ruin.[56]

The sight of those who were enlightened by spiritual reason, in contrast, was more restrained with respect to "seeing" miracles. Oriented in life to both body and soul, those guided by spiritual reason saw beyond the mere physical aspects of life. In Ignatii's view, such people embraced virtues—especially patience and humility—that "a mind set on the flesh" usually could not recognize or appreciate. Accordingly, those who were enlightened by spiritual reason did not react to bodily illness as a tragedy, but were aware of the virtues that illness might cultivate. Hence, a miracle would not necessarily be sought in or perceived as an unexpected or unexplainable cure—in the marvel or in the display of wondrous power. Instead, the miracle, in the eyes of those enlightened by spiritual reason, would be found in the salvific consequence of an act, event, or phenomenon. For Ignatii, genuinely miraculous events or phenomena were replete with meaning; their primary purpose was to guide a person toward the Word of God as communicated in Scripture—a function they served, in his estimation, even in the Gospel narratives. Never an end in themselves, miracles were above all meant to be contemplated, and for this reason were sometimes referred to as "signs."[57] Since those guided by spiritual reason were acutely aware of the power of a living God, maintained Ignatii, they resisted seeking "signs," since they understood the risks of deception involved in doing so. Indeed, as Ostroumov and other Orthodox thinkers maintained before their fellow believers, the seeking of miracles was a sign of a misguided religious consciousness and suggested unbelief rather than belief.[58]

While Ignatii's observations were addressed primarily to fellow monastics and Orthodox Christians at large, the discussion of perception and discernment with regard to miracles was somewhat different when addressed to nonbelievers. According to Glagolev, divine causality and activity within the world could be perceived only if a person was open to its existence. If a person remained deaf and mute to God's "good callings," he maintained, such divine activity, though objectively present, would remain beyond a person's field of vision. In other words, to an untrained eye, a miracle appears as an "ordinary" natural phenomenon. It remains "hidden" and "inaccessible."[59] A "trained eye"—cultivated in part by faith—however, sees the world in qualitatively different terms. In an attempt to articulate for the modern mindset the sensibilities associated with the experience of a miracle, Bishop Feofan of Kronstadt compared these sensibilities with those that inspired artists and composers in their work, where an enigmatic "special gift" accounted for a special "sight" or "perception." No less of "genius" was at work, in Bishop Feofan's estimation, when the matter came to genuine religious experience.[60] In other efforts to explain the character of perception that lent itself to discernment of miracles, Orthodox authors spoke about the "moral-psychological sensibility" and the "disposition of the soul" that conditioned and allowed a person to see the miraculous.[61]

The well-known theologian, philosopher, priest, and graduate of Moscow Spiritual Academy Pavel Florenskii addressed the issues of perception, faith, and miracles in an essay entitled "About Superstition and Miracle," penned in 1903, the year before he enrolled at the Academy and during his final year as a mathematics student at Moscow State University. Writing in reaction to the popularity of spiritualism and occultism in Russian society at that time, Florenskii maintained that neither superstition nor miracle lay in the "fact" of a phenomenon or event, but in the mode of their apprehension, in a person's relation to the fact.[62] Florenskii identified three such modes or "world views" (*mirovozrenii*)—religious, scientific, and superstitious. A person with a religious world view, Florenskii argued, often perceived things and events as "transparent" to divine activity. A person envisaged a thing as a "transparent membrane" through which he or she would claim to behold the working power of God. Such a religious mode of perception, he maintained, resulted in the assertion of miracle. Miracles are dependent on faith, in Florenskii's estimation, insofar as "faith" was understood to relate to the working power of the Good (*Blagoi Sily*).[63]

According to Bishop Ignatii, the ability to perceive genuine miracles was linked not merely to faith, but also to a particular level of spiritual development. He considered the notions of "true" and "false" miracles in terms of the development of a "spiritual" in contrast to a "fleshly" sight. Florenskii was no less interested than Ignatii in matters of inner development and human constitution that accounted for different modes of apprehension of the world. Instead of characterizing sight in terms of "spiritual" and "fleshly," however, Florenskii distinguished between "religious" and "superstitious" world views. In his estimation, miracles were inherent to the religious world view, while "anti-miracles" (*otritsatel'nye chudesa*) characterized the superstitious world view. The distinction between the two—miracle and anti-miracle—lies in a person's inclination to discern the power of good or the power of evil.

According to Florenskii, a person who held a religious world view "saw" a miracle when he or she discerned the will of "Him through whom all things came into being" within a seemingly arbitrary event or phenomenon.[64] Addressing primarily those involved in spiritualism, Florenskii maintained that those who held a "superstitious" world view, in contrast, operated with a different vision, and saw things in terms of evil or impure forces. Whereas a person with a religious world view perceived a "divine moment" in the miracle, a person with a superstitious world view experienced a heightened perception of "an evil moment," with a resulting sense of dread, aversion, and disgust once the "moment" has passed. Other authors, such as the priest Petr Smirnov, conceived of false miracles as those "unusual" and "supernatural" events or acts whose results were destructive, false, and impure.[65]

Florenskii acknowledged that not all people conceived of the world in such enchanted terms. Between the religious and the superstitious world views, therefore, he proposed a third, more neutral mode of comprehending the world—the scientific. According to a scientific mode of perception, as Florenskii defined it, things are distinguished from their causality and are considered in and of themselves, in value-free terms. In such a world view, insofar as they are attributed to a divine cause, miracles lay beyond the scope of interest and perceptual range.[66] Indeed, as the anonymous priest P-skii maintained, inasmuch as miracles might be a part of nature but did not belong to nature, they remained outside the bounds of strictly scientific explanation.[67] On the other hand, Florenskii agreed with other Orthodox thinkers that just because a person deemed an occurrence a miracle did not mean that it necessarily defied rational, scientific explanation. The two were not mutually exclusive. Faith and reason and faith and knowledge, insisted Florenskii, were not antithetical categories.[68] As Pavel Svetlov maintained, it was neither science nor knowledge that was at odds with the faith, but "bad philosophy that cloaks itself in the name of science."[69] Not only did phenomena deemed miraculous not detract from the sciences, but, as Glagolev maintained, in some cases they helped to further scientific inquiry.[70] Indeed, according to Florenskii, even the resurrection was a natural phenomenon since all eventually would be subject to its law; as yet, however, it was a lone example thereof. In Florenskii's estimation, simply because something may not be rationally demonstrated or ever rationally explained does not lead to the conclusion that it was impossible and held no place in the scientific world view.

Conclusion

Frustrated by the continued efforts on the part of diocesan officials to convince them of the "ordinary" (*obyknovennaia*) nature of their newly found icon of the Mother of God named "The Joy of All Who Sorrow" and to thwart their veneration of it, peasant parishioners from the Saint Nicholas church in the diocese of Eniseisk in 1912 penned a letter to the ober-procurator of the Holy Synod calling for what can be read as a philosophical truce with their detractors: "Let the icon for some be ordinary," they wrote, "but we cherish it as a blessing."⁷¹ It is impossible to know with which group Orthodox academic thinkers who wrote about miracles and modernity in the late nineteenth and early twentieth century would have sympathized in this particular case or in numerous other cases like it. Conditioned by the Orthodox spiritual heritage to avoid "rumors of miracles," as expounded by Ignatii (Brianchaninov), and aware of the Christian responsibility to "dispel superstition and false beliefs and to explain the seemingly miraculous quality of natural phenomena," Russia's academic theologians were potentially no less critical than their modern European counterparts of claims about the miraculous.⁷²

At the same time, by defending the notion and possibility of miracles against modern detractors, Russia's academic theologians pushed the boundaries of the debates surrounding them. In addition to political issues of authority, power, and control already embedded in institutional discourse about miracles, academic theologians shed light on the other, more foundational epistemological, anthropological, and historical issues at stake. In doing so, they offered intellectual and conceptual credibility to a host of sensibilities found among the Orthodox faithful that otherwise could easily be dismissed by modern standards as obscurantist and steeped in "the murk of ignorance."⁷³ In particular, since miracles begged the definition of knowledge as much as understandings of God and nature, and since, as the priest and graduate of the Kiev Spiritual Academy Petr Linitskii recognized, knowledge is power, the subject of miracles—and the experiences reportedly associated with them—remained tenaciously relevant in the modern world.⁷⁴

Insofar as they have considered Russian religious thought in terms of "contemporary philosophical expression of the ideals of the culture of Russian Orthodoxy," most twentieth-century historians and intellectual historians of Russia have tended to focus on the rich intellectual heritage left by such luminaries of Russian society as Sergei Askol'dov, Sergei Bulgakov, Vladimir Solov'ev, and Sergei Trubetskoi.⁷⁵ Russian religious thought has tended to be identified primarily with thinkers who received their primary education in secular institutions of higher learning. Despite the fact that many such religious thinkers were active Orthodox believers, students of Russian history often conceived of their thought as part of an intellectual community distinct from the Orthodox Church both as an institution and as a community of faith. Consequently, in the past two decades, in order to understand the culture of Russian Orthodoxy as it was lived and practiced, historians of Russia have broadened their conceptualization of what constitutes "thought" and have sought the voices of those, such as the parishioners from the Saint Nicholas parish in the Eniseisk diocese, whose beliefs and rituals defined lived Orthodox culture at any given time. Conspicuously absent for the most part from both lines of investigation has been in-depth consideration of the voices from the theological academies and their graduates. As the subject of miracles indicates, many Orthodox academically trained thinkers were deeply steeped in tradition yet actively engaging the modern cultural and philosophical trends influencing all levels of Russian society. Their voices, no less than those of their university-trained counterparts, seminary-trained consistory bureaucrats, and parish priests, monastic guides, and ordinary laymen and women, belong to the rich legacy of modern Russian religious thought.

NOTES

1. The record of this case can be found in Rossiiskii gosudarstvennyi istoricheskii arkhiv (RGIA), f. 796, op. 195, d. 1430, ll. 1–175.

2. RGIA, f. 796, op. 195, d. 1436, l. 60.

3. Ibid., l. 7.

4. For the notion of "theology of the streets," see Robert Orsi, *The Madonna of 115th Street: Faith and Community in Italian Harlem, 1880–1950* (New Haven, CT: Yale University Press, 1985), 219.

5. As examples, see Gregory L. Freeze, "Institutionalizing Piety: The Church and Popular Religion, 1750–1850," in *Imperial Russia: New Histories for the Empire*, ed. Jane Burbank and David L. Ransel (Bloomington: Indiana University Press, 1998), 210–49; Vera Shevzov, "Icons, Laity, and Authority in the Russian Orthodox Church, 1861–1917," *Russian Review* 58 (January 1999): 26–48.

6. Alexander V. Muller, ed. and trans., *The Spiritual Regulation of Peter the Great* (Seattle: University of Washington Press, 1972), 15. See also P. V. Znamenskii, "Zakonodatel'stvo Petra Velikago otnositel'no chistoty very i blagochestiia tserkovnago," *Pravoslavnyi sobesednik*, no. 12 (December 1864): 290–340. For more recent discussion, see Paul Bushkovitch, "Popular Religion in the Time of Peter the Great," in *Letters from Heaven: Popular Religion in Russia and Ukraine*, ed. John-Paul Himka and Andriy Zayarnyuk (Toronto: University of Toronto Press, 2006), 146–64; Simon Dixon "Superstition in Imperial Russia," *Past and Present*, Supplement 3 (2008): 209, 218; Eve Levin, "False Miracles and Unattested Dead Bodies: Investigations into Popular Cults in Early Modern Russia," in *Religion and the Early Modern State: Views from China, Russia, and the West*, ed. James D. Tracy and Marguerite Ragnow (Cambridge: Cambridge University Press, 2004), 260.

7. As examples, see Himka and Zayarnyuk, *Letters from Heaven*; Eve Levin, "*Dvoeverie* and Popular Religion," in *Seeking God: The Recovery of Religious Identity in Orthodox Russia, Ukraine, and Georgia*, ed. Stephen K. Batalden (DeKalb: Northern Illinois University Press, 1993), 29–52; Stella Rock, *Popular Religion in Russia: "Double Belief" and the Making of an Academic Myth* (New York: Routledge, 2007); Vera Shevzov, "Letting 'the People' into Church: Reflections on Orthodoxy and Community in Late Imperial Russia," in *Orthodox Russia: Studies in Belief and Practice under the Tsars*, ed. Valerie

A. Kivelson and Robert H. Greene (University Park: Pennsylvania State University Press, 2003), 59–77.

8. For a good overview of the genesis of this thesis, see Gordan Graham, "Religion, Secularization, and Modernity," *Philosophy* 67, no. 260 (April 1992): 183–97. As examples, see Gregory L. Freeze, "Subversive Piety: Religion and the Political Crisis in Late Imperial Russia," *The Journal of Modern History* 68, no. 2 (June 1996): 308–50. Robert H. Greene, *Bodies Like Bright Stars: Saints and Relics in Orthodox Russia* (DeKalb: Northern Illinois University Press, 2010), 55–64; Nadieszda Kizenko, *A Prodigal Saint: Father John of Kronstadt and the Russian People* (University Park: Pennsylvania State University Press, 2000), 281–85; Christine D. Worobec, "Miraculous Healings," in *Sacred Stories: Religion and Spirituality in Modern Russia*, ed. Mark D. Steinberg and Heather J. Coleman (Bloomington: Indiana University Press, 2007), 22–43.

9. For articulation of this sentiment, see E. Smirnov, "Slavianofily i ikh uchenie v otnoshenii k bogoslovskoi nauke," *Strannik*, no. 2 (February 1877): 203. While virtually absent from Western historiographical treatment of Russian religious thought until relatively recently, Russia's spiritual academies and their theologians, historians, and philosophers have been gaining increasing attention, especially in post-Soviet Russia. For examples, see V. A. Tarasova, *Vysshaia dukhovnaia shkola v Rossii v kontse XIX–nachale XX veka* (Moscow: Novyi khronograf, 2005); Paul Valliere, *Modern Russian Theology: Bukharev, Soloviev, Bulgakov* (Edinburgh: T&T Clark, 2000), 35–106; Vera Shevzov, "The Burdens of Tradition: Orthodox Constructions of the West (late XIX–early XX cc.)," in *Orthodox Constructions of the West*, ed. George Demacopoulos and Aristotle Papanikolaou (New York: Fordham University Press, 2013), 83–101; N. Iu. Sukhova, *Vertograd nauk dukhovnyi: Sbornik statei po istorii vysshego dukhovnogo obrazovaniia v Rossii XIX–nachala XX veka* (Moscow: PSTGU, 2007); N. Iu. Sukhova, *Vysshaia dukhovnaia shkola: Problemy i reformy vtoraia polovina XIX v.* (Moscow: PSTGU, 2012).

10. Orthodox academic thinkers often outlined the tenets of modernity's challenges in essays that broadly discussed the "philosophy of the times." See, for example, P. Linitskii, "Filosofiia nashego vremeni," *Vera i razum*, no. 11, bk. 1 (October 1891): 287–304.

11. As examples, see Gotthold Lessing, *Lessing's Theological Writings*, trans. Henry Chadwick (Stanford, CA: Stanford University Press, 1957); David Friedrich Strauss, *The Life of Jesus, Critically Examined*, 2 vols., trans. George Elliot (Cambridge: Cambridge University Press, 2010).

12. A. Kriazhimskii, "Vozmozhno li razgranichenie sfer religioznoi i nauchnoi?" *Strannik*, no. 11 (October 1915): 121–22. See also S. S. Glagolev, "Bor'ba za sviatoe: Vstupitel'naia lektsiia po osnovnomu bogosloviiu, prochitannaia v Moskovskoi Dukhovnoi Akademii 9 sentiabria, 1914," *Bogoslovskii vestnik*, no. 9 (September 1914): 5; Ostroumov, *Mysli o chudesakh* (Kiev: Khristianskaia mysl', 1916), 35. This essay was originally published in the journal *Khristianskaia mysl'* (Christian Thought), which was conceived as a journal of "Orthodox self-awareness." The journal sought to track religious trends in Russia and abroad.

13. Ostroumov, *Mysli o chudesakh*, 36. See also Glagolev, "Bor'ba za sviatoe," 5.

14. As examples of this voluminous literature, see A. Bronzov, "Znachenie voskreseniia Khristova dlia nashei nravstvennoi zhizni," *Khristianskoe chtenie*, no. 4 (April 1900): 523–50; A. Druzhinin, "Uchenie Fikhte mladshego o voskresenii i iavleniiakh Khrista," *Vera i razum*, no. 6, bk. 1 (June 1884): 41–58; no. 7, bk. 2 (July 1884): 112–30;

E. I. Loviagin, "Sobytie voskreseniia Iisusa Khrista," *Khristianskoe chtenie*, no. 4 (1869): 527–61; M. M. Tareev, "Voskresenie Khristovo i ego nravstvennoe znachenie," *Bogoslovskii vestnik*, no. 5 (May 1903): 1–45; no. 6 (June 1903): 201–17.

15. N. Dobronravov, "O voskresenii Gospoda nashego Iisusa Khrista i ego iavleniiakh po voskresenii," *Pravoslavnoe obozrenie*, April 1891, 679–95; I. A. Glebov, "Kakaia dolzhna byt' apologiia very v Khristovo voskresenie?," *Khristianskoe chtenie*, no. 5 (May 1908): 779–92.

16. Victoria Frede, *Doubt, Atheism, and the Nineteenth-Century Russian Intelligentsia* (Madison: University of Wisconsin Press, 2011), 11.

17. Loviagin, "Sobytiia voskreseniia," 559. For similar observations, see I. P-skii, "Vera v chudo," *Dushepoleznoe chtenie*, no. 11 (November 1879): 341; Sergei Glagolev, "Chudo i nauka," *Bogoslovskii vestnik*, no. 6 (June 1893): 479; I. A. Orfanitskii, "Chto takoe chudo?," *Vera i tserkov*, no. 1 (January 1902): 66; Aleksandr Vvedenskii, *Religioznye somneniia nashikh dnei*, 2 vols. (Odessa: Tip. L. Nitche, 1914), 1:161.

18. Glagolev, "Bor'ba za sviatoe," 20.

19. Aleksandr Bertash and A. A. Naseko, "D'iachenko," in *Pravoslavnaia entsiklopediia* (Moscow: Pravoslavnaia entsiklopediia, 2007), 19:518–20; "Orfanitskii, Ioann Alekseevich," *Bogoslov.ru*, http://www.bogoslov.ru/persons/46309/index.html; "Ostroumov, Stefan Ivanovich," *Novomucheniki i ispovedniki Russkoi Pravoslavnoi Tserkvi XX veka*, http://www.pstbi.ru/cgi-htm/db.exe/ans/nm/?HYZ9EJxGHoxITYZCF2JMTdG6XbuCs S9UfiCgfe6UYS8Zt8oh66WWc8qiceXb**. For details concerning Ostroumov's arrest, see V. A. Korostelev, "Krest'ianskie vosstaniia v Riazanskoi gubernii v 1918," *Istoriia, kul'tura, i traditsii Riazanskogo kraia*, http://www.history-ryazan.ru/node/7495.

20. "Loviagin, Evgraf Ivanovich," *Biograficheskii slovar'*, http://dic.academic.ru/dic.nsf/biograf2/8146; "Sergei Glagolev," *Biograficheskii slovar'*, http://dic.academic.ru/dic.nsf/biograf2/3786; "Pavel Svetlov," *Biograficheskii slovar'*, http://dic.academic.ru/dic.nsf/biograf2/11424.

21. "Predtechenskii, Andrei Ivanovich," *Biograficheskii slovar'*, http://www.biografija.ru/show_bio.aspx?id=109084. Occasionally, as in the instance of his essay on the meaning and significance of miracles in Christianity, Predtechenskii wrote under the pseudonym A. Ramushevskii.

22. These include Nikolai Dobronravov, Pavel Florenskii, Sergei Glagolev, Stefan Ostroumov, and Feofan, the bishop of Kronstadt (Vasilii Stepanovich Tuliakov).

23. I. M. Bogoslovskii-Platonov, "O chudesakh," *Dushepoleznoe chtenie*, no. 6 (May 1871): 34–38; P-skii, "Vera v chudo," 341–56; Petr Smirnov, *Chudesa v prezhnee i nashe vremia*, 2nd. ed. (Moscow: Tip. I. D. Sytina, 1895); Platon Tarnavskii, "O chudesakh v nashe vremia," *Strannik*, no. 12 (December 1864): 118–22.

24. See, in particular, A. Ramushevskii, "Mesto i znachenie chudes v sisteme khristianstva," *Khristianskoe chtenie*, no. 3 (September–December 1863): 410–61; and the comprehensive work of Feofan, Episkop Kronshtadtskii, *Chudo: Khristianskaia vera v nego i eia opravdanie* (Petrograd: Sinodal'naia tip., 1915). The essay by Ramushevskii was also published under the author's real name, A. Predtechenskii, as an appendix to his *Chto razumnee: Vera ili neverie* (St. Petersburg: Tip. Departamenta udelov, 1864).

25. Bernice Glatzer Rosenthal, "A New Spirituality: The Confluence of Nietzsche and Orthodoxy in Russian Religious Thought," in Steinberg and Coleman, *Sacred Stories*, 331.

26. Ignatii (Brianchaninov), *O chudesakh i znameniiakh* (Iaroslavl: Tip. Gub. zem. upravy, 1870). Initially, the talks were directed at his fellow monastic brethren and published in a volume entitled "Ascetic Sermons"; in an introduction to their publication in 1866, however, Bishop Ignatii noted that these sermons were intended for all Orthodox Christians who desire "to familiarize themselves with the ascetic life according the mind of the Fathers and the Church." Ignatii's views will be discussed in more detail below.

27. Ostroumov, *Mysli o chudesakh*, 35.

28. Sukhova, *Vertograd*, 172.

29. Tareev, "Voskresenie Khristovo," 1–2.

30. Ramushevskii [Predtechenskii], "Mesto i znachenie chudes," 412. For overviews of the debates concerning miracles in modern Western thought, see Colin Brown, "Issues in the History of the Debates on Miracles," in *Cambridge Companion to Miracles*, ed. Graham H. Twelftree (Cambridge: Cambridge University Press, 2011), 273–90; Colin Brown, *Miracles and the Critical Mind* (Grand Rapids, MI: William B. Eerdmans Publishing, 1984); Ralph Del Colle, "Miracles in Christianity," in Twelftree, *Cambridge Companion*, 235–53; Mary Hesse, "Miracles and the Laws of Nature," in *Miracles: Cambridge Studies in their Philosophy and History*, ed. C. F. D. Moule (London: A. R. Mowbray, 1965), 33–42.

31. Ostroumov, *Mysli o chudesakh*, 19.

32. Ramushevskii [Predtechenskii], "Mesto i znachenie chudes," 427.

33. P-skii, "Vera v chudo," 356; Feofan, *Chudo*, 167–76; Glagolev, "Chudo i nauka," 479; Ostroumov, *Mysli o chudesakh*, 21; Ramushevskii [Predtechenskii], "Mesto i znachenie chudes," 419.

34. Ramushevskii [Predtechenskii], "Mesto i znachenie chudes," 424–25; P. Svetlov, "Izlechenie psikhicheskim vliianiem i chudesnye istseleniia: Bibleisko-apologeticheskii ocherk," *Khristianskoe chtenie*, nos. 7–8 (July–August 1896): 53–54.

35. Ramushevskii [Predtechenskii], "Mesto i znachenie chudes," 424.

36. Ostroumov, *Mysli o chudesakh*, 8–9; Grigorii D'iachenko, *Dukhovnyi mir* (Moscow: I. D. Sytin, 1900), 134–35, 210–11.

37. Ramushevskii [Predtechenskii], "Mesto i znachenie chudes," 427–28. For parallel views, see Bogoslovskii-Platonov, "O chudesakh," 36; Feofan, *Chudo*, 106; Ostroumov, *Mysli o chudesakh*, 4.

38. D'iachenko, *Dukhovnyi mir*, 209; Feofan, *Chudo*, 105.

39. S. Ostroumov, "O chudesakh, kak priznak istinnoi tserkvi," *Vera i razum*, no. 6, bk. 1 (May 1896): 490.

40. Glagolev, "Chudo i nauka," 484.

41. I. Nikolin, "O sverkhestestvennom otkrovenii," *Dushepoleznoe chtenie*, chast' 2 (1902): 65.

42. Smirnov, *Chudesa*, 4; D'iachenko, *Dukhovnyi mir*, 209.

43. Orfanitskii, "Chto takoe chudo," 80.

44. Glagolev, "Chudo i nauka," 511; D'iachenko, *Dukhovnyi mir*, 136–37.

45. Feofan, *Chudo*, 314.

46. Ibid., 316–18.

47. Nikolin, "O sverkhestestvennom otkrovenii," 63.

48. Vissarion, "Znachenie chudes v dele very vo Khrista i khristovu tserkov," *Dushepoleznoe chtenie*, chast' 2 (1902): 14.

49. Svetlov, "Izlechenie psikhicheskim vliianiem," 37.

50. Ostroumov, *Mysli o chudesakh*, 5.

51. Nikanor, Arkhiepiskop Khersonskii, "Protiv otritsaiushchikh dostovernost' chudes," in *Sovremennye religioznye i tserkovno-obshchestvennye voprosy v reshenii ikh vydaiushchimisia dukhovnymi i svetskimi pravoslavno-russkimi pisateliami* (St. Petersburg: Slovo, 1903), 110–11.

52. Ostroumov, *Mysli o chudesakh*, 5; Ramushevskii [Predtechenskii], "Mesto i znachenie chudes," 411.

53. Ignatii (Brianchaninov) borrows the notion of "a mind that is set on the flesh" from the Epistle of Paul to the Romans. See Romans 8:8.

54. Ignatii, *O chudesakh*, 9.

55. Ibid., 6–7, 23–24.

56. Ibid., 46.

57. Smirnov, *Chudesa*, 4.

58. Ostroumov, "O chudesakh," 493–94.

59. Glagolev, "Chudo i nauka," 484; Feofan, *Chudo*, v; Ostroumov, *Mysli o chudesakh*, 5.

60. Feofan, *Chudo*, iv. The priest I. A. Orfanitskii made a similar comparison between religious and aesthetic sensibilities. Orfanitskii, "Chto takoe chudo?," 89.

61. Orfanitskii, "Chto takoe chudo?," 87; Glagolev, "Bor'ba za sviatoe," 20; Ostroumov, *Mysli o chudesakh*, 6.

62. Pavel Florenskii, "O sueverii i chude," *Novyi Put'*, no. 8 (1903): 61–121. For a reprint of this essay, see Pavel Florenskii, "O sueverii," *Filosofskie nauki*, no. 5 (1991): 87–108. For an overview of the history of spiritualism and the occult in modern Russia, see Maria Carlson, *"No Religion Higher than Truth": A History of the Theosophical Movement in Russia, 1875–1922* (Princeton, NJ: Princeton University Press, 1993), 3–38; Ilya Vinitsky, *Ghostly Paradoxes: Modern Spiritualism and Russian Culture in the Age of Realism* (Toronto: University of Toronto Press, 2009).

63. Florenskii, "O sueverii," 93.

64. Here, Florenskii draws on John 1:4.

65. Smirnov, *Chudesa*, 5.

66. Florenskii, "O sueverii," 95–96; Ostroumov, *Mysli o chudesakh*, 10.

67. P-skii, "Vera v chudo," 356.

68. Kriazhimskii, "Vozmozhno li razgranichenie sfer," 1115–27.

69. Pavel Svetlov, *Religiia i nauka* (St. Petersburg: Tip. Aleksandro-Nev. o-va trezvosti, 1912), 4.

70. Glagolev, "Chudo i nauka," 495; P-skii, "Vera v chudo," 356.

71. RGIA, f. 796, op. 195, d. 1436, l. 17.

72. Ostroumov, "O chudesakh," 494.

73. P-skii, "Vera v chudo," 341.

74. Linitskii, "Filosofiia nashego vremeni," 287.

75. Judith Deutsch Kornblatt and Richard F. Gustafson, eds., *Russian Religious Thought* (Madison: University of Wisconsin Press, 1996), 3.

Chapter 6

"The Light of the Truth"

Russia's Two Enlightenments, with Reference to Pavel Florenskii

RUTH COATES

The essays in this collection bear witness to a fundamental tension within Russian Orthodoxy of the modern period. Indeed this tension arises from Russia's engagement with modernity from the late seventeenth century onward, and is fundamentally about Orthodoxy's response to modernity. In the broadest terms it can be characterized as the tension between reason and faith, but this alone is insufficient. The question as to the relationship between reason and faith has been posed since the dawn of Christianity. Given the historical context, it is more productive to view this tension as existing between two diametrically opposed conceptions of enlightenment, as first highlighted by the semioticians Iurii Lotman and Boris Uspenskii: "The determining significance for eighteenth-century culture of the words 'enlightenment' and 'enlightener' [*prosveshchenie* and *prosvetitel'*] is well known. These two words were the basis for the most fundamental ideas of the 'Age of Reason.' However, they were not neologisms—they were known in pre-Petrine Russia. 'To enlighten [*prosveshchati*]... means: to christen, to consider worthy of Holy Baptism.' It is in this sense that the word *prosvetitel'* is used in the Church canticle addressed to Saint Vladimir: 'O teacher of Orthodoxy and enlightener of all Rus, you have enlightened all of us with baptism.'"[1] Lotman and Uspenskii draw our attention to the fact that both the eighteenth-century European Enlightenment and the Eastern Orthodox Church privilege light as a metaphor for truth while at the same time entertaining very different conceptions as to the nature of "truth," its source and content.

My purpose in this chapter is to explore the differences between Russia's two Enlightenments in the context of Russian religious culture (particularly religious-intellectual culture) of the imperial period, and specifically in light of emerging research—showcased in this volume—into the relationship of the Church intelligentsia to the European Enlightenment. I will argue that the principal intellectual alternative to the values and aspirations of the Western religious Enlightenment, an alternative that I will term the Orthodox Enlightenment, arose in the form of the discourse of contemplative monasticism: the ascetical writings of the *Philokalia*. Finally, I will analyze how the religious philosopher Pavel Florenskii (1882–1937) draws on Philokalic theology in his polemical apology for the Orthodox Enlightenment, *The Pillar and Ground of the Truth* (*Stolp i utverzhdenie istiny*, 1914). I will suggest that Florenskii's unique status as a member of the lay intelligentsia who on entry into the Church brought with him the cultural and intellectual experience of the secular outsider is what made it possible for him to be the first Orthodox churchman to mount a sustained philosophical and theological challenge to the values of the religious Enlightenment. While I aim to place the Philokalic tradition, the related tradition of spiritual eldership (*starchestvo*), and Florenskii's relationship with these on a sound historical footing, my primary approach in this essay is to explore the conceptual relationship between the term "enlightenment," the theological framework shared by the Philokalic texts in each and all of their specific historical redactions (Greek, Slavonic, and Russian), and the conceptual framework employed by Florenskii in his critique of "rational faith." As a result, I will establish the intellectual historical importance of the *Philokalia*, a seminal text in modern Russian Orthodox belief and practice, to this important representative of the early twentieth-century Russian religious renaissance.[2]

Two Enlightenments

Both parts of Lotman and Uspenskii's formulation require further comment. The eighteenth century is known as the *siècle des Lumières*. For the ideologues of the Enlightenment, the French philosophes, the term *lumières* had become synonymous with *connaissances*, "knowledge" (commonly rendered in the plural in French). Jacques Roger has adduced evidence that the plural *lumières* originally came into use in deliberate contradistinction to the singular *la lumière*, which until the beginning of the eighteenth century denoted the divine light proceeding from God. Roger observes that the biblical source text for this concept is the prologue to John's Gospel: "In him was life, and the life was the light of all people. The light shines in the darkness, and the darkness did not overcome it. . . .

The true light, which enlightens everyone, was coming into the world" (John 1:4–5, 9).[3] Later in the eighteenth century the singular *lumière* was recouped in polemical usurpation of its theological meaning to convey the light of ideal Reason, by means of which the *raisonneurs* struggled against the forces of darkness, that is: ignorance, prejudice, superstition, and fanaticism ("enthusiasm").[4] In relation to Christianity, this meant the principled opposition to such "irrational" aspects of belief and practice as the sacraments, the priestly hierarchy, dogma, ritual, and mysticism.[5]

Citing John's Gospel, Roger fails to point out that the divine light there described is Christ, the Word of God:[6] this is an essential point for Orthodoxy.[7] From an Orthodox point of view, the Enlightenment ideologues were substituting reason for Christ as the source of truth. While they understood enlightenment to mean liberation from prejudice and superstition through the exercise of discursive reason, Orthodox believers have always understood it as liberation from sin and death through the revelation of God in Christ. Lotman and Uspenskii's reference to the sacrament of baptism as the means by which Russians were enlightened must be understood in this context. Following the Church Fathers, Orthodoxy understands baptism as the sacrament in which the convert receives the Holy Spirit for the first time, symbolically dying and being resurrected into a new, spiritual life in Christ. This is the first step on the way to the ultimate goal of the Christian life as the Orthodox Church conceives it: deification, or the attainment of holiness, and thus immortality, through the grace of God.[8] Deification becomes possible for humans only after the incarnation, death, and resurrection of Christ, who is the prototype of deified humanity. The deified state is verbally represented through light imagery in the works of the Greek Doctors of the Church and the Desert Fathers, and, through them, in the Orthodox liturgy.

Though light imagery may be found throughout the liturgical corpus,[9] the core text, theologically speaking, is that of the Feast of the Transfiguration.[10] This feast commemorates the event, related in all three synoptic Gospels, when Jesus takes the disciples Peter, James, and John up a mountain (in Orthodox tradition—Mount Tabor) and reveals his divinity to them visually: in Matthew's account "his face shone like the sun, and his clothes became dazzling white" (Matthew 17:2). In the liturgy for the feast, emphasis is laid on this event as the revelation of the prototype of the deified humanity that Jesus is about to make possible through his sacrificial death and resurrection: "For in his mercy the Saviour of our souls has transfigured disfigured man and made him shine with light upon Mount Tabor"; "On Mount Tabor He makes bright the weakness of man and bestows enlightenment upon our souls"; "Today Christ on Mount Tabor has changed the darkened nature of Adam, and filling it with brightness He has made it godlike."[11]

Truth conceived as light in the Orthodox sense not only differs from the Enlightenment's rationalistic conception: it presents a challenge to reason in several distinct ways, which bear brief enumeration. First, truth is lodged in a personality: "I am the way, and the truth, and the life" (John 14:6), Christ declares of himself. Discursive reason aspires to objectivity and is in principle impersonal in nature. Second, that personality is an embodied entity, a psychosomatic organism, whereas rational thought operates on the formal and abstract plane. Third, access to truth depends on revelation, on the initiative of a transcendent Other: in Christian terminology, on grace. This places human reason in a subordinate attitude of waiting ("waiting on the Lord"). The characterization of reason as "proud," frequently encountered in Russian religious thought, has to do with its insistence on its autonomy and rejection of this subordinate position. Fourth, truth is revelatory not of some theoretical and axiologically neutral state of affairs, but of one's own debased condition, the correction of which depends not on the reason, but on the will. Finally, truth is disclosed as personally transformative, as the "darkened nature of Adam" is conformed to the "godlike."

The opposition of these two interpretations of enlightenment presented the intellectuals of Russian Orthodoxy of the imperial period with a choice between accommodating Russia's historical confession to Enlightenment ideals, on the one hand, and intellectually defending its ancient mystical-sacramental foundations, on the other. Three of the contributors to the present volume together provide a clear picture as to the forms taken by the choice of the former. In Elise Wirtschafter's words, "the pan-European religious Enlightenment ... grew out of efforts to find a reasonable faith, neither excessively enthusiast nor rigidly doctrinaire, capable of sustaining belief in an age of ongoing scientific discoveries and new societal priorities."[12] As Sean Gillen asserts, such a reasonable faith, stripped of its irrational appurtenances, found scholarly expression in theism, culminating in the philosophy of Immanuel Kant from the *Critique of Judgment* (1790) onwards.[13] Randall Poole's lucid exposition of Kant's thinking on religion and Christianity makes plain that for Kant, "pure religious faith" consists solely in the individual's free obedience to the moral law, and that revealed religion, as expressed in the empirical historical confessions, must be superseded by natural religion, "proceed[ing] from morality and pure reason, principles on which a true universal church must be founded."[14] As his work of the same name implies, Kant's religious ideal is religion within the boundaries of reason alone. Despite the ideal status of reason in much Enlightenment thought, its appropriation and dissemination is seen, by Kant and others, in historicist and progressivist terms as the cumulative victory of rational truth over irrational falsehood. Religion, if it is to be progressive, must accommodate itself[15] to reason and science; it must become "modern." Wirtschafter, Gillen, Poole, and also Rampton, for this volume, demonstrate how from the eighteenth century to the Bolshevik Revolution certain educated Orthodox, both within the Church (Platon [Levshin], Kudriavtsev-Platonov) and outside it (Solov'ev,[16] the liberals Novgorodtsev, Sergei Kotliarevskii, and Struve), assimilated the spirit of the Western religious Enlightenment and, in their different ways, promoted a modern, moral-rational Orthodoxy capable—as they saw it—of meeting the needs of contemporary believers and the modern Russian state.[17]

The "modernizing" tendency within Russian Orthodoxy inevitably created a fundamental divide between the ecclesiastical academy and popular piety. In recent years much research has been devoted to "lived Orthodoxy," that is, the beliefs and practices of the Orthodox faithful; popular religion. Commenting on the wealth and diversity of Russian religious culture of the imperial period, the historian Laura Engelstein has asserted that "the Orthodox spectrum was broad enough to embrace a range of styles, from the intellectual articulations of the ecclesiastical academies, to the spiritual rigor of the contemplative life, to the social outreach of the monasteries, to the improvisational piety of the peasants." Engelstein resists a typology of Orthodox cultural forms based on social class and suggests instead that we view these as "different registers of the creed."[18] In the light of the discussion above, however, this attractive proposition can be accepted only in part. Precisely those aspects of Orthodoxy that the Enlightenment rejected as irrational were central to the practices of "lived Orthodoxy": the veneration of icons and relics; processions and pilgrimages; confession and participation in the Eucharist; holy foolishness and spiritual eldership, and so on. At the same time, these same practices are united by a common sacramentalism that is central to the Orthodox conception of enlightenment, and that is justified theologically by the patristic understanding of Christ as God incarnate: the saving grace of God is mediated through the material world and deifies that world. This idea is indeed encapsulated in the Nicene Creed. Thus, to the extent that the ecclesiastical academy embraced Enlightenment ideals, it may be argued, it distanced itself from the Christ-centered faith of popular Orthodoxy, and thereby did in fact create a divide based on social class, at least insofar as this was defined by one's degree of learning.

Nevertheless, not all educated Orthodox embraced the Western religious Enlightenment. Over the course of the nineteenth century, numerous individuals within the priestly hierarchy and the spiritual academies, among them significant figures such as Metropolitan Filaret (Drozdov), and Bishops Ignatii (Brianchaninov) and Feofan (Govorov), resisted what was seen as the Protestantization of Orthodoxy in the name of what Georges Florovsky, among others, has called a "theology of the heart."[19] According to Florovsky, this "theology of the heart," introduced in the reforms to the ecclesiastical schools of 1814 in the form of an instruction to educate the "'inner man' by imparting a living and well-founded personal conviction in the saving truths of faith"[20] (a departure from the rote learning favored in the prereform schools), was for some decades colored, even in its best representatives, by German Pietistic and mystical influences. In due course, however, under the influence of the nineteenth-century revival of contemplative monasticism in Russia, this gave way to a focus on the mystical asceticism of the Greek Desert Fathers.[21] It is hard to exaggerate the importance of this revival for Russian Orthodox culture and religious thought, both lay and ecclesiastical, from the middle of the nineteenth century to the present day. More than any other facet of Orthodox culture, it proved capable of challenging the Western religious Enlightenment, both as a practice that embodied all the features of Orthodox enlightenment, and as a "philosophy" for which there was a specific "language," a set of concepts made available to philosophical discourse in the collection of texts on Orthodox mystical-ascetic practice known as the *Philokalia*.

Spiritual Eldership and the *Philokalia*

The practice of Eastern Christian mystical asceticism is known as Hesychasm (from the Greek *hesychia*: stillness), its practitioners as Hesychasts. At its core is devotion to silent "prayer of the heart,"[22] and its sought-for objective is an experience, in this life, of deification, or transfiguration by divine (uncreated, immaterial) light. Those Hesychasts who over many years have achieved spiritual perfection and been rewarded by mystical union in this sense are known as spiritual elders (*startsy*). These exercised great authority over the common people, but because this authority rested on their charisma as saints their relationship with the institutional Church authorities was often fraught.[23] The *startsy* carried out two roles that reflected their authority: they acted as spiritual directors to neophyte Hesychasts, and they carried out a ministry of prayer, advice, and healing to laypeople of all classes.

The historical context for spiritual eldership in Russia has now been expertly written up in Irina Paert's recent study, which makes full use of preexisting sources in addition to providing substantial new material from archival research and offering a range of interpretative strategies for understanding the phenomenon.[24] Spiritual eldership is an ancient phenomenon dating back to the earliest Desert Fathers. It enjoyed a renaissance in the thirteenth and fourteenth centuries that culminated in the successful theological defense of hesychastic practice by Gregory Palamas, bishop of Thessalonica (1296–1359), who was himself a practicing Hesychast, from attacks from Byzantine humanist quarters.[25] It was at this time that this mystical type of asceticism was introduced to Russia. Having fallen into abeyance in Russia and elsewhere in the early modern period, it enjoyed a second revival in the eighteenth century as a result of the efforts of Greek monks to counteract the influence of the Enlightenment on the Orthodox Church (the Kollyvades movement). This revival was driven by the publication in 1782 of a collection of writings on mystical ascetic practice encompassing the fourth to the fifteenth centuries under the title of the *Philokalia*. A shorter collection in Slavonic translation prepared by the Ukrainian elder Paisii Velichkovskii (1722–94) appeared in Moscow in 1793 (the *Dobrotoliubie*). Russian translations followed, the most comprehensive from 1877 by Feofan (Govorov) the Recluse.[26] The *Philokalia* enjoyed far greater influence in Russia than it did in Greece.[27] Its dissemination went hand in hand with the above-mentioned remarkable flowering of Hesychasm and spiritual eldership in the Russian monasteries, which continued to the Bolshevik Revolution.[28] In the nineteenth century certain Russian elders, the most famous of which are probably Saint Serafim of Sarov (1754/59–1833) and the elders Lev, Makarii, and Amvrosii of the Optina Pustyn' hermitage, achieved iconic status and attracted the attention of a wide range of figures from the secular elite.[29] Of course, the reception of Philokalic spirituality in Russian monasticism involved change as well as continuity. In Paert's account, a more moderate approach to ascetic discipline than that recommended by Paisii was adopted by the Russian elders, particularly in regard to diet and ritual, and particularly with respect to expectations of lay adopters of the prayer of the heart. They "advocated the interiorization of spiritual life," possibly echoing the wider early nineteenth-century interest in "inner Christianity."[30] As stated above, the Philokalic writings are (together with the Liturgy) the fullest written expression that we have of the Orthodox conception of enlightenment,[31] so their dissemination in the Age of Enlightenment constituted a clear challenge to the burgeoning hegemony of the new rationalism.[32]

The title page of the Greek *Philokalia* states that the purpose of the writings it contains is that "through ethical philosophy, in accordance with praxis and contemplation, the intellect is purified, illuminated and perfected." As Louth has pointed out, these words contain "a wealth of meaning."[33] The Philokalic texts constitute a "philosophy," not in the Enlightenment sense of rational enquiry but in the sense of the quest for personal moral perfection. It is an experiential rather than an intellectual philosophy. The role of the "intellect" (*nous*) is at the center of this experiential philosophy, but not in the modern sense as the faculty of reasoning. In the *Philokalia*, *nous* retains its Platonic meaning of "the organ of contemplation (*theoria*)": it "does not function by formulating abstract concepts and then arguing on this basis to a conclusion reached through deductive reasoning, but it understands divine truth by immediate experience, intuition, or 'simple cognition.'"[34] In the conceptual framework of the *Philokalia*, *nous* is distinguished from *dianoia*, a term that is closer to the modern concept of "reason" as "rational thought."[35]

The quest for moral perfection is predicated upon the belief that human beings are fallen. By virtue of their fallenness, they are separated from God. Thus, the motivation for the quest is to overcome that separation and experience closeness to God once more, to "know" God in experience. Again following the Platonic model, the Philokalic writings hold that the organ that apprehends God is the intellect, which, in the words of Andrè-Jean Festugière, "aspires to a union where there is total fusion, the interpenetration of two living things";[36] hence the need for the purification of the intellect through "praxis and contemplation." The intellect is conceived as the higher part of the soul, as opposed to the passionate lower part. "Praxis," the ascetic struggle against the passions, is directed at subordinating the lower part of the soul to the higher, to achieve a state of dispassion (*apatheia*) that is the prerequisite for contemplation. Nevertheless, the intellect, too, requires discipline. In its fallen state it is distracted by the world of the senses, and must through prayer be gathered to a state of "attention" (*prosochi*) or "watchfulness" (*nipsis*).

In addition to the Platonic notion of "intellect," the *Philokalia* engages intensively with the biblical concept of "heart" (*kardia*). Its usage has little in common with the heart's modern association with the emotions. The "heart" is "the spiritual centre of man's being, man as made in the image of God, his deepest and truest self."[37] Again, "it is the centre of the human person, the source of everything that we are."[38] In one sense, the relationship between "intellect" and "heart" in the Philokalic texts reflects the uncertain relationship between Platonic and biblical mysticism in the Greek tradition. In another, though, a synthesis is achieved by the idea that the rightful place of residence of the intellect is in the heart, that their separation is a mark of fallenness, and their integration a mark of healing and salvation. Thus, the hesychastic mystics articulated the struggle against distraction as the effort to "return the mind to the heart." Palamas describes the relationship in the following way: "Consequently, when we seek to keep watch over and correct our reason by a rigorous sobriety, with what are we to keep watch, if we do not gather together our mind, which has been dissipated abroad by the senses, and lead it back again into the interior, to the selfsame heart which is the seat of the thoughts?"[39] The aim of hesychastic prayer was through the elimination of extraneous thoughts to bring about the "descent" of the mind into the heart, to achieve "prayer of the heart," in which the whole person, not just the mind, participates. Consequently, when union with God occurs, it is not merely an intellectual event, but an experience that overwhelms the whole person as a psychosomatic organism.

The Philokalic Fathers were highly reticent about the event of mystical union. Saint Symeon the New Theologian (tenth century) is a rare exception. What is clear is that the intellect cannot achieve union by its own efforts through contemplation: contemplation, prayer, can only prepare the contemplative to receive God as the latter freely and supernaturally reveals himself (through grace). Furthermore, mystical union is neither a sensory nor an intellectual experience, though it paradoxically engages body and mind. In Palamas's words, it is "an illumination immaterial and divine, a grace invisibly seen and ignorantly known."[40] This "illumination" is *theosis*, or divinization: not knowledge about God, but participation in God. Hence, in the *Philokalia*, knowledge of the truth is an encounter with the personal God. Finally, to return to the metaphor of light, mystical union in the Orthodox tradition is experienced as a "vision" of the divine light not exteriorly, but as infusing the visionary, who is transfigured as Christ was transfigured in the Gospel narrative: "For in his mercy the Saviour of our souls has transfigured disfigured man and made him shine with light."

Florenskii and Orthodox Enlightenment

The most radical and influential appropriation of Philokalic discourse for the purpose of rejecting secular Enlightenment rationalism and the Western religious Enlightenment in favor of a culture founded on Orthodox enlightenment emerged as late as 1914, with the publication of *The Pillar and Ground of the Truth* (henceforth: *Pillar and Ground*) by Pavel Florenskii, the outstanding polymath and religious philosopher of the early twentieth century.[41] This contention does need some defending. Why did a breakthrough not come earlier? Why did it not come from within the academy? (Florenskii cannot be considered a typical academy figure. He received a secular education, taking a degree in mathematics in 1904 before entering the Moscow Spiritual Academy as a relatively new convert. It was his post-graduate research, from which *Pillar and Ground* developed, that earned him a teaching position in the academy from 1908. He became a priest in 1911.) Possibly it was difficult for academics at the spiritual academies to appropriate a discourse that came from a source that was both external to them and in some sense represented a challenge to their authority in matters of faith. Possibly the prevailing ethos of rationalistic moralism was experienced as too powerful to take on philosophically.[42] Those among the higher clergy who favored the "theology of the heart" spent most, if not all, of their lives outside academia, as bishops or abbots, and drew upon the Philokalic corpus for pastoral purposes: in sermons, letters, and treatises on the ascetic path. We should also consider the widely held perception by the lay intelligentsia in the nineteenth and early twentieth centuries that the institutional Church was out of touch with the intellectual debates, and even the religious longings, of wider society.[43] To the extent that this perception was true, it was perhaps to be predicted that a *philosophical* riposte to the Western religious Enlightenment would require an extra-institutional intellectual experience.

In many respects, the Slavophile Ivan Kireevskii's essay of 1856 "On the Necessity and Possibility of New Principles in Philosophy" ("O neobkhodimosti i vozmozhnosti novykh nachal dlia filosofii") is the best attempt prior to Florenskii's work to use insights drawn from spiritual eldership and the Philokalic corpus to revolutionize philosophical practice in Russia by returning it to its patristic roots.[44] Though space does not permit a detailed analysis here, it can be shown that Kireevskii was well aware of the distinction between secular enlightenment (*filosofiia*) and Christian enlightenment (*liubomudrie*), that he privileged the latter, and that his formulation "integral knowledge" (*tselostnoe znanie*) owes a great deal to the Philokalic teaching about the return of the mind to the heart. Nevertheless, Kireevskii's essay is open to criticism in the respect that, despite its repudiation of "Western rationalism," on the level both of content and of form it remains within the rationalistic paradigm. Kireevskii challenges reason with reason, resisting the introduction into his discourse of theological concepts such as sin, repentance, and ascesis, and his "integral knowledge" remains a cognitive, rather than a personal and experiential, approach to truth.

Kireevskii's essay was written under the influence of German metaphysical idealism, Hegel and Friedrich Wilhelm Joseph von Schelling, which perhaps accounts for his tendency to treat reason and faith as essentially a single entity, with rationality (discursive reason) and faith ("higher" or "believing" reason) located on a continuum. As Sergei Khoruzhii has pointed out, Florenskii appears essentially uninterested in Hegelian dialectical reason, engaging much more actively and consistently with Kant (and, to a lesser extent, with neo-Kantianism).[45] Florenskii, as it were, ignores developments after the Enlightenment in order to take on Enlightenment rationalism itself, which he sees as the major enemy of Orthodoxy. Thus, though he writes in the early twentieth century, his work engages intensively with the eighteenth. He calls the eighteenth century "the century of the [rationalist] intelligentsia *par excellence*," and Kant "the greatest representative of the *intelligentsia*" (215).[46] This raises the interesting possibility that Florenskii's attack on rational faith and on Kant was directed, at least in part, at the very academy that he was joining.

In promoting Florenskii as the champion of Orthodox enlightenment, Christ-centered as this is, I must address the criticism, leveled by Florovsky, and after him Khoruzhii, that Christ is unpardonably absent from the vision of *Pillar and Ground*.[47] Without attempting a detailed refutation of Khoruzhii's argument, which is trenchant and substantial, I would assert that, so far as Florenskii's treatment of reason is concerned, the allegation does not stand. As will become clear from the analysis below, Florenskii fully embraces the idea that the path to true knowledge is through Christ (13), indeed, through the ascetic self-renunciation that is "co-crucifixion with Christ" (48). Furthermore, his major thesis that Christian truth is antinomical and therefore unacceptable to logic-based rationality rests on the doctrine of the consubstantiality of Christ with the Father, that is, the presence in Christ of both divine and human natures.[48] Florenskii asserts that this doctrine, when it was first formulated, dealt a "death blow" to rationality (41). It is hard to reconcile this substantial fact with Khoruzhii's allegation that the Christological theme "is almost completely absent" from *Pillar and Ground*.[49]

During his student days Florenskii drew a great deal from his relationship with his spiritual father, the uneducated *starets* Isidor of the Gethsemane Skete, which was attached to the Trinity-Sergius Monastery and close therefore to the Moscow Spiritual Academy in Sergiev Posad. Avril Pyman suggests Florenskii was motivated in this choice by his growing admiration of the common people as "the living embodiment of elemental popular culture, creative in a way the disunited, analytically minded intelligentsia could no longer hope to be."[50] This bears relation to Florenskii's claim, in *Pillar and Ground*, that the common people are instinctively drawn to the spiritual elders (5). After Isidor's death in

1908, Florenskii wrote a tender memoir of him.[51] The eighth letter of *Pillar and Ground* is addressed to him, and in the tenth Florenskii says of him: "Full of grace and made beautiful by grace, he gave me the most solid, the most undeniable, the purest perception of a spiritual person I have had in my entire life" (233).

The image of the Orthodox ascetic is absolutely central to *Pillar and Ground*. The spiritual elder is established at the outset in the preface "To the Reader" as the exemplar par excellence of the work's leading idea, stated in the first line, that "living religious experience [is] the sole legitimate way to gain knowledge of the dogmas" (5). Introducing his chosen term "ecclesiality" to convey this experience, Florenskii clearly explicates its connection to asceticism:

> But the life of the Church is assimilated and known only through life—not in the abstract, not in a rational way. . . . What is ecclesiality? It is new life, life in the Spirit. What is the criterion of the rightness of this life? Beauty. Yes, there is a special beauty of the spirit, and, ungraspable by logical formulas, it is at the same time the only true path to the definition of what is orthodox and what is not orthodox.
>
> The connoisseurs of this beauty are the spiritual elders, the *startsy*, the masters of the "art of arts," as the holy fathers call asceticism. . . . The Orthodox taste, the Orthodox temper, is felt but it is not subject to arithmetical calculation. Orthodoxy is shown, not proved. (8–9)[52]

On open display here is a life/rationality dichotomy. Orthodox truth transcends the capacity of "arithmetic" to conceptualize it. With "ecclesiality," "the pretensions of the rational mind (*rassudok*) are tamed, [and] great tranquility descends into our reason (*razum*)" (7). Not logical, but "biological and aesthetic" criteria most closely approach an adequate conceptualization of the life of the Church (8).[53] The *startsy*, who, to use Saint Serafim of Sarov's expression, have through ascetic endeavor "acquired the Holy Spirit," most fully "know" this life and realize its beauty. They are saints, *prepodobnye*, who have restored the image of God in man and achieved "likeness" to Christ. They are the "lights" of the Church, who show the way for the faithful to follow.

The first six letters of *Pillar and Ground* are occupied with various aspects of this "taming" of the "pretensions of the rational mind" that is demanded by faith and successfully executed by the *starets*, and thus explicitly deal with the relationship between the Enlightenment and the Orthodox concepts of truth.[54] In the first, "Two Worlds," the problem is announced with reference to the eleventh chapter of the Gospel of Matthew as that of "knowledge, the problem of the insufficiency of rational knowledge [*poznanie rassudochnoe*] and the necessity of spiritual knowledge [*poznanie dukhovnoe*]" (12). True knowledge can be acquired only through and from Jesus Christ, who bids us cast off "the cruel yoke and hard, unbearable burden of science" (13). In the second, "Doubt," Florenskii's excursus into the etymology of terms for "truth" is designed to reinforce the notion of a distinct Orthodox truth, the content of "spiritual knowledge." In the Russian understanding, according to Florenskii, the word "truth" (*istina*), related to the verb "to be" (*est'*), which itself derives originally from the Sanskrit root denoting the breath, is "existence that abides, that which lives, living being, that which breathes." Here as elsewhere in the work Florenskii asserts the congruence of Russian popular belief (lived Orthodoxy) and high philosophical culture: "Truth as the living being *par excellence*" is a conception shared by the Russian people and Russian philosophy, as the latter's "distinctive and original feature" (16).

Florenskii's distinction between "rational" and "spiritual" knowledge consistently engages a distinction between "rationality" and "reason."[55] Only the first, discursive reason, or *rassudok*, is inimical to the life of the spirit. This is because rationality rejects what does not conform to the norms of logic and therefore rejects "life," Orthodox truth, which is in its very essence antinomical.[56] "Reason" (*razum*), on the other hand, is treated by Florenskii as the Neptic Fathers (the ascetic authors of the Philokalic texts) treated *nous*, the intellect, that is, as the higher part of the soul in which the image of God resides.[57] This, once purified, is the organ that contemplates the divine. It is to the *nous* that Florenskii is referring when he argues for the integral connection between reason and being, describing the former as "an organ of man, his vital activity, his real power, logos" (55). Florenskii sees rationality and reason as implacably opposed to one another: "Life, flowing and non self-identical, might be reasonable; it might be transparent for reason.... But, precisely for this reason, life would be non-conformable with rationality, opposed to rationality. It would rip apart the limitedness of rationality. And rationality, hostile to life, would in turn rather seek to kill life than agree to receive life into itself" (24). There is no smooth transition between rational knowledge (*episteme*) and spiritual knowledge (*gnosis*). Rather, "reason must become emancipated from its limitedness within the confines of rationality," and this can only happen by renouncing rationality in an act of intellectual ascesis (*podvig*) (45).

Thus, the rational mind is treated by Florenskii as an intrinsic part of the "flesh," the fallen human being as a psychosomatic organism.[58] It partakes in the egoism, the pretension to autonomy that according to Paul is the hallmark of atheism in the sense of the rejection of God (Romans 1:21–22). Florenskii graphically writes of Eunomius's objection to the Cappadocian Fathers that the doctrine of Christ as one Person in two natures was "impossible" as "a cry of the flesh, a cry of rationality, a rationality that wanders about the elements of the world and egotistically trembles in fear for its integrity, a rationality that is self-satisfied despite its total inner disintegration, a rationality that dares, in its infinite fear of the smallest pain, to adapt very Truth to itself, to its blind and meaningless norms" (46). To this extent rational thought for Florenskii is rather more than the Neptic Fathers' *dianoia*, which is regarded neutrally as one of the faculties of the higher soul, though inferior to the *nous*;[59] it is more like the passions that must be overcome in order to achieve the attention necessary for the pursuit of *gnosis*. Like the passions, rational thought, if given its head, leads to the disintegration of the personality, to the madness of skepticism. Remaining within a Pauline framework, Florenskii suggests that rationality has little choice: either it is "saved" through the ascesis of faith, through self-renunciation, or it perishes: "Either the Triune Christian God or the dying in insanity" (47). Once sacrificed, however, "rationality is transformed into a new essence" (47) as it finds its ground in the "supralogical" (48).

The fourth letter, "The Light of the Truth," concerns itself with the nature of spiritual knowledge, with the question as to "how and by virtue of what the philosopher is received by Heaven" (55).[60] Despite remaining with the term "philosophy," it is clear that Florenskii is now using this in a sense closer to that of the patristic "theology," that is, as "active and conscious participation in or perception of the realities of the divine world."[61] Here, the spiritual elder becomes the true philosopher. As we shall see, in his deliberations Florenskii draws extensively upon the theology disclosed in the spirituality of the *Philokalia*; his understanding of knowledge as union is founded on the Hesychasts' experience of mystical union with the personal God, as is demonstrated by the passage on light with which the letter concludes.

Firstly, Florenskii insists on the primacy of the ontological over the purely cognitive in acts of spiritual knowledge, which follows from the integral relationship between reason (*nous*) and being: "the act of knowing is not only a gnoseological but also an ontological act, not only ideal but also real. Knowing is a real *going* of the knower *out* of himself, or (what is the same thing) a real *going* of what is known *into* the knower, a real unification of the knower and what is known" (55). He explicitly traces the roots of this realistic conception of knowledge in "the ancient, realistic understanding of life" (57), advocating it polemically as a Christian—that is, Orthodox and Russian—philosophy of identity (*homoousian* philosophy) in contradistinction to the modern, Western, rationalistic philosophy of similarity (*homoiousian* philosophy) (60). Spiritual knowledge overcomes the law of identity to assert the real merging of subject and object in knowledge. Palamas, the theologian of Hesychasm, likewise asserted the real unification of the contemplative with what is contemplated against nominalist adversaries who maintained that only symbolic knowledge of God was possible.[62]

Secondly, spiritual knowledge is knowledge of persons: "Thus, knowing is not the capturing of a dead object by a predatory subject of knowledge, but a living moral communion of persons, each serving for each as both object and subject. Strictly speaking, only a person is known and only by a person" (55–56). In the Christian world view, truth is personal: the living God is Truth.[63] It follows that "essential knowing of the Truth [is] the real entering into the interior of the Divine Triunity, and not only an ideal touching of the Triunity's outer form" (56).

Finally, spiritual knowledge is transformative: to know God is in a very specific sense to become god-like: "true knowledge, knowledge of the Truth, is possible only through the transubstantiation of man, through his deification [*obozhenie*], through the acquisition of love as the divine essence" (56). Here is a clear statement of the Orthodox doctrine of deification as participation in the divine. The only false note is sounded by the word "essence," where Palamite theology would emphasize that only the energies of God are participable, his essence remaining inaccessible. The hesychastic tradition as expressed in the *Philokalia* maintains that the purified intellect may experience union with God in the Holy Spirit. Nevertheless, despite the ascetic labor of preparation, such an experience occurs only through the grace of God, and here Florenskii remains orthodox: Spiritual knowledge "arises in the soul from the free revelation of Trihypostatic Truth, from the grace-giving visitation of the soul by the Holy Spirit. This visitation begins in a volitional act of faith, which is absolutely impossible for human selfhood and is accomplished through 'attraction' by the Father Who is in heaven" (70; cf. 62).

The Hesychast experienced union with God as a "vision" of the divine (immaterial) light. Florenskii clearly had this in mind when he entitled his chapter on spiritual knowledge "The Light of the Truth." Nevertheless, he saves the discussion of light for the closing passage of the letter, where it is treated with an exceptionally high degree of lyricism and constitutes something of a coda to the foregoing analysis, a hymn of praise to the Orthodox expression of light mysticism in the liturgy, the writings of the Desert Fathers, and finally the nineteenth-century eyewitness account of the transfiguration of Saint Serafim of Sarov. The passage contains all the essential elements of the Orthodox mysticism of light. The spiritual master "sees in his heart [*vnutri serdtsa*] the 'spiritual light,' the 'light of Tabor.' And he himself becomes spiritual and beautiful" (70). Thus the saint is transfigured through the indwelling of the divine as Christ was transfigured before the apostles in the Gospel story. The end of spiritual knowledge, its fullest expression, is light, which for Florenskii is identical with beauty: "That is why the holy fathers called asceticism, as the activity directed at the contemplation of the ineffable light by means of the Holy Spirit, not a science and not even a moral work, but an art, and not just an art, but art par excellence, the 'art of arts'" (72). In this way Florenskii returns to his initial thesis that the criterion for life in the Spirit is beauty.

The closing passage of "The Light of the Truth," which consists almost entirely of quotation of religious texts, points up an important issue relating to the problematic relationship between philosophical discourse and Christian (Orthodox) truth. It is an issue of which Florenskii appears keenly aware. He starts out by conceding that, though his original intention for *Pillar and Ground* was "to use no references, only my own words," by the end of the project "it appeared that I had to discard everything of my own and publish only the works of the Church" (6). The logic of conversion dictates that the philosopher subordinate his own ideas (and Russian religious philosophy is clear that modern philosophical discourse is profoundly individualistic, despite its claims to objectivity) to the word of the Church, which becomes internally persuasive for the convert.[64] Thus, an extreme view would be that Florenskii is able to retain his own discourse only to the extent that he has not yet completed his own ascesis. Florovsky harshly indicts Florenskii for subjectivism, claiming that he "remained subjective even when he wished to be objective."[65] Part of what he means by this is that Florenskii speaks for himself rather than the Church. Florovsky is also critical of what we might call the hybridity of *Pillar and Ground*, the influence on it of the romanticism and aestheticism of early Russian modernism.[66] No concession is made to the important point that Florenskii, himself a recent convert, is writing, by his own admission, for "catechumens," those on the threshold of conversion, whose language is still that of the secular world. Florenskii is effectively acting as a guide for outsiders, and an interpreter, attending to each discourse and translating each in terms of the other. This gives him permission to indulge his formidable intellect while also drawing on the textual resources of the Orthodox Church. As for the modernist features of the work, it can be argued that it is only by virtue of these that Florenskii is able to challenge Enlightenment rationalism on the level of form in addition to that of content. *Pillar and Ground*'s eclectic mixing of genres and discourses, its adoption of the epistolary form, the "'concretely general, symbolically personal'" persona of the narrator:[67] all these make a virtue of early modernism's rejection of "positivism" and embrace of aestheticism in order to overcome the gap between objectivism and subjectivism, theoretical and experiential knowledge, scholarship and the spiritual poetry of the soul in the interests of articulating Orthodox enlightenment.

NOTES

This essay is based on material presented in Ruth Coates, "Russia's Two Enlightenments: The *Philokalia* and the Accommodation of Reason in Ivan Kireevskii and Pavel Florenskii," *SEER* 91, no. 4 (October 2013): 675–702. Copyright 2013 by *The Slavonic and East European Review*. Used by permission of the publisher.

1. Ju. M. Lotman and B. A. Uspenskij, "The Role of Dual Models in the Dynamics of Russian Culture (up to the End of the Eighteenth Century)," in *The Semiotics of Russian Culture*, ed. Ann Shukman (Ann Arbor: Michigan Slavic Contributions, 1984), 19. G. D'iachenko's *Polnyi tserkovno-slavianskii slovar'* of 1899 (Moscow: Tip. Vil'de) gives for the entry *Prosveshchenie* "Svet, osveshchenie, prosveshchenie" (light, illumination, enlightenment) and also "Kreshchenie" (baptism), as found in the *ekten'ia* for the Feast of Epiphany (which in the Orthodox rite celebrates the baptism of Christ). Earlier dictionaries confirm the association with baptism. Shishkov's brainchild, the *Slovar' tserkovno-slavianskago i russkago iazyka* (St. Petersburg: Tip. Imp. Akad. nauk), compiled between 1827 and 1847 and published in 1847, gives alongside the neutral "Osiianie svetom" (radiating light) and "Obogashcheniia uma poznaniami" (enrichment of the mind with knowledge), "Prazdnik Bogoiavleniia" (the Feast of Epiphany) and "Kreshchenie." The six-volume *Slovar' Akademii Rossiiskoi* of 1789–94 (Moscow: MGU) gives "Prazdnik Bogoiavleniia" as the third meaning after "Osiianie" and "Nastavlenie; ochishchenie razuma ot lozhnykh predosuditel'nykh poniatii, zakliuchenii. Protivopolagaetsia nevezhestvu" (Instruction; the cleansing of the reason from false prejudicial concepts, conclusions. The opposite of ignorance). Interestingly, despite the Enlightenment ring to this latter definition, the quotation used to illustrate it is from 2 Timothy 1:10: "Iavl'sheisia blagodati nyne prosveshcheniem Spasitelia nashego Iisusa Khrista" ("[grace] has now been revealed through the appearing of our Savior Christ Jesus"). The 1806–22 edition retains these three definitions, and adds "Kreshchenie." As late as V. Dal"s *Tolkovyi slovar' zhivago velikorusskago iazyka* (2nd ed. [Moscow: M. O. Vol'f, 1882]) there is no definition of "Prosveshchenie" as referring to the age of Enlightenment. This corresponds with the situation in Germany, where it was only at the end of the nineteenth century that it became the norm to understand *Aufklärung* in the first instance as the historical epoch of that name (Otto Brunner, Werner Conze, and Reinhart Kosellek, eds., *Geschichtliche Grundbegriffe: Historisches Lexikon zur politisch-sozialen Sprache in Deutschland* [1972, repr., Stuttgart: Klett-Cotta, 2004], 1:244, 341).

2. Andrew Louth makes a useful distinction between the material and the noetic reception of the *Philokalia*, commenting that the latter "is a much more subjective matter;

in exploring what is meant by noetic reception we shall encounter claims that really constitute challenges to what we consider Orthodoxy to be, what we consider theology to be." Andrew Louth, "The Influence of the *Philokalia* in the Orthodox World," in *The Philokalia: A Classic Text of Orthodox Spirituality*, ed. Brock Bingaman and Bradley Nassif (New York: Oxford University Press, 2012), 50. My attempt to relate Florenskii's thought to Philokalic theology can I think be seen as an exercise in exploring the *Philokalia's* noetic reception. For an overview of the Russian religious renaissance, see Ruth Coates, "Religious Renaissance in the Silver Age," in *A History of Russian Thought*, ed. William Leatherbarrow and Derek Offord (Cambridge: Cambridge University Press, 2010), 169-93.

3. Biblical quotations are from the New Revised Standard Version.

4. Jaques Roger, "La lumière et les lumières," *Cahiers de l'Association internationale des études françaises*, no. 20 (1968): 167-77.

5. According to Horst Stuke, the German term *Aufklärung* was used up to the end of the seventeenth century in a primarily meteorological sense as a translation of the Latin *serenitas* (fair weather). Over the course of the eighteenth century, first the verbal form (by 1720) and later the noun (from the 1760s) became connected with the notion of shedding light on matters previously obscure, and was applied initially to the human mind in general, and subsequently to the reasoning faculty specifically. Stuke surmises that the development was prompted by the need to correctly translate into German the French terms, used by Leibniz, *éclairer*, *éclaircir*, and *éclaircissement*. Well into the nineteenth century it was used synonymously with *Erleuchtung* and *erleuchten*. Stuke points out that Leibniz used the terms to refer to *lumen naturale* and *lumen divinum* alike. He sees "the age-old, traditionally rich and multiform matrix of ideas attaching to the religious-metaphysical doctrine of light" as one of two main sources (the other is Cartesian epistemology) of the semantic content of *Aufklärung*, while expressing caution about viewing these as exhaustive. Brunner et al., "Aufklärung," in *Geschichtliche Grundbegriffe*, 1:247-49.

6. Cf. John 8:12: "Again Jesus spoke to them, saying, 'I am the light of the world. Whoever follows me will never walk in darkness, but will have the light of life.'"

7. Affirmed in the *Slovar' Akademii Rossiiskoi* of 1789-94, and of 1806-22, which includes in its definitions of "Svet": "pridaetsia nazvanie synu Bozhiiu. *Iako svet pride v mir*. Ioan. III. 19. *Ne de toi svet, no da svidetel'stvuet o svete*. Ioan. I. 8." (name given to the son of God. "[T]he light has come into the world" [John 3:19]. "He himself was not the light, but he came to testify to the light" [John 1:8]).

8. The literature on deification (Gk: *theosis*) is extensive. For an introduction to the subject, see Norman Russell, *Fellow Workers with God: Orthodox Thinking on Theosis* (Crestwood, NY: St. Vladimir's Seminary Press, 2009). On baptism, see 127-29.

9. Florenskii declared that "[t]he idea of the light that is full of grace is one of the few fundamental ideas of the whole liturgy." Pavel Florenskii, *The Pillar and Ground of the Truth*, trans. Boris Jakim (Princeton, NJ: Princeton University Press, 1997), 71. He cites "almost at random": the troparion of Saint Sergius of Radonezh, "vselisia v tia Presviatyi Dukh, Ego zhe deistviem svetlo ukrashen esi" ("The Holy Spirit has entered you; by the Spirit's action you are adorned with light"); the Christmas troparion, "Rozhdestvo tvoe Khriste Bozhe nash, vozsiia mirovi svet razuma" ("Thy birth, O Christ our God, has shed upon the world the light of reason"); the Sunday canon of the 6th tone, "Liuboviiu

ozari, moliusia, videti tia Slove Bozhii" ("With love illuminate me, I pray, that I may see Thee, Word of God"); Matins, 1st antiphon of the 2nd tone, "Na nebo ochi pushchaiu moego serdtsa k Tebe Spase, spasi mia Tvoim osiianiem" ("I cast my heart's glance heavenward, toward Thee, O Savior, save me with Thy radiance"); Saint Symeon the New Theologian, Seventh Prayer for Holy Communion, "Ne ibo est' edin, s toboiu Khriste moi, svetom trisolnechnym, prosveshchaiushchim mir" ("For I am not alone, I am with Thee, my Christ, the light of three suns illuminating the world"); the prayer of dismissal, "Khriste, svete istinnyi, prosveshchaiai i osviashchaiai vsiakago cheloveka, griadushchago v mir, da znamenuetsia na nas svet litsa tvoego, dav nem uzrim svet nepristupnyi" ("Christ, the true light, who lights and sanctifies every man who comes into the world, let the light of Thy face be a sign upon us that we may see the unapproachable light"); and the holy martyr Afinogen, evening song to the Son of God, "Svete tikhii sviatyia slavy, bezsmertnago Ottsa, nebesnago, sviatago blazhennago, Iisuse Khriste: Prishedshe na zapad solntsa, videvshe svet vechernii, poet Ottsa, Syna i Sviatago Dukha Boga. Dostoin esi vo vsia vremena pet' byti glasy prepodobnymi, Syne Bozhii zhivot daiai: tem zhe mir Tia slavit" ("O tranquil light of the holy glory of the immortal Father, heavenly, holy, blessed, O Jesus Christ. Having come at the setting of the sun, having seen the evening light, we sing the Father and the Son and the Holy Spirit, God. Thou, the Son of God, giver of life, art worthy at all times of being sung by the voices of saints. Thus the world praises Thee"). P. A. Florenskii, *Stolp i utverzhdenie istiny* (1914; repr., Moscow: Pravda, 1990), 1:1:96–97, 1:2:659.

10. See Andreas Andreopoulos, *Metamorphosis: The Transfiguration in Byzantine Theology and Iconography* (Crestwood, NY: St. Vladimir's Seminary Press, 2005). The *Slovar' tserkovno-slavianskogo i russkago iazyka* (1847) illustrates the verb *prosveshchat'sia* with a quotation from Matthew's account of the Transfiguration: "I prosvetisia litse ego iako solntse" ("and his face shone like the sun" (Matthew 17:2). The *Slovar' Akademii Rossiiskoi* of 1789–94 illustrates the noun "svet" from the same verse: "Rizy zhe ego bysha bely, iako svet" ("and his clothes became dazzling white").

11. *The Festal Menaion*, trans. Mother Mary and Kallistos Ware (South Canaan, PA: St. Tikhon's Seminary Press, 1998), 468, 469.

12. Elise Kimerling Wirtschafter, "Orthodoxy and Enlightenment in Catherinian Russia: The Tsarevich Dimitrii Sermons of Metropolitan Platon," in this volume.

13. Sean Gillen, "V. D. Kudriavtsev-Platonov and the Making of Russian Orthodox Theism," in this volume.

14. Randall A. Poole, "Kant and the Kingdom of Ends in Russian Religious Thought (Vladimir Solov'ev)," in this volume.

15. Gillen, "V. D. Kudriavtsev-Platonov."

16. Poole's reading of Solov'ev is likely to prove controversial. It entirely brackets out the sacramental-mystical dimension in Solov'ev's work, as it does his debt to Schelling.

17. To the list of North American scholars sympathetic to this basic orientation should be added Patrick Michelson, whose unpublished PhD thesis, "'The First and Most Sacred Right': Religious Freedom and the Liberation of the Russian Nation, 1825–1905" (PhD diss., University of Wisconsin–Madison, 2007), documents the spiritual academies' recovery of the Greek Fathers, arguing at the same time that these were read in such a way as to promote the moral autonomy and perfectibility of the self, very Kantian preoccupations.

18. Laura Engelstein, "Old and New, High and Low: Straw Horsemen of Russian Orthodoxy," in *Orthodox Russia: Belief and Practice under the Tsars*, ed. Valerie A. Kivelson and Robert H. Greene (University Park: Pennsylvania State University Press, 2003), 30.

19. Georges Florovsky, *Ways of Russian Theology*, part 1, trans Robert L. Nichols (Belmont, MA: Nordland, 1979), 220. Florovsky writes of an enduring "tragic schism in Russian ecclesiastical society" between "spiritual askesis" and "moralism": *Ways of Russian Theology*, part 2 (Vaduz: Büchervertriebsanstalt, 1987), 174. First published as *Puti russkogo bogosloviia* (Paris, 1937).

20. Florovsky, *Ways*, 1:220.

21. Ibid., 229.

22. This consisted of the invocation of the name of Jesus in the Jesus Prayer. See Kenworthy, in this volume, for the connection of this prayer to the Name-Glorifiers controversy of the early twentieth century. For the relationship of the Jesus Prayer to the *Philokalia*, see Mary B. Cunningham, "The Place of the Jesus Prayer in the *Philokalia*," in Bingaman and Nassif, *The Philokalia*, 195–202.

23. See Irina Paert, *Spiritual Elders: Charisma and Tradition in Russian Orthodoxy* (DeKalb: Northern Illinois University Press, 2010). While engaging with Weber's dichotomy between "traditional" and "charismatic" forms of authority, Paert is careful not to oversimplify the picture in the Russian case. Though the Church did make periodic attempts to rein in, regulate, or subdue the practice of eldership, it also sometimes fostered it, whether in genuine support for spiritual renewal, to help in the fight against religious dissent, or to appropriate the symbolic capital of eldership in order to validate an institution that was coming under increasing attack from the forces of secularization and revolution.

24. Ibid.

25. See John Meyendorff, *A Study of Gregory Palamas*, trans. George Lawrence (Crestwood, NY: St. Vladimir's Seminary Press, 1998). First published as *Introduction à l'étude de Grégoire Palamas* (Paris: Éditions du Seuil, 1959).

26. For the history of the translation and material reception of the *Philokalia*, see G. E. H. Palmer, Philip Sherrard, and Kallistos Ware, trans. and ed., *The Philokalia: The Complete Text*, 4 vols. (London: Faber and Faber, 1979–), 1:11–13; Bishop Kallistos of Diokleia, "The Spirituality of the *Philokalia*," *Sobornost* 13, no. 1 (1993): 6–11; and Kallistos Ware, "St. Nikodimos and the *Philokalia*" (9–35), John Anthony McGuckin, "The Making of the *Philokalia*: A Tale of Monks and Manuscripts" (36–49), and Louth, "The Influence of the *Philokalia*" (50–60), all in Bingaman and Nassif, *The Philokalia*.

27. Kallistos, "The Spirituality of the *Philokalia*," 20.

28. Paert, *Spiritual Elders*, chapters 2–5.

29. Chetverikov notes visits by the writers Pamfil Iurkevich, Nikolai Gogol', V. Solov'ev, A. K. Tolstoy, L. N. Tolstoy, and Dostoevsky, among others. Sergii Chetverikov, *Starets Paisii Velichkovskii*, trans. Vasily Lickwar and Alexander I. Lisenko (Belmont, MA: Nordland, 1980), 313.

30. Paert, *Spiritual Elders*, 82–90, 85.

31. In the delineation of Philokalic "philosophy" that follows, I treat the Philokalic texts as an internally cohesive whole, notwithstanding the fact that the Greek, Slavonic, Russian, and other editions of the Philokalia differed to a greater or lesser extent in the

number and authorship of texts selected. In doing so I emulate contemporary specialists in Orthodox spirituality such as Andrew Louth ("The Theology of the *Philokalia*," in *Abba: The Tradition of Orthodoxy in the West*, ed. John Behr, Andrew Louth, and Dimitri Conomos [Crestwood, NY: St. Vladimir's Seminary Press, 2003], 351–61), and, more recently, Rowan Williams ("The Theological World of the *Philokalia*," in Bingaman and Nassif, *The Philokalia*, 102–21).

32. Louth, "The Theology of the *Philokalia*," 352. Louth points out that Kant's *Critique of Pure Reason* appeared within a year of the *Philokalia*, in 1781.

33. Ibid., 357.

34. Palmer, Sherrard, and Ware, *Philokalia*, 1:362. Williams employs "intelligence" for *nous* "on the grounds that 'intellect' has for most readers a narrower and more conceptually focused sense than 'intelligence.'" Williams, "Theological World of the *Philokalia*," 295n7.

35. Palmer, Sherrard, and Ware, *Philokalia*, 1:364.

36. Quoted in Andrew Louth, *The Origins of the Christian Mystical Tradition: From Plato to Denys*, 2nd ed. (Oxford: Oxford University Press, 2007), xv.

37. Palmer, Sherrard, and Ware, *Philokalia*, 1:361.

38. Louth, "The Theology of the *Philokalia*," 359. For an extensive survey of the term "heart" in biblical usage, see P. I. Iurkevich, "Serdtse i ego znachenie v dukhovnoi zhizni cheloveka, po ucheniiu slova Bozhiia" (1860), in *Filosofskie proizvedeniia* (Moscow: Pravda, 1990), 69–103.

39. Gregory Palamas, *The Triads*, ed. John Meyendorff, trans. Nicholas Gendle (New York: Paulist Press, 1983), 43.

40. Ibid., 57.

41. See Avril Pyman's recent biography: Avril Pyman, *Pavel Florensky: A Quiet Genius; The Tragic and Extraordinary Life of Russia's Unknown Da Vinci* (New York: Continuum, 2010).

42. Iurkevich's essay (n38, above) is of great interest from this point of view, but he seeks a rapprochement between science and faith, ultimately revealing himself as a religious enlightener. He does not refer to the *Philokalia* and is negatively inclined toward mysticism. Iurkevich taught both at the Kiev Spiritual Academy and at Moscow University.

43. This view was held, for example, by Dmitrii Merezhkovskii and his circle at the time of the Religious-Philosophical Meetings (1901–3). See Florovsky, *Ways*, 2:252–58; Olga Matich, *Erotic Utopia: The Decadent Imagination in Russia's Fin de Siècle* (Madison: University of Wisconsin Press, 2005), 212–35.

44. *Polnoe sobranie sochinenii I. V. Kireevskago v dvukh tomakh*, ed. Mikhail Gershenzon (Moscow, 1911; repr., Westmead, Farnborough: Gregg International Publishers Limited, 1970), 1:223–64. Kireevskii's spiritual director was the elder Makarii of the Optina Hermitage (*Pustyn'*), with whom he enjoyed an extensive correspondence. Kireevskii studied Eastern patristic literature under Makarii's guidance, and collaborated with him in the translation into Russian and publication of a series of patristic works, including key texts on the theology and practice of Hesychasm. For biographical information on Kireevskii, see Abbott Gleason, *European and Muscovite: Ivan Kireevsky and the Origins of Slavophilism* (Cambridge, MA: Harvard University Press, 1972).

45. S. S. Khoruzhii, *Mirosozertsanie Florenskogo* (Tomsk: Vodolei, 1999). Khoruzhii is sharply critical of Florenskii's neglect of Hegel, which he believes greatly undermines the former's opposition of "rational" and "spiritual" knowledge. He argues that, as a former scientist, Florenskii is drawn to, and indeed dependent on, Kantian rationality, which is the model of reason best suited to the natural sciences: in seeking to overcome it, he does battle with himself (74–86).

46. Florenskii, *Pillar and Ground*, 215. Henceforth page references to this work are given in parentheses in the text.

47. Florovsky, *Ways*, 2:278–80; Khoruzhii, *Mirosozertsanie Florenskogo*, 89–96.

48. The Council of Nicaea in 325 produced the formulation "consubstantial [*homoousion*] with the Father" and captured it in the Nicene Creed. See Norman P. Tanner, ed., *Decrees of the Ecumenical Councils*, vol. 1, *Nicaea I to Lateran V* (London: Sheed and Ward, 1990), 5. The Council of Chalcedon in 451 applied the same adjective to Christ's relationship to humanity: Christ is "consubstantial with the Father as regards his divinity, and the same consubstantial with us as regards his humanity." It famously acknowledged in Christ "two natures which undergo no confusion, no change, no division, no separation" (Tanner, *Ecumenical Councils*, 86). Khoruzhii correctly points out that the Chalcedonian formula is not mentioned directly by Florenskii (*Mirosozertsanie Florenskogo*, 91). But Chalcedon merely clarified the relationship of the divine and human natures in Christ, while Nicaea I, which Florenskii makes a great deal of, established the more fundamental position that Christ was both human and divine.

49. Khoruzhii, *Mirosozertsanie Florenskogo*, 90.

50. Pyman, *Pavel Florensky*, 46.

51. Ibid. The memoir, *Sol' zemli* (Salt of the Earth), was first published in 1908 and 1909 in the journal *Khristianin* (The Christian). Now in P. A. Florenskii, *Sochineniia v cheterekh tomakh* (Moscow: Mysl', 1996), 1:571–637.

52. It is worth noting that Louth ends his article "The Influence of the *Philokalia* in the Orthodox World" by quoting this passage, with the comment: "There we find a succinct statement of the true philokalic tenor of theology; it is in tracing that that we trace the noetic influence of the *Philokalia*" (60).

53. Mikhail Bakhtin makes a related point, in my view, when he points out that "in its concreteness and its permeatedness with an emotional-volitional tone, [the world of art] is closer than any of the abstract cultural worlds (taken in isolation) to the unitary and unique world of the performed act," i.e., to lived experience (M. M. Bakhtin, *Toward a Philosophy of the Act*, trans. and ed. Vadim Liapunov and Michael Holquist [Austin: University of Texas Press, 1993], 61). For Bakhtin's relationship to the theology of the *Philokalia*, see Ruth Coates, "Bakhtin and Hesychasm," *Religion and Literature* 37, no. 3 (2005): 59–80.

54. For detailed analysis of Florenskii's philosophical argumentation in these chapters, see Robert Slesinski, *Pavel Florensky: A Metaphysics of Love* (Crestwood, NY: St. Vladimir's Seminary Press, 1984); Frank Haney, *Zwischen exakter Wissenschaft und Orthodoxie: Zur Rationalitätsauffassung Priester Pavel Florenskijs* (Frankfurt am Main: Peter Lang, 2001); and Frank Haney, "Gestaltungen des Tranzendenten: Pavel Florenskijs Unendlichkeitsbegriff" (127–46), Wolfgang Ullmann, "Florenskijs Beiträge zu einer Logik der Diskontinuität" (147–60), and Ludwig Wenzler, "Intuition und Diskursivität: Grundvollzüge von Rationalität bei Pavel Florenskij" (107–26), all in *Pavel*

Florenskij: Tradition und Moderne, ed. Norbert Franz, Michael Hagemeister, and Frank Haney (Frankfurt am Main: Peter Lang, 2001).

55. Jakim's excellent translation consistently renders *razum* as "reason" and *rassudok* as "rationality," or "rational mind" (see his footnote *e* in Florensky, *Pillar and Ground*, 7). For this reason I refrain from providing the Russian in the text from this point.

56. On antinomy in Florenskii, see Slesinski, *Metaphysics of Love*, chap. 5. Bethea's summary is helpful: "[Florenskii's] way is to *visualize* two separate and as it were self-canceling categories and then to show, against logic (*rassudok*), how these categories can suddenly occupy the same space in a privileged 'crossover zone.'" David M. Bethea, "Florensky and Dante: Revelation, Orthodoxy, and Non-Euclidean Space," in *Russian Religious Thought*, ed. Judith Deutsch Kornblatt and Richard F. Gustafson (Madison: University of Wisconsin Press, 1996), 115.

57. Russell, *Fellow Workers with God*, 80.

58. Palmer, Sherrard, and Ware, *Philokalia*, 1:361: I have in mind "flesh" defined as "fallen and sinful nature in contrast to human nature as originally created and dwelling in God; man when separated from God and in rebellion against Him."

59. Palmer, Sherrard, and Ware, *Philokalia*, 2:334.

60. This is the essay that engages with Philokalic discourse most directly. It is here we find direct evidence of Florenskii's familiarity with the Greek *Philokalia* of 1782, with Feofan's five-volume Russian anthology in four editions (he quotes from the introduction to the first volume of the fourth edition, of 1905), as well as with the broader Philokalic tradition as reflected, for example, in the popular work of 1884, *Otkrovennye rasskazy strannika dukhovnomu svoemu ottsu* (known in the West as *The Way of a Pilgrim*) and its sequel. See Florenskii, *Pillar and Ground*, 472nn134-35.

61. Palmer, Sherrard, and Ware, *Philokalia*, 1:367.

62. It is reasonable to suppose that Florenskii had read Palamas's defense of the Hesychasts. The evidence for this in *Pillar and Ground* is in Florenskii's note 128, in which he links the light of Tabor, described in correct Palamite terms as "the energy of the Triune Divinity," to the hesychastic vision. He provides a list of critical treatments of the controversy over Hesychasm that include Igumen Modest's work of 1860, *Sviatoi Grigory Palama, Mitropolit Solynsky, pobornik pravoslavnogo ucheniia o Favorskom svete i o deistviakh Bozhiikh*. He also lists the protagonists in the controversy and refers the reader to the volumes of Migne where their works can be found (468-69).

63. See the etymology of *istina*, discussed earlier in this chapter.

64. See Bakhtin's discussion of internally persuasive discourse in his essay "Discourse in the Novel," in *The Dialogic Imagination: Four Essays by Mikhail Bakhtin*, ed. Michael Holquist (Austin: University of Texas Press, 1988), 342-46.

65. Florovsky, *Ways*, 2:277.

66. Ibid., 279-81.

67. Richard F. Gustafson, "Introduction," in Florenskii, *Pillar and Ground*, xii, quoting from Florenskii's defense of his master's dissertation, of which *Pillar and Ground* is the development. Gustafson's essay offers a good summary of the Symbolist features of the work.

PART III

Thinking Orthodox in Society and Culture

Chapter 7

Written Confession and Religious Thought in Early Nineteenth-Century Russia

NADIESZDA KIZENKO

The development of written confession in Russia breaks down a number of conventions. The boundaries between speaking and writing, reading and listening, theology and devotion, autobiography and literature, absolver and penitent, rarely seem as porous as they do in the written exchanges between elite Russian women and their confessors from the mid-1820s to the mid-1850s. These texts suggest that Russian religious thought did not exist as the exclusive province of hierarchs and theologians. Rather, the theology of confession became the joint production of confessors and penitents alike. The insights clerics gleaned through confession informed both their notions of sin and their subsequent writing. Similarly, confession provided penitents like Natal'ia Fonvizina and Ekaterina Novosil'tseva an occasion to both internalize and articulate Christian teaching, and to construct and reconstruct their life stories. The confessional texts they produced became a shared project that would form religious thought, religious practice, and Russian literature.

This interpenetration of genres is all the more remarkable given the stereotypical impressions of Russian religiosity in the early nineteenth century. Both memoirs and scholarship suggest that, throughout the eighteenth and nineteenth centuries, the Russian elite regarded parish clergy as socially inferior, not fit to mingle with.[1] Elite penitents and father confessors literally spoke different languages—French and somewhat halting Russian on the part of the penitents, Church Slavonic-inflected Russian and occasional Latin on the part of the clergy.² In such a context, one might expect confession for the Russian elite to be a perfunctory exercise. Indeed, it was partly the opportunity to have better confessions from men perceived as social equals that prompted Russian noblewomen including Countess Varvara Golovina, Anastasie de Circourt (née Khliustina), Madame de Ségur (née Rostopchina), and Sofia Svetchina to convert to Roman Catholicism at the turn of the nineteenth century.³

This is the conventional wisdom. The documents discussed in this chapter, however, show something different. By the middle of the nineteenth century, some educated Russian lay people turned to writing to go beyond sacramental confession as currently practiced. Noblemen like the young Iosif Vielogorskii prepared for their sacramental confessions with a thorough, unsparing written examination of conscience.⁴ The educated laywomen discussed here went even further. They asked Church hierarchs, monastic elders, and even parish priests to receive their confessions in writing. The texts they produced were something new. Although nuns had sometimes penned written confessions in the late eighteenth century, those documents focused on obtaining absolution in absentia.⁵ In their explicit request for absolution, they reflect the criteria for a written confession laid out by the French historian Alphonse Michel.⁶ But the laywomen discussed here did not simply describe their sins and seek absolution, as did the nuns; nor was their confession a private exercise, as was Vielogorskii's. Instead, they entered into a dialogue with, and themselves offered advice to, their clerical interlocutors. The texts they produced show that confession may have been a more important force in Russian religious thought than previously suspected.

Historical Context

There was little in previous Russian Orthodox practice to suggest that written confession might arise. In fact, with the exception of literate deaf-mutes, the written confession in nineteenth-century Russia was not meant to exist.⁷ Annual auricular, or spoken, sacramental confession was the norm: it became a legal as well as religious requirement for Russian Orthodox Christians in the seventeenth century, as it had for Roman Catholics at the 1215 Council of Trent.⁸ Historians and theologians regard this requirement as a crucial moment in reflecting and creating a new, peculiarly "modern," sense of the accountable individual.⁹ Confession became the focus for several goals: the instruction and the churching of the Orthodox population, increased bureaucratic control over parishes and monasteries, and attempted control over what people were thinking and doing. The sacrament of confession was thus both educational and potentially punitive.¹⁰

These mechanisms worked. Sermons, memoirs, police records, paintings, children's books, the lives of the saints—all testify in different ways that, by the nineteenth century, *govenie*, the process of preparation for annual confession and communion, had become an important marker of most people's religious lives. Russian Orthodox Christians were expected to spend a week preparing for their confession by attending church services morning and night, performing works of charity, reading or listening to the prayer rule before confession, and seeking to avoid worldly distractions. After going to confession on the evening before they meant to go to communion, people were expected to abstain from all food and drink until they partook of the Eucharist at the following morning liturgy. Most people scheduled their *govenie* for the end of the first week of Great Lent. Schoolchildren stood in line with their classmates; peasant children with their parents; soldiers with their regiments. Thus, although confession was a private conversation between penitent and priest, its ritualized timing and performance also made the sacrament a communal action that most Orthodox Christians in the Russian Empire undertook at the same time.[11]

Russian Orthodox Christianity, moreover, did not reproduce the Roman Catholic practice of the anonymous confessional booth, introduced in the late sixteenth century.[12] Instead, the penitent and priest stood next to one another. Although a portable screen might separate them from penitents waiting their turn, and although they spoke quietly, they might still be overheard. At absolution the priest put his arm around the penitent's shoulders as he covered the penitent's bowed head with his stole. Thus, the sacramental confession in Russia was more physically intimate and less anonymous than it was in the contemporary Roman Catholic world. This may be another factor in why written confession developed in Russia: if penitents had something particularly shameful to confess, or wished a longer conversation than a long line of penitents would allow, they might seek out either a priest who did not know them, or the distance offered by the written word.[13]

Theology of Confession

Mid-nineteenth-century Russians learned to confess, and priests learned to confess them, from a variety of sources. The services of Great Lent guided penance through seven weeks of themes including those of the Prodigal Son (the loving father forgives the errant child who has squandered his inheritance) and the Dread Judgment (all sins will be made public, and all will account for their own sins).[14] High-ranking clerics, such as Metropolitan Platon (Levshin) and Archpriest Vasilii Bazhanov, the confessor of the imperial family, discussed confession in their published sermons.[15] Priests could draw on penitentials—the lists of questions to ask at confession classified by the age, sex, clerical or marital status, and occupation of the penitent—they had consulted from the fourteenth century onward, and which had regularly changed in response to changing social realities.[16] The standard modern clerical guide to confession, however, was *On the Duties of Parish Priests* (*O dolzhnostiakh presviterov prikhodskikh*), first published in 1776 and reprinted twenty times by 1833. Drawing as it did on Church law, the Bible, and the holy fathers from Augustine to John Chrysostom, the book was literally a canonical text. It remained required reading in seminaries through the middle of the nineteenth century.[17]

According to *Duties*, confession was the most difficult of all the sacraments for the priest and the one requiring the most art: thirty pages were devoted to its discussion, more than four times the space allotted to the others (baptism and marriage, the next closest, got only six). The priest-confessor was compared to a physician healing people's souls and cutting away their "ulcerous, gangrenous" wounds, instructing penitents to place all hope in the crucified Christ and his grace, with Judas as a counter-example: "He repented and confessed his sin, and returned the pieces of silver, but, as he did not seek God's mercy, his confession was of no use, and this wretch received a noose round his neck instead of absolution."[18] Although free will is not mentioned explicitly, penitents are expected to choose to sin no more. Priests are reminded that the grace of God will always accept the penitent, and that they are not judges, but only witnesses of the penance of their flock; their task is service, not domination. This may have been a tacit rebuke to those who criticized the change in the wording of the absolution formula introduced by Metropolitan Petro Mohyla in 1646, from the original deprecative, declarative formula used elsewhere in Orthodoxy ("May *God* forgive you"), to the indicative, imperative one from Latin practice giving more power to the priest ("*I* forgive and absolve you").[19] As an explicit counter to Roman Catholic teaching on confession, Russian priests were told that while such good works as prayer, fasting, and charity were useful penances, in no way could they be considered satisfaction for sins: "By bringing Himself as a sacrifice, Christ fulfilled this forever." Indeed, precisely because Orthodoxy did not recognize the notion of satisfaction (a point that the guide emphasized), truly sorry penitents could be released without any formal penance at all. The Russian clerical guide to confession thus confirms theological thought's traditional contrast between the "therapeutic" Orthodox Christian approach and the legal righting of a wrong characteristic of Scholasticism.[20]

Laypeople had their own devotional texts instructing them in confession. The works of Saint Tikhon of Zadonsk (1724–83, canonized 1861) drew on Pietist and Anglican traditions to introduce new devotional models to Russian Orthodox readers.[21] As in the Roman Catholic world, spiritual biographies, catechisms, edifying correspondence (both real and invented), and written "conversations" (both real and invented), included confession among their subjects. Particularly relevant for the documents discussed in this chapter were the works of Archbishop Dimitrii (Tuptalo) of Rostov, published extensively throughout the first half of the nineteenth century. They included: *Spiritual Medicine for Confused Thoughts* (1826); *A Prayer of Confession to God from a Person Who Has Set Himself on the Path of Salvation* (1827); *General Confession of Sins Spoken before the Priest by the Penitent* (1840); and *On the Confession of Sins and Holy Communion* (1858). Both Natal'ia Fonvizina and Countess Natal'ia Apraksina copied out these meditations on repentance and confession as part of their spiritual discipline—a practice that may have prompted at least one of them to put her own confessions in writing.[22] In short, by the beginning of the nineteenth century, confession in Russia had become a part of established religious practice and the subject of a large theological and devotional literature. Educated lay people would turn it into a literary genre.

The Confessions of Natal'ia Fonvizina

The written confessions of Natal'ia Fonvizina are as extraordinary as their writer. Fonvizina, the wife of the Decembrist Mikhail Fonvizin, chose to leave her children to accompany her unloved husband into Siberian exile in 1825. This heroic action would give her and the other Decembrist wives an aura of secular martyrdom.[23] After her return from Siberia in 1849, Fonvizina undertook to set down a confession that would cover her entire life, from her earliest childhood recollections to the present. She would write several versions of her confession, each more detailed than the last. Fonvizina's confessions contain rich details about early to mid-nineteenth-century religious beliefs, magical practices, and the relation of a well-born woman to Orthodox clerics. Taken together, they are the longest written confessions in nineteenth-century Russia, and perhaps the longest confessions ever written in literary Russian. They provide one of the earliest examples of how people absorbed Russian religious thought and transformed it into life-writing. Nevertheless, despite the hopes of their writer for a broader audience and their brief mention in works on the Decembrists, these rare sources have remained almost entirely unstudied.[24]

What prompted Fonvizina to write her confessions at all? Chiefly the same impulse that others would give later in the nineteenth century: a sin "too shameful" to share with one's local priest. Besides adultery, incest, and a chronic infatuation with men of the cloth, Fonvizina writes of having been plagued all her life by masturbation (which she calls by its Church Slavonic term, *malakia*) from the age of eleven. This activity, which she regards as her greatest sinful passion, is the only one she never mentioned at her spoken confessions. Tellingly, she was able to confess her chronic sin only when she realized that she could write it down on a piece of paper, rather than saying it out loud. She planned to hand over silently the paper with the single word that was her written confession to a confessor she was encountering for the first time in the Kievan Caves Monastery (*Lavra*). However, when the confessor routinely asked her whether she had anything particular weighing down on her soul, the act of having written the sin down proved liberating: rather than giving him the paper, she was finally able to utter the name of the sin she had carried unspoken since childhood, and for the first time in her life gave a full spoken confession.[25]

The matter might have ended there. Because Fonvizina felt herself falling back to her old urges, however, she began to despair of a single absolution as a means of permanent release. It then occurred to her that if she wrote her lifetime confession to her new father confessor, she might at last find spiritual peace.[26] This notion was remarkable, given that a retrospective "life" confession was not a standard exercise for Orthodox laity: it was typically limited to such religious life-changing occasions as priests before ordination, nuns and monks before tonsure, and converts embracing Orthodox Christianity (such as the fiancées of the Russian emperors).[27] On the other hand, the written life confession containing a particularly grievous sin does occur in Orthodox hagiography: A sinful woman brings Saint Basil the Great her written transgressions, but asks him not to read them, and cleanse them through his prayer alone.[28] It also, one might note, had a secular model in the celebrated *Confessions* of Jean-Jacques Rousseau.[29] Thus Fonvizina would have had familiar models from both the lives of the saints and Western letters. Her confessor gave her his blessing to write her confessions to him—and so began her compositions.[30]

A summary of Fonvizina's first five pages suggest something of her confessions' density and intensity. Echoing the emphasis on feeling and Christianity of the heart discussed by Oliver Smith in this volume, she writes that God called her to himself from her earliest years, and that she felt this bond not in the sense of "formal, ritual piety," but as something she felt "from the depths of [her] heart." This is not to say that she thinks the heart can be trusted: her heart was also the source of her "essentially evil, fornicatory [*bludnichei*] nature." This unchaste nature first made itself known when she began using her dolls for masturbation. She describes her chronic sin in ambivalent terms. On the one hand, it turned her from a weak and sickly child into a glowing, healthy one; on the other, it made her independent of men, but also made her long for a pure, higher love. She is careful to emphasize that when this activity began she did not regard it as being particularly important—but, from the perspective of her middle age, using the language of Romans 1:25, she now interprets masturbation to mean that she "worshipped the creature [that is, herself] rather than the Creator."[31]

At thirteen, Fonvizina read Metropolitan Filaret (Drozdov)'s *Extended Catechism*: this text, so central in forming generations of clerics and thinkers, was thus not limited to pupils in Church schools.[32] Upon learning from the *Catechism* that God was invisibly present everywhere, Fonvizina began to fear that he would tell her mother of her secret habit and of her thoughts. She had the novel idea of going to church to early liturgy to commission a *moleben* prayer service for God to forget her. The priest, who did not think he could be hearing her correctly, understood her to mean that she would like a *moleben* to the Savior. Fonvizina then decided to turn the rite to her purpose by inverting the petitions, saying "Lord, *don't* have mercy," instead of the usual "Lord, have mercy" (*Gospodi ne pomilui* instead of *Gospodi pomilui*). Convinced that her "prayer" worked, she became, as she puts it, "a devil," insolent and vexing to one and all. Only when her mother urged her to go to confession and communion during the Dormition fast (her mother, unusually, went to confession and communion during all four fasting periods of the Orthodox Church) did Fonvizina experience a change of heart. For the first time, she saw a dead child her own age laid out in a coffin:

> I looked seriously at my life, recognized myself as being guilty before my parents, begged their forgiveness, confessed my sins at confession (except my usual sin), and for the first time in full conscience communed of the Holy Mysteries. The Lord Himself became known to me—O supreme Love!—I became utterly transfigured—where did all my earthly loves go at the revelation of this all-consuming love—whence did prayer come? It was as if my eyes, my hearing, and my understanding opened—suddenly I began to understand everything they sang and read in church. My love for the Creator of the world first resembled earthly love—I blushed when I mentioned Him or His name—I was jealous of the holy martyrs Catherine and Barbara, weeping inconsolably that I had gray eyes while these holy

virgin brides probably had black eyes, as they were beauties. I somehow understood that He could be the spiritual bridegroom of so many brides and they all love Him and He loves all of them, that He is the light of the world—but all these ideas were kind of stupid and earthly. With this new love the habit of fleshly sin left me[33]—I did not even remember it! I became quiet, meek, thoughtful, and silent, as if I no longer lived on this earth, I forgot all earthly needs, I asked my mother for a Russian Psalter and a Russian Gospel.[34]

This brief selection, typical of the rest of Fonvizina's confessions in its overwrought style and abundance of detail, shares a number of elements with other contemporary sources. The notion of the Savior as Bridegroom recurs in Orthodox liturgy, the life accounts of nuns, and troparia hymns to virgin martyrs. Fonvizina shares the jealousy the *vitae* of the "brides of Christ" attribute to their heavenly bridegroom. Her request for a Psalter and a Gospel in vernacular Russian suggests that she wants access to Holy Writ in easily understandable form and that she knows these texts are available, as indeed they had been since 1819 and 1822, respectively, with the establishment of the Russian Bible Society.[35] She also writes of disguising herself as a boy so that she could run away to a monastery—a trope from the lives of female monastic saints.[36] Perhaps coincidentally, Rousseau's *Confessions* share a similar emphasis on childhood and shameful actions committed in one's youth.[37]

Fonvizina's family became so alarmed by the change in her that they secured Synodal permission for her to marry her uncle. Despite her marriage and the birth of two children, Fonvizina sustained her intense prayer and confessions, to the amazement of her confessor, who expressed naïve surprise that so young a married woman could reach such heights of prayer. At the same time, she began carrying on a passionate illicit correspondence with a young deacon, which the two "blasphemously" passed to one another on notes of names attached to blessed *prosphora* bread. (In an illustration of how such temptations could affect clerics, the deacon began to stumble in saying his petitions whenever she came to church.) Interestingly, the infatuation does not seem to have affected Fonvizina's deliberations on whether to follow her sentenced husband to Siberia, or to stay with her children. Although her family urged her to stay, both her Saint Petersburg confessor and the schemamonk Mikhail of the Trinity-Sergius Monastery (*Lavra*) in Moscow supported her decision to accompany her husband.[38]

In Siberia, she encountered other temptations. God "abandoned her for her pride" in having sacrificed herself for her husband. She began to explore the occult, using magical incantations from a French novel called *The Devil's Notebook*, and swore herself to the Devil.[39] She learned to cast spells from a Siberian girl who had known shamans. She refused to recite the "Our Father," saying, "How can I ask to be delivered from the evil one when it is the evil one that I love?" She describes an affair with Ferdinand Vol'f, a Lutheran convert from Judaism, consoling herself with the thought that it was "less bad to sin with one of the circumcised." She felt so guilty over the affair that she was glad when she miscarried "its fruit," her last child, who was stillborn. Although she continued to read the Old Testament in French, she felt too sinful to read the Gospels.[40]

With a second fleshly sin, Fonvizina's attitude to confession became more complicated. "Like Cain," she evaded confessing those sins: when she went to confession, she assumed disguises, or went to priests who did not know her, or hid behind a kerchief, speaking "like a common woman." On one occasion, when her husband suspected she had something on her mind and thought that confessing would do her good, she went, but lied outright when asked about sins against the fourth commandment. At that communion, she dared not swallow the Gifts.[41]

A turning point came during a Paschal service when Fonvizina swooned at Father Petr, a twenty-five-year-old priest "whose gold vestments were like those of an angel," and decided he might be her salvation. The role of confession in a priest's life, both as confessor and as penitent, here becomes evident. When Fonvizina revealed her previous affair to Father Petr at confession, he became attracted to her (one might note that mutual attraction between priest and penitent was a staple of Protestant anticlerical polemics).[42] Although Father Petr resisted consummating the relationship, hearing her confessions became a temptation for him; on one such occasion, he had to push Fonvizina away, comparing her to the wife of Potiphar who had tempted Joseph, and nearly dropped the chalice at liturgy the next day. To save Father Petr "from her own wiles," Fonvizina attempted suicide by drinking poison, but, together with her husband, he rescued her in the nick of time.

Father Petr finally found a solution for the situation he understood to be spiritually damaging for all concerned: when the Fonvizins moved to Tobol'sk, he gave her his written confession to give to her confessor there. As he explained, he knew he needed to confess his sin of being attracted to her, but he also knew that the local clerical confessor bore him a grudge, and feared that making an honest confession might damage his family.[43] He therefore asked Fonvizina to pass his written confession along to another priest in the new location, and to relay whether he had been absolved.

Two things are important here. First, whether or not she had ever read Rousseau or the Life of Saint Basil the Great, Fonvizina encountered and transmitted a written confession from an Orthodox priest. It is thus not surprising that she might later have adopted this idea. Second, as Father Petr's example shows, Russian Orthodox priests, like their Roman Catholic counterparts, clearly felt the effects of confession as *penitents*, not only administrators of penitence, and indeed feared potentially greater disciplinary consequences than did laypeople.[44] It took Fonvizina a year to find a confessor whom she might trust with the document. After her husband's friend recommended a priest, Fonvizina first evaded him so that she could go to confession to him as an unknown party to report the near-adultery, and only then go to "regular" confession to her parish priest, thus not incriminating herself. The confessor, Father Stefan Znamenskii, told her that he would bear the penance of the other priest, and to relay to Father Petr that he had been absolved; her own penance was to recite the penitential Psalm 50, with twenty-five prostrations. Fonvizina's gratitude at her own absolution took an unexpectedly dark turn:

> A holy, prayerful spirit reached the depths of my breast and turned it into fire like the one hidden by Jeremiah and found after Babylonian captivity ... I no longer sought mercy for myself. I gave myself up to impartial Justice, and rejoiced that the Lord had judged me for my deeds—to be glorified before angels and men! I recalled a prayer from the works of Dimitrii of Rostov: "O Lord, if Thou wouldst have me in light, bless Thee. If Thou wouldst have me be in darkness, bless Thee again. If Thou wouldst destroy me for my transgressions, glory to Thy Righteous Judgment ..." Only such feelings of unselfish love and full turning myself over to God could satisfy my heart—my soul would not accept all the other prayers about forgiveness or mercy.[45]

Later, Fonvizina developed this unsparing understanding of justice, rather than mercy, in more explicitly theological terms: "I reached the conclusion that all of God's qualities are perfect, and none outweighs another. For example, His mercy is not greater, nor more powerful, than His justice. *But all deeds demand satisfaction—this is what the mystery of redemption consists of.* Whereas I, judged even in human terms, cannot be forgiven, but am subject to Hell, because I freely sought out Hell. So I ask only one thing—to preserve my abjection humbly in Hell, and not to murmur. As the Psalm says, if I go down to Hades, Thou are there."[46]

This bleak interpretation of Christian redemption is peculiar to Fonvizina. It ignores the message of Metropolitan Platon's sermons, of Russian pastoral guides to confession, of contemporary Orthodox texts, of the absolutions she received, and for that matter the New Testament itself. Her original interpretation is all the more striking given the wide range of her religious reading, her friendships with Orthodox bishops, and her knowledge of Orthodox liturgy. After all, she read the Bible in different translations. Her confessions are filled with quotations from the Psalms and the Book of Job. She adored the hymns of Passion Week, especially "Behold, the Bridegroom Comes at Midnight," "Thy Bridal Chamber," and, more unusually, the song of the Israelites from the Vespers of Great and Holy Saturday. Archbishop Vladimir (Aliavdin) of Tobol'sk had such esteem for her religious acumen that he had her draw icons for an iconostasis and compose an exegesis of the Lord's Prayer. She befriended Hieromonk Makarii (Glukharev), missionary to Altai and spiritual child of Metropolitan Filaret (Drozdov). Her spiritual confidant, the Decembrist Pavel Bobrishchev-Pushkin, tried to teach her to pray according to the *Philokalia*.[47] Thus, while Fonvizina's confessions suggest that some of the Russian elite in the beginning of the nineteenth century had a greater knowledge of religious texts and Orthodox services, and were more intensely engaged with confession, than may have been suspected, this knowledge did not necessarily inflect their notions of grace.

Fonvizina's confessions also suggest that, unlike the writers of other confessions and examinations of conscience, she was not particularly interested in either education or discipline. Although she addresses her confessions to a priest, they do not reflect any acknowledgment that someone has read them and offered spiritual counsel. Instead, each subsequent version only provides more of her interpretations and more autobiographical detail. Other written confessions show that their writers knew the template of the Orthodox auricular confession, and generally followed it.[48] But, with the exception of classifying her sins by the commandments they violated, Fonvizina mostly ignored the conventions of the spoken confession, using the pretext of confessing her sins to set down different, increasingly elaborate, versions of her entire life story.

Can these texts be trusted? Given that Fonvizina's friends and husband expressed alarm about her instability and attempted suicide, some aspects of her confessions, particularly her supposed affair with Vol'f, need to be treated with caution.[49] But, whatever their veracity, Fonvizina's confessions reveal a great deal about the religious texts used by some nineteenth-century elite Russians, their preoccupation with confession, and their notions of redemption. Fonvizina saw her life, and her written confessions, as ultimately witnessing the kind of mercy shown to holy harlots.[50] As she wrote in one of the last versions of her confession: "I conceal neither my falls nor God's care for my sinful soul, nor yet the Lord's mercies which have poured forth and still pour forth on my sinful soul . . . God is glorious in His saints, but even more so in His sinners."[51] Acknowledging her shame, she nonetheless believes that her confessions testify to her ultimate redemption. In this sense, despite Fonvizina's apparent lack of spiritual instruction, her confessions appear to have "worked."

Unfortunately, although some letters from priests to Fonvizina have survived, none appears to be a response to her confessions.[52] While Fonvizina mentions one letter from Father Petr, it appears to be his plea for *her* spiritual counsel, which she provides and which, she notes with satisfaction, "contained much that was strong and was useful for him."[53] It is not clear who her confessor-correspondent was; she addresses him only as "Father" (*Batiushka*). It is not even clear that she mailed the confessions: all that survive are the copies she kept for herself.

Here we come to the central problem. The written confession, whether that of Natal'ia Fonvizina, the eighteenth-century nun Fedotia, the Slavophile Natal'ia Kireevskaia, or the late nineteenth-century correspondents of the holy Father Ioann (Sergiev) of Kronstadt, is a supremely private autobiographical narrative.[54] Of all the writers of confessions, Fonvizina was the only one to express hope that her texts might be published. But, consciously or unconsciously, most scholars encountering written confessions have maintained a respectful confessional "seal." And thus the pattern of only one surviving side is typical for the written confession. Moreover, partly because of the tradition that a confession ought to remain secret, and partly because the spiritual father was usually better known than his spiritual child, it is far more characteristic for the responses to written confessions to survive, than the written confessions themselves.[55] The comments of the celebrated Bishop Feofan (the Recluse) on the confessions of his many spiritual children, for example, fill volumes, while their names are usually given only with a discreet initial.[56]

This might seem to bring us to Carolyn Heilbrun's argument that women's lives and the stories of those lives have been steeped in the language and power of men—or, in this case, that women's confessional texts were literally displaced by those of their confessors.[57] But, as Jodi Bilinkoff has noted in her study of texts produced by and about holy Roman Catholic women and their confessors, confessional exchanges were more nuanced.[58] In this context it is instructive to note that Fonvizina compared herself to Saint Mary of Egypt, whose *Life* was prescribed reading at the regularly attended Matins service in the fifth week of Great Lent. This allusion is an apt model both for Fonvizina's own confessions and for the problems of authorial voice. After all, although Saint Mary's *vita* was written by someone else, it claims to contain her life confession, narrated directly by her, and contains graphic accounts of her sexual addiction from the age of twelve. The hero is the vivid Mary herself; a distant second her confessor and admirer, Abba Zosima (to whom Providence introduces Mary precisely to teach him a lesson about thinking he has attained spiritual heights because of his life of unblemished ascetic virtue); and the narrator, named only as Saint Sophronius, is mentioned only at the end.[59] Natalia Fonvizina, by contrast, is both the author and the subject of her life confession; though her confessor, too, serves largely to provide communion and listening rather than counsel.

Another warning against reading confessional texts only in terms of power and authorship, and perhaps the best pendant to Fonvizina's confessions, is the lengthy correspondence, lasting from 1822 to 1849, of the widowed Ekaterina V. Novosil'tseva, née Countess Orlova, with her spiritual director, Metropolitan Filaret of Moscow.[60] Like Fonvizina, Novosil'tseva would confess to different priests in person. Unlike Fonvizina, however, Novosil'tseva was not tormented by sins she deemed too shameful to confess. She was thus secure enough to seek out both education and discipline from one of the most celebrated hierarchs of imperial Russia. Indeed, she began the correspondence largely to better prepare for spoken sacramental confession. Filaret obliged, often advising her on her sacramental confessions, which she would analyze and describe in detail before and after they took place. On some occasions, he absolved her in writing.[61] Thus, despite the injunction to maintain confessional secrecy, if penitents wished additional guidance, they felt free to share what they had confessed to someone else.

The Filaret-Novosil'tseva correspondence shows how fruitful such an exchange could be. On the face of it, it seems to reproduce the pattern typical of many others. Only his side of the correspondence remained in the family archive and only it was published many decades later. Novosil'tseva's voice thus appears to be silent. But, quite apart from Novosil'tseva's spiritual growth, these responses show what a confessor could learn from his spiritual child. And it could be a great deal. As with the correspondence between Natal'ia Kireevskaia and her father confessor, shared reading figures prominently. Filaret asks Novosil'tseva to tell him the title of the daily meditations of Saint François de Sales published by the Synod; he expresses curiosity in *Voltaire as a Christian*, a book she has recommended; he advises her on how to translate Patristic texts; he approves her ideas about newly baptized converts to Orthodox Christianity; he comments on her opinions about Capodistrias and the Greek revolution (but when she asks Filaret his opinion on Rousseau, he warns her against him).[62] The Filaret-Novosil'tseva correspondence suggests that, for a learned hierarch or archimandrite, letters to an educated spiritual "daughter" on improving her sacramental confession were not a matter of one-sided, top-down direction. Instead, they provided a private space where bishops could explore some intellectual interests, learn what their audience was reading, and write with an informality and candor that is less evident in their public writing, their homilies, and their exegeses of Scripture.[63] Archbishops Tikhon (Zadonskii) and Platon (Fiveiskii) both thought that priests should draw on what they learned at confession to compose their homilies and sermons: Metropolitan Filaret (Drozdov) seems to have applied this principle.[64] His emphasis on having such essential texts as the Bible and the Extended Catechism available in vernacular Russian comes partly from his conviction that his flock needed them for growth in their spiritual lives.[65]

Conclusion

The first half of the nineteenth century in imperial Russia saw a mutually affirming and mutually reproducing phenomenon. Educated women and the clerics to whom they confessed read many of the same mystical and devotional texts on repentance, collaborated on the publication or translation of those texts, and formed their confessions based on those texts. Priests and laypeople alike could turn to written confession when they felt the subject matter was too shaming to be spoken. Sometimes, as with Natal'ia Fonvizina and Iosif Vielogorskii, the act of writing could be more important than receiving absolution. In other cases, as with Ekaterina Novosil'tseva, an initial wish to confess better in spoken form could turn into a lifelong correspondence, sometimes accompanied by absolution, and sometimes not. Confessors took seriously their obligation "to bind and to loose." They shared their spiritual children's belief that confession was a time to tell the truth. In written confessions, however, the relationship was one of two parties who were embarked on a shared quest—that of the pursuit of salvation and growth in the spiritual life—rather than that of superior to subordinate. Particularly striking in the letters of the spiritual fathers to their charges is the sense that they welcomed this collaborative aspect of their religious life, and that, in their letters, they could maintain the devotional life that first drew them to the clerical life. A father-confessor might even seek counsel from his penitent. The written confession and the response to it became a key part of the spiritual autobiography and biography of both parties.[66] Written confession continued to develop in parallel with other trends in Russian Orthodoxy and Russian secular culture. Dostoyevsky, Tolstoy, and Chekhov introduced representations of confession to Russian literature. In the late nineteenth century, as Russian society became ever more literate, the practice of the written confession became more widespread and more representative of varied class backgrounds.[67] In the Soviet period, with the closing of churches and monasteries and the limits on public religious practice, written confessions became a greater part of the private piety of those who remained religious.[68] In the twenty-first century, the sacrament of confession, and written confessions, are more central to Russian Orthodox practice than ever.[69] Future studies may show that, like their mid-nineteenth-century predecessors, they both reflect and influence Russian religious thought.

NOTES

1. See Laurie Manchester, *Holy Fathers, Secular Sons: Clergy, Intelligentsia, and the Modern Self in Revolutionary Russia* (DeKalb: Northern Illinois Press, 2008), 14–15, 24–28.

2. Gregory L. Freeze, *The Russian Levites: Parish Clergy in the Eighteenth Century* (Cambridge, MA: Harvard University Press, 1977).

3. For a discussion of conversion motives, see *The Memoirs of Countess Golovine: A Lady at the Court of Catherine II* (London: D. Nutt, 1910); Sophie Swetchine, *Madame Swetchine: Journal de sa conversion, méditations, et prières* (Paris: A. Vaton, 1863). For a survey of Russian attitudes to Catholicism, see Olga Tsapina, "'Us and Them': The Image of Catholicism in 18th-Century Russia," in *Culture and Identity in Eastern Christian History*, ed. Russell E. Martin and Jennifer B. Spock, Ohio Slavic Papers 9/Eastern Christian Studies 1 (Columbus: Ohio State University, 2009), 343–73.

4. Iosif Vielogorskii, "Bednyi Iosif: Dnevnik. Pis'ma," *Nashe nasledie* 46 (1998): 38–55.

5. See, for example, the 1775 confessions of the nun Fedotia to Archimandrite Aleksandr of Eniseisk, in Rossiiskii gosudarstvennyi arkhiv drevnikh aktov (RGADA), f. 7 (Preobrazhenskii Prikaz), op. 1, d. 2400a, ll. 1–130b.

6. Alphonse Michel, "Confessions et absolutions données par écrit," *Revue d'histoire et de litterature religieuses* 7, no. 1 (March 1921): 58–72.

7. S. V. Bulgakov, *Nastol'naia kniga dlia sviashchenno-tserkovno-sluzhitelei* (Kiev: Tip. Kievo-Pecherskoi Lavry, 1913), 1102–3.

8. *Polnoe sobranie zakonov Rossiiskoi imperii s 1649 goda* (St. Petersburg: Pechatno v Tipografii II Otdeleniia Sobstvennoi Ego Imperatorskogo Velichestva Kantseliarii, 1830), 1:312, pt. 15: 367. In Russian Orthodox practice, children partook of communion from the time they were baptized in infancy. From the age of seven, confession before communion became obligatory.

9. Peter Brooks, *Troubling Confessions: Speaking Guilt in Law and Literature* (Chicago: University of Chicago Press, 2000), 92.

10. See Viktor Zhivov, "Pokaiannaia distsiplina i individual'noe blagochestie v istorii russkogo pravoslaviia," in *Druzhba: Ee formy, ispytaniia, i dary* (Kiev: Dukh i litera, 2008), 303-43.

11. For a descriptive account contemporary with the texts discussed here, see V. I. Dolitskii, "Ob ispovedi," *Khristianskoe chtenie* 10 (1843): 89-93. For hierarchs' acknowledgment of the shared, cyclical aspect of *govenie*, see Feofan (Vyshenskii), *O pokaianii, ispovedi, prichashchenii sviatykh Khristovykh tain i ispravlenii zhizni: Slova preosviashchennago Feofana vo sviatuiu chetyredesiatnitsu i prigotovitelnyia k nei nedieli*, 5th ed. (Moscow: Izd. Afonskago Russkago Panteleimonova monastyria, 1896), 265.

12. Annemarie Kidder, *Making Confession, Hearing Confession: A History of the Cure of Souls* (Collegeville, MN: Liturgical Press, 2010), 169.

13. Jean Delumeau notes that Roman Catholics similarly preferred to confess their worst sins to a priest who did not know them. See Delumeau, *Le péché et la peur: La culpabilisation en Occident, 13e-18e siècles* (Paris: Fayard, 1983).

14. *The Lenten Triodion*, trans. Mother Mary and Kallistos, bishop of Diokleia (London: Faber and Faber, 1978).

15. Platon (Levshin), *Polnoe Sobraniie Sochinenii* (St. Petersburg: Izd. P. Soikina, n.d.), 138, 147, 200-203, 514-17; Vasilii Bazhanov, *Pouchitel'nyia slova i rechi protoiereia Vasiliia Bazhanova*, 2nd ed. (St. Petersburg: V voennoi tip., 1837), 80-115, 237-50.

16. See M. V. Korogodina, *Ispoved' v Rossii v XIV-XIX vekakh: Issledovanie i teksty* (St. Petersburg: D. Bulanin, 2006), 335-551.

17. The 1776 edition, attributed to Archbishop Georgii (Konisskii) of Mogilev and Bishop Parfenii (Sopkovskii) of Smolensk, may be consulted online at http://www.stsl.ru/manuscripts/staropechatnye-knigi/255?fnum=5. A recent reprint edition is *O dolzhnostiakh presviterov prikhodskikh* (Moscow: Izd. Sretenskogo monastyria, 2004).

18. *O dolzhnostiakh*, 47-48.

19. For the new wording, which became standard in Russian prayer books published from Patriarch Nikon onward, see *Evkhologion ili Trebnik* (Kiev: Great Lavra, 1646; repr. Kyiv: Informatsiino-vydavnychyi tsentr Ukrains'koi Pravoslavnoi Tserkvi, 2004), 1:387. For a modern condemnation of it, see Georges Florovsky, *Puti russkogo bogosloviia* (Paris, 1937), 49. In Roman Catholic practice, theologians' definitions of what precisely brought about the penitent's reconciliation shifted in the thirteenth century from pure contrition to assigning an efficacious role to absolution. See Bernhard Poschmann, *Penance and the Anointing of the Sick* (Freiburg: Herder, 1964), 157-93.

20. For a survey of this argument, see Alfons Brüning, "Peter Mohyla's Orthodox and Byzantine Heritage: Religion and Politics in the Kievan Church Reconsidered," in *Von Moskau nach St. Petersburg: Das russische Reich im 17. Jahrhundert* (Berlin: Osteuropas Institut, 2000), 63-90.

21. For example, Tikhon's essay on repentance emphasized the sentiments that should accompany it, barely mentioning the sacrament of confession as such. 'O pokaianii,' in his *Sochineniia* (St. Petersburg: Tip. Ivana Glazunova, 1826), 4:3-58. See also Andrey V. Ivanov, "The Saint of Russian Reformation: Tikhon of Zadonsk and Protestant Influences in the 18th-Century Russian Orthodox Church," in *Religion and Identity in Russia and the Soviet Union: A Festschrift for Paul Bushkovitch*, ed. Nikolaos A. Chrissidis et al. (Bloomington, IN: Slavica, 2011), 81-106.

22. For Apraksina's handwritten devotional texts, see RGADA, f. 18, op. 1, d. 975, ll. 1-360b.

23. The poet Nikolai Nekrasov would help canonize the Decembrist wives' image in his poem, *Russkie zhenshchiny* (Moscow: Gos. Izdat. Detskoi lit-ry, 1946).

24. I am grateful to Anna Biel for introducing me to Fonvizina's confessions, and to Marina Sidorova of Gosudarstvennyi arkhiv rossiiskoi federatsii (GARF) for making them available on short notice. GARF, f. 279 (Diary and Confessions of Natal'ia Fonvizina), op. 1, d. 303 (henceforth Fonvizina). For a discussion of Fonvizina's text in the context of Decembrist wives' memoirs, see Anna Biel, "Sacrifice in the Name of Sacred Duty: The Representations of the Decembrist Wives in Russian Culture, 1825–Present" (PhD diss., State University of New York at Albany, 2011), 333–68.

25. Fonvizina, l. 143.

26. Fonvizina, l. 93, 147–48.

27. Metropolitan Antonii (Khrapovitskii), "Priniatie sviashchenstva" (*Strannik*, April–May 1896), in *Uchenie o pastyrie, pastyrstvie, i ob ispovedi* (New York: Izd. Severo-Amerikanskoi i Kanadskoi eparkhii, 1966), 99–101.

28. *Zhitiia sviatykh, na russkom iazykie izlozhennyia po rukovodstvu Chet'ikh-Minei sv. Dimitriia Rostovskago* (Moscow: Sinodal'naia tip., 1904), 5:1:19–50.

29. Jean-Jacques Rousseau, *Confessions*, http://www.gutenberg.org/files/3913/3913-h/3913-h.htm. I am grateful to Marina Soroka for this suggestion.

30. Fonvizina, l. 17.

31. Fonvizina, ll. 18–20.

32. Filaret (Drozdov), *Prostrannyi khristianskii katikhizis pravoslavnoi kafolicheskoi vostochnoi tserkvi* (Berlin: Izd. V. Siial'skii i A. Kreishman, 1845); http://krotov.info/library/05_d/ro/zdov_01.htm.

33. Fonvizina later added: "but not for long," l. 22.

34. Fonvizina, ll. 21–22.

35. See Stephen K. Batalden, *Russian Bible Wars: Modern Scriptural Translation and Spiritual Authority* (New York: Cambridge University Press, 2013).

36. See the Lives of Saint Mary/Marinos and Saint Matrona of Perge, in Alice-Mary Talbot, ed., *Holy Women of Byzantium: Ten Saints' Lives in English Translation* (Washington, DC: Dumbarton Oaks, 1996), 1–64.

37. Rousseau, *Confessions*, books 1–2.

38. Fonvizina, ll. 23–25.

39. The Devil figured more prominently in French literature of the first half of the nineteenth century than any other character. Max Milner, *Le Diable dans la littérature française de Cazotte à Baudelaire, 1772–1861* (Paris: Corti, 1960), 2:484.

40. Fonvizina, ll. 69, 88.

41. Ibid., ll. 32, 54.

42. Stephen Haliczer, *Sexuality in the Confessional: A Sacrament Profaned* (New York: Oxford University Press, 1996), 184–203.

43. Although confessions were meant to be secret, one never knew for sure. The headmaster of the future bishop Ignatii Brianchianov, for example, called him in for questioning when his confessor understood his 'spiritual turmoil' to refer to sedition. See "Episkop Ignatii Brianchianinov," in *Zhizneopisaniia otechestvennykh podvizhnikov blagochestiia 18 i 19 vekov* (Moscow: Tipo-lit. I. Efimova, 1908), 310–15.

44. For confession-related disciplinary measures applied to priests, see National Archive of Tatarstan (NART), f. 4 (Religious Consistory of Kazan'), d. 5096 (On the

absence of priests at confession, 1851–53), ll. 1–38. For this argument in the Roman Catholic context, see Philippe Boutry, *Prêtres et paroisses au pays du curé d'Ars* (Paris: Les Éditions du Cerf, 1986), 441–51; Thomas N. Tentler, *Sin and Confession on the Eve of the Reformation* (Princeton, NJ: Princeton University Press, 1977), xx.

45. Fonvizina, ll. 24–320b., 156.

46. Ibid., ll. 88–89. The reference is to Psalm 139:8.

47. Ibid., ll. 40, 57, 320b., 93, 112, 380b., 52, 1240b., 154, 99–101, 73.

48. See the written confessions to Father Ioann (Sergiev) in Tsentral'nyi gosudarstvennyi istoricheskii arkhiv (TsGIA), f. 2219, op. 1, d. 31.

49. See Biel, "Sacrifice," 351–56.

50. Fonvizina, ll. 38, 52–53.

51. Ibid., ll. 91.

52. For letters from Archpriest Petr Filitsyn, see Otdel rukopisei, Rossiikaia gosudarstvennaia biblioteka (OR RGB), f. 319 (the Fonvizins), kn. 4, 1840–54, d. 1.

53. Fonvizina, l. 92.

54. Natal'ia Kireevskaia, the wife of the celebrated Slavophile Ivan Kireevskii, took part in translating and publishing the classic *Philokalia* text that Bobrishchev-Pushkin had urged Fonvizina to read. Her confession to her spiritual elder, Makarii of the Optina Hermitage (*Pustyn'*), was published in Sergii Chetverikov, *Optina Pustyn': Istoricheskii ocherk i lichnyia vospominaniia* (Paris: YMCA Press, 1926), 149–50.

55. See Irina Paert, *Spiritual Elders: Charisma and Tradition in Russian Orthodoxy* (DeKalb: Northern Illinois University Press, 2010), 71–102.

56. See, for example, *Sobranie pisem sviatitelia Feofana* (Moscow: Tip. I. Efimova, 1899), 5:122.

57. Carolyn Heilbrun, *Writing a Woman's Life* (New York: Ballantine Books, 1988), 11–12.

58. Jodi Bilinkoff, *Related Lives: Confessors and Their Female Penitents, 1450–1750* (Ithaca, NY: Cornell University Press, 2005), 1–31.

59. "The Life of St. Mary of Egypt," in Talbot, *Holy Women of Byzantium*, 65–97.

60. Filaret (Drozdov), *Pis'ma vysokopreosviashchennago Filareta Moskovskago k Ekaterine Vladimirovne Novosil'tsevoi* (Moscow: Russkaia Pechatnia, 1911).

61. Filaret, *Pis'ma*, 49, 115, 125. For his analysis of a bad confession on her part, see the letter of August 1822, 6–7.

62. Ibid., 10, 44, 83, 133, 137, 190. The editor adds that de Sales's *Introduction à la vie devoté* was particularly well known in Russia.

63. T. B. Vergun, "Svt. Filaret v opyte kratkogo analiza dukhovnoi situatsii v Rossii pervoi chetverti XIX v.," in *Pervye Dmitrievskie Chteniia* (St. Petersburg: RTP, 1997), 27–37.

64. Tikhon (Zadonskii), "Pribavleniie k dolzhnosti sviashchennicheskoi o taine sv. Pokaianiia," in *Sochineniia* (St. Peterburg: Tipografii Ivana Glazunova, 1825–26); Platon (Fiveiskii), *Napominanie sviashchenniku ob obiazannostiakh ego pri sovershenii tainstva pokaianiia* (Kostroma, 1859; Moscow, 1861 and 1895; repr., St. Petersburg: Voskresenie, 2004), 56–65.

65. See "O dogmaticheskom dostoinstve i okhranitel'nom upotreblenii grecheskogo 70 tolkovnikov v slavianskikh perevodov sviashchennogo pisaniia," *Pribavleniia k tvoreniiam sviatykh ottsov v russkom perevode* 17 (1858): 452–84.

66. Bilinkoff, *Related Lives*, 1–31.

67. Nadieszda Kizenko, "Written Confessions and the Construction of Sacred Narrative," in *Sacred Stories: Religion and Spirituality in Modern Russia*, ed. Mark Steinberg and Heather J. Coleman (Bloomington: Indiana University Press, 2007), 93–118.

68. Aleksei Beglov, "Asketicheskaia pis'mennost' epokhi gonenii kak sistema marginalii," *Al'fa i Omega* 1, no. 54 (2009): 121–25.

69. Maksim Kozlov, *Klir i mir: Kniga o zhizni sovremennogo prikhoda* (Moscow: Khram Sviatoi Muchenitsy Tatiany pri MGU, 2008), 123.

Chapter 8

Anagogical Exegesis

The Theological Roots of Russian Hermeneutics

OLIVER SMITH

This chapter examines the conceptual and emotional apparatus with which Russians approached the reading of texts during an era in which a secular literary culture began to challenge the dominance of religiously enculturated interpretative paradigms. It looks, firstly, at the interpretation of Holy Scripture in the school of Metropolitan Platon (Levshin, 1737–1812) and, secondly, at the nineteenth century's most celebrated literary critic, Vissarion Belinskii (1811–48), concentrating particularly on his interpretation of the nascent "secular scriptures" of poet Alexander Pushkin. While not seeking to underplay the profound changes that took place in the critical writing of this period, particularly with regard to stylistics and philosophical content, its goal is to identify a common hermeneutic that passed from the Russian religious academies to "secular" literary criticism (wherein lay the first seeds of Russian philosophy) and thence to inform a great deal of what it meant to "do philosophy" in a Russian key.

ANAGOGY AND METROPOLITAN PLATON

Anagogy (from the Greek *anagein*, "to lift up"), alongside allegory and tropology, is one of the three spiritual meanings of Scripture that supplement its literal, or historical, meaning as propounded by John Cassian, who inherited the term from the Chaldean Oracles and Neoplatonic thinkers such as Iamblichus.[1] In Cassian's handling, allegory functions as an interpretation of the Old Testament under the lens of the New, reading prefigurations of Christ, the Church and its sacramental life into earlier salvation history, while tropology expounds a certain moral meaning of practical relevance to the individual Christian. Anagogy differs from these two in that it "climbs up from spiritual mysteries to the higher and more august secrets of heaven."[2] The philosopher Gustav Shpet later classified the anagogical meaning as that "suprameaning" that attains to an understanding of reality as it appears "in the context of eternal or divine truth."[3]

In Russia, anagogy as a means of interpreting Scripture was first expounded by Dimitrii (Tuptalo) of Rostov (1651–1709) in his *Inquiry into the Sectarian Faith of Brynsk* (*Rozysk o raskol'nicheskoi Brynskoi vere*, 1709; first edition published in 1745). Dimitrii's work demonstrates, contrary to the widespread opinion that the late seventeenth-century schism between Old Believers and Orthodox in Russia was to the detriment of theology and biblical studies,[4] that it forced the more enlightened among the Orthodox to reconsider their own tradition, often leading to the reclamation of ancient hermeneutic paradigms that might have otherwise remained dormant. Dimitrii follows Cassian and medieval exegetes in dividing the meanings of Scripture into "written" (literal) and "spiritual," as well as in associating the three spiritual meanings with the three theological virtues of faith, love, and hope. The term "anagogy" itself, he writes, is difficult to translate into Russian, although were he to do so he suggests the parse "highest reason" (*vyshnii razum*), which "signifies something belonging to the life eternal, which we anticipate, or the Church, triumphant in the heavenly places, to which we hope to come."[5]

Anagogy, then, to collate these rather vague attempts at a definition, is concerned with a path of ascent from the earthly to the heavenly plane that is effected through the practice of a higher form of reason. As such, it informed not only the reading of Scripture. It was the central principle of Byzantine art, as well as the ancient Russian art forms that drew on it, which sought to realize the "gradual ascent from the depiction of the external aspect of things to their archetype, to the spiritual, divine essence invisible to the eye alone."[6] It is important to stress the *gradual* nature of the ascent. While anagogy took the believer into a realm inaccessible to the empirical gaze, it did so not through ecstatic transferal but through a prolonged and, at least in part, conscious interaction with the external form acting as the gateway to this realm. The central component of Orthodox worship, the icon itself, is the anagogical medium par excellence, lifting the soul with whom it comes into communication away from the mundane toward a higher, spiritual reality in the context of the gradual progression of the liturgy or private life of prayer.

Besides the obvious resonance of anagogy with the liturgical life of Orthodoxy, its eventual emergence as a religio-philosophical principle in Russia owed much to the influence of Pseudo-Dionysius the Areopagite. From the first Slavonic translations of the *Corpus Areopagaticum* in the fifteenth century to their official recognition by the Russian Church through inclusion in Metropolitan Macarius's *The Great Menologion* (*Velikie Chet'i-Minei*) in the sixteenth and beyond,[7] the influence of Dionysius on both Russian Orthodox and non-Orthodox thought was immense. The impact of his corpus, characterized by one critic as "the first text in the history of ancient Russian thought that one may without exaggeration describe as 'philosophical,'"[8] can readily be discerned in the early attempts of Russian theologians to express their faith in philosophical terms.[9]

Dionysius had written in his *Celestial Hierarchy* of both word and image as facilitators of an ascent to the divine sphere. Theology, he argued, often employed a form of "poetic symbolism" as a "means of ascent fitting and natural to [human intelligence] by framing the sacred Scriptures in a manner designed for our upliftment."[10] Sacred imagery itself, meanwhile, may in the Areopagite's view have an even more direct effect by stimulating the mind, which would otherwise find no foothold in the "discordant and diverse symbols" of the celestial natures, to "leave behind all material attachments, and training it by means of that which is apparent to aspire to the supramundane ascent."[11] What has been called Dionysius's "anagogical process of interpretation"[12] found its continuation on Russian soil in the shape of Metropolitan Platon, in whom, as philosopher Petr Kalitin has argued, "anagogy acquired a metaphysical significance."[13] The incorporation of the anagogical method within Platon's metaphysics is best approached through Henri de Lubac, the preeminent scholar of early Christian exegesis in modern times, who proposes the following definition: "Anagogy realizes the perfection both of allegory and of tropology, achieving their synthesis. It is neither 'objective' like the first, nor 'subjective' like the second. Above and beyond this division, it realizes their unity. It integrates the whole and final meaning. It sees, in eternity, the fusion of the mystery and the mystic. In other words, the eschatological reality attained by anagogy is the eternal reality within which every other has its consummation."[14]

Anagogy, according to de Lubac, is not so much the "highest spiritual" sense in opposition to other senses; rather, it is that sense in which all others receive their final meaning, realizing that unity of earthly and heavenly, individual and cosmic, that is the mark of God's kingdom. The model here is one of incorporation of levels of meaning rather than sublation in the manner of the Hegelian

Aufhebung, which suggests transcendence, rather than integration. The mysteries of allegory, writes de Lubac, "leave the heart unchanged," while tropology "appropriates," interiorizes them for us.[15] The essence of anagogy is that it removes this disjunction between the individual, "subjective" interiorization of the mystery of faith and its external, "objective" existence in the historical life of the Church in the form of dogma and ritual. In anagogy, that which is received *is* that which is experienced; the objective and subjective components coincide.

Such a conjunction of objective and subjective (de Lubac's "fusion of the mystery and the mystic") permeates Platon's sermons. For Platon, God was known in two ways: through natural means and through revelation. Yet the question of the appropriate relationship between these two, and the preservation of an adequate distinction between revealed and natural theology, which had so exercised medieval theologians such as Aquinas,[16] concerned Platon not in the least. Natural theology for him was not, as it has been primarily understood in the Western tradition, the investigation of religious truths using human reason and its faculties of logic alone.[17] The natural knowledge of God, for Platon the *prius* of all theological reflection (including the interpretation of revelation), was instead accessible through the turning inward of the person. In a Church that had, within the living memory of some, been rocked by division over the external observances of the Orthodox faith, he attempted to redirect the attention of his listeners away from what he saw as an excessive concern with externalities toward a Christianity of the heart guided by the prerogatives of inner life. Here, again, the impetus given Russian theology by the schism is easy to discern. "Piety is not sewn into one's dress, just as the inner virtue of the soul does not hang from the hair," Platon wrote in his *Admonition to the Schismatics* (*Uveshchanie k raskol'nikam*).[18]

In knowing oneself, and especially one's own heart through prayer, God reveals himself as the one who has made residence in that heart through the cross of Christ. This is what Platon called the experience of the "inner cross," which, as Paul has it, "is foolishness to those who are perishing" (1 Corinthians 1:18). Only in understanding the cross in its "dual" (*dvoiakii*) aspect—inner and external—can the Christian task of anagogy, the conformation of subjective reality with the objective truth of Scripture, be engaged. The "wise" of this world, precisely because they are directed toward the world, have knowledge only of the external cross and, in their inability to perceive its inner dimension, fail to recognize its true nature. "These wise men, not attaining that inner hiddenness, consider the cross of Christ as folly, and laugh to their demise. But we faithful, entering through the inner curtain, discern in this cross the great wisdom of God, as well as God's salvific power."[19]

Platon's metaphorical use of the passage referring to an inner partition, which echoes the entry through the curtains of the Holy of Holies in the Jewish Temple, sets up a fundamental consonance between the Word of God in Scripture and the self-witness of the human heart, which makes known its "innate desire for sovereign Good, or absolute bliss." The law of God is to be found, therefore, first of all "in my conscience, and from there one can also find it in the Ten Commandments of the Lord."[20]

The revealed law of God thus concurs with the empirical, or natural, self-witnessing of the human heart, into whose most interior dimension the catechesis is meant to lead. Salvation history, with its central point as the cross, is in this understanding not the rote learning, or even recitation, remembrance, or glorification of the saving acts of God, but the inner experience of the same through the inner adoption had through faith, defined as the "reception of the Gospel in the heart," and prayer, defined as "the ascension of our thought and heart to God."[21] The historical search for the God of Israel, with its culmination in the Incarnation, is recapitulated in the opening of the heart to its own present, and eventual, citizenship in heaven. This process, which involves the heart not in a metaphorical but a direct sense, is the core of the anagogical method: the bringing into correlation of the mystic and mystery—the subjective strivings of the exegete and the objective revelation of Scripture—through ascent to God.

Ascent through Feeling

Platon's school would later become known by two descriptors, the "school of the learned monks" and "school of believing reason,"[22] yet to judge from his sermons Platon himself seems to have modified his conviction in the autonomy of reason he inherited from the Western Enlightenment only later in life. Indeed, Platon's own intellectual and religious development in many ways mirrors the remarkable changes witnessed during the last quarter of the eighteenth century in Russia, when a system of theological instruction largely derived from German theologies was reconceived, adapted, and reforged into something more consonant with the Orthodox theological heritage. In 1785, for example, Platon had argued that "the more enlightened thinking becomes, and the more solidly reason operates, the less are one's concepts of good and evil prone to err. If one here follows the senses, this is tantamount to throwing enlightened thinking into confusion, or diverting reason from its authentic path."[23]

This simplistic, binary opposition of sense perception as necessarily something base, to reason as something elevated, begins to fade from his published works in the 1790s. Far from a negative category, sensory perception later becomes for Platon the vehicle that brings the reason of the mind to the heart through anagogical ascent, an ascent that draws its emphasis from the example of Byzantine liturgical aesthetics:[24] "the feelings themselves, being struck by the majesty of the Church, elevate thought to an excellent conception of the majesty of God, and captivate the heart with fear and love toward Him."[25] The terminus of this movement he describes in a sermon of 1800, when he rejects both a purely conceptual path to truth as well as a conceptual understanding of its goal. Here he puts in first place "spiritual feelings," which "have their own eyes to discern truth from falsehood."[26] Such "spiritual feeling" he associated with a "higher reason," accessible through the heart, echoing Dimitrii's earlier description of the anagogical path to truth. "The goodly Christian who has reached such a high level where he can discern truth from falsehood and good from evil, then ascends to the highest level of reason and knowledge of the glory of God [which] consists in the fact that it is acquired not through thinking and the concept alone, but that we begin to feel it in our hearts also."[27]

It may be of some relevance that Platon's move away from a naïve belief in Enlightenment reason, so typical of the intellectual climate under Catherine the Great's "enlightened" absolutism, coincided with the years in which his pupil, Iakov Nikol'skii, worked on the Slavonic translation of the *Philokalia*. There is little proof, however, to suggest that the metropolitan was considerably influenced by the work. Even in his later years, the theologians Platon returns to time and again are Gregory of Nazianzus, Basil the Great, and John Chrysostom, rather than those who stand at the wellspring of Hesychasm.

In a number of later sermons from 1805-6, Platon expounds on his understanding of anagogical ascent. It should not, he argues, be compared to an elevation through the celestial hierarchies (as in Dionysius) but should rather be seen as "ascent within one's own heart."[28] Such a path, Platon stresses, is not an *ascension* (*voznesenie*; as that of Christ) nor an *elevation* (*vozvyshenie*, as in the kings of the Bible), but precisely a long and gradual *ascent* (*voskhozhdenie*) that occurs "little by little, in stages."[29] While the arena for this movement is the heart, and the end result similar to the kind of prayer described in the *Philokalia*, there is little resonance with the central operation described in the latter—the descent of the mind into the heart[30]—which is realized by a prior withdrawal from the world of sensory perception.[31] Nor is there a sense, as in Dionysius, of such a gradual ascent enabling a "return" to the simplicity of the Godhead.[32]

In Platon, to the contrary, there is no *ekstasis*, no detachment of the intellect from the lower powers to dwell in the intoxicating rapture of pure spirit. Platon does not acknowledge the possibility of a transferal from human to angelic being in this life, as does, say, Evagrius,[33] and argues for the central and enduring significance of the liturgy to "arouse our spirit and, striking at our feelings call our inner being to life. We are not angels. Our spirit cannot act on its own if the corporeal feelings are in no way moved." The mind and intellect, according to Platon, are only set in motion by the external stimuli of the phenomenal world: "what imprints itself on the mind the more strongly is usually that which first strikes against our feelings." The ramifications of this are that the corporeal aspects of human being are not so much instrumentalized, to be discarded when their purpose has been fulfilled, as *incorporated* within the structural dynamics of ascent. "The union of the soul with the body," wrote Platon, "demands that the inner movements of the soul disclose themselves in the external actions of the body."[34]

Platon, then, spoke of a process that involved the whole person, body and soul, in a movement toward the spirit contained within the heart, which involved the joint efforts of sensual perception and thought. Such ascent has as its goal not the transcendence of the limited and sinful self but its constantly renewing integration within God's kingdom. This is so precisely because the ascent leads toward the infinite, there can be no finite resolution. Speaking of the distinctions in spiritual experience and knowledge described by Paul in Colossians 2:8 (the "elemental spiritual forces" and the spirit of Christ), Platon claims that "even in the spirit itself there should be ascent. From what to what? From spirit to spirit." Should even the humility of Christ's spirit be attained, however, there is still further to ascend: to a perpetual dwelling in the imperative that Christ addresses to each individual: "repent." In the lived experience of the Christian, repentance is thus both the first and last word. Or, in the words of Platon, it is both "the height" toward which we are aiming and "the first step in our elevation from baseness."[35]

The immutability of human sin means that there is no rung in the spiritual ladder whereby we may declare it powerless against us; possessed of sensual souls and bodies, there always remains a door open to sin. Yet, through the transformation of the human body into an instrument of anagogical ascent, rising to God *through* rather than *against* sensuality by the practice of perpetual repentance, the human person *is* deified, not in some imagined terminus but in the very dynamic of ascent itself. In such a way, Platon presents the ever-moving, uncertain path of anagogy over and above any statically conceived destination as the essential core of adoption to God through faith.[36]

Scripture as the Gate of Ascent

For Platon, Scripture itself mirrored the twofold conception of the human being as embodied soul, or ensouled body, discussed in the previous section. "Holy Scripture," he wrote, echoing the teaching on the literal and spiritual meanings of the Bible, "is like a human being, which consists of body and soul: the body is the visible and the soul the invisible, and most noble, part." For him, the goal of all Christian life is "to ascend into a knowledge and a feeling [*vozchuvstvie*] of oneself," and he writes in many places of the significance of church architecture, iconography, liturgy, and prayer as enablers of such ascent. By far the greatest attention, however, he ascribes to the Scriptures. "The mother in her womb conceives a child, while the diligent student conceives in his heart the word. And whosoever conceives the word of God receives Christ also. The genuine listener, therefore, conceives Christ in his heart."[37] Expounding on 2 Corinthians 3,[38] Platon defines the righteous not, in the first place, as those who are perfected in virtue, or those who follow the divine commandments to the letter, but as the "animate word of God"[39]—those who have incorporated the Scriptures, and in particular the Gospel, into their heart and actualized its twofold structure—literal and spiritual, body and soul—within their own selves. Let us take two examples of Platon's exegesis to see what this might look like in concrete terms. In the first, he brings to mind the story of David and Michal, daughter of Saul, from the Second Book of Samuel (2 Samuel 6):

> Is this not the flesh: to seek God in faraway places, as if God took more delight in a particular place than in your heart . . . ? All of this occurs because in reading Holy Scripture you catch only the surface, while the inner mystery is left untouched. The flesh senses, but the soul does not discern. Sense the flesh, certainly, but only so that you may feel the soul itself. Here is a memorable example for you to follow. David, when he carried from the house of Abinadab the Ark of the Lord . . . sang with the organ, and was transformed from a King into a sacred cantor. . . . His soul plays, and this play moves his body as well. His heart leaps, and this leaping moves his legs too. . . . By this, he endeavors to do all he can to win God's favor, and gives over his entire self to this sacred act. This deed of David's was as praiseworthy as it was zealous. However, it failed to impress Michal, the daughter of Saul, who saw instead in this play something vulgar. She had not reckoned with the hidden spirit, neither with what it had played before the Lord.[40]

Platon here transforms a narrative scene from the Hebrew Scriptures into a doorway opening onto living exegetical practice. The "folly" of David, which gave life and rhythm to his flesh, becomes a hermeneutic expressing a twofold movement. On one hand, we see the play of the "hidden spirit" of David himself as the incarnation of the divine wisdom of the Spirit of God while, on the other, it is through the subjective movement of the exegete in love and faith, who unites with David in the play of his soul, that such spiritual discernment becomes possible. A fundamental sympathy is thus set up where the exegete discerns in the other only what he himself has come to accept as the wisdom had through grace. The central point here is that the anagogical aspect of the Scriptures does not lie in themselves, just as the anagogical aspect of the liturgy does not somehow reside objectively in the rites or iconography; rather, it dwells in their very *interpretation*. The place of ascent, therefore, is not the Word of God itself, nor the heart of its reader, but the hermeneutic that unites the one to the other.

The second example sees Platon take the Gospel as his starting point. "God sent his son into the womb of the Most Holy Virgin," Platon says in a rich sermon of 1787, and continues: "but he also sent his Spirit into our hearts." The history of the Incarnation is for him not only located in first-century Palestine, but involves the adoption of each individual to God through the Spirit. Here we have to do not with mere analogy—one event prefiguring, or signifying, another—but with the unity of inner and external realities whose experience is accessible to the human being through ascent. Platon goes on to equate such personal experience of the Gospel with Paul's Trinitarian formula that "God has sent the Spirit of his Son into our hearts, crying 'Abba, Father!'" (Galatians 4:6), and distinguishes between a cry audible to the ears and one audible to the heart. This "inner cry of the heart is all the louder the stronger the feeling and movement of the heart," and elevates its possessor to a realm beyond the confines of language or *ratio* (reason): "the feeling of this cry transcends not only all words, but also all concepts."[41] Here, then, we have to do with a process involving adoption into the passion of God where the human being not only contemplates the divine but ascends to a knowledge of God enjoyed from within the intensity of God's revelation to Godself. Such is the anagogical arc: in the passion of the heart's cry, the objective word of Scripture is unfolded as the lived content of one's own, never complete, adoption to God.

An Anagogical Reading of Belinskii

There are many conscious and indirect heirs to the anagogical method worked out by Platon's school: the sophiological movement in Russian religious thought, particularly Pavel Florenskii's late *Filosofiia kul'ta* (*Philosophy of Cult*);[42] Boris

Vysheslavtsev's theory of the "transfigured Eros";[43] Viacheslav Ivanov's development of symbolism and its application in his collection of verse *Cor ardens*;[44] in the academy, Mikhail Tareev's "philosophy of the heart."[45] We conclude by looking at Vissarion Belinskii, that half-atheist, half-believer yet with anything but an agnostic's ambivalence, not because his ideas exhibit the closest possible convergence with the churched thinkers previously treated but because, although he stands at the source of a philosophical tradition in Russia independent of the Church, the method and overall structure of his thinking continue a style of philosophizing, and a conception of the human search for truth, that resonate with previous Russian models. We use the word "resonate" here not in order to point to certain commonalities of imagery, discourse, or ideational paradigms, which are possible to discover in sources belonging to a common tradition, but rather to uncover a more fundamental likeness at the structural level of thinking itself, in spite of often radical divergences in the content that emerges from it.

Belinskii, of course, rarely indulged in biblical exegesis, yet his mature literary criticism of the 1840s, particularly his essay cycle on Pushkin (*Sochineniia Aleksandra Pushkina*, 1843–46), exhibits a relation to text and its interpretation that it would be no exaggeration to call a spiritual hermeneutics of a very Russian vintage. At the most basic level, his criticism mirrors the split into literal and spiritual meanings of Scripture in its desire to "understand poetry not merely as something external but in its inner essence."[46] He was convinced that reading itself, especially those forms of poetry and literature he considered "true," had a strongly pedagogic function, not in the limited sense of moral or civil formation but in the sense of the multifaceted, inner development of human personality. "Reading his works," Belinskii wrote of Pushkin, "one can in the most excellent way cultivate in oneself the human being."[47] These rather generic points of similarity, however, which Belinskii shares with many other critics, are set in the context of a wider hermeneutic governing the nature of spirit's indwelling in poetry, and of its reception by the reader, that closely mirror the anagogical trajectory with which we have so far been concerned.

After Lenin's proclamation of Belinskii as a "precursor to the complete supplanting of the gentry by the *raznochintsy* in our freedom movement,"[48] the critic's status as strident denizen of the future cemented the fissure he is frequently understood to have opened up between religious and secular models of thinking in Russia. Indeed, in the popular mind as well as in academic prose, the association of Belinskii with a Westernizing, and therefore secularizing, mindset has become a commonplace.[49] Yet even a cursory reading of his contradictory oeuvre reveals that Belinskii can be described as a "secular" thinker only in the limited sense that he wrote from a position outside the Church.[50] His pieces of literary criticism and *publitsistika* (social and political journalism) are littered not only with language that appropriates religious terminology but with philosophical content that rests on an explicit recognition of the transcendent.[51]

It is often easy to forget how much Belinskii influenced the course of Russian literature, naming its dwarves and giants often before they were aware of it themselves. A large part of the history of Russian literature up to that point, according to him, had been concerned with the gradual shedding of the incidental and its replacement by the essential. By the incidental, he largely had in mind the "false forms of the rhetorical poetry of the preceding era," beginning with Mikhail Lomonosov. Rhetoric to him represented the falsification of language and thought, language reveling in its own superficial glint yet wholly barren underneath. The main distinction between false and true poetry for him, therefore, consisted in the difference between verse that derived from "rhetorical thought" and that which derived from "poetic thought." The derivation of rhetorical poetry he described as a "separation from life and a falling away from reality; its character—falsity and generic aspects."[52] It was this generic nature of rhetorical poetry that most appalled Belinskii, who was to lay at the foundation of his demands for true poetry the demand of *narodnost'*, unwisely translated as nationality or national character, and more capably as specificity, differentiation, the very stuff of life.

Belinskii's obsession with the "truth" of a poetic work should not be interpreted from a formal perspective as the disclosure of a certain set of objective criteria. Nor, however, should we seek his criterion for truthfulness in the reader's response alone. While poetry, like the philosophical and theological traditions Russia had adopted from the West, was for Belinskii a "transplant rather than a native fruit,"[53] Russia's inheritance was not a set of rhetorical devices but above all potential access to a certain "mystery." While this mystery itself was universal, the route to it necessarily lay through the national, the personal, the specific, and its mediator was the poet-priest, who disclosed its nature to the uninitiated.[54]

For Belinskii, it was precisely Pushkin who "was called to be the living incarnation of this mystery in Rus'," yet peculiarly the great weight of his criticism is dedicated not to this ineffable mystery but to the *route* along which the poet ascends to it, and by which the critic also must travel. Just as the theology of the eighteenth century gradually reconceived its German heritage, so in Belinskii Russian criticism begins to reappropriate the legacy of German aesthetics in a more creative manner. At a time when Belinskii himself had turned away from the legacies of Hegelianism and Romanticism, he sees the core of the Pushkinian revolution in Russian poetry in the widening of the scope of the poetic eye to encompass all life, not merely its rarefied or romanticized forms. "Of the previous poets," he writes, "not one would have resolved to speak in verse of a beer mug, and a punchbowl would have seemed prosaic to every one of them; in verse back then one spoke not of mugs, but of vials, not of beer, but of Ambrosia and other noble, albeit non-existent, beverages." For Pushkin, however, "there was no such thing as base nature. . . . He whose poetry trembles in the face of the prose of life, who can only be inspired by higher objects, is no artist. For a real artist, wherever there is life, there is poetry."[55] As Platon incorporated all aspects of corporeal being within the dynamics of ascent, so the true poet discards nothing characteristic of life in his attempt "to incarnate the heavenly in the earthly and to illumine the earthly by the heavenly."[56]

The predominance of the artwork over "life" is the defining mark, in Belinskii's view, of what he called "German impersonal universalism," which "acknowledging everything, itself cannot become nothing; it posits art as a goal in itself and, in so doing, divests itself of any correlation with life which is always higher than art, since art is only one of the many manifestations of life." Art cannot be higher than life, in Belinskii's view, since its very content is life, which it discloses to the reader in its most intense aspect. In this context, he compares Pushkin's significance for Russia to that of Goethe for Germany. "[Pushkin] contemplated [nature] incredibly faithfully and vividly but did not delve into its mysterious language. For this reason he paints nature but does not reason on it. . . . For Goethe, nature was an open book of ideas; for Pushkin it was a living picture, full of an inexpressible but silent charm."[57]

This comparison with Goethe may at first glance appear not to be in Pushkin's favor. Yet, while he held a high opinion of Goethe, what Belinskii is arguing is that the German poet allowed the thinker in himself to outweigh the poet. Pushkin, by contrast, in creating what Belinskii calls "painting in poetry," never rushes beyond the immediacy of the sensual perception of nature to posit a suprasensory unity in thought. The stuff of life moves in the verse of Pushkin, but is not captured as a human possession. "The heavenly bodies may very well form harmonious worlds: yet it is not only by this that they elevate the soul of the person who contemplates them, but by the poetry of their mysterious glimmer, the marvelous beauty of the living play of their pale, fiery rays."[58] While the elevation of the soul occurs through sensing the natural world as filtered through poetic perception, its destination is not, for Belinskii, some transcendental perception of the oneness of nature, as he believed it was for Goethe, but rather the very mystery itself: life, unmediated by human *ratio*. Poetry, then, was not a petrified vision of a harmonious universe but the human spirit itself in the process of ascent "toward somewhere, to some forever enchanting yet never attainable realm."[59] For Belinskii, Goethe was the embodiment of the Romantic spirit, while Pushkin was the archetype of his particular brand of "realism."

The romantic-realist distinction was one of the core elements in the famous conflict between Belinskii and the Russian revolutionary philosopher and onetime close friend Mikhail Bakunin, whom the former believed to have conformed to the ideals of Romanticism, with its exaltation of the infinite at the expense of the finite. "True life is only that which flows from the feeling of the absolute," wrote Bakunin in 1837. "Anything that is said or done outside this feeling is insignificant and without reality."[60] For Bakunin, as for Goethe in Belinskii's handling, the "feeling of the absolute"—a precognitive, supraindividual intuition of the oneness of nature and being—is the starting point for any exploration of "truth." For Belinskii, to begin from such a point was to leap to the finish line having neglected to run the race. It is not in the assertion that the heavenly bodies comprise a single, harmonious world that the individual is drawn into their mystery, but in the concrete interaction of their play of lights and shapes with his or her empirical and psychological experience. It is this that Pushkin gives us: not the objective presence of a harmonious cosmos beyond the subject-object divide but the baffling concatenation of subjective and objective *realia* in lived experience, never steady and never complete. What is received as the content of this experience (the "mystery") is not a vision of harmony or oneness but precisely what is experienced itself: the precarious ascent of the human spirit in its fleshly being.

If this is the content of the revelation disclosed by Pushkin in his capacity as artist—a holding of the mystery before the eyes of the reader without allowing it to become objectified through human thought—the critic's vocation was of a similar kind: to preserve this non-objectified vision in the full integrity of its original articulation. Such criticism was possible only, according to Belinskii, by "penetrating to the hidden spirit [*sokrovennyi dukh*]" of the poet. The first step toward this goal governs a close analogue to the anagogical path of the "inner cross": the kenotic emptying of self, the divestiture of all preheld concepts and ideas, precisely the kind of movement that German criticism, which can never "make itself nothing," can never fulfill. "Any investigation demands without fail the kind of cold-bloodedness and dispassionateness only possible for a human being under the condition of the full negation of one's individuality for the duration of the investigation."[61]

Yet this is not where the matter rests. Instead, self-divestiture is the beginning for a wider hermeneutic movement, which forges the "critic" in the real sense of the word. "When you have finished your study, penetrated to the hidden spirit of his poetry and grasped the mystery of his individuality, your individuality once more reclaims its rights and you are transformed from a prisoner into a judge." Criticism, paradoxically, can never begin from the critic him or herself. Instead, the critic is only born when the preservation of a measure of critical remove is wholly discarded and he enters into that space in which the artwork itself originated. Belinskii uses the word "judge" here not in a dispassionate sense—the executor of a preordained law—but in the same sense as we are judges of our very selves. For the process of penetrating the hidden spirit of the poet involves our entering into that place where the spirit plays, unfolds, and interacts with our own spirit. "To live through the works of a poet means to carry, to feel through in one's soul all the wealth, the depth of its content, to become afflicted by its sicknesses, to suffer through its grief, to reexperience the bliss of its joy, its victory and hopes."[62] The critic's attainment of poetic truth, therefore, is not a sudden revelation but a slow, gradual, and difficult journey involving the full apparatus of the psychological and spiritual self, for which the external form of the poetic word is the gateway.

In a characteristic outburst to his friend Vasilii Botkin, Belinskii defines the nature of his search as critic in even starker terms: "I need that," he wrote, "in which the condition of the spirit of the human being becomes visible, where he is breathless with the waves of trembling rapture and in them drowns the reader, never allowing him to break free."[63] It is this unsteady, fecund interpretive space Belinskii discovers in the concept of "pathos," which he borrows from classical thought through the prism of Hegelian aesthetics, yet into which he pours a strikingly different content. "By 'pathos' is also understood passion, the kind associated with the boiling of the blood, with the stimulation of the entire nervous system, just like every other passion. But pathos is always passion enflamed in the soul of the human being by an idea, and always striving toward the idea. Consequently, it is a purely spiritual, moral and heavenly passion. Pathos turns the purely intellectual possession of an idea into love for the idea, full of energy and passionate striving. In philosophy, the idea is fleshless; through pathos it turns into an act, a real fact, living consciousness."[64]

Through the critic's adoption into the pathos of the poet, according to Belinskii, the way is opened to reading verse as the "revelation, the realization of the soul."[65] Such a reading is never possible as the result of Hegelian "pathos," which the German philosopher differentiated from "passion" as something "trifling and low," true pathos being "an inherently justified power over the heart . . . well considered and wholly deliberate."[66] Belinskii's model of criticism, as opposed to that of Hegel, runs counter to what John Caputo has called the "classical metaphysical assumption" lying behind much German idealism that "becoming is a process to be interpreted, not a process to be intensified, magnified, and made more elastic and electric."[67] In returning the sense of a *passion* of the spirit" to his conception of pathos, understood as a living-through that enters into the torturous, antinomic experience of the artist to glimpse that "grain of truth in a soul transfigured by grace,"[68] Belinskii's approach resonates with the non-resolved, perpetual movement of Platon and his school and its approach to reading Scripture. As in the anagogical ideal, we have here a certain bridging of the subjective (internal)—objective (external) divide, which at the same time never arrives at a sublimation into some higher, objectified third. The mature Belinskii described himself as being "equally little as internal a person as an external one; I stand on the border of these two great worlds."[69] Much of Russian philosophy would operate on the border of these worlds, where hermeneutics creates ever new perspectives and the unsteady, gradual ascent toward truth continues.

NOTES

1. See John Cassian, *The Conferences* (New York: Paulist Press, 1985), 160–61. On the term's development within Neoplatonism, see Paul Rorem, *Biblical and Liturgical Symbols within the Pseudo-Dionysian Synthesis* (Rome: Pontifical Institute of Mediaeval Studies, 1984), 106–16.

2. Cassian, *Conferences*, 160.

3. Gustav Shpet, *Esteticheskie fragmenty*, http://www.magister.msk.ru/library/philos/shpet01.htm, section 4.1. The most famous definition of the four senses belongs to Augustine of Dacia: "The literal sense teaches what happened, the allegorical what you believe. The moral what you should do, the anagogical where you are going." On this saying see, for example, Earl Miner, *Comparative Poetics: An Intercultural Essay on Theories of Literature* (Princeton, NJ: Princeton University Press, 1990), 111. The rediscovery and development of the fourfold sense in the West is largely attributable to the influence of Henri de Lubac's seminal *Medieval Exegesis*. For a wider discussion of the specifically Orthodox understanding of "truth," see the chapter by Ruth Coates in the present volume.

4. "For more than a century" after the schism, writes Alexander Negrov, "Orthodox theologians and teachers of the Bible were more preoccupied with defending various opinions on scholasticism . . . than with the problem of Bible interpretation." Alexander Negrov, *Biblical Interpretation in the Russian Orthodox Church* (Tübingen: Mohr Siebeck, 2008), 57.

5. Dimitrii (Tuptalo), *Rozysk o raskol'nicheskoi brynskoi vere* (Moscow: Sinodal'naia Tipografiia, 1855), 369–70.

6. V. G. Vlasov, *Novyi entsiklopedicheskii slovar' izobrazitel'nogo iskusstva*, 10 vols. (St. Petersburg: Azbuka-Klassika, 2004–10), vol. 2 (2005), http://slovari.yandex.ru/~книги/Словарь%20изобразительного%20искусства/Восхождение.

7. See Aleksandr Gorskii and Kapiton Nevostruev, eds., "Opisanie Velikikh Chet'ikh-Minei Makariia mitropolita Vserossiiskago," *Chteniia v Imperatorskom obshchestve istorii i drevnostei Rossiiskikh* (1884) 1:1–65.

8. Vladimir Mil'kov, Andrei Makarov, and Anna Smirnova, "Areopagatiki—traditsiia bytovaniia na Rusi," *Istoriko-filosofskii ezhegodnik* 1 (2000): 213.

9. For an account of Dionysius's influence on twentieth-century Russian thought, see Paul Gavrilyuk, "The Reception of Dionysius in Twentieth-Century Eastern Orthodoxy," in *Re-Thinking Dionysius the Areopagite*, ed. Sarah Coakley and Charles M. Stang (Malden, MA: Wiley-Blackwell, 2009), 177–94.

10. Dionysius the Areopagite, "The Celestial Hierarchy," *Esoterica* 2 (2000): 151.

11. Ibid., 156.

12. Rorem, *Biblical and Liturgical Symbols*, 58.

13. Mikhail Maslin, ed., *Russkaia filosofiia: Entsiklopediia* (Moscow: Algoritm, 2007), 18. Platon himself, it should be noted, does not use the term anagogy in his published works.

14. Henri de Lubac, *The Four Senses of Scripture*, vol. 2 of *Medieval Exegesis* (Grand Rapids, MI: Eerdmans, 2000), 187.

15. Ibid., 132, 174.

16. For Aquinas, though the subject matter of natural and revealed theology was identical—God and the things of God—the former was inferior to the latter in that it "considers creatures in themselves and leads us from them to the knowledge of God, the first consideration is about creatures, and the last of God: whereas in the teaching of faith which considers creatures only in their relation to God, the consideration about God takes the first place, and that about creatures the last." *The Collected Works of Thomas Aquinas: Summa Contra Gentiles* (Charlottesville, VA: InteLex, 1993), 2:7.

17. For an account of Kudriavtsev-Platonov's later elaboration of the "religious sense" within the bounds of natural theology, see Sean Gillen's chapter in the present volume.

18. Platon, *Pouchitel'nye slova pri vysochaishem Dvore Eia Imperatorskago Velichestva . . . Ekateriny Alekseevny* (Moscow: Senatskaia tipografiia, 1763–1806), 6:64.

19. Ibid., 2:105, 9:249.

20. Ibid., 6:155, 170.

21. Ibid., 6:163, 193.

22. Both terms were first used by Sergei Glagolev in his survey of the first hundred years of the Moscow Spiritual Academy. See Sergei Glagolev, *Pamiati pochivshikh nastavnikov* (Sergiev Posad: Tipografiia I. I. Ivanova, 1914), v.

23. Platon, *Pouchitel'nye slova*, 12:231.

24. Note here the similarity with the Areopagite: "the uplifting takes place by means of the formations; the movement is not away from the images as undesirable but precisely through them as the means to a higher realm." Rorem, *Biblical and Liturgical*

Symbols, 54. Further, "the realm of symbols is not merely an optional means through which one may be uplifted; it is the *only* means" (ibid., 105, emphasis in original).

25. Platon, *Pouchitel'nye slova*, 20:316.

26. Ibid., 19:252.

27. Ibid., 19:247. The influence of the preeminent Russian theologian of the early eighteenth century, Tikhon (Zadonskii) (1724–83), is important here. In Tikhon, writes Esiukov, "a dominant role is allocated not to reason alone, but to the 'rational' heart, or 'the reason of the heart', a reason 'filtered' through the heart." Al'bert Esiukov, *Chelovek i mir v pravoslavnoi prosvetitel'skoi mysli Rossii vtoroi poloviny XVIII veka: Istoriko-filosofskie ocherki* (Arkhangel'sk: Pomorskii gosudarstvennyi universitet im. M. V. Lomonosova, 1998), 167. On Platon as synthesizer of Orthodox and Enlightenment principles, see Elise Kimerling Wirtschafter's chapter in the present volume.

28. Platon, *Pouchitel'nye slova*, 20:316–17.

29. Ibid., 20:316. The passage Platon is interpreting to his listeners here is from Psalm 84:6, which in Slavonic reads: "Blazhen muzh, emuzhe est' zastuplenie u tebe: voskhozhdeniia v serdtsy svoem polozhi" ("Blessed is he who dwells in your care; whose ascents are in his heart" [*Bibliia*, 1762, 291]). In another place, he writes that "it is impossible for us to suddenly ascend into the newness of the new, heavenly dispensation, but must here begin in advance, even if little by little, to renew ourselves." Platon, *Pouchitel'nye slova*, 19:263.

30. For a representative example from the *Philokalia*, see Symeon the New Theologian on prayer (*Philokalia*, 4:69–75). The significance of the *Philokalia* in Russia after Platon was immense; see Ruth Coates in this volume.

31. See, e.g., Ilias the Presbyter: "If the intellect does not become detached from all sensible things, it cannot rise upward and realize its true dignity." *Philokalia*, 3:43.

32. See Rorem, *Biblical and Liturgical Symbols*, 102–3.

33. "The monk becomes equal to the angels through prayer," writes Evagrius Ponticus. *Philokalia*, 1:68.

34. Platon, *Pouchitel'nye slova*, 12:37–38, 7:132, 17:99–100.

35. Ibid., 19:237, 20:317.

36. On repentance in Platon, see P. V. Kalitin, *Uravnenie russkoi idei* (Moscow: Editorial URSS, 2002), 93.

37. Platon, *Pouchitel'nye slova*, 5:245, 14:591, 8:154.

38. "You are a letter of Christ . . . written not with ink but with the Spirit of the living God, not on tablets of stone but on tablets of human hearts."

39. Platon, *Pouchitel'nye slova*, 17:341.

40. Ibid., 9:251–52.

41. Ibid., 14:349, 352, 355.

42. Pavel Florenskii, *Filosofiia kul'ta: Opyt pravoslavnoi antropoditsei* (Moscow: Mysl', 2004).

43. Boris Vysheslavtsev, *Etika preobrazhennogo Erosa* (Moscow: Respublika, 1994); Vladimir Bykov, *Russkaia teurgicheskaia estetika* (Moscow: Ladomir, 2007), 408–16.

44. Viacheslav Ivanov, *Cor ardens* (Moscow: Skorpion, 1911).

45. Mikhail Tareev, *Khristianskaia filosofiia* (Moscow: Tipografiia Izdatel'skoi komissii Mosk. Soveta sold. dep., 1917).

46. Vissarion Belinskii, *Sochineniia Aleksandra Pushkina* (Moscow: Khudozhestvennaia literatura, 1985), 241. The inability to separate external form from spiritual content, in Belinskii's view, was the chief misdemeanor of the critically attuned reader. The frequent comparison of Pushkin to Byron, for example, was for Belinskii based on the failure to see through "external similarity of form" to the complete lack of any commonality in the "spirit of their talent." Ibid., 223.

47. Ibid., 260.

48. V. I. Lenin, *Sochineniia*, 45 vols. (Moscow: GIPL, 1941–67), 20:223. The term *raznochintsy* literally means persons of various social ranks or, in this case, persons who have consciously overcome the established legal and social order of the old regime.

49. Isaiah Berlin, for example, described Belinskii as a "moralist, secular and anticlerical through and through. Religion was to him a detestable insult to reason, theologians were charlatans, the Church a conspiracy." Isaiah Berlin, *The Power of Ideas* (Princeton, NJ: Princeton University Press, 2000), 83.

50. In two articles published in the journal *Molva* (Rumor) in 1836, Belinskii attacks the "proliferation of secularity [*svetskost'*] in literature" spearheaded, in his view, by popular journals such as *Moskovskii nabliudatel'* (The Moscow Observer). The critic is not speaking in support of institutional or dogmatic Christianity but rather against the attempt to found literary studies in a resolutely this-worldly paradigm. "'Secularity' never mixes with speculation and ideality [*myslitel'nost'*] . . . lifelessness is the most striking aspect of the character of all 'secular' distortions, secular literatures and 'secular' journals." Vissarion Belinskii, "Priznaki myslitel'nosti i zhizni v Moskovskom nabliudatele," *Molva* 10 (1836): 270.

51. Mikhail Epstein has written of Belinskii's "religious atheism," or "quasi-religiosity," yet the drawback of such an approach is that it necessitates understanding the critic's discourse surrounding the transcendent either as mere posturing or, at best, a deluded appeal to realms outside the real constraints of his world view. See Mikhail Epstein, "The Demise of the First Secularization: The Church of Gogol and the Church of Belinsky," *Studies in East European Thought* 58, no. 2 (2006): 97–98.

52. Belinskii, *Sochineniia Aleksandra Pushkina*, 31.

53. Ibid., 239.

54. The conflation of poet and priest, or oracle, with its roots in classical mythology, is a commonplace in Belinskii's work. "In that moment when he reproduces in word, paint or sound the remarkable phenomena that mystically accompany his soul, the artist is also a priest, a servant of god." Vissarion Belinskii, *Polnoe sobranie sochinenii* (Moscow: Izdatel'stvo Akademii nauk, 1953–59), 2:244.

55. Belinskii, *Sochineniia Aleksandra Pushkina*, 240, 211, 257–58.

56. Belinskii, *Polnoe sobranie*, 5:557.

57. Belinskii, *Sochineniia Aleksandra Pushkina*, 224, 271.

58. Ibid., 272, 242.

59. Belinskii, *Polnoe sobranie*, 4:493.

60. Cited in L. Ginzburg, *O psikhologicheskoi proze* (Leningrad: Sovetskii pisatel', 1971), 119.

61. Belinskii, *Sochineniia Aleksandra Pushkina*, 228, 225.

62. Ibid., 228, 230.

63. Belinskii, *Polnoe sobranie*, 12:24.
64. Belinskii, *Sochineniia Aleksandra Pushkina*, 232.
65. Ibid., 237.
66. G. W. F. Hegel, *Aesthetics: Lectures on Fine Art*, trans. T. M. Knox (Oxford: Clarendon Press, 1988), 1:232.
67. John D. Caputo, "The Absolute, the Perverse Core of Hegel, and Radical Theology," in *Hegel and the Infinite: Religion, Politics, and Dialectic*, ed. Slavoj Žižek, Clayton Crockett, and Creston Davis (New York: Columbia University Press, 2011), 60.
68. Belinskii, *Sochineniia Aleksandra Pushkina*, 27.
69. Cited in Ginzburg, *O psikhologicheskoi proze*, 107.

Chapter 9

Kant and the Kingdom of Ends in Russian Religious Thought (Vladimir Solov'ev)

RANDALL A. POOLE

Perhaps more than most of the world's great religious philosophers, Vladimir Solov'ev was concerned to reconcile faith and reason. As he put it in one of his better-known statements, his aim was "to justify the faith of our fathers by raising it to a new level of rational consciousness."[1] His first major effort to construct a synthesis of faith and reason was *Principles of Integral Knowledge* (*Filosofskie nachala tsel'nogo znaniia*, 1877), which proceeds from Ivan Kireevskii's concept of "believing reason." In Solov'ev's view, the contemporary state of religion in Russia and elsewhere in Europe was very far from the integration of faith and reason that he sought. In *Lectures on Godmanhood* (*Chteniia o bogochelovechestve*, 1877–81), he deplores it as a "pitiful thing."[2] Faith had become irrational and blind. His task in *Lectures on Godmanhood* and in his subsequent works was to justify and modernize religion, to show that it is reasonable, in two related senses: first, that the divine principle (God or the absolute), since it is known primarily through inner moral-religious experience or consciousness, is a truth of reason and not merely one of revelation; and, second, that reason (in addition to its "theoretical" task) has the practical task of conforming and perfecting human and earthly nature to the divine principle. Solov'ev's reconciliation of faith and reason,[3] his effort to make religion modern and progressive, places him squarely within the tradition of nineteenth-century liberal theology.[4] In a way that has not been fully appreciated, his project took shape under the decisive influence of Immanuel Kant, whose moral religion or religion of pure reason laid the foundations of liberal theology.

Solov'ev knew Kant's philosophy very well. It was a fundamental frame of reference for him; he argued for and against it in many places in his works. As a student at Moscow University he translated Kant's *Prolegomena to any Future Metaphysics*.[5] In *Principles of Integral Knowledge*, he called Kant's theory of space and time "truthful and sublime," his "eternal merit."[6] He devoted many pages of his doctoral dissertation (soon recognized as a fundamental work), *Critique of Abstract Principles* (*Kritika otvlechennykh nachal*, 1880), to the defense of Kant's rational ethics, which he regarded as normative.[7] There he adopted Kant's conception of human dignity and of personhood (namely, that they consist in self-determination or autonomy), which conception he retained for the rest of his life and which forms the "human principle" of his mature philosophical system. In his great work of moral philosophy, *Justification of the Good* (*Opravdanie dobra*, 1897), Solov'ev extolled Kant's principle of autonomy and his formulation of the moral law as "one of the greatest achievements of the human mind."[8] He also wrote the standard encyclopedia article on the German philosopher. In it he appraised Kant as one of the truly pivotal figures in the history of human thought, whose life divides that history into two periods, pre-Kantian and post-Kantian.[9] Clearly Kant made a very deep impression on Solov'ev.[10]

The Russian philosopher accepted the premise of Kant's moral religion, namely, that the primary grounds of faith are in morality (or in moral-religious experience). He understood morality in wholly Kantian terms as the human capacity for self-determination and perfectibility according to the moral law. For Kant the moral law was a basic and irreducible fact of reason (PrR 164/5:31).[11] Theism followed from it—or more precisely from infinite human perfectibility toward the ideal of "holiness," the complete conformity of the will with the moral law—in the form of the postulates of immortality and the existence of God (PrR 243-44/5:129).[12] Solov'ev's approach was more straightforward. He identified the moral law with human consciousness of the absolute or with the "image" of God, but the image had precisely the same role as Kant's moral law: it was the ideal driving human perfectibility toward it (perfectibility being our "likeness" to God). This dynamic formed the central concept of his religious philosophy, Godmanhood,[13] which strikingly combines patristic ideas of the "image and likeness" and of *theosis* with Kant's theology of moral perfectibility (as I shall call it here). Godmanhood was Solov'ev's version of the kingdom of God. He followed Kant in thinking that the kingdom of God could come only through the kingdom of ends, Kant's famous ideal of a moral order whose members recognize each other as persons or ends-in-themselves. Kant conceived the kingdom of ends as an ethical community of "a people of God" (the Church)

(R 134/6:99).[14] As this chapter will show, it was the model for Solov'ev's social ideal of "free theocracy."

Faith and Reason:
Solov'ev's Divine and Human Principles

In 1878 Solov'ev delivered his soon famous *Lectures on Godmanhood* to packed audiences in Saint Petersburg. They were a vastly impressive effort to "justify the faith of our fathers" and to defend his philosophical approach to religion. His subject, he tells us, is the philosophy of religion. His method, which followed directly from his philosophical idealism, was a type of natural theology that proceeded from analysis of human consciousness.[15] He believed that basic religious ideas, beginning with the idea of the absolute, were intrinsic or natural to human consciousness and that their further development also took place largely by reason.[16] He spoke of "religious consciousness" in a way that gave it primacy over revelation. Such consciousness includes two sources of faith: ordinary moral-religious experience or religious feeling, and extraordinary mystical experience (such as his own visions of Sophia).[17] He called human consciousness of the absolute (in one form or another) the divine, religious, or mystical principle in man. The divine principle is the "object" of faith, but Solov'ev emphasized that true faith comes from within and that we become aware of its object through inner moral-religious experience, rather than primarily through external media such as revelation in any traditional sense. His insistence on the inner nature of faith, that the "object" of faith can be only an ideal intrinsic to consciousness, not something extrinsic to it or positively given, is closely tied to his Kantian conception of self-determination and personhood.

Lectures on Godmanhood is an awe-inspiring presentation of the core concepts, main arguments, and overall approach of Solov'ev's mature religious philosophy. He starts with the assertion that "religion is the connection of humanity and the world with the absolute principle and focus of all that exists" (1). Contemporary humanity had largely lost this connection, but Solov'ev believed that it could be restored—and restored on a higher metaphysical level. With this hope he slightly modifies his definition: "Religion is the reunification of humanity and the world with the absolute, integral principle" (10). By "integral" he means that the absolute is the "unity of all" (*vseedinstvo*), but a unity that fully respects the autonomy of its constituent parts, each of which must freely enter into it. So conceived, the absolute is "all-one" and its essence is "all-unity," the term that designates Solov'ev's metaphysics. His tenth lecture provides a succinct statement of his overall conception. "The divine principle,"

Solov'ev says, "is the eternal all-one." From it emerges the cosmic process, the meaning and goal of which is the gradual realization in itself of all-unity, the incarnation of the divine idea in the world, "the deification (*theosis*) of all that exists" (135–37). "Why," Solov'ev asks, "is the realization of the divine idea in the world a gradual and complex process, and not a single simple act?" He answers in one word: "freedom" (138). He means, ultimately, that an *achieved* state of all-unity and deification is higher than one given in a simple act of divine fiat or grace. That is the meaning of Godmanhood: the free human realization of the divine idea in the world.

Clearly it is humanity that has the task of freely achieving the reunification or reintegration of everything in absolute all-unity, in which all will be one in God. Our task is to "consciously and freely turn to the divine principle and enter into a perfectly free and deliberate union with it" (17). Such a divine-human union is possible because human beings themselves have an absolute, divine significance (equality being a condition of genuine, free union). Solov'ev locates this absolute significance (he calls it "negative absoluteness") in the human ability "to transcend every finite, limited content, not to be limited by it . . . but to demand something greater" (17). He regarded this capacity for "infinite development" (or for perfectibility, as he will refer to it in later works) as the distinctive human property: he called it the human principle. He recognized it as the source of absolute human value, human dignity, and human rights. His understanding of it is based on Kant's conception of morality as self-determination (see below), and it is central to his whole system.[18] Infinite human striving implies an ideal end giving direction to the whole process, which ideal was for him, in the final instance, the positive absolute of all-unity, the perfect "fullness of being" that is to be achieved by humanity (23). In his tenth lecture Solov'ev calls this ideal (i.e., human consciousness of the all-one absolute) the *image* of God in us; our *likeness* to God is the "formal limitlessness of the human I" (our capacity for self-determination, infinite development, and perfectibility) by which we can "spontaneously will to be like God" (142).[19] But by the end of the second lecture Solov'ev already had arrived at his momentous conclusion: when belief in God (as the positive absolute of perfection) and belief in humanity (as the negative absolute of perfectibility) "are carried consistently to the end and actualized in full, they meet in the one, complete, integral truth of Godmanhood" (24).[20]

Solov'ev's argument is that the divine principle is a genuine reality "that is asserted by the infinite striving of the human I" (23–24). Though its reality is "asserted" by infinite human striving toward it, the divine principle remains only an object of faith. Solov'ev was concerned to keep it that way, for otherwise (i.e., were it positively given or revealed in the manner of empirical objects) it could not be the *ideal* that motivates—indeed makes possible—human striving and perfectibility, which is the very condition of Godmanhood (the free human realization of the divine). Obviously relying on Kant (though without referring to him), he writes that the reality of God (and of the external world in general) "cannot be deduced from pure reason," because we know only phenomena, not things in themselves. Their reality can be taken only on faith (30–31). Such faith (at least in God, ourselves, and other persons) is justified, however, by inner moral-religious experience. "That God *is*, we believe, but *what* God is, we experience and try to know," Solov'ev writes. "Of course, without belief in the reality of their object, the facts of inner religious experience are only fantasy and hallucination." But with faith, they "are known as the actions of the divine principle upon us, as its revelation in us" (32–33).[21] Note that Solov'ev's understanding of faith required him to redefine revelation as the content of inner religious experience, as the gradual development of the divine principle in human consciousness, in contrast to traditional notions of revelation as an external miracle in which God suddenly reveals himself to a passive humanity.[22] His overall approach to faith is well conveyed by Hebrews 11:1 ("the substance of things hoped for, the evidence of things not seen").[23]

Reason has two different roles in Solov'ev's religious philosophy, both closely tied to his idea of faith. The first is rational analysis of the data of moral-religious experience. As he says in *Lectures on Godmanhood*, reason has the role of "*organizing* religious experience into an integral, logically connected system," ultimately into a philosophy of religion (33).[24] The second role is essential to his system. It is conveyed by Kant's concept of "practical reason," that is, the capacity of reason to determine the will by its own ideals such as (for Kant himself) the moral law and (for Solov'ev) the absolute or the image of God. Practical reason is the power of self-determination or, as Kant also calls it, autonomy. It is what he understood by morality.[25] His most influential account of morality as self-determination or as rational autonomy is *Groundwork of the Metaphysics of Morals* (1785). In *Critique of Abstract Principles*, Solov'ev explicates Kant's work at length and embraces its main ideas as his own.[26] He regarded rational autonomy as the distinctive human quality, indeed as the quality that makes us persons. In his view (as in Kant's), it is the peculiar nature of human (and other rational) beings that they are capable of acting according to ideals of pure reason (rather than only by natural inclination), of self-determination according to these ideals, and of infinite development or perfectibility toward them.

Reason, in this sense of what might be called "ideal self-determination," is the middle, properly human principle in Solov'ev's tripartite conception of human nature. The other two are the material and divine principles.[27] "Human beings are not limited to a single principle," Solov'ev writes. "They have in themselves both the elements of material being that unite them with the natural world, and an ideal consciousness of all-unity that unites them with God. Moreover, they are not confined to either; human beings are, as free *I*'s, capable of determining themselves in one manner or another with respect to the two sides of their essence."[28] The human principle is the capacity to "become" more (or less) than we presently are, to infinitely perfect (or degrade) ourselves. Solov'ev calls this the "essentially human attribute."[29]

It bears emphasizing that the middle, human principle of self-determination is deeply indebted to Kant's ethics. This is most obvious in *Critique of Abstract Principles*, but it is evident in other works as well. For example, in "The Meaning of Love" ("Smysl liubvi," 1892–94) Solov'ev wrote that rational human consciousness is formed by "universal ideal norms" and a "sense of truth" by which we evaluate the phenomena and facts of life. "Considering his actions with this higher consciousness, man can infinitely perfect his life and nature *without leaving the boundaries of human form*. And therefore, he is indeed the supreme being of the natural world and the effective end of the world-creative process."[30] Though Solov'ev does not refer to him here, Kant as well declared, on the basis of our perfectibility, that the "human being is the final end of creation,"[31] "God's final end in creating the world" (PrR 245/5:130). To the extent that the core of Solov'ev's system is self-determination and human perfectibility according to the ideals of pure reason, then that core is Kantian. The Russian philosopher also followed his German predecessor in thinking that practical reason (rational autonomy) is the source of human dignity and of personhood itself. It is what makes human beings ends-in-themselves. "Kant better than any other philosopher established the principle of the moral person," he wrote.[32]

Solov'ev incorporated Kantian autonomy within a religious metaphysics that has often been seen (ever since E. N. Trubetskoi's 1913 study) as strongly influenced by Schelling (to whom, however, Solov'ev seldom refers), in particular by the German philosopher's conception of the cosmos as a theogony of the suffering God in the process of becoming.[33] In *Lectures on Godmanhood*, as we have seen, Solov'ev elaborates a similar idea of the self-realization of the divine absolute (all-unity) in cosmic and human history. Trubetskoi held that Schelling's "pantheism" and "gnosticism" were the main sources of Solov'ev's "metaphysical utopianism," which caused him to displace human freedom and responsibility for evil to the theogonic world-process.[34] I would maintain that Solov'ev's Kantian focus on human autonomy mitigates his "metaphysical utopianism."[35]

Solov'ev's Kantianism enables him to achieve the reconciliation of faith and reason that is the very heart of his project. As "ideal self-determination," the human principle of (practical) reason depends on ideals such as the moral law or the divine principle: without them, genuine *self*-determination and perfectibility cannot take place. Reason alone, not anything external, can give the ideals that make possible self-determination or autonomy (and therefore also, for Kant and Solov'ev, personhood itself). Ideals, by their nature, cannot be positively given in the manner of empirical objects. They are a matter of faith. This is the intricate relationship between faith and reason, between the divine and human principles, in Solov'ev's religious thought.

Godmanhood

Solov'ev's concept of Godmanhood is a further development of his philosophical anthropology; it projects the ever fuller realization of the divine principle by the human one. Godmanhood is the autonomous, progressive realization of the divine principle by and in humanity and, through humanity, in nature. It describes both the ongoing process of human perfectibility (in which sense Godmanhood is already underway) and the culmination of the process in *theosis*. In *Critique of Abstract Principles*, Solov'ev wrote that rational autonomy is the necessary formal means for the realization of the divine idea, which "must enter into the *process* of rational consciousness and be recognized by human reason."[36] The divine principle must be *humanly* realized. The material principle, too, has an integral part: "If the form of freedom and rationality in the realization of the divine idea is given by the human principle, then the material basis for this realization is nature, first of all the natural element of every human being.... As the source of the real force behind the [divine] idea, our material being must not be suppressed; it must be developed and cultivated as necessary means of the higher end. This end is the realization, i.e., the full embodiment, of the divine principle, the mutual spiritualization of matter and materialization of spirit."[37] Here Solov'ev formulates a succinct definition of the human being (in union with the rest of humanity): a being containing in itself the divine idea (all-unity or the absolute plenitude of being) and realizing this idea by means of rational freedom in material nature.[38]

In November 1880, seven months after the defense of *Critique of Abstract Principles*, Solov'ev delivered his inaugural lecture in philosophy at Saint Petersburg University, "The Historical Tasks of Philosophy" ("Istoricheskie dela filosofii"). It frames the value of philosophy in terms of his conception of human nature. The new professor declared the true principle of Christianity to be

Godmanhood: "the inner union and interaction of the divine with man, the inner birth of the divine in man." He then specifies that "the divine content must be appropriated by a human being *from within himself*, consciously and freely," through the fullest development of human rationality. Philosophy has served this purpose, "the development of a human being as a free and rational person." It has also served to illuminate the higher meaning of the material principle in human nature. Above all "it has liberated the human person from external violence and given it inner content." What is the source of the liberating process of philosophy? It is the essential property of human consciousness that Solov'ev identified in *Lectures on Godmanhood* as "negative absoluteness," on account of which it, consciousness, is not satisfied with any limit, external determination or content, "so that all the goods and blessings on earth and in heaven have no value, if they have not been acquired by it on its own and do not comprise what is its own. And this inability to be satisfied with any outward content of life, this striving toward the ever more inward fullness of being, this force that is destructive of all alien gods, this force already contains, in possibility, that toward which it strives—the absolute fullness and perfection of life."[39] This process—what I have called "ideal self-determination"—is the essence of philosophy and also of human personhood itself. Philosophy, Solov'ev says, makes a person more human. "Philosophy, realizing the properly human principle in man, for that very reason also serves both the divine and material principles, bringing one and the other *into the form of free humanness*."[40]

The Russian philosopher S. L. Frank wrote that with the concept of Godmanhood, Solov'ev extended the Chalcedonian dogma of Christ the God-man's two natures to all of existence.[41] Indeed Solov'ev often does employ, in a range of contexts, the Council of Chalcedon's formula that Christ's divine and human natures abide in him "without division or confusion."[42] These pervasive references make clear the impact that Chalcedon had on his thought. Solov'ev drew on other patristic sources as well, in particular on the doctrine of *theosis*.[43] His concept of Godmanhood combines Chalcedonian Christology with the doctrine of *theosis* and gives them a modern philosophical development, specifically a Kantian one (I would argue) that emphasizes the autonomy of the human principle relative to the divine.

Gustafson and other scholars have argued persuasively that Solov'ev's understanding of Chalcedon owed a lot to Maximus the Confessor. Gustafson recalls that Maximus "was the major intellectual force behind the resolution of the heresy of monothelitism. He shaped the central arguments for the two natures and the two wills—divine and human—in Christ, the Godman, which thereby preserved in the face of the divine the human freedom so important to Solov'ev." The Russian philosopher's appreciation of Maximus's dyotheletism and of Kantian autonomy go hand-in-hand. Gustafson himself writes that Solov'ev fitted Maximus into "a nineteenth-century philosophical theology, expressed in the language not of Greek patristics but of German idealism," though Gustafson has Schelling in mind more than Kant.[44]

Solov'ev's emphasis on human autonomy is evident even in his Christology per se. Certainly he thought that the divine nature of Christ was an ontological reality and not just an ideal, but nonetheless he emphasized that even Christ's divinity had to be autonomously realized by his humanity. The self-limitation of the Godhead in the incarnation (kenosis) enabled Christ *to attain to theosis* (which took the form of resurrection) by perfectly submitting or conforming his rational human will to his divine will.[45] As Oliver Smith puts it, "The humanity of Christ is 'spiritualized' or divinized not despite his humanity but because of it."[46] In view of his emphasis on the need for the autonomous exercise of Christ's rational human will (which need would seem to preclude foreknowledge of his divine nature), Solov'ev may well have been among those who have thought that no one was more surprised at the resurrection than Jesus himself.

Solov'ev and Kant's Theology of Moral Perfectibility

Godmanhood might be construed as a process theology of human perfectibility and of its transcendent culmination in *theosis*. It is Solov'ev's version of the kingdom of God, which, he always stressed, will not come in its full glory until human beings have prepared it through their own perfectibility. It will come, Solov'ev says, only through what Kant called the kingdom of ends. In *Justification of the Good*—the very concept of which is infinite human perfectibility toward the kingdom of God—he wrote that the kingdom of God cannot be expected by the immediate action of God, for "God has never acted immediately"—a striking comment meant to reinforce the necessity of free human participation in God's work. "In man's consciousness and in his freedom is the inner possibility for each human being to stand in an independent relation to God," Solov'ev continues, "and therefore to be His direct end [*tsel'*], to be a citizen possessed of full rights in the kingdom of ends" (149–50).

The kingdom of ends is Kant's ideal of a moral community of persons who recognize each other as ends-in-themselves. The concept is at the very center of his philosophy and figures in various ways in his major works that deal with morality and religion.[47] It refers not only to persons as ends-in-themselves but also to the moral ends that they pursue (G 83/4:433). In it, persons strive toward a perfection in which their will would be wholly determined by (or be in complete conformity with) the moral law, a state that Kant calls "holiness of will" (G 88/4:439; PrR 238/5:122). This is the deepest sense in which the kingdom is "admittedly only an ideal" (G 83/4:433).[48] The kingdom of ends is headed by a sovereign, who from what Kant says can only be God (G 83–84/4:434). Like Solov'ev after him, Kant held that the kingdom's sovereign respects the autonomy of its other members: "It now follows of itself that in the order of ends the human being (and with him every rational being) is an end in itself, that is, can never be used as a means by anyone (not even by God) without being at the same time himself an end" (PrR 245/5:131).

Solov'ev embraced Kant's ideal of the kingdom of ends as his own. He explicated the concept at several points in *Critique of Abstract Principles*. "If every subject is a moral agent," he writes, "and everyone else as an end-in-itself is the object of its action, then the general result of the moral activity of all subjects will be their organic unity in the kingdom of ends."[49] He describes his own vision of the ideal society ("free theocracy") as the practical unity of all, "by virtue of which all are the end . . . for each and each for all" (viii). In *Justification of the Good*, as we have seen, he says that the kingdom of God can be achieved only through the kingdom of ends: "Universal history is the realization of this possibility for everyone. Those who take part in it attain to actual perfection through their own experience, through their interaction with other human beings. This perfection attained by oneself, this full, conscious, and free union with the Divine, is precisely what God ultimately wants—the unconditional good" (150). Here as well Solov'ev seems to draw directly on Kant, who wrote in *The Metaphysics of Morals*: "It is a contradiction for me to make another's *perfection* my end and consider myself under obligation to promote this. For the *perfection* of another human being, as a person, consists just in this: that he *himself* is able to set his end in accordance with his own concepts of duty" (MM 518/6:386). In Solov'ev's words, "Perfection is not a thing which one person can make a gift of to another" (150–51).

According to Kant, the perfectibility of persons in the kingdom of ends consists in their pursuit of perfect virtue or "holiness," that is, the complete conformity of the will with the moral law (PrR 238/5:122). He says that this is a state, however, that human beings can never achieve, not even in the afterlife. We are capable only of what Kant calls "*endless progress*" toward holiness. Because it is endless so must persons be to pursue it; hence Kant's postulate of immortality (PrR 238/5:122). The moral law always remains as an ideal, it drives endless progress toward it, and therefore it always enables the "ideal self-determination" that is a condition of morality and of personhood itself. Kant's theology of moral perfectibility—"endless progress" toward holiness and the postulates therefrom of immortality and of the existence of God[50]—seems to have made quite an impression on Solov'ev, who advanced his own concept of infinite perfectibility in *Justification of the Good*. He preferred to speak of the divine principle or divine image in us, which he thought was a more robust version of Kant's moral law. Moreover, he sharply criticized Kant for merely postulating the soul's immortality and the existence of God instead of recognizing that they are immediate realities of moral-religious experience (134–39). But for Solov'ev the "image" of God functions as the ideal just like Kant's moral law, while the human "likeness" to God is our capacity for self-determination and infinite perfectibility according to the image or ideal (145, 152). In one passage he calls the image of God the power of representation (of absolute perfection) and the likeness of God the power of striving (to achieve it). This "double infinity" belongs to everyone. "It is in this that the absolute significance, dignity, and worth of human personhood consist, and this is the basis of its inalienable rights" (176). In another passage, perhaps the most capacious in *Justification of the Good*, he wrote: "The absolute value of man is based, as we know, upon the *possibility* inherent in his reason and his will of infinitely approaching perfection or, according to the patristic expression, the possibility of becoming divine (*theosis*)" (296).

Solov'ev's type of dynamic, synergetic interpretation of the "image and likeness" had been advanced by Christian humanists since the Eastern Church fathers.[51] He drew widely on this tradition but modernized it with Kant. The modern elements are three. First is the emphasis itself on infinite perfectibility or "endless progress."[52] Second is the idea that perfectibility is achieved not through mystical, monastic, or ascetic withdrawal from society but through the full, integral development of society. Solov'ev closely followed Kant's social philosophy (see below), which culminates in the kingdom of ends, where human development becomes ready for the advent of the kingdom of God. Third is the link to human rights.[53] In these ways Solov'ev was a full-fledged modern liberal, even a "new liberal."[54]

Like Solov'ev after him, Kant specifies that the end of creation is "[h]umanity . . . in its full moral perfection" (R 103/6:60). This ideal humanity is personified in Jesus Christ, whom Kant evokes through a number of biblical phrases (R 104/6:60–61). For Kant, Christ is both ideal humanity, in God, and also the ideal that we are to realize in ourselves: "Now it is our universal duty to *elevate* ourselves to this ideal of moral perfection," which is given by pure reason and which therefore does not need revelation or miracles for validation.[55] Both Kant and Solov'ev found powerful biblical expression of their ideal in Matthew 5:48: "Be perfect even as your Father in heaven is perfect."[56] They gave the verse the same meaning, namely, infinite perfectibility toward the ideal of holiness.

While human perfectibility rests on self-determination and is in that sense an individual responsibility, it cannot take place outside of human society and community. For both Kant and Solov'ev, moral perfectibility is the path to the kingdom of God, but for neither is it an individualistic path. The kingdom of God is to come through the ethical community of the kingdom of ends, which both philosophers thought of as the Church. Solov'ev called it "free theocracy."

Given his understanding of the path to the kingdom of God, Kant's conception of religion falls within his social philosophy.[57] His exposition can be found in *Religion within the Boundaries of Mere Reason*. He argues that law and the state are the necessary foundations of any ethical community for they make possible civilization and thus all higher moral and spiritual development (R 130–31/6:94–95). This advance to civilization is made by people subjecting themselves to juridical laws, which limit, by coercion if necessary, "the freedom of each to the conditions under which it can coexist with the freedom of everyone else" (R 133/6:98).[58] By contrast, the pure laws of the kingdom of ends are those of virtue; they are freely and inwardly accepted, which is what distinguishes an ethical from a political community. Laws of virtue, though inwardly given by pure practical reason, are also recognized as divine commands. This enables members of the kingdom of ends autonomously to do God's will and autonomously to follow his commands. "Hence an ethical community is conceivable only as a people under divine commands, i.e., as a people of God" (R 134/6:99). A people of God does not, Kant cautions, form a theocracy, which historically refers not to an ethical community but to a political one based on external clerical power (R 134/6:99–100). But surely the concept of a people of God under the laws of virtue suggests a type of pure, free theocracy.[59]

The ethical community of a people of God, the kingdom of ends, is a "never fully attainable idea." Though ultimately it is the transcendent kingdom of God, we must work toward it as though its realization depended on our efforts (R 135/6:100). Kant called it the Church: as transcendent ideal it is the *Church invisible* and as "the actual union of human beings into a whole that accords with this ideal" it is the *Church visible*. Existing historical churches are poor approximations even to the Church visible; they must be transformed into the "true (visible) church ... that displays the (moral) kingdom of God on earth inasmuch as the latter can be realized through human beings" (R 135/6:101). According to Kant, the true visible Church would be: (1) universal, one, and united in its essential purpose; (2) morally pure ("of the nonsense of superstition and the madness of enthusiasm" or fanaticism); (3) free both in the internal relations of its members (i.e., without a hierarchy) and in its external political relations; (4) unchangeable in its constitution of secure a priori principles (in the idea of its end); and (5) centered not in the historical, ecclesiastical faiths of revelation but in *pure religious faith* embraced by all (R 135–37/6:101–3). The kingdom of God will come when "the very form of a church is dissolved; the vicar on earth enters the same class as the human beings who are now elevated to him as citizens of Heaven, *and so God is all in all*" (R 162/6:135, italics added).

Solov'ev first presented his social philosophy in comprehensive form in *Critique of Abstract Principles*. From its foundations in external right to the kingdom of ends, it closely follows (though without acknowledgement) Kant's in structure and logic.[60] Solov'ev's ideal of free theocracy surely recalls Kant's notion of a "people of God." In advancing the ideal, no doubt the Russian philosopher drew on Kant's statement of the distinction between the Church invisible (as transcendent ideal) and the Church visible (as its approximation), and on his enumeration of the qualities of the true visible Church.

Of those qualities, Kant devoted particular care to elucidating the idea of "pure religious faith," which is essentially the same as his concept of moral religion or religion of pure reason, all based on his view that the moral law and infinite human perfectibility toward that ideal entail theism. He thought that Christianity was in its "true first purpose" a pure religious faith (R 159/6:131; 181/6:158). Its founder, the teacher of the Gospel, "announced himself as one sent from heaven while at the same time declaring, as one worthy of this mission, that servile faith ... is inherently null; that moral faith, which alone makes human beings holy 'as my father in heaven in holy' and proves its genuineness by a good life-conduct, is on the contrary the only one which sanctifies" (R 156/6:128). Despite these foundations, Christianity soon veered off in another direction. Salvation was sought not in moral perfectibility according to the ideal of holiness, but in various "counterfeits" or surrogates for pure religious faith. Kant devotes the fourth part of his treatise to unmasking these counterfeits, which seek to replace self-determination with "dependence on the historical and statutory part of the church's faith as alone salvific" (R 176/6:153). These counterfeits for pure moral faith include miracles, revelation, dogma, orthodoxy, hierarchy, "priestcraft," and all the other external forms of "ecclesiastical, statutory faith" that together amount to a "delusion of religion" (R 188/6:168). Kant describes the counterfeit service of God as fetishism, idolatry, and coercion over conscience (R 197/6:179; 202/6:185). Nonetheless he believed that "in the end religion will gradually be freed of all empirical grounds of determination.... Thus at last the pure religion of reason will rule over all, 'so that God may be all in all'" (R 151/6:121, italics added).

Solov'ev's conception of religion bears striking similarities to Kant's idea of pure religious faith. The similarities are especially obvious in two essays from 1891, "On the Reasons for the Collapse of the Medieval Worldview" ("O prichinakh upadka srednevekovogo mirosozertsania") and "On Counterfeits" ("O poddelkakh"). In the first he remarks "how small is the significance of faith in the Divine as an external supernatural fact"; he castigates those who take an "easy, cheap" approach to salvation "through dead faith and works of piety—*works* and not *work*"; and he deplores "the monstrous doctrine that the only means to salvation was faith in dogma."[61] The title of the second echoes that of the fourth part of *Religion within the Boundaries of Mere Reason*, which Solov'ev must have taken to heart. In this short essay he argues that various counterfeits for the "pure morality" of the Christian religion have no salvific value. True Christianity consists in what Jesus taught: that "the Kingdom of God, perfected in the eternal divine idea ('in heaven'), potentially inherent in our nature, is necessarily at the same time something *perfectible* for us and through us."[62]

Conclusion

At every level the kingdom of ends is a kingdom of ideals. Therefore it must be taken on faith and realized by reason. With Solov'ev, it became the social ideal of Russian liberalism, as understood by neo-idealists like Pavel Novgorodtsev.[63] In *Problems of Idealism* (*Problemy idealizma*, 1902) Novgorodtsev called the kingdom of ends the supreme good of the moral world.[64] He and other Russian neo-idealists understood with Solov'ev that personhood, the foundational liberal value, depends on the ideal—whether the moral law, the divine principle, or the image of God—because it depends on self-determination. Therefore it also depends on faith, for once the ideal is positively given it is no longer an ideal but a fact, and with that true self-determination is no longer possible. This insight informed the Russian neo-idealist critique of every type of positivism, whether of religious fundamentalism, of scientism, or of necessitarian forms of utopianism like orthodox Marxism, all of which undermined personhood at its very foundations. Though they agreed with Solov'ev (and with Kant) on the ideal structure of personhood, Novgorodtsev and other Russian liberal theorists (notably Boris Chicherin and Evgenii Trubetskoi) criticized "free theocracy" as a dangerous utopia, especially for the threat they thought it posed to freedom of conscience.[65] Curiously, they seem to have missed the extent to which the great religious philosopher, in his social ideal, was following Kant in thinking that the earthly form of the kingdom of the ends was the "true (visible) church . . . that displays the (moral) kingdom of God on earth inasmuch as the latter can be realized through human beings" (R 135/6:101).

NOTES

1. *Istoriia i budushchnost' teokratii* (1887), in *Sobranie sochinenii Vladimira Sergeevicha Solov'eva*, ed. S. M. Solov'ev and E. L. Radlov, 2nd ed., 10 vols. (St. Petersburg: Prosveshchenie, 1911–14), 4:243. As early as 1873, he wrote (in a letter to E. V. Romanova) that his task was "to bring the eternal content of Christianity into a new form suitable to it, i.e., an absolutely rational one." Vladimir Solov'ev, *"Nepodvizhno lish' solntse liubvi . . .": Stikhotvoreniia, proza, pis'ma, vospominaniia sovremennikov*, ed. Aleksandr Nosov (Moscow: Moskovskii rabochii, 1990), 174. According to Oliver Smith, this letter "reads like a manifesto for the philosopher's future activity." By 1877, he had decided to devote himself (in Smith's words) to a philosophical "grounding of the known—whether through mystical, logical, or empirical knowledge—in that most human of principles, reason." From then on, his philosophical works were concerned "with a metaphysics that searches for its basis in rational principles already present, to some degree, in human consciousness." Oliver Smith, *Vladimir Soloviev and the Spiritualization of Matter* (Boston: Academic Studies Press, 2011), 25, 30.

2. Vladimir Solovyov, *Lectures on Divine Humanity*, trans. Peter P. Zouboff, rev. and ed. Boris Jakim (Hudson, NY: Lindisfarne Press, 1995), 2.

3. Compare to earlier, Enlightenment projects to find a reasonable faith, such as Father Platon's in Russia. See Elise Kimerling Wirtschafter's chapter in this volume.

4. Paul Valliere, "Theological Liberalism and Church Reform in Imperial Russia," in *Church, Nation and State in Russia and Ukraine*, ed. Geoffrey A. Hosking (London: Macmillan, 1991), 108–30; Paul Valliere, *Modern Russian Theology: Bukharev, Soloviev, Bulgakov; Orthodox Theology in a New Key* (Grand Rapids, MI: William B. Eerdmans, 2000); Greg Gaut, "Christian Politics: Vladimir Solovyov's Social Gospel Theology," *Modern Greek Studies Yearbook* 10/11 (1994–95): 653–74. For a seminal analysis of Solov'ev's prominent place in the history of Russian liberalism (related to but distinct from his liberal theology), see Andrzej Walicki, *Legal Philosophies of Russian Liberalism* (Oxford: Oxford University Press, 1987).

5. S. M. Luk'ianov, *O Vl. S. Solov'eve v ego molodye gody: Materialy k biografii*, 3 vols. (Petrograd: Senatskaia tipografiia, 1916–21), 1:351, 358–60. The translation was published later, in 1889, by the Moscow Psychological Society; a second edition appeared in 1893. There is a recent edition: Immanuel Kant, *Prolegomeny ko vsiakoi budushchei metafizike, mogushchei vozniknut' v smysle nauki* (Moscow: Progress-VIA, 1993).

6. Vladimir Solovyov, *The Philosophical Principles of Integral Knowledge*, trans. Valeria Z. Nollan (Grand Rapids, MI: William B. Eerdmans, 2008), 162, 92.

7. See note 26 below. He gives his overall evaluation of Kant's ethics as normative and as the last word in subjective (pure or formal) ethics in chapter 11 of *Critique of Abstract Principles: Kritika otvlechennykh nachal*, in *Sobranie sochinenii*, 2:110-16.

8. Vladimir Solovyov, *The Justification of the Good: An Essay on Moral Philosophy*, trans. Natalie A. Duddington, ed. and annot. Boris Jakim (Grand Rapids, MI: William B. Eerdmans, 2005), 135. At points I have modified the Duddington translation in accordance with the Russian text: *Opravdanie dobra: Nravstvennaia filosofiia*, in *Sobranie sochinenii*, 8:3-516.

9. Vladimir Solov'ev, "Kant," in *Entsiklopedicheskii slovar' Brokgauza i Efrona*, vol. 14 (2), reprinted in V. S. Solov'ev, *Sochineniia v dvukh tomakh*, ed. A. V. Gulyga and A. F. Losev, 2nd ed., 2 vols. (Moscow: Mysl', 1990), 2:441-78, here 441.

10. Studies of Kant's influence on him include Aleksandr I. Vvedenskii, "O mistitsizme i krititsizme v teorii poznaniia V. S. Solov'eva," *Voprosy filosofii i psikhologii* 12, no. 1, bk. 56 (1901), reprinted in Vvedenskii, *Filosofskie ocherki* (Prague: Plamia, 1924), 45-71; S. A. Chernov, "Krititsizm i mistitsizm (Obzor kantianstva v zhurnale 'Voprosy filosofii i psikhologii')," in *Kant i filosofiia v Rossii*, ed. Z. A. Kamenskii and V. A. Zhuchkov (Moscow: Nauka, 1994), 119-20, 139-42; V. V. Lazarev, "Kategoricheskii imperative I. Kanta i etika V. Solov'eva," in Kamenskii and Zhuchkov, *Kant i filosofiia*, 42-80; Alexander Haardt, "Personal'nost' v morali i prave: Vstrecha Vl. Solov'eva s I. Kantom," in *Personal'nost': Iazyk filosofii v russko-nemetskom dialoge*, ed. A. Haardt and N. S. Plotnikov (Moscow: Modest Kolerov, 2007), 149-65; A. Haardt, "Kants Personalitätsprinzip als Grundlage der Rechtsphilosophie Vladimir Solov'evs: Ein Meilenstein in der russischen Kantrezeption des 19. Jh.," in *Die Aktualität der Philosophie Kants*, ed. K. Schmidt, K. Steigleder, and B. Mojsisch (Amsterdam/Philadelphia: John Benjamins, 2005), 37-57.

11. References to Kant are to *The Cambridge Edition of the Works of Immanuel Kant*, in this case to the volume *Practical Philosophy*, trans. and ed. Mary J. Gregor, intro. Allen Wood (Cambridge: Cambridge University Press, 1996). This volume contains, among Kant's works that I have used here, *Groundwork of the Metaphysics of Morals* (G), *Critique of Practical Reason* (PrR), and *The Metaphysics of Morals* (MM). The first page reference is to the Cambridge edition, the second to the standard German edition of Kant's works, *Kants gesammelte Schriften* (as indicated in the margins of the Cambridge edition).

12. Thus Wood claims that "Kant is fundamentally a *religious* thinker." Allen W. Wood, *Kant's Ethical Thought* (Cambridge: Cambridge University Press, 1999), 318. On the development of philosophical theism in Russia, see Sean Gillen's chapter in this volume.

13. *Bogochelovechestvo*, also translated as theanthropy, divine humanity, or the humanity of God.

14. Kant, *Religion and Rational Theology*, trans. and ed. Allen W. Wood and George di Giovanni (Cambridge: Cambridge University Press, 1996), which includes *Religion within the Boundaries of Mere Religion* (R).

15. Solovyov, *Lectures on Divine Humanity*, 33; subsequent page citations are made parenthetically in the text. As Valliere puts it, "Like all the idealists Soloviev regarded human consciousness as the mysterious fact with which philosophy must begin." *Modern Russian Theology*, 124.

16. Evgenii Trubetskoi gives a good account of Solov'ev's view that all human thought testifies to and presupposes the absolute as its transcendental and ontological condition. E. N. Trubetskoi, *Mirosozertsanie V. S. Solov'eva*, 2 vols. (Moscow: Put', 1913), 1:94–104.

17. Judith Deutsch Kornblatt, *Divine Sophia: The Wisdom Writings of Vladimir Solovyov* (Ithaca, NY: Cornell University Press, 2009). Recently V. F. Boikov, too, has emphasized the primacy of mystical experience (though not of an exclusive mysticism) for Solov'ev. According to him, "universal mystical experience is the foundation . . . of Solov'ev's philosophy. In relation to experience, philosophy is the power of individual reason that raises the intuitions of mystical experience to the level and form of universal reason." V. F. Boikov, "The Nightingale Song of Russian Philosophy," *Russian Studies in Philosophy* 46, no. 1 (Summer 2007): 35–63, here 39–40. This article translates the valuable introduction to V. F. Boikov, ed., *Vl. Solov'ev: Pro et contra (Lichnost' i tvorchestvo Vladimira Solov'eva v otsenke russkikh myslitelei i issledovatelei)*, 2 vols. (St. Petersburg: Izd. Russkogo Khristianskogo gumanitarnogo instituta, 2000–2002).

18. Perfectibility is the first of the "central teachings" identified by Jonathan Sutton in *The Religious Philosophy of Vladimir Solovyov: Towards a Reassessment* (New York: St. Martin's Press, 1988).

19. Solov'ev returns to the "image and likeness of God" in *Justification of the Good*, where he puts it more simply: the image is our consciousness of divine perfection and the likeness is our capacity for perfectibility according to the image (145, 152, 176–77).

20. Solov'ev soon revised this distinction between positive (divine) and negative (human) absoluteness. In *Critique of Abstract Principles*, he distinguishes rather between two poles of the absolute. The first is self-subsistent (God), the second is in the process of becoming (man), "and the full truth can be expressed by the word 'Godmanhood.'" *Sobranie sochinenii*, 2:315–24, quotation at 323.

21. Solov'ev returned to the inner sources of faith in *Justification of the Good*. In his analysis of moral experience he found three "primary data of morality" (shame, compassion, and reverence) that he believed to be indubitable grounds for accepting the realities experienced through them: ourselves as supramaterial beings, fellow persons, and God, respectively. Reverence is the highest datum, so for him moral experience was really moral-religious experience. "In true religious experience," he writes, "the reality of that which is experienced is immediately given; we are directly conscious of the real presence of the Deity, and feel Its effect upon us" (142).

22. See Valliere, *Modern Russian Theology*, 150–51.

23. One of the places where Solov'ev alludes to this verse is his essay "The Jews and the Christian Problem" (1884), which is recently translated in *Freedom, Faith, and Dogma: Essays by V. S. Soloviev on Christianity and Judaism*, ed. and trans. Vladimir Wozniuk (Albany: State University of New York Press, 2008), 43–88, here 53.

24. He also considers the analytic role of reason in *Justification of the Good* (and in many other works). See Randall Poole, "Vladimir Solov'ëv's Philosophical Anthropology: Autonomy, Dignity, Perfectibility," in *A History of Russian Philosophy: Faith, Reason, and the Defense of Human Dignity*, ed. Gary M. Hamburg and Randall A. Poole (Cambridge: Cambridge University Press, 2010), 146.

25. He regarded "autonomy of the will" as the supreme principle of morality (G 89/4:432).

26. He closely paraphrases and directly translates large parts of the *Groundwork*. Solov'ev, *Sobranie sochinenii*, 2:44–62. In addition to these two chapters, he devotes three more, plus an appendix, to Kant's ethics and conception of rational autonomy, drawing also on (paraphrasing and quoting at length) the *Critique of Pure Reason* and the *Critique of Practical Reason*. *Sobranie sochinenii*, 2:62–72, 89–116, 371–97. See Poole, "Vladimir Solov'ëv's Philosophical Anthropology," 137–41.

27. "The conjunction of these three elements forms the actual human being, and the properly human principle is reason (*ratio*), the relationship of the two others." Solovyov, *Lectures on Divine Humanity*, 158. For additional statements of his three principles of human nature, see *Sobranie sochinenii*, 2:158–60, 172–74, and (in the context of his Christology) *Spiritual Foundations of Society* (*Dukhovnye osnovy zhizni*, 1882–84) in *Sobranie sochinenii*, 3:368–74.

28. Solovyov, *Lectures on Divine Humanity*, 142.

29. Solovyov, *Justification of the Good*, lv. Solov'ev makes clear here that the choice to degrade ourselves is to "become lower and worse than the animal," since normal human beings cannot simply divest themselves of morality and revert to an animal state. It is still self-determination, but a "diabolical" one. Twenty years later, Evgenii Trubetskoi, writing in the context of the Great War and the Russian Revolution, called this "beast-manhood." See E. N. Trubetskoi, *Smysl zhizni* (Moscow: Sytin, 1918; Berlin: Slovo, 1922), 246; Randall Poole, "Religion, War, and Revolution: E. N. Trubetskoi's Liberal Construction of Russian National Identity, 1912–20," *Kritika: Explorations in Russian and Eurasian History* 7, no. 2 (Spring 2006): 195–240.

30. This essay is included in *The Heart of Reality: Essays on Beauty, Love, and Ethics by V. S. Soloviev*, ed. and trans. Vladimir Wozniuk (Notre Dame, IN: University of Notre Dame Press, 2003), 83–133, quotation at 92.

31. Kant, *Critique of the Power of Judgment*, ed. Paul Guyer, trans. Paul Guyer and Eric Matthews (Cambridge: Cambridge University Press, 2000), 302 (5:435). See the section below, "Solov'ev and Kant's Theology of Moral Perfectibility."

32. Vladimir Soloviev, "The Social Question in Europe," in *Politics, Law, and Morality: Essays by V. S. Soloviev*, ed. and trans. Vladimir Wozniuk (New Haven, CT: Yale University Press, 2000), 35n.

33. On Schelling and Solov'ev, see Trubetskoi, *Mirosozertsanie Vl. S. Solov'eva*, 1:52–59, 383–94; P. P. Gaidenko, *Vladimir Solov'ev i filosofiia Serebrianogo veka* (Moscow: Progress-Traditsiia, 2011), 69–91; Paul Valliere, "Solov'ëv and Schelling's Philosophy of Revelation," in *Vladimir Solov'ëv: Reconciler and Polemicist*, ed. William van den Bercken, Manon de Courten, and Evert van der Zweerde (Leuven: Peeters, 2000), 119–29.

34. Trubetskoi, *Mirosozertsanie Vl. S. Solov'eva*, 1:89–90. Gaidenko's interpretation of Solov'ev's Schellingianism is similar.

35. See Randall A. Poole, "Utopianism, Idealism, Liberalism: Russian Confrontations with Vladimir Solov'ev," *Modern Greek Studies Yearbook: A Publication of Mediterranean, Slavic, and Eastern Orthodox Studies* 16/17 (2000/2001): 43–87.

36. Solov'ev, *Sobranie sochinenii*, 2:173.

37. Ibid., 173–74.

38. Ibid., 174.

39. "Istoricheskie dela filosofii," in *Sobranie sochinenii*, 2:410; 2:411–12; 2:412.

40. Ibid., 413. For other readings of Solov'ev's famous lecture, see A. F. Losev, *Vladimir Solov'ev i ego vremia* (Moscow: Progress, 1990), 139–42; Edith W. Clowes, *Fiction's Overcoat: Russian Literary Culture and the Question of Philosophy* (Ithaca, NY: Cornell University Press, 2004), 103–4.

41. Vladimir Solovyov, *A Solovyov Anthology*, ed. S. L. Frank, trans. Natalie Duddington (London: SCM Press, 1950), 15–16. Konstantin Mochul'skii, *Vladimir Solov'ev: Zhizn' i uchenie* (Paris: YMCA-Press, 1951), 10, also notes that Godmanhood is a modern philosophical development of Chalcedon.

42. Judith Deutsch Kornblatt shows this in her essay "Vladimir Solov'ev on Spiritual Nationhood, Russia and the Jews," *The Russian Review* 56 (April 1997): 157–77.

43. As Richard Gustafson writes, Solov'ev made *theosis* "the cornerstone of his theology of Godmanhood." See his seminal essay, "Soloviev's Doctrine of Salvation," in *Russian Religious Thought*, ed. Judith Deutsch Kornblatt and Richard F. Gustafson (Madison: University of Wisconsin Press, 1996), 31–48, quotation at 39.

44. Gustafson, "Soloviev's Doctrine of Salvation," 46–47.

45. Solovyov, *Lectures on Divine Humanity*, 158–63; Solov'ev, *Dukhovnye osnovy zhizni*, in *Sobranie sochinenii*, 3:370–74.

46. Smith, *Vladimir Soloviev*, 119.

47. Mainly: *Groundwork of the Metaphysics of Morals* (1785), *Critique of Practical Reason* (1787), *Critique of the Power of Judgment* (1790), *Religion within the Boundaries of Mere Reason* (1793), and *Metaphysics of Morals* (1797).

48. Allen W. Wood, *Kant's Moral Religion* (Ithaca, NY: Cornell University Press, 1970), 127: people cannot "attain to the moral perfection in *deed* which would be required actually to bring about a Kingdom of Ends."

49. Solov'ev, *Sobranie sochinenii*, 2:70 (see also 59–60, 114, 116).

50. The postulate of the existence of God is somewhat more complicated. It follows from Kant's premise that persons deserve happiness proportionate to their endless progress or perfectibility toward holiness (which can only mean perfect happiness); only God can provide such happiness (PrR 240/5:124).

51. Patrick Lally Michelson has reconstructed the history of the idea of "similitude anthropology"—free "assimilation to God" and "moral deification"—and its Russian reception in "In the Image and Likeness of God: The Patristic Tradition of Human Dignity and Freedom in Nineteenth-Century Russia," the first chapter of his excellent doctoral dissertation, "'The First and Most Sacred Right': Religious Freedom and the Liberation of the Russian Nation, 1825–1905" (University of Wisconsin–Madison, 2007), 29–92.

52. The idea of infinite perfectibility can be found in patristic works such as Gregory of Nyssa's *The Life of Moses* (for which example I am indebted to T. Allan Smith of the University of Toronto), but Solov'ev's version has more in common with the Enlightenment idea of progress.

53. Vladimir Wozniuk, "Vladimir S. Soloviev and the Politics of Human Rights," *Journal of Church and State* 41, no. 1 (Winter 1999): 33–50.

54. Walicki, *Legal Philosophies*, 195–98, 203–5.

55. Kant says that anyone who asks for "miracles as credentials . . . thereby confesses to his own moral unbelief." But moral faith "can validate miracles, if need be, as effects coming from the good principle" (R 105/6:62–63). Solov'ev shared these sentiments entirely.

56. Kant quotes it in somewhat recast form (R 108/6:66). Solovyov, *Justification of the Good*, 147.

57. Wood, *Kant's Moral Religion*, 191.

58. Cf. Solov'ev in *Critique of Abstract Principles*: The equality of all before the law actually means that "all are equally *limited* by law, or all equally limit each other; this means there is no inner or positive unity among them, only their correct division and demarcation" (*Sobranie sochinenii*, 2:167).

59. According to Stephen Palmquist, for Kant the true end of religion "is to bring into being something which might best be called a 'theocracy,' provided we take this term literally rather than in its common meaning." See Palmquist, "'The Kingdom of God Is at Hand!' (Did *Kant* really say *that*?)," *History of Philosophy Quarterly* 11, no. 4 (October 1994): 421–37, here 427.

60. See Poole, "Vladimir Solov'ëv's Philosophical Anthropology," 143–44.

61. The essay is translated in Frank, ed., *A Solovyov Anthology*, 60–71, quoted here at 61, 65, 67; and in Wozniuk, ed., *Freedom, Faith, and Dogma*, 159–70.

62. The essay is translated in Wozniuk, ed., *Freedom, Faith, and Dogma*, 147–57, quoted here at 147, 151.

63. See Vanessa Rampton's chapter in this volume.

64. Randall A. Poole, ed. and trans., *Problems of Idealism: Essays in Russian Social Philosophy* (New Haven, CT: Yale University Press, 2003), 305.

65. Chicherin devoted an entire book to criticizing Solov'ev's theocratic project: B. N. Chicherin, *Mistitsizm v nauke* (Moscow: Tip. Martynova, 1880). As a Hegelian, Chicherin maintained that the highest form of human community was the state, not the Church, so his criticism is not surprising. For Trubetskoi's criticism, see his *Mirosozertsanie Vl. S. Solov'eva*, 1:173–78, 531–85. Novgorodtsev directs the brunt of his criticism not at Solov'ev himself, but at the very idea of theocracy. See his *Ob obshchestvennom ideale*, 3rd ed. (Berlin: Slovo, 1921), 17–19, 40.

Chapter 10

Religious Thought and Russian Liberal Institutions

The Case of Pavel Novgorodtsev

VANESSA RAMPTON

In imperial Russia, liberal preoccupations and Orthodox faith did not cluster naturally together. What Paul Valliere has called "the culture of wholeness" associated with the Orthodox Christian concern for moral unity within society, and individual self-realization within a community of believers, was often in direct tension with certain liberal predispositions toward the world.[1] Liberals, as presented in this essay, are characterized not so much by their commitment to "the culture of wholeness," but rather by their conscious engagement with what they perceive to be the inevitable conflicts of values that arise between different members of society.[2] In the liberal view, Orthodox support for integralism and merging the religious and secular spheres of life could present a direct challenge to the dynamic repositioning between sometimes competing goods and values, arising from the fact that concepts such as liberty and equality are not the same for all members of society. The desire of liberals to associate individual dignity with objective legal standards coexisted uneasily with Orthodoxy's traditional aspirations to organize society according to values such as love, mercy, and humility. Religious respect for miracle, revelation, and ritual had no value for liberals concerned with cultivating the ability of individuals to use reason independently from traditional superstitions and faiths.

Despite these preliminary differences, small but important groups of thinkers actively sought to explore the potential affinities between a liberal concern with irreconcilable values and Orthodox belief in turn-of-the-century Russia, and introduced Orthodox terms and categories into institutional settings where we would not necessarily expect them. The Liberation Movement (*Osvoboditel'noe dvizhenie*) of 1900 to 1905, an eclectic oppositional movement crucial for the development of Russian liberalism, contained several prominent members who sought to further a vision of social and political reform based on Orthodox principles.³ The foundation of the Constitutional Democratic (Kadet) Party (Konstitutsionno-demokraticheskaia partiia) in 1905, and the emergence of a politically coherent liberal movement that demanded freedom of conscience and religious liberty, occurred simultaneously with the revival of a new interest in the currents of spirituality deriving from Orthodoxy and religious dissent, a phenomenon galvanized by the decrees on religious tolerance of April 1905 and October 1906.⁴ In an ecclesiastical context, meanwhile, liberal concepts were refined and redefined by a number of parish clergy who attempted to offer a new synthesis between Orthodoxy and social life based on their desire to confer increased rights and freedoms on the clerical estate.⁵ Several influential faculty members and former students at Russia's four spiritual academies, religious institutions of higher education that played an important role in the development of philosophy in the nineteenth century, sought to combine their interest in rational, scientific, and individualistic concepts with their theological commitments.⁶ Many of them were acquainted with the Moscow Psychological Society (Moskovskoe psikhologicheskoe obshchestvo, 1885–1922), a learned society where prominent philosophers such as Vladimir Solov'ev (1853–1900) and Boris Chicherin (1828–1904) were engaged in elaborating a liberal social philosophy rooted in the divine value of the person.⁷ Evidently, some of the multiple Orthodoxies mentioned in the introduction to this volume had the ability to establish and sustain a broadly liberal world view. In particular, the idea of social commitment and desire to formulate a flexible answer to the most pressing problems of Russian society cut across different strands of the country's intellectual life, and blurred the categories and concerns of liberal and religious thinkers. As I shall argue in this essay, a particularly good example of a religious liberal attempt to formulate a non-dogmatic defense of the idea of individual dignity can be found in the career and writings of Pavel Ivanovich Novgorodtsev (1866–1924).⁸

Novgorodtsev was one of the outstanding legal philosophers of his generation, a member of the Psychological Society and the Kadet Party, as well as a devout Orthodox believer. While his religious faith remained only implicit in many of his early academic articles and published works (often printed in the Psychological Society's journal, *Questions of Philosophy and Psychology* [*Voprosy filosofii i psikhologii*, 1889–1918]), it defined the contours of his attempt to articulate a liberal social philosophy in late imperial Russia. For Novgorodtsev, religious belief played a crucial role in providing the liberal political project with an enduring foundation; only by acknowledging that there is a higher authority than human beings themselves can we avoid utopian approaches to personhood and freedom, and recognize that the individual and society interact in a permanent, fruitful tension. Much of his early work was concerned with the potential of religious belief to sustain his vision of an anti-utopian social philosophy. In his later years, in the wake of war, revolution, and emigration, he addressed more explicitly in his writings the benefits of a specifically Russian Orthodox (as opposed to Western Christian) approach to religious belief, and argued for involving the Russian Orthodox Church in the project of rebuilding Russian society. Novgorodtsev's work can thus be approached as a vehicle to illuminate more broadly the place of religious concepts in the institutional settings normally associated with the development of liberalism in Russia, such as the Moscow Psychological Society, the Liberation Movement, the Kadet Party, and the Russian Juridical Institute (Russkii iuridicheskii institut), which he founded in Prague in the early 1920s.

My aim in this article, to contextualize and analyze how Novgorodtsev attempted to reconcile the principles of Orthodox belief with a liberal philosophy of social development in revolutionary Russia, goes beyond the context of Slavic studies to illustrate some of the fundamental tensions and affinities between religious and liberal approaches to freedom and selfhood.[9] Trained in European philosophy, Novgorodtsev himself devoted much attention in his work to demonstrating that divisions within the intelligentsia concerning the proper relationship between religion and politics were not unique to Russia, but rather a concrete manifestation of broader conflicts between dogmatic utopians and liberal pragmatists, secular and religious alike. From this perspective, his defense of liberalism and humanistic Orthodoxy in a hostile environment can be seen as a particularly vivid illustration of a broader concern with the power of religion to advance and celebrate a non-dogmatic vision of social progress. Yet Novgorodtsev's own insights into the relationship between religion and liberalism also illustrate some of the difficulties of repudiating dogma entirely. Toward the end of his career, his sense of the urgent need for the renewal of Russian society based on Orthodox principles led him to adopt some of the utopian modes of thought he had devoted much of his early work to discrediting. This selective blindness at the end of his life is very significant because it sheds light on the delicate relationship between religion, liberalism, and dogma, as well as on the difficulty of finding a middle way between the extremes of dogmatism and skepticism.

Personhood

Before I proceed to an analysis of those aspects of Novgorodtsev's writings that have a clear affinity with Russian religious thought more broadly, a word about terminology is in order. Imported into Russia by the 1820s, as of the mid-1860s the words *liberal* and its derivative *liberalizm* took on a firmly pejorative connotation: liberals were identified with men of leisure, who had a superficial interest in using European culture to reform their country, without wanting to incur any risks to their own social position.[10] The negative association with the label was such that not even members of the Kadet Party (Novgorodtsev included), who clearly sympathized with liberal ideas of Western origin and associated politics with the notion of a permanent balance between sometimes competing goals, attached the label "liberal" willingly to themselves.[11] In contrast to liberal, the term Orthodox (*pravoslavnyi*) was a far more ubiquitous means of self-identification, and until the nineteenth century was closely connected with the idea of Russian (*russkii*) national identity.[12] But despite its widespread use, publically identifying one's philosophical beliefs with the official Church was more controversial for liberally inclined thinkers, in part because of the former's long-standing association with the tsarist regime. As we shall see, it was primarily in the period following the Russian Revolution of 1917 that Novgorodtsev engaged more explicitly with specifically Orthodox, rather than more generally religious, categories such as humility and contemplation, and made provocative claims about the universal significance of the Orthodox Christian Church. While I apply the terms "liberal" and "Orthodox" retrospectively to Novgorodtsev's work and dispositions during the period, it is important to remember that they remain sensitive indices of the culture to which they belong.

The synthesis Novgorodtsev elaborated in the first decades of the twentieth century between religious belief and liberal principles is best understood in reference to a larger movement concerned with refuting positivist social theories and orchestrating what has been described as a "revolution of the spirit," involving "a new kind of human being—spiritual, aesthetic, sensitive, and loving—the very opposite of rationally calculating economic man—and a new society based on the ideal of *sobornost'* (a collective body in which the elements retain their individuality)."[13] Novgorodtsev played a crucial role in this endeavor through his association with the revival of neo-idealism and philosophical liberalism in the Russian Silver Age. A member of the Psychological Society, he was well acquainted with the attempts of Chicherin and Solov'ev (but also of Sergei Trubetskoi [1862–1905], Evgenii Trubetskoi [1863–1920], and Sergei Kotliarevskii [1873–1939]) to derive liberal social principles from an idealist approach to ethics, epistemology, and ontology. Novgorodtsev also knew and collaborated with four philosophical thinkers renowned for their unorthodox intellectual trajectory from Marxism to idealism and liberalism: Petr Struve (1870–1944), Semen Frank (1877–1950), Sergei Bulgakov (1871–1944), and Nikolai Berdiaev (1874–1948).[14] Together with Struve, he organized the symposium *Problems of Idealism* (*Problemy idealizma*, 1902) that would serve as the manifesto of neo-idealist liberalism.[15]

In their attempt to reject positivism and articulate new conceptions of personhood (*lichnost'*), Novgorodtsev and like-minded thinkers were inspired by Kant's views on selfhood, but also by theological ideas about the divine element within individuals.[16] The Kantian contention that human beings are authentically persons because they benefit from the ability to act in the light of moral conscience, rather than simply material urges or desires, which is also an indication of their freedom, has an important affinity with theological notions of the special status and dignity of individuals; both philosophies have been used to argue that human beings are ends-in-themselves and ought never to be treated merely as a means.[17]

For neo-idealists, consciousness of absolute moral principles revealed by reason constitutes a link with a realm of noumenal being, distinct from the phenomenal world. While Kant always claimed that this suprasensible realm of being was unknowable, his assertion that its existence constitutes the proof of freedom, God, and immortality inspired Russian philosophers in their attempt to link Kantian personalism and Christian belief.[18] By pushing further the metaphysical conclusions of the Kantian ideas of autonomy and theism, a number of thinkers with liberal sympathies posited a transcendent ontological reality, in Novgorodtsev's words a realm of "free, creative, uncaused being," the existence of which makes possible a higher synthesis that joins all aspects of human life.[19] For many Psychological Society professors, this religiously inspired vision, in which human dignity takes on an objective, theistic dimension, is what confirms the worth and vocation of the human person. The reality of a "divine principle" (*bozhestvennoe nachalo*) that "rises above human life at an inaccessible height," Sergei Kotliarevskii wrote, is what confers on individuals their unique worth and also confirms their intrinsic equality.[20] Semen Frank and Petr Struve also used the idea that "the human person is sacred" (*sviatynia*) to substantiate the claim that no individual "could be used as a means by other people nor to achieve any objective goals outside themselves."[21] In supplementing the Kantian ethical principle of individual dignity by giving it explicitly metaphysical or religious roots, Novgorodtsev and his neo-idealist colleagues saw themselves as providing a more robust justification of the absolute value of the human person.

For Novgorodtsev in particular, the ontological foundations of personhood offered one way of overcoming what he saw as an irresolvable dualism in Kant's thought, namely that the Kantian separation of material necessity and spiritual freedom offered little in the way of concrete, tangible guidance for individual moral behavior.[22] It is the existence of a transcendental absolute—what Novgorodtsev claims we experience as a "living God in our spirit"—that has the ability to provide moral guidance in a concrete historical epoch.[23] By revealing the individual's link with God, and the "absolute principle of the good," religion supports the idea of eternal striving toward an unattainable goal, the same justification Novgorodtsev had already identified for politics.[24] And yet the moral but also inherently social aspects of religious principles such as love, harmony, and solidarity have both the potential to endow the notion of "ought" with content, as well as infuse and direct social life and progress.[25] Thus conceived, the "divine" element in each individual person is realized in his or her earthly vocation: individuals become persons in the fullest sense of the word by seeking to approximate God.

Freedom

This personalist theory in which individual dignity is rooted in transcendent being had a particular significance for ways of thinking about freedom in late imperial Russia. For religious liberals, freedom is not something created by human powers and aspirations alone, but rather granted by a divine being. Yet the fact that freedom is bestowed on humans by God and measured against his will does not diminish in any way its authenticity or significance. On the contrary, it is thanks to the awareness of higher values, located in "the spiritual depths" of human consciousness, that freedom can be said to constitute an authentic choice, and preserves its meaning.[26] The exercise of moral freedom plays a crucial role in the recognition of a supreme religious authority.

As Novgorodtsev elaborated his views on freedom, he was inspired by both Vladimir Solov'ev's social philosophy and his religious ideal. Though Randall Poole's study in this volume is devoted to the Kantian roots of Solov'ev's philosophy, it is worth emphasizing in this context the extent to which Novgorodtsev saw Solov'ev as crucially supplementing Kant's thought and its implications for freedom. Solov'ev, Novgorodtsev argued in 1901, had gone beyond Kant's emphasis on abstract principles by attempting to "elucidate the extent and strength of the power of the good, and uncover its existence in all fundamental practical relationships which compose individual and collective life."[27] He had therefore become a "partisan of living social Christianity," who sought the embodiment and justification of the good in reality.[28] Inspired by his predecessor, Novgorodtsev drew out the concrete, social implications of his religious view of personhood to justify a positive conception of freedom, emphasize that the right to a dignified existence must be enshrined in law, and argue that various obstacles to achieving freedom—including material insufficiencies and economic dependency—must be removed.[29] Moral religion, in this view, helps persons become aware of their intrinsic equality, and thus become alive to the importance of exercising freedom in accordance with the demands of solidarity.[30] By linking a vision of autonomous and moral-religious principles to the idea of an ethical community, Solov'ev provided Novgorodtsev with an influential model of how the Kantian principle of human dignity might be embodied in reality.

Despite the emphasis Solov'ev placed on the positive idea of individual self-determination ("freedom to"), Novgorodtsev was particularly concerned to demonstrate that it exists in constant interaction with the idea of "freedom from," in the negative sense of independence from any kind of dependency.[31] Indeed, his careful distinction between these divergent types of liberty was what marked his identity as a liberal, and differentiated him and his colleagues from other groups on the political spectrum. In Novgorodtsev's case, his religious world view, based on the absolute principle of personhood, inspired his notion of a liberal social philosophy characterized by a fruitful tension between positive and negative freedom, and also underpinned some of his ambivalences toward the Orthodox Church. Part of the reason he valued a sphere of external freedom was because of its significance for moral and spiritual life; he believed that a sphere of non-interference guaranteed by law is necessary for the development of internal, moral freedom, and thus of personhood and culture. A significant number of his academic efforts were directed toward demonstrating the importance of law for liberalism and, by implication, arguing that the spiritual freedom ostensibly granted by Orthodoxy cannot exist under autocracy. "Without requisite guarantees from the law and the state," Novgorodtsev wrote in 1905, moral freedom "remains a mere fiction."[32] Underlying this claim is his fundamentally non-dogmatic notion of historical progress: he observes that if seeking the truth amounts to an eternal quest, and the "truth has yet to be fully revealed, and there are no limits to searching for it," a realm of non-interference protected by law is what enables each individual to find her or his own, unique truth.[33] Novgorodtsev recognized the importance of allowing inner, spiritual freedom to be guaranteed in visible, public ways in the history of the development of liberalism. In his lectures on the history of the philosophy of law, he emphasizes that the principle of freedom of conscience and its derivatives were the first applications of the idea of negative freedom in the sense of an inviolable human right.

As a philosophical idealist, Novgorodtsev believed that the "absolute form can never be filled by an adequate content, and the moral call can never be satisfied by an achieved result."[34] Moral autonomy is required to uncover the absolutism of the moral law, while its empirical content is worked out in reference to concrete historical circumstances. His religiously inspired concern with enriching this "absolute form" led him in the direction of natural law, which he defined as "the sum total of ideal, moral notions about law."[35] Thus conceived, natural law derives from the highest moral norms associated with the absolute significance of personhood. As the earthly expression of the transcendental values of human dignity, freedom, and equality, it provides a just, objective standard for social and political life. That this task is also a religious one is explicit in Novgorodtsev's description of the instauration of a regime of law as a "sacred achievement of individuals."[36] It was on these premises that he endorsed a constitutional state based on natural law as the one best suited to the self-realization of Russian citizens.[37]

Reactions to 1905 and Its Aftermath

As opposition to tsarism mounted in the early twentieth century, the question of how new approaches to freedom and selfhood could be implemented in practice took on a new urgency for large portions of Russian society, including academics, churchmen, and students. At that time, the special circumstances of tsarist oppression blurred many of the distinctions between liberally inclined thinkers and other movements, who found common cause within the Liberation Movement under the claims of liberation (*osvobozhdenie*) from tsarist institutions. A concern for positive liberty as described above had many obvious affinities with a progressive, democratic stance and the desire of left-wing movements to enact major social reforms for the benefit of peasants and workers, as well as the resources of religious philosophy to provide an adequate basis for a more just society.

The widespread unrest and revolutionary ferment among students, industrial workers, peasants, and national and religious minorities confronted political actors with some of the internal contradictions of freedom, just as they were in the process of establishing Russia's only significant liberal party, the Kadet Party, in the second half of 1905.[38] Landowners defending their "inalienable rights" clashed with peasants who perceived their situation as legalized oppression, defenders of freedom of conscience were confronted with the question of how to make citizens identify with a view of the state as a national and spiritual whole, and some of those who were opposed to autocratic government nevertheless conceded that the rights and liberties they prized could not be guaranteed in times of social unrest and economic disturbances. In a polarized political environment, moreover, Kadet Party members were divided as to whether the main threat to freedom came from political forces further to their left or to their right. The official response to the turmoil, expressed in a series of decrees and manifestos and codified in the Fundamental Laws of April 1906, committed the government to introducing basic civil liberties (including the freedom of religion), political rights, and a democratically elected Duma (parliament) that would benefit from full legislative powers. Yet these concessions, which were granted reluctantly by the tsar, were perceived as too little too late and failed to pacify the country as expected.

Deeply engaged in the reform movement, Novgorodtsev and his liberal colleagues experienced firsthand the turmoil of Russia's first revolution, the flawed constitutional experiment, and the need to adapt a theory of liberalism to Russian specificities.[39] Their practical knowledge of the limits of tsarist constitutionalism to guarantee freedom and of the dangers posed by social unrest and economic disturbances to individual self-realization reinforced their sense of the importance of linking freedom with religion, culture, and community. In the aftermath of 1905, Novgorodtsev and some of his associates, including Frank, Struve, and Kotliarevskii, sought to popularize the notion that formal ideas of law and political freedom are useless foundations for liberalism if they are divorced from religious principles and cultural renewal.[40] Culture—what Frank and Struve defined as "the sum total of absolute values created and produced by humankind and constituting its spiritual-social essence [*dukhovno-obshchestvennoe bytie*]"—verges on religious experience because it provides the framework within which individual creative activity approximates absolute values.[41] Seen in this light, the liberation of Russia cannot be accomplished by politics alone, but rather depends on culture and creative (*sozidatel'nyi*) impulses that make the principles of freedom and equality immune to instrumentalization by politicians.⁴²

One corollary of this new approach to culture and the disillusionment concerning the prospects of imposing radical social equalization from above, was an emphasis on the cultivation of the individual personality, its religious convictions and beliefs, as a prerequisite to the liberation of society. In this view, free moral self-perfection is better placed to further respect for the rule of law and political forms than any kind of top-down social reorganization, advocated by some socialists. Social equality cannot be imposed from without, but rather is reinforced at the national level by the interplay in individual life between spirituality and cultural practices. Related to this claim is the notion that democracy must necessarily be accompanied by certain social and psychological attitudes to be able to provide freedom worthy of each person's individual destiny. Drawing on the religious notion of the responsibility for oneself and the world, in the period immediately following 1905 Novgorodtsev advocated a more individualist application of positive freedom, informed by his understanding of the potential of religious belief to regenerate society. Echoing Frank and Struve, he now highlighted the importance of individual self-perfection in the light of ideals that reside not "in the cultural and social manifestations of the personality, but in the depths of its own consciousness, in its moral and religious needs."⁴³

In the context of the resurgence of religious and millenarian thought that directly followed the failed Revolution of 1905,⁴⁴ Novgorodtsev was careful to distinguish his social ideal from any form of biblical or prophetic utopia, and this is also what most distinguishes his mature religious thought from the Western Christian tradition and gives it a decidedly Orthodox flavor. In the aftermath of 1905 he wrote two major treatises, *Crisis of Contemporary Legal Consciousness* (*Krizis sovremennogo pravosoznaniia*, 1909) and *On the Social Ideal* (*Ob obshchestvennom ideale*, 1911–16), condemning the rise of utopian thought in Russia and emphasizing the unparalleled value of the non-dogmatic element of religious consciousness as the foundation of a better and more robust social order. Time and again in these publications, he emphasizes the anti-utopian aspect of bringing together the earthly and divine, and excludes the possibility of the material realization of the kingdom of God on earth. Freedom, he affirms, is fundamentally incompatible with the idea that humankind is "approaching the final, blissful stage of its existence" and that there exists a "salvatory truth" (*spasitel'naia istina*) "that will lead people to this highest and last epoch [*peredel*] of history."⁴⁵ He stressed that his ethics supports a philosophy of history that conceives of religious experience as constituting the link between the earthly and the divine, while practice teaches that the ideal can never be more important than reality, and there is no single answer to the problem of individual freedom and society. In *On the Social Ideal*, he wrote: "To construct a life without God and without power [*vlast'*], without the ties that constrain [*stesniat'*] individual being and without any restrictions on freedom . . . would mean the destruction of the foundations of society and of freedom. Understanding the interactions between human beings without recognizing their overall unifying ties is impossible: by rejecting the moral nature of life in society, we reject society itself, and along with this deny the existence of the problem of society."[46] Novgorodtsev was convinced that moral freedom's links with a higher power were also the justification for its limitation in earthly affairs. In particular, individual awareness of the extent to which freedom is God-given has an inherently social aspect: the ultimate equality of individuals confirms the freedom of all, and thus the necessary limitation of the power of one person over another.

It seems plausible that this commitment to the anti-utopian quality of religious belief was directly supported by Novgorodtsev's experience of liberalism in the Russian context. At the height of controversy between peasants and landowners in 1905 he observed that the ideas of the rights of the individual person (*pravo chelovecheskoi lichnosti*), human dignity, and freedom "eliminate the idea of inalienable property rights, replacing it with the principle of public legal regulation of acquired rights and a necessary reward to their holders in case of their infringement."[47] In other words, the requirements of the fullest development of personhood imply a new answer to the problem of freedom and equality based on historical circumstances. Four years later, Novgorodtsev developed a policy platform he called "equality as a starting point" (*ravenstvo iskhodnogo punkta*), designed to make sure that all individuals have the opportunity to fulfill their destinies. Inspired by the difficulties of guaranteeing freedom in Russia's unequal society, he observed that individual rights and freedoms gain in relevance only once this preliminary equality has been established.[48] Overseeing the liberation of individual citizens by guaranteeing their dignity is incumbent on the state and, according to Novgorodtsev, it is a lawful state, not a socialist one, that is best able to ensure that freedom will be approached as an eternal compromise, a constantly evolving dualism of the concrete historical process and spiritual consciousness. If religious principles such as piety and reverence can guide individual life and promote creativity, they offer no one version of freedom to which individuals must adhere. The absolute worth of individual rights does not preclude their limitation and readjustment in the light of moral impulses and feelings of solidarity. This seemed to him the essence of the liberal task in Russia, and was supported by his understanding of the nature of religious consciousness.

War, Revolution, Emigration

In his later years, during emigration in Prague, Novgorodtsev further elaborated on the insights of his earlier works concerning the link between religion and politics using the idioms and motifs of religious thought. Several of his articles— with titles such as "The Essence of the Russian Orthodox Consciousness" ("Sushchestvo russkogo pravoslavnogo soznaniia," 1923), and "The Orthodox Church and its Relationship to the Spiritual Life of New Russia" ("Pravoslavnaia tserkov' v ee otnoshenii k dukhovnoi zhizni novoi Rossii," 1922)—made more explicit the relationship he posited between a specifically Orthodox Christian religious ideal and the achievement of freedom in society. While this change in vernacular has been noted, it is generally accepted that these later writings constitute an obvious continuity with his earlier thought; his student I. A. Il'in (1883–1954) observed after his death that "Pavel Ivanovich did not 'become' in his last years a religious man, he always was one. The wise depths of Russian Orthodoxy, revealed to him in years of strife and suffering, imparted not the first, but a new and, I believe, final form of his religiosity."[49] It is certainly true that Novgorodtsev's work in his later years became more explicitly concerned with the merits of Russian Orthodoxy, but a close reading of these later texts suggests that it is here that we have the clearest examples of his selective blindness regarding the possible utopian dimensions of his own religious liberalism. It is questionable, for example, whether he fully repudiated the idea of historical inevitability in his vision of Orthodoxy facilitating the movement of history upward through contradictions to ultimate unity.

During this period, Novgorodtsev was particularly concerned with linking specifically Russian cultural ideals and the Eastern Christian consciousness, and exploring their potential for helping to overcome both national and global crises. He underscores the fact that, in contrast to other national traditions, the Russian Orthodox consciousness provides significant doctrinal support for the principle of positive freedom and the "equality as a starting point" that he had identified as a key notion of the liberal tradition. The principle of "love in Christ," the essence of Orthodoxy, has the "beneficent property of elevating individual consciousness from insularity, alienation, and isolation to collectivity [*sobornost'*], wholeness, and universality."[50] Orthodoxy, according to him, provides an opportunity to genuinely overcome excessive individualism and solitude, and promote a more balanced view of freedom founded on solidarity.

Novgorodtsev singles out Orthodoxy's aspiration to universal unity and brotherhood as its unique contribution to world culture. He argues that in contrast to both Catholic and Protestant traditions, Orthodoxy's closeness to the original first principles of Christianity, and the idea of love in Christ, enable it to overcome national insularity in the name of a higher religious synthesis.[51] The Orthodox mind, he writes, "searches for and expects the Kingdom of God as real but attainable under certain miraculous conditions, the Kingdom of God cannot be built on earthly activity; nevertheless all earthly life must be infused with the idea of this expected Kingdom."[52] The humility and contemplativeness that represent the essence of the Orthodox consciousness recognize "the inscrutable mysteries of Divine Providence" and therefore do not make the mistake of considering individual reason to be the sole justification for social organization.[53] Only by relativizing human reason in the light of its "eternal and universal foundation" can we clearly see that "human history has always moved, and always will move, through growing contradictions, through the conflict of opposing principles to higher complexity. It achieves unity in the relative fusion of multi-faceted differences and growing ties, and not in an absolute reconciliation of contradictions."[54]

To the extent that Orthodoxy affirms that there are such things as universal and absolute values, while simultaneously denying that such values can ever be fully harmonized, Novgorodtsev's support for the doctrine is fully compatible with the core premises of his liberalism. Yet his willingness to entertain the possibility of the advent of the kingdom of God in certain miraculous circumstances, his claim that one particular way of life can take on a global dimension, and his desire to present this development as historically inevitable, bear witness to a certain amount of selective blindness as to the utopian elements of his own theory. This oversight is particularly important in revealing the difficulty of the struggle to find a middle way between the extremes of dogmatism and skepticism, a project with which Novgorodtsev was engaged throughout his life.

Conclusion

In the Soviet Union, religiously oriented liberalisms that defended the principles of individual self-improvement and culture were denounced as fundamentally reactionary and so heretical that Novgorodtsev and the majority of his colleagues were forced into emigration. Yet by explicitly associating his theory of liberty with the idiom and motifs of religious thought, Novgorodtsev was also attempting to highlight the potential of religion to play a progressive role in a liberal, democratic political order. The bulk of his work suggests that a theological framework could ensure that freedom would not degenerate into anarchy, while offering a non-dogmatic vision of social progress. Partly in response to the rise of political and religious utopianism in Russian society, liberals were particularly sensitive to freedom and toleration, and antipathetic to closing ranks around any system of beliefs. In one of his works written in 1909, Struve observes that contemporary liberalism has ceased to be a political theory that requires dogmatic faith or a credo;[55] Novgorodtsev's approach to liberalism and religion in his early work could be described in the same terms. Despite his confidence in the non-dogmatic essence of religion, he did not regard it as any less real as a guiding principle for achieving social and political freedom. While the spiritualization of individual life remains an unattainable ideal, it was the fundamental concept according to which everyday clashes between freedom and equality must be resolved. That Novgorodtsev did not live to see his project of reconciling the claims of religion with a liberal approach to freedom come to fruition in Russia does not make it any less relevant for a broader reassessment of what we mean when we talk about religious thought in Russia or elsewhere.

NOTES

1. Paul Valliere, "Theological Liberalism and Church Reform in Imperial Russia," in *Church, Nation and State in Russia and Ukraine*, ed. Geoffrey A. Hosking (London: Macmillan, 1991), 109.

2. This approach to liberalism is further clarified in the following essays: Jeremy Waldron, "Theoretical Foundations of Liberalism," *Philosophical Quarterly* 37, no. 147 (1987): 127–50; Bernard Williams, "Liberalism and Loss," in *The Legacy of Isaiah Berlin*, ed. Ronald Dworkin, Mark Lilla, and Robert B. Silvers (New York: New York Review Books, 2001), 91–103. For a minority view that liberal values can be harmonized, see the work of Ronald Dworkin, for example his "Do Liberal Values Conflict?," in Dworkin, Lilla, and Silvers, *The Legacy of Isaiah Berlin*, 73–90.

3. The primary representative of this tendency was Dmitrii Nikolaevich Shipov (1851–1920); it also included Nikolai Alekseevich Khomiakov (1850–1925) and Mikhail Aleksandrovich Stakhovich (1861–1923). Among the extensive literature on the Liberation Movement (referred to from its inception as the Liberal Movement), see Shmuel Galai, *The Liberation Movement in Russia, 1900–1905* (Cambridge: Cambridge University Press, 1973); K. F. Shatsillo, *Russkii liberalizm nakanune revoliutsii, 1905–1907 gg.: Organizatsiia, programmy, taktika* (Moscow: Nauka, 1985).

4. Surveys of the religious revival during this period include Christopher Read, *Religion, Revolution and the Russian Intelligentsia, 1900–1912: The Vekhi Debate and Its Intellectual Background* (London: Macmillan, 1979); Nicolas Zernov, *The Russian Religious Renaissance of the Twentieth Century* (London: Darton, Longman & Todd, 1963).

5. Gregory L. Freeze coined the term "clerical liberalism" to describe this movement. See his *The Parish Clergy in Nineteenth-Century Russia: Crisis, Reform, Counter-Reform*

(Princeton, NJ: Princeton University Press, 1983), 389-97. On liberalism within the established Church, see also I. K. Smolich, *Istoriia russkoi tserkvi, 1700-1917* (Moscow: Izdatel'stvo Spaso-Preobrazhenskogo Valaamskogo monastyria, 1994-97).

6. Examples include Mikhail Mikhailovich Tareev (1866-1934), Ivan Vasil'evich Popov (1867-1938), Pavel Vasil'evich Tikhomirov (1868-1925), and Aleksei Ivanovich Vvedenskii (1861-1913). For a study of the "religious enlightener" V. D. Kudriavtsev-Platonov, see Sean Gillen's essay in this volume. On the various theological and philosophical positions within the academies, see V. A. Tarasova, *Vysshaia dukhovnaia shkola v Rossii v kontse XIX-nachale XX veka: Istoriia imperatorskikh pravoslavnykh dukhovnykh akademii* (Moscow: Novyi kronograf, 2005).

7. On the Psychological Society, see Martha Bohachevsky-Chomiak, "Filosofiia, religiia i obshchestvennost' v Rossii v kontse 19-go i nachale 20-go vv," in *Russkaia religiozno-filosofskaia mysl' XX veka*, ed. Nikolai P. Poltoratskii (Pittsburg, PA: University of Pittsburgh, 1975), 54-67; Randall A. Poole, "The Moscow Psychological Society and the Neo-Idealist Development of Russian Liberalism, 1885-1922" (PhD diss., University of Notre Dame, 1996).

8. Randall Poole argues in his essay in this volume that Solov'ev followed Kant in rejecting a dogmatic conception of religion; this approach has much in common with Novgorodtsev's. Good introductions to Novgorodtsev's thought include George F. Putnam, *Russian Alternatives to Marxism: Christian Socialism and Idealistic Liberalism in Twentieth-Century Russia* (Knoxville: University of Tennessee Press, 1977); Andrzej Walicki, "Pavel Novgorodtsev: Neo-Idealism and the Revival of Natural Law," in *Legal Philosophies of Russian Liberalism* (Notre Dame, IN: University of Notre Dame Press, 1992), 291-341; A. N. Litvinov, ed., *Problemy filosofii prava: Sbornik statei; K 140-letiiu co dnia rozhdeniia Pavla Ivanovicha Novgorodtseva* (Lugansk: RIO LGUVD, 2006); I. A. Katsapova and S. I. Bazhov, *Filosofskoe mirovozzrenie P. I. Novgorodtseva* (Moscow: Institut filosofii Rossiiskoi Akademii Nauk, 2007).

9. For an intellectual project articulated in the context of the Russian Enlightenment that has many interesting points of connection with Novgorodtsev's, see Elise Wirtschafter's essay in this volume.

10. For a detailed account, see Charles E. Timberlake, "Introduction: The Concept of Liberalism in Russia," in *Essays on Russian Liberalism*, ed. Charles E. Timberlake (Columbia: University of Missouri Press, 1972), 1-17.

11. Boris Chicherin, mentioned below, was one of the few midcentury thinkers who liked to apply this label to himself.

12. See Geoffrey Hosking, *Russia: People and Empire, 1552-1917* (Cambridge, MA: Harvard University Press, 1997), 211-13.

13. "Introduction," in *A Revolution of the Spirit: Crisis of Value in Russia, 1890-1918*, ed. Bernice Glatzer Rosenthal and Martha Bohachevsky-Chomiak, trans. Marian Schwartz (Newtonville, MA: Oriental Research Partners, 1982), 1.

14. For an account of this process by one of its protagonists, see Sergei Bulgakov's *Ot marksizma k idealizmu* (St. Petersburg: Obshchestvennaia pol'za, 1903). Petr Struve's collection of articles *Na raznye temy (1893-1901 gg.): Sbornik statei* (St. Petersburg: Tipografiia Doma prizren, 1902) traces his intellectual evolution.

15. See Randall A. Poole, ed., trans., and intro., *Problems of Idealism: Essays in Russian Social Philosophy* (New Haven, CT: Yale University Press, 2003).

16. For a discussion of the meanings of *lichnost'* in Russian history, see V. V. Vinogradov, "Lichnost'," in *Istoriia slov: Okolo 1500 slov i vyrazhenii i bolee 5000 slov, s nimi sviazannykh*, 2nd ed., ed. N. Iu. Shvedova (Moscow: Institut russkogo iazyka RAN, 1999), 271–309. See also Derek Offord, "*Lichnost'*: Notions of Individual Identity," in *Constructing Russian Culture in the Age of Revolution, 1881–1940*, ed. Catriona Kelly and David Shepherd (Oxford: Oxford University Press, 1998), 13–25.

17. See Immanuel Kant, *Groundwork of the Metaphysics of Morals*, ed. Mary Gregor and Jens Timmerman (Cambridge: Cambridge University Press, 2012), 40. On the Kantian conception of liberty see, in particular, Charles Taylor, "Kant's Theory of Freedom," in *Conceptions of Liberty in Political Philosophy*, ed. Zbigniew Pelczynski and John Gray (London: The Athlone Press, 1984), 100–122; Patrick R. Frierson, *Freedom and Anthropology in Kant's Moral Philosophy* (Cambridge: Cambridge University Press, 2003).

18. Randall Poole develops this argument in his essay "The Neo-Idealist Reception of Kant in the Moscow Psychological Society," *Journal of the History of Ideas* 60, no. 2 (1999): 319–43. For an analysis of Kant's own views of religion, see Poole's essay in this volume.

19. P. I. Novgorodtsev, "K voprosu o sovremennykh filosofskikh iskaniiakh. (Otvet L. I. Petrazhitskomu)," *Voprosy filosofii i psikhologii* 14, no. 1, bk. 66 (1903): 138.

20. S. A. Kotliarevskii, "Predposylki demokratii," *Voprosy filosofii i psikhologii* 16, no. 2, bk. 77 (1905): 125.

21. P. B. Struve and S. L. Frank, "Ocherki filosofii kul'tury. 2. Kul'tura i lichnost'," *Poliarnaia zvezda* 3 (1905): 174. Struve's first expression of this idea is contained in his introduction to *Sub"ektivizm i individualizm v obshchestvennoi filosofii*, by N. A. Berdiaev (1901; repr., Moscow: Astrel', 2008).

22. See, for example, P. I. Novgorodtsev, "Nravstvennaia problema v filosofii Kanta," *Voprosy filosofii i psikhologii* 12, no. 2, bk. 57 (1901): 304–6.

23. P. I. Novgorodtsev, "Kant, kak moralist," *Voprosy filosofii i psikhologii* 16, no. 2, bk. 77 (1905): 25.

24. P. I. Novgorodtsev, *Ob obshchestvennom ideale*, 3rd ed. (Berlin: Knigoizdatel'stvo Slovo, 1921), 95.

25. See Novgorodtsev's "Ideia prava v filosofii Vl. S. Solov'eva," *Voprosy filosofii i psikhologii* 12, no. 1, bk. 56 (1901): 124; and "Pravo i nravstvennost'," in *Sbornik po obshchestvenno-iuridicheskim naukam*, ed. Iu. S. Gambarov (St. Petersburg: Popov, 1899), 118.

26. See, for example, P. Struve and S. Frank, "Ocherki filosofii kul'tury. 1. Chto takoe kul'tura?," *Poliarnaia zvezda* 2 (1905): 110.

27. Novgorodtsev, "Ideia prava," 125.

28. Ibid.

29. P. I. Novgorodtsev, "Dva etiuda I. Pered zavesoi. II. Pravo na dostoinoe chelovecheskoe sushchestvovanie," *Poliarnaia zvezda* 3 (1905): 218. See also part 3 of Solov'ev's influential work *Opravdanie dobra: Nravstvennaia filosofiia Vladimira Solov'eva* (St. Petersburg: Tipografiia Stasiulevicha, 1897). On Solov'ev's conception of freedom, see Andrzej Walicki, "Vladimir Soloviev: Religious Philosophy and the Emergence of the 'New Liberalism,'" in *Legal Philosophies*, 165–212.

30. See also E. N. Trubetskoi, "Filosofiia prava Prof. L. I. Petrazhitskogo," *Voprosy filosofii i psikhologii* 12, no. 2, bk. 57 (1901): 30–33; S. A. Kotliarevskii, "Politika i kul'tura," *Voprosy filosofii i psikhologii* 17, no. 4, bk. 84 (1906): 365.

31. Kant was one of the first to formulate this distinction, which was formalized in the late 1950s in Isaiah Berlin's essay, "Two Concepts of Liberty," and further developed in a number of studies. See Howard Caygill, *A Kant Dictionary* (Oxford: Blackwell Publishing, 1995), 207; Frierson, *Freedom and Anthropology*, 13–30.

32. Novgorodtsev, "Ideia prava," 119.

33. P. I. Novgorodtsev, *Lektsii po istorii filosofii prava: Ucheniia novogo vremeni, XVI–XIX vv.*, 2nd ed. (Moscow: T-vo. Pechatnia S. P. Iakovleva, 1912), 107.

34. P. I. Novgorodtsev, "Ethical Idealism in the Philosophy of Law (On the Question of the Revival of Natural Law)," in Poole, *Problems of Idealism*, 309.

35. P. I. Novgorodtsev, *Istoricheskaia shkola iuristov, ee proiskhozhdenie i sud'ba* (Moscow: Universitetskaia tipografiia, 1896), 9.

36. Novgorodtsev, "Ideia prava," 128.

37. See primarily his long article "Goduarstvo i pravo," *Voprosy filosofii i psikhologii* 15, no. 4, bk. 74 (1904): 397–446; 15, no. 5, bk. 75 (1904), 508–38.

38. A number of representatives of the propertied classes split off from the Kadets to form the Union of October 17, a party based on the premise that cooperation with the tsarist authorities was necessary for the advent of social reform in Russia, and whose members were less committed to a tension between positive and negative liberty than the Kadets. See Shmuel Galai, "The True Nature of Octobrism," *Kritika: Explorations in Russian and Eurasian History* 5, no. 1 (2004): 137–47.

39. For historical details of the period see Abraham Ascher, *The Revolution of 1905*, 2 vols. (Stanford, CA: Stanford University Press, 1988). Novgorodtsev participated in the Liberation Movement, was a member of the Kadet Party from its inception, and was elected to the First State Duma in 1906. By signing the Vyborg appeal in 1906, a text that advocated passive resistance as a response to the government's dissolution of the Duma, he became ineligible for future election, though he remained an active party member. For additional details on his political activities during this time, see Laurent Cauderay, "Die Partei der konstitutionellen Demokraten und das liberale Weltbild von Pavel Ivanovic Novgorodcev" (PhD diss., University of St. Gallen, 2004).

40. This view was expressed in the *Landmarks* (*Vekhi*) symposium published in 1909. See Marshall S. Shatz and Judith E. Zimmerman, ed. and trans., *Vekhi—Landmarks: A Collection of Articles about the Russian Intelligentsia* (Armonk, NY: M. E. Sharpe, 1994). See also Kotliarevskii, "Filosofiia kontsa," *Voprosy filosofii i psikhologii* 24, no. 4, bk. 119 (1913): 318; Kotliarevskii, "Predposylki demokratii," 119–20; Kotliarevskii, "Partii i nauka," *Poliarnaia zvezda* 5 (1906): 354–55.

41. Struve and Frank, "Ocherki filosofii kul'tury. 1," 110.

42. See also S. A. Kotliarevskii, "Politika i kul'tura," *Voprosy filosofii i psikhologii* 17, no. 4, bk. 84 (1906): 358, 364–65.

43. P. I. Novgorodtsev, *Vvedenie v filosofiiu prava: Krizis sovremennogo pravosoznaniia* (St. Petersburg: MVD Rossii Sankt-Peterburgskii Universitet, 2000), 259, 266; the book was first published in serial form in *Voprosy filosofii i psikhologii* between 1906 and 1908, and in book form in 1909.

44. Concise surveys that put this phenomenon in context include Bernice Glatzer Rosenthal, "Religious Humanism in the Russian Silver Age," and Robert Bird, "Imagination and Ideology in the New Religious Consciousness," both in *A History of Russian Philosophy 1830–1930: Faith, Reason and the Defense of Human Dignity*, ed. G. M. Hamburg and Randall A. Poole (Cambridge: Cambridge University Press, 2010), 227–47, 266–84.

45. Novgorodtsev, *Ob obshchestvennom ideale*, 3.

46. P. I. Novgorodtsev, appendix to *Ob obshchestvennom ideale*, in *Voprosy filosofii i psikhologii*, nos. 4–5 (1917): 127–54, http://www.philosophy.ru/library/vehi/ideal.html.

47. Novgorodtsev, "Dva etiuda," 220.

48. Novgorodtsev, *Vvedenie v filosofiiu prava*, 286.

49. Cited by Poole, "Editor's Introduction," in *Problems of Idealism*, 17.

50. P. I. Novgorodtsev, "Sushchestvo russkogo pravoslavnogo soznaniia," in *Pravoslavie i kul'tura: Sbornik religiozno-filosofskikh statei*, ed. V. V. Zen'kovskii (Berlin: Russkaia kniga, 1923), reprinted as "The Essence of the Russian Orthodox Consciousness," in Glatzer Rosenthal and Bohachevsky-Chomiak, *Revolution of the Spirit*, 256, translation modified.

51. Pavel Novgorodtsev, "Pravoslavnaia tserkov' v ee otnoshenii k dukhovnoi zhizni novoi Rossii," *Russkaia mysl'* 43, bks. 1 and 2 (1922): 195–96.

52. Novgorodtsev, "The Essence," 266, translation slightly modified. See also "Pravoslavnaia tserkov'," 197.

53. P. I. Novgorodtsev, "On the Paths and Tasks of the Russian Intelligentsia" (1918), in *Out of the Depths (De Profundis): A Collection of Articles on the Russian Revolution*, trans. and ed. William F. Woehrlin (Irvine, CA: Charles Schlacks, 1986), 189.

54. Ibid., 188.

55. P. B. Struve, "Religiia i sotsializm," *Russkaia mysl'* 8 (1909): 153. It must be noted, however, that Struve's liberalism became inconsistent during this period, as he became increasingly attracted by a chauvinistic Russian nationalism.

Chapter 11

What Is Beauty?

Pasternak's Adaptations of Russian Religious Thought

MARTHA M. F. KELLY

In a central scene in Boris Pasternak's *Doctor Zhivago* (*Doktor Zhivago*, 1956), we witness through the eyes of the eponymous protagonist a folk healer healing a sick cow named "Beauty" (*Krasava*). Zhivago is surprised to find himself captivated by the "nonsensical" spell the healer Kubarikha improvises from ancient chronicles, "transformed through layer upon layer of distortion into apocrypha." Despite the absurd distortions of her text, it inspires in Zhivago a luminous vision of his love, Lara, and he suddenly envisions her figure enfolded and defined by a "simple and swift line." Moved by the healer's art, the imagination of the doctor-poet progresses from Beauty the sick cow to his "fabled beauty" (*krasota pisanaia*), Lara—and from Lara to the beauty of his poetic renditions of her.[1] The object of his erotic affections inspires his greatest literary work, the cycle of his poems with which the novel ends. In this detail as in so many others in *Doctor Zhivago*, perceived beauty fuels the erotic imagination, which in turn clothes the mundane and incongruous in the beautiful. In this passage Boris Pasternak uses wit to set in relief one of the key issues in his novel: the role of beauty in personal and cultural transformation.

In this essay I will read *Doctor Zhivago* as an exploration of the significance of beauty in the Russian novel—and of how the novel might use its own beauty fruitfully to extend the work of Russian religious culture and religious-philosophical thought. We find multiple discussions in Pasternak's fictional-poetic work on art and its effects, and the novel stands as a representation of how erotic desire inspires an author to create beauty. Here I will speak of beauty, via Pasternak and Vladimir Solov'ev, as artistic effects that clothe the ordinary in the ideal as a way to draw out the ideal essence of the ordinary. But nowhere does the author take for granted the role of beauty; through philosophical dialogue and figurative means, *Doctor Zhivago* asserts its philosophy of beauty as its central achievement. How are we to understand what is at stake in this issue for Pasternak? To whom is he responding? And what does he present as his own contribution to the problem?

Answers to these questions lie not only in the immediate cultural-historical context of the novel, but, as we will see, also in its literary context—that is, in the novel genre as it evolved in Russia. *Doctor Zhivago* is perhaps best known for the political scandal it provoked when Pasternak was awarded the Nobel Prize after the novel was published abroad.[2] The prize—which Pasternak ultimately turned down—was viewed by the Soviet authorities as a political gesture in light of the novel's critical treatment of Marxist ideology. Yet the work's political threat lurked not only on the level of character and plot, but also in its very rendering; while Pasternak had attempted to simplify the complex style of his earlier work, nevertheless his folding of the (highly personal) lyrical mode, with its idiosyncratic comparisons and associative leaps, into the realist setting could not but incur official disapproval. As Lazar Fleishman points out, even in the context of the cultural "Thaw" that followed Stalin's death and its toleration of publications criticizing Soviet life, Pasternak's novel stood out as radical both for its ideas and its formal qualities.[3] In many ways, though, Pasternak's refusal to exorcise his lyrical mode with its accompanying complexity represented not only a challenge to Socialist Realist doctrines, but also to long-standing debates over the role of beauty in the novel.

The novelist to whom Pasternak most directly responds is Lev Tolstoy— whose presentations of beauty in the novel differ starkly from Pasternak's, even while the novelists share some similar concerns—and even while Pasternak spoke of Tolstoy's particular influence on him.[4] Like the Soviet authorities, Tolstoy and Pasternak are profoundly concerned with art's effects on society. Yet Tolstoy increasingly conveys a deep suspicion of beauty's overwhelming force, which to him deprives a person of his ability to respond ethically. Indeed, in his aesthetic treatise "What Is Art?" ("Chto takoe iskusstvo," 1897–98) the writer provocatively expels the category of beauty (understood as art's attractive effects), painting it as a dangerous force to which he prefers art's more controlled constructions.[5] In his novel *Resurrection* (*Voskresenie*, 1899), to which Pasternak was especially responding, regeneration occurs when beauty (art's force) is replaced with philosophical truth claims. Pasternak, on the other hand, overtly prefers beauty to philosophy in his novel and suggests that this potent force bears the means for social renewal. A major point of difference lies in their presentation of the erotic, with which both associate beauty: for Tolstoy the force of eros draws the individual away from common concerns, whereas for Pasternak it enables the individual to foster new visions of humanity as a whole. Both authors use depictions of eros to portray how art should or should not function: for Tolstoy if art's effects overwhelm the beholder, they short-circuit moral action, whereas for Pasternak precisely the overwhelming potency of art can move the beholder to creative acts that sustain society. In their analogy of the erotic and the beautiful these authors echo a long philosophical tradition beginning with Plato. But Pasternak especially has in mind something much more recent: the emergent Russian religious-philosophical tradition. Vladimir Solov'ev, in particular, indicated the importance of artists in realizing humanity's fullest potential. He himself deploys philosophical and artistic means together to convey his vision of the world. In *Doctor Zhivago* Pasternak leverages the achievements of Solov'ev and others to reclaim a place in the realist novel for beauty as he understands it.

In the sections that follow I will show how Pasternak essentially reverses Tolstoy's move from art to philosophy in order to establish the primacy of beauty in the regeneration of individual and social life. Pasternak achieves this reversal through fictional, philosophic, and poetic means, but in each aspect he traces a repeating trajectory: experiences of beauty inspire undetermined responses, new creative endeavors that extend beauty further into life. One fictional approach both authors take is to represent narratively how ideas affect life; and both use the Orthodox liturgy as their fictional testing ground, showing how characters respond to their liturgical experiences. Tolstoy's characters are mesmerized by the liturgy, whereas it inspires Pasternak's characters, who go on to tell their own stories about it. As they present it, the liturgy uses beauty to body out religious tradition in ever new contexts; therefore it supplies a tangible, native, everyday illustration of art's effects. But they also both use fiction's figural means, here, too, borrowing from the liturgy.[6] Both novelists use the figure of Mary Magdalene in their work to represent beauty's seductive powers as either destructive or regenerative, and more generally they use Orthodox liturgy to represent beauty's lived effects. As we will see, Pasternak uses Mary Magdalene to advocate a spiritual path that embraces sensuality's attraction, while Tolstoy uses her figure to promote the desiccation of sensuality (or beauty) as the path to redemption. Significantly, Pasternak deploys one further approach that Tolstoy here avoids: a poetical extended visual metaphor for beauty's effect. Adapting a set of images of the female body from the work of Vladimir Solov'ev, who firmly believed that poets can save society, the twentieth-century poet-turned-novelist figuratively demonstrates how the eros-like force of beauty extends into and reshapes the world through acts of human creativity.

Beauty in the Tolstoyan Novel

Pasternak's acquaintance with Tolstoy is too well known to repeat here, but a word of explanation is due on the comparison I will draw here between *Doctor Zhivago* and *Resurrection*, rather than the more obvious *Kreutzer Sonata* (*Kreitserova sonata*, 1899), mentioned in Pasternak's novel along with Solov'ev's "The Meaning of Love" ("Smysl liubvi," 1892–94). Pasternak had a familial relationship to *Resurrection* because Tolstoy asked Pasternak's father, Leonid, to illustrate its initial, serialized version.[7] Pasternak's title—which one could translate "Doctor of the Living"—itself invites comparison with Tolstoy's final novel. What is more, Pasternak himself compared the complicated publishing situation of his novel to that of *Resurrection*.[8] Also, Pasternak may have been following Solov'ev's example: as Judith Kornblatt has shown, Solov'ev, too, polemicizes with this very text, in a move to criticize Tolstoy's diminishment of the novel in favor of rationalistic and moralistic discourses that discourage critical engagement in reading and life alike.[9] In my comparison I will point out several parallels Pasternak creates between his novel and *Resurrection*, but the chief point of engagement is found in the Mary Magdalene figure that both novels use to illustrate their views on beauty.

In *Resurrection*, Tolstoy tells the story of a degenerate aristocrat, Nekhliudov, who experiences moral regeneration after he encounters a woman he ruined many years before, Katia Maslova, and witnesses the fearful consequences of his actions.[10] The novel proceeds with Nekhliudov's participation as juror in a murder trial, in which Maslova, now a prostitute, is wrongfully convicted and sentenced to labor in Siberia. In perhaps his most infamous passage in the novel— a passage that eventually helped ensure the author's excommunication from the Orthodox Church in 1901—Tolstoy depicts the recently convicted Maslova attending the liturgy in the prison church.[11] In this passage he throws down the gauntlet not only to the Church, but also to those who would embrace beauty for its intoxicating powers—a moral hazard he describes in "What Is Art?" At this point in his thought and work, Tolstoy recommends extreme caution with the force of artistic effects, going so far as to identify the term "beauty" with art that deprives the individual of moral agency, enchanting him.[12] Accordingly, he presents both Church ritual and contemporary high-brow art alike as wielding beauty irresponsibly: for him they are morally harmful and foster degeneration rather than regeneration. (Some artists—e.g., unspoiled peasants and himself, post-*Anna Karenina*—might be trusted with art's force, but not most educated writers.) I will quote at some length in order to help establish how Tolstoy stakes out his claims about beauty in *Resurrection*.

> The service began.
>
> The service involved the priest dressing up in a peculiar and very uncomfortable brocade garment, cutting up bread and laying bits of it onto a dish, then putting them into a chalice with wine, all the while reciting various names and prayers. Meanwhile the deacon first of all read out and then sang at various intervals with a choir of prisoners an incessant stream of different Slavonic prayers, the prayers being difficult to understand in themselves and made worse so by being read and sung too quickly. The main content of the prayers consisted of a desire for the welfare of the sovereign emperor and his family. Prayers were said many times on this subject. . . . Apart from that there were readings by the deacon from the Acts of the Apostles in such weird and strangulated tones that they were totally incomprehensible, and very clear readings by the priest from Saint Mark's Gospel in which it was stated that Jesus Christ, after his resurrection and before flying up to heaven to sit at the right hand of his father, appeared first to Mary Magdalene, out of whom he had cast seven devils, and then to eleven disciples. . . . What the service seemed basically to be about was that the priest cut up bits of bread and put them into wine and then, by certain manipulations and prayers, turned them into God's body and blood. . . . The main action took place when the priest took a napkin in both hands and, with a smooth and measured movement, waved it over the saucer and the golden cup.[13]

Tolstoy begins his account with the priest's vestment, and his description of it offers a key to his critique of the liturgy as a prime example of how beauty counteracts moral progress. That is, the outfit with its expensive brocade is awkward both functionally and aesthetically; it hampers the priest's movements and therefore looks ridiculous, ill-fitting. The text of the liturgy is like the garment, as Tolstoy presents it—ornate and awkward, not suited to its presumed purpose: difficult to understand, chanted too hurriedly to discern, in "weird and strangulated tones"—as well as not aptly addressed to the convicts' needs, who must sit through and gesture to the rhythm of prayers said for the political order that has put them where they are.

In a way, though, the arcane and awkward elements of the service serve a particular purpose. For the earnest narrator the obfuscating qualities of the ornamentation create a kind of hocus-pocus, promising magic results. The image of the liturgy as illusionism finds its most pointed expression in the napkin the priest waves above the elements, a gesture meant to signify their transformation into Christ's body and blood. As the passage continues, the priest covers the elements with his napkin and then uncovers them to signify that the conjuring trick has worked. Here again the fabric of the ritual obfuscates. The narrator describes how despite their skepticism, the convicts nonetheless believe in some kind of "mysterious force" (*tainstvennaia sila*) that will bring them good things in the distant future if they submit to it.[14] For the narrator, as for Tolstoy, what is really going on is something sinister but not essentially mysterious.

Tolstoy uses the Gospel reading in the service to debunk the beauty of the liturgical texts and gestures, and to assert his own, more cautious model. In particular he gestures at the method of the didactic story, and here we see a recessed image of his own book: the Gospel story tells of Christ and Mary Magdalene, and likewise Tolstoy is telling a parable of a fallen woman who finds salvation and serves as a model of religious conversion.[15] (In the novel a character refers to prostitutes—including Maslova—as "Magdalenes."[16]) Preferring Gospel to liturgy, he prefers, then, story to poetry as a spiritual teaching method.[17] We see in Nekhliudov's conversion, with which Tolstoy ends his novel, that he also values the Gospels for the "simple and clear commands" they offer, commands that one can fulfill "in practice."[18] But it is in his use of the Mary Magdalene figure that we can best discern the attitude to beauty against which Pasternak later revolts. For Tolstoy's Magdalene figures conversion as emerging only when one dispenses with the erotic and turns instead to the philosophic. In the Gospel story, as we see, Christ casts "seven devils" out of Mary Magdalene, saving her soul by saving her from sex and its destructive passions. In "What Is Art?," Tolstoy prefers "Mary of Egypt not in the day of her beauty, but in the day of her repentance."[19] Likewise in *Resurrection* Maslova's conversion involves a divestment of her seductive qualities, which she has consciously used to her advantage in the past. When, after two months of the march to Siberia, Nekhliudov sees how she has grown sunburned, thin, and wrinkled, he feels a sacred tenderness (*umilenie*) and is freed from his earlier "sensual love" for her.[20] It is through the desiccation and obscuring of the female body that Nekhliudov loses interest in her as a love object and thereby steps out on his own path to redemption. That is, her loss of beauty and its attraction frees him to act in accordance with considered moral precepts.

PASTERNAK'S REFIGURATION OF BEAUTY

Pasternak wittingly takes quite the opposite tack: for him beauty regenerates. His novel *Doctor Zhivago* tells the story of a doctor and poet, Iurii Zhivago, who experiences firsthand and tries to understand—through poetry and philosophic discourse—the major events of Russia's early decades in the twentieth century: the 1905 and 1917 Revolutions and the Civil War. Zhivago writes a cycle of poems that present his personal life as emblematizing this period, and in the novel's prose his dialogue and thoughts serve especially to frame this relationship.[21] The fact that comes most to define his personal life is his adulterous relationship with Lara, a Mary Magdalene figure whom he first encounters when she is sixteen and entangled in a damaging and surreptitious affair with a predatory lawyer.[22] The blossoming of Zhivago and Lara's relationship accompanies the disruption of Zhivago's family life: it is his family's decision to leave Moscow for the Urals that throws him together with Lara irrevocably. His new relationship with Lara, then, represents the disruption of the established social order, but also the conception of a new one. Zhivago's poems and prose meditations on Lara emphasize that it is precisely the overwhelming force of her beauty that feeds his reconstructive visions and rhythms. While Tolstoy eschews beauty, as he understands it, Pasternak pursues, embraces, succumbs to it, responds to it.

I will discuss Pasternak's Mary Magdalene more below, but first I will show how the author uses figural methods to construct a positive picture of beauty's seductive powers. Of course Pasternak follows Tolstoy's line in some ways, not least in how he uses figures emblematically; but here as in other aspects he uses Tolstoy's tools in a kind of corrective to Tolstoy's novel. As we have seen, Tolstoy uses the aesthetic category of fittingness to judge the validity of artistic forms. In seminal passages where Pasternak targets Tolstoy and teachings associated with him, the modernist author also works with this category. But whereas Tolstoy depicts cultural refinements as a whore's seductive garb, Pasternak positively prefers characters who both propound and inhabit poetry, in all its complexity.[23] The two characters of this ilk whom he uses most *directly* in his polemic with Tolstoy are Zhivago's uncle, Nikolai Vedeniapin, and Sima Tuntseva, a Siberian townswoman and friend of Lara's, whom, as both Lara and Zhivago reflect at different moments, has been deeply influenced by Vedeniapin's thought.[24] Vedeniapin is a composite fictional turn-of-the-century religious philosopher, whom Pasternak bases partly on Solov'ev. Zhivago's uncle the philosopher takes the protagonist into his care when he is orphaned as a child, and Zhivago later reflects on how his uncle's thought has influenced his poetry. In this detail alone we find a move from the philosophical to the creative, but we also find a similar trajectory in the parallel figure of Sima Tuntseva, a relatively uneducated provincial who takes Vedeniapin's thought and uses it to understand liturgy and life alike. In such figures we find Pasternak's novelistic demonstration of the path he advocates—that is, the move from philosophy to art.

Pasternak borrows from Russian religious thought not only in these figures, but also in the ways he uses their ideas to undergird the very shape of his novel, its repeated trajectory toward free, creative response. As we find in his reflections, Zhivago sees in Vedeniapin's work "a new interpretation of Christianity" that leads "directly to a new conception of art," and he associates his own poetic craft with Vedeniapin's religious philosophy. Vedeniapin speaks above all of the importance of the individual over the group; cultures are sustained by inspired individuals who act freely—that is, not from compulsion but from an overwhelming experience of love.[25] For Vedeniapin, life's vital force is sustained by love between people; this love "fills up the heart of man" and overflows into creative endeavors. While his stance is hardly an expression of official Orthodoxy, Vedeniapin points to Christ, who he feels emblematizes this love, which feeds the "free personality" and inspires him to a "life as sacrifice"; he posits these two principles as central to his thought. (Indeed, these principles shape Pasternak's novel as a whole.) Accordingly Vedeniapin deplores the impulse of individuals to align themselves with groups and particular figures: "Solov'ev or Kant or Marx."

Or Tolstoy. We see how Pasternak compares Solov'ev with Tolstoy most clearly in Vedeniapin's encounter with a Tolstoyan acquaintance, a certain Vyvolochnov, described as "a fat man in a gray peasant shirt."[26] Vyvolochnov pays Vedeniapin a visit, interrupting Vedeniapin's bemused thoughts about how the teenage Zhivago and his two closest friends seek to combat sensuality by clinging to ideas they draw from Solov'ev's essay "The Meaning of Love" and Tolstoy's *The Kreutzer Sonata*.[27] Here we find an example of how Pasternak uses the index of fittingness. While Vedeniapin himself reflects Solov'ev's thought, this earnest adherence, of course, directly controverts Vedeniapin's belief in individual inspiration and freedom. Philosophy, then, bears fruit only when it inspires a free, creative, and critical response—an insight that seems lost on Vedeniapin's Tolstoyan friend. Almost immediately upon the Tolstoyan's arrival, Vedeniapin reflects on him as a blind follower in whom the ideas of "the genius" "had settled down to enjoy a long, unclouded rest, growing hopelessly shallow." For the Tolstoyan philosophical teachings seem an end in themselves. But while Vedeniapin objects to blind adherence to any thinker or group, he seems to harbor special suspicion of those who believe, per Tolstoy, that "the more a man devotes himself to beauty the further he moves away from goodness"—a view reflected in "What Is Art?" Here Vedeniapin places himself not against, but in the line of Solov'evian thought, with its emphasis on beauty as a means to transformation.

Vyvolochnov comes on business, but he and Vedeniapin cannot resist arguing over their respective positions, and in this dialogue Pasternak lays out his polemic most directly. Vyvolochnov accuses Vedeniapin of "decadence," of supporting a philosophy that overvalues beauty and therefore abandons social reform. He mocks, "And you think . . . the world will be saved by beauty [*Mir spaset krasota*], is that it? Dostoevsky, Rozanov, mystery plays, and whatnot?"[28] Vedeniapin counters, "'I think that if the beast who sleeps in man could be held down by threats—any kind of threat, whether of jail or of retribution after death—then the highest emblem of humanity would be the animal tamer in the circus with his whip, not the prophet who sacrificed himself. But don't you see, this is just the point—what has for centuries raised man above the beast is not the cudgel but music: the irresistible power of unarmed truth, the powerful attraction of its example.'" This exchange serves as the perfect commentary to Pasternak's revision of the Tolstoyan narrative. In *Resurrection*, Tolstoy, too, rejects threats "of jail or of retribution after death," to use Vedeniapin's words, as effective or moral means of regeneration; nonetheless he does advocate an ascetic self-restraint that Pasternak overtly rejects and that one might associate with Vedeniapin's "animal tamer" image, especially given the prominence in ascetic discourse of imagining the passions as wild beasts. Pasternak, on the other hand, goes as far as to indicate that following this "music" no matter where it leads—even into adultery—is precisely "what has raised man above the beast" for centuries. If Tolstoy believes man should use rules to master passionate forces, Pasternak believes that passion impels individuals toward their most lasting achievements.

Sima Tuntseva is another (albeit self-taught) philosopher figure in the novel, and one who speaks out against the aesthetics of the "animal tamer." After Zhivago returns from his captivity by the partisans, he and Lara renew their affair. Lara finds herself in turmoil. At this time her friend Sima offers her a discourse on her philosophical views, focusing especially on liturgical accounts of Mary Magdalene; in a non-traditional reading of these liturgical passages she finds in these texts both a depiction and validation of Magdalene's passionate nature. For her, Magdalene's passion expresses life's vital force, which the liturgy preserves and sustains. Thus Sima indirectly speaks to Lara's situation and validates her choice to pursue passion. In particular Sima takes aim at Church traditions of asceticism with which Tolstoy's views align, protesting especially against a group of Lenten readings that elevate the "reining in of the senses and the mortification of the flesh."²⁹ She describes these texts—the ones Tolstoy would surely prefer—with great distaste, as deprived of beauty: "curiously flat and clumsy and without the poetry of other spiritual writings." When she surmises that they were probably written by "fat-bellied" monks, we are reminded of Pasternak's incongruously fat and also physically awkward Tolstoyan, Vyvolochnov, with whom Vedeniapin debates the power of beauty. Her attack on this kind of asceticism, like Pasternak's attack on Tolstoy, proceeds ultimately via aesthetics; for her, this attention to "various infirmities of the flesh and to whether it is fat or famished" is simply "repulsive."³⁰ For her, moral teachings on their own are a dead end; they inspire no productive response.

Instead, she presents a Mary Magdalene figure whose sensual nature facilitates her redemption. Pasternak outlines an alternative approach to Tolstoy's in Sima's reading of a particular liturgical service: the service for Holy Wednesday, in which Mary Magdalene is a central figure. Remarking on "what genuine passion there is" in the text, Sima recounts Mary Magdalene's letting down her hair to wipe Christ's feet dry after she has anointed them with myrrh and with her tears. In Sima's reading this act becomes an erotic gesture, and one that redeems feminine beauty as a whole. Sima cites (in her own, modern Russian) a moment in the liturgy when Magdalene compares herself to Eve: "'Let me kiss thy most pure feet and water them with my tears and dry them with the hair of my head, which covered Eve and sheltered her in its rushing waves when she was afraid in the cool of the day in paradise.'"³¹ Eve uses her hair to "shelter" her nakedness, yet the sensuality of the image of her hair's "rushing waves" seems to amplify rather than conceal her body. In her passionate act of wiping Christ's feet with her hair, Magdalene redeems Eve's seductive beauty and the "covering" that amplifies it. Likewise in her impassioned interpretation of liturgy through a religious-philosophical lens, Sima both brings the liturgy to life and redeems Lara. We might see her, then, as a figure of the novel itself, how it takes moments of beauty and draws them into restorative visions of life.

In his interest in the power of the erotic and all that amplifies the flesh's beauty, Pasternak remains true to the legacy of the prerevolutionary period he reinvokes and to common themes in its public discussions. He was one of many to attend some of the Religious-Philosophical Meetings initiated in 1901 by members of the intelligentsia in hopes of establishing dialogue with representatives of the Russian Orthodox clergy. The meetings were held regularly from 1901 to 1903 and served—for a few years, at least—as one of the only forums in which intelligentsia and clergy alike could freely address social, cultural, and political topics in a public setting. Many of the discussions, transcripts of which were published in the journal *A New Way* (*Novyi put'*), centered on the importance of art and the need for the Church to embrace new forms of culture. In part this is what one of the meeting's key organizers, Dmitrii Merezhkovskii, meant when he used the term "holy flesh" (*sviataia plot'*) in a paper he read for the tenth meeting on Nikolai Gogol'.[32] This phrase, however, came to be particularly understood as referring to the intelligentsia's desire to consecrate eroticism in its many forms. One Church figure taking part in the meetings, in flat disagreement with Merezhkovskii's presentation of flesh, objected that the Christian does not consecrate but rather "vanquishes the flesh, that is, his sinful disposition."[33] And yet others representing the Church's views spoke positively of a "Christian culture of the flesh" and lamented overly strict applications of ascetic ideals.[34]

As the meetings progressed, discussions focused increasingly on questions around sex, with the intelligentsia calling on the representatives of the Church to articulate and defend their positions. The intelligentsia viewed this topic as revealing of both the Church's attitude to human culture and also its attitude to questions of conscience, seen in its application of dogma to real-life situations. Olga Matich has written extensively on the debates over sex in the Religious-Philosophical Meetings, emphasizing an overarching question of whether the Church considers celibacy superior to marriage.[35] As Matich shows, and as readings of the meeting transcripts reveal, both sides of the discussions evinced uncertainty and ambivalence over the role of sex in the life of individuals and society. Some members of the intelligentsia—most notably Vasilii Rozanov—propounded the physical aspects of sexuality, while others, like Merezhkovskii, privileged rather the power of erotic desire. Clergy responded in varying ways, some arguing that the Church positively views sex in the context of procreation and others, as we see above in the comment on "vanquishing" the flesh, largely identifying sexuality with sin.[36] Pasternak's novel comprises a continuation of these debates, in all their complexity.

The Place of the Poetic in a Novel about Beauty

But we find Pasternak's innovation in the novel genre—the way he moves beyond Tolstoy—in his use of the poetic, and it is here that he most boldly adapts religious-philosophical thought. As we have seen, Pasternak's novel figures the Solov'evian affirmation of eros as a force for positive transformation. But *Doctor Zhivago* also figures the poetic itself, morphing the seductive force of the female body into an emblem of how art affects those who encounter it. Here I will not speak primarily of the cycle of poems that ends the novel; rather,

I will show one way in which the poetic plays out in the novel's very prose, in the form of an extended visual metaphor. At numerous moments in the novel Zhivago (or the narrator focalizing through him) imagines a line (often pictured as fabric) that wraps around Lara's body and projects out in an arc that echoes and amplifies her contours. This abstracted figure comes to represent the force of beauty as it reaches into and touches the world around it. It is the kind of figure the later Tolstoy would deplore—not only for its amplification of the erotic, but also for the obscurity of its reference and the interpretive subjectivity it encourages. As though Pasternak's ending his novel with poems rather than moral principles is not a clear enough statement about his preference for poetry over philosophical truth claims, he introduces into his prose this lyrical element that demands the reader's interpretive engagement well before the narrative winds down.

In his privileging of the poetic Pasternak follows Solov'ev's borrowed dictum that precisely beauty will save the world; but fascinatingly, he goes as far, I would argue, as to adapt this visual metaphor from the religious philosopher himself, and perhaps also from his successor, Pavel Florenskii. In both these philosophers' works we find such an abstracted image, pictured in fabric covering a beloved body and expressing its essence. In "The Meaning of Love," that very essay loved by the young Zhivago and discussed by Vedeniapin, Solov'ev writes, "In the arrangement of the physical world (the cosmic process) the divine Idea only adorned the kingdom of matter and death with a shroud of natural beauty from without: through humanity, through the activity of its universally rational consciousness, it must enter into this kingdom *from within*, in order to vivify nature and immortalize its beauty."[37] Solov'ev begins his essay with a discussion of the insufficiency of natural beauty—that is, it casts beauty as a mere aid for propagation and therefore fails to express spiritual immortality. Hence natural beauty appears as a "shroud," rather than the light-bearing garments we will see in Florenskii's icons. In "The Meaning of Love," Solov'ev describes a "cosmic process" by which "the force directing the life of humanity," or "Divine Providence," takes possession of individuals so that they may work out the transformation of mankind and all of creation into an "all-unity ideal" (*vseedinyi ideal*).[38] Unlike the "shroud" of natural beauty, the beauty clothing the new humanity will radiate *"from within."*

But in his images of an arcing fabric Pasternak—like Solov'ev—presents more than a divine life force; both seek to represent man's own creative engagement with the world's transformation. Elsewhere in "The Meaning of Love," Solov'ev writes more about how individuals co-create the world's new beauty, by their responses to love; his discussion of this cooperative process especially sheds light on Pasternak's own creative project. For Solov'ev the force that initiates the "cosmic process" comes to individuals in the form of love.[39] This life/love force wells up of its own accord, a "divine gift"; but its outward manifestation is the fruit of spiritual labor, the recipient's active response to grace. The extension of this force into the world very much depends on the individual's creatively channeling it, as Solov'ev writes, "toward higher aims."[40] Solov'ev tries to give us some sense of what this creative cooperation might look like, and here we discover another fabric image, when he describes "the concrete form of this imagination, the ideal image in which I wrap the beloved person in a given moment."[41] This "ideal image," then, constitutes an embodiment of the universal life essence, in the enticing form of a particular beloved. The creative lover works passion into beauty with eternal significance. He helps transform the shroud into a living fabric.

Pasternak takes this very figure and uses it to picture how philosophical and literary genres can complement one another. In "The Meaning of Love," Solov'ev himself was responding to Tolstoy, and especially his *Kreutzer Sonata*, which famously denounces sex and sexual attraction.[42] For Solov'ev, the novel, at least as represented by Tolstoy, holds little promise as a way to transform life. Solov'ev associates "everyday prose" with mere sex.[43] He speaks in "The Meaning of Love" of Tolstoy's works—*Anna Karenina* (1878), "The Death of Ivan Il'ich" ("Smert' Ivana Il'icha," 1889), *The Kreutzer Sonata*—as splendid embodiments of the deathly emptiness of immorality and coarse pleasure-seeking.[44] To this depiction, he proclaims, "I have nothing to add." Instead, he aims to depict the extension of the life force into all the world, which Tolstoy's works, by virtue of their subject matter, cannot do. "Is it possible," Solov'ev writes, "without horrific sadness, even to imagine the infinitely continuing existence of any high-society lady, or any sportsman, or card player?" He leaves it to poets, instead, to figure, or prophesy, "a universal restoration of life and beauty."[45]

In his creative exploration of the relations between philosophy and literature, meanwhile, Pasternak seems to be taking a leaf from Solov'ev's book. Judith Kornblatt has written on Solov'ev's literary polemic with *Resurrection* in "Three Conversations" ("Tri razgovora," 1900), and the polemic she describes parallels Pasternak's with Tolstoy. For Solov'ev, as Kornblatt describes him, Tolstoy reduces fiction to an elaboration of philosophy's "fixed, declarative" stance, whereas Solov'ev uses fiction to set literature and philosophy in conversation and thereby to foster a more "interpretive," interactive relationship to truth.[46] The kind of prose Tolstoy offers hollows out reality, simplifying it and reducing it to only its most obvious and rationally acceptable outlines. As such, it leaves no room for the mystery and the work of the imagination, humanity's active, creative participation in the world's transformation. Instead, Solov'ev brings together literature and philosophy so that literature "makes real/embodies/incarnates" the philosophy.[47] Pasternak, then, extends Solov'ev's task, using one of Solov'ev's own images as an emblem for the endeavor.

Florenskii further develops the thought of Solov'ev in ways that suggest how far-reaching this metaphor of world-transforming beauty as fabric might be. As Steven Cassedy shows in the first *Russian Religious Thought* volume, Florenskii's embrace of materiality permeates all his work.[48] Given Pasternak's own study of philosophy and participation in a philosophical discussion group with Andrei Belyi and others in the 1910s, it is difficult to imagine that he did not know Florenskii's early work, especially his sensational 1914 *The Pillar and Ground of the Truth* (*Stolp i utverzhdenie istiny*).[49] Pasternak could not have known the shorter work *Iconostasis*, which was not published until 1977, and then only in part.[50] But Susanna Witt persuasively argues that Pasternak may well have known the text of one of Florenskii's lectures on the icon, specifically on the topic of "inverse perspective."[51]

In 1922 Pavel Florenskii composed *Iconostasis*, a short and accessible work aimed at presenting the icon to modern readers in its spiritual, philosophical, and material dimensions.[52] Materiality comprises one of his central concerns, and he goes to great lengths to demonstrate how in the icon medium constitutes far more than message: the icon does not simply convey information between sender and receiver, it institutes a new reality in those who let it address them. Its medium constitutes nothing less than a transfiguration of the earthly, its permeation by God's light, his uncreated energies.

In one of his most illuminating passages Florenskii explains to his interlocutor, Sophia Ivanova, the significance of clothing in the icon. He begins by mocking Vasilii Rozanov, whose concerns centered on the body and who, as mentioned above, was a central figure in the Religious-Philosophical Meetings. Florenskii remarks ironically that Rozanov "somewhere says that in the Kingdom of God everyone will be naked."[53] Clothes in the icon, Florenskii contends, signify nothing less than the essence of the holy person himself, his transformed, deified flesh. They are "the covering woven by their acts of spiritual discipline, or *podvig*."[54] As such, the saint's clothing represents "earthly accident" that "beautifully highlight[s]" these actions and thus "disclose[s] the body's constitution." The ornament reveals the essence. "A nude figure," he writes, "is therefore not obscene or ugly; rather, it is metaphysically less intelligible." The formal accidents, in other words, that comprise beauty in a work of art reveal its deepest meaning. This view of beauty characterizes his project as a whole: the iconostasis (a screen covered in icons) may seem to function simply to conceal the altar area, but for Florenskii its consecrated materiality reveals the worlds hidden behind the trappings of ritual structures.

In his dialogue, reflections, and poems, Zhivago validates the power of the beauty that swathes and amplifies the female figure, "accident" that embodies essence. As his thought and art develop he holds ever more firmly to the power of attraction to transform the self and the world; as he writes in his journal, "Forward steps in art are governed by the law of attraction." Soon thereafter he begins his affair with Lara. This principle is one he has adapted from Vedeniapin, who, as we saw above, propounds "music" by which histories and civilizations advance; but increasingly it takes on a palpable shape for him: the shape of Lara. It is not until Zhivago and his family uproot their lives and move to the Urals that we begin to see what was originally Vedeniapin's idea interpreted, performed, bodied out. The "new order of things" that Zhivago heralds back in Moscow begins to take shape along the seductive lines of Lara's form.[55]

Once he begins to acknowledge to himself his love of Lara, Zhivago sees her body as the vector of the force of attraction he has before now only theorized about. The first such image occurs to him after Zhivago has moved with his family from Moscow to the Urals, near where Lara is living in the town of Iuriatin. Even as he tries to build a new, safe world for his family, he begins drifting toward Lara by that very "force of attraction" he notes in his journal reflections on art. In a first concrete step toward a relationship with her, he furtively notes down her address from a slip she has left in the library and goes to visit her at her home. Here he finds her fetching water at a well (a near biblical image of an adulteress Christ addresses [John 4]) and marvels at her movements. He sees a "fluidity [*plavnost'*] in everything she does, as if she had taken a running start early in life, way back in her childhood, and now everything she does follows this momentum, easily, naturally. This quality is in the line of her back when she bends down and in her smile as it parts her lips and rounds her chin, and in her words and thoughts."[56] In the thoughts leading up to this image, Zhivago describes how "lightly" and "effortlessly" Lara does everything, and with what "ardor." Here Zhivago imagines a kind of arc that describes flight, and he sees that forceful yet effortless trajectory in all she does and says—and even thinks. This is the body that we have been waiting for, the one Tolstoy would not—could not?—produce: at once natural and attractive.

This quality of a forceful but natural vector increasingly associates itself in Zhivago's imagination with the image of fabric, and this fabric becomes a figure of his art. During his captivity with the partisans his thoughts turn increasingly, irrevocably to Lara. One such reverie begins as Zhivago witnesses the activities of the folk healer, Kubarikha, singing and then speaking of witchcraft and then weaving a spell over the sick cow "Beauty." Kubarikha incorporates numerous images of fabric and weaving into her discourse. As Zhivago listens raptly to the "nonsense" of her spell he begins to adapt her images into a vision of Lara: "How he loved her! How beautiful she was! In exactly the way he had always thought and dreamed and wanted! Yet what was it that made her so lovely? Was it something that could be named and analyzed? No, a thousand times no! She was lovely by virtue of the matchlessly simple and swift line that the Creator had, at a single stroke, drawn all around her, and in this divine form she had been handed over, like a child tightly wrapped in a sheet after its bath, into the arms of his soul."[57] In this image we seem to find a novelistic rendering of what Solov'ev proposes in "The Meaning of Love": "the concrete form of this imagination, the ideal image in which I wrap the beloved person in a given moment."[58]

The novelist goes further. He imaginatively takes this line, this fabric that seems to enwrap Lara, and extends it into a grandiose emblem of her, into his adapted image of the *pokrov* (Mary's protective veil over the children of God), which becomes a figure for his artistic embodiments of religious-philosophical concepts. We read, "Like a message on a breadth of cloth [*plakat na bol'shushchem polotnishche*] stretched between buildings across a city street, there hung before him in the air, from one side of the forest glade to the other, a blurred, greatly magnified phantom [*prizrak*] of a single, astonishing, idolized head."[59] As I have argued elsewhere, Pasternak combines in this image the *pokrov* with the floating head from the icon "not made by hands" [*nerukotvornyi*], also known as the *mandylion*.[60] Traditionally the *mandylion* was a fabric on which Christ's face imprinted itself, marking the cloth with the healing powers of his presence. Edith Clowes has also pointed to the similarity of this "banner" with those carried in religious processions; the image of "stretched . . . across a city street," though, resonates with other *pokrov* images in the novel.[61] Using this type, Pasternak offers us his most literal image of what Florenskii and Solov'ev discuss: the fabric or adornment that shares in the essence of what it adorns, whose beautiful accidents entice the beholder into real union with the one beheld and with the world.

This image and those that echo it attune us to the way Pasternak develops the female figure across his novel; Zhivago's art launches itself from the line of the female body, from mother to lover. The novel itself begins on the eve of the

Feast of the *Pokrov*, the Virgin's Intercession, when Zhivago's mother is buried. When we first glimpse the young Zhivago, he is standing on his mother's grave, as though to speak, or howl.[62] That night a blizzard brings a knocking at the window that awakens the boy, and he watches how "turning over and over in the sky, length after length of whiteness unwound over the earth and shrouded it."[63] This image of snow covering the earth reappears in several of the Zhivago poems as nature's temporary way of adorning and covering a naked earth.[64] Here we find that shroud Solov'ev describes, an incomplete expression of beauty. But Pasternak does not stop here. Later in the novel, as we have seen, a similar covering wraps itself around Lara in Zhivago's reveries, "like a child tightly wrapped in a sheet after its bath." Pasternak associates the mother image with a "shroud," with death; but he associates the lover with brand new life. Notably, he also associates Tonia, his wife, with Mary the Mother of God (*Bogomater'*), and Lara with Mary Magdalene.[65] What is more, he associates his Magdalene figure throughout with new and clean clothes: her mother runs a sewing workshop; we often see Lara doing laundry and sewing; and Lara and Zhivago's illegitimate child, Tanya, becomes a laundress. We see in these mundane details how Pasternak works to infuse poetry into the most prosaic, immortalizing sheer materiality.

His cycle's penultimate poem, "Magdalene," presents this enwrapping fabric as a line into new life—one that extends in a passionate line from beloved to lover and beyond. In the poem Magdalene speaks of embracing Christ's feet as she washes them: "I have buried them in my hair, as in the folds of a burnous."[66] Here the seductive covering of Magdalene's hair swaddles Christ's feet, an erotic adaptation of the motherly image of protection. This figure embodies the very force that bears Christ through grave into resurrection—an image suggested both by the poem and by a dream Zhivago has early on in the novel, just as he recovers from a bout of typhus. "Magdalene" ends with an image of the female figure reaching out—like her hair, like her arms embracing Christ—and saying that during Christ's time in the tomb, literally, "I will grow into Resurrection" (*Ia do Voskresen'ia dorostu*).[67] Likewise in Zhivago's feverish dream, he is writing a poem called "Turmoil" ("Smiatenie") in which he describes "neither the entombment nor the resurrection but the days between"—days he himself is experiencing. "Near him, touching him, were hell, dissolution, corruption, death, and equally near him were the spring and Mary Magdalene and life. And it was time to awake. Time to awake and get up. Time to rise from the dead."[68]

In *Doctor Zhivago*, Pasternak envisions Russia, like the ailing doctor, as ready to emerge from its time of turmoil and rise from the dead, but only as it reappropriates its native cultural resources. As we see in this passage but also in the cycle of poems and throughout the novel, Pasternak pictures how, using philosophical tools, one might creatively leverage the beauty found in Russia's primary religious tradition, a task Per-Arne Bodin and others have begun to describe.[69] By making the Orthodox liturgy speak into the lives of contemporary characters and inspire new poetry he underscores how art—far from leading to decadence—carries out a religious work, which is to say a work of resurrection, of restoration. Neither Pasternak nor the religious philosophers on whom he draws can be described in any simple way as representing the views of the Orthodox Church. And yet they insist that the work they do bears every relevance to how ideas, including religious ones, work themselves out in society. That is, they see human creativity as necessary to channel Russia's moral and cultural resources, from its religious traditions to its philosophical traditions. While its embodiments necessarily extend outside the bounds of religious and philosophical discourses, nevertheless these creative appropriations alone ensure the vitality of the individual and society.

In *Doctor Zhivago* the erotic line of the fabric that launches from the female form stretches out into creative acts that will bear individuals and culture through "the days between." In the novel it culminates in a poetic cycle; how different from the five guiding principles that conclude Tolstoy's novel. In *Resurrection*, the protagonist boils his experiences down to ethical maxims; in *Doctor Zhivago*, the protagonist distills his experiences into suggestive images, resonant phrases. Tolstoy seeks to move his reader away from art into life, abandoning his narrative once his protagonist reaches conversion; Pasternak, on the other hand, leaves the reader to weave connections, to try to grasp that arc by which love propels "everyday prose" into poetry. By enticing the reader's imagination, Pasternak positions the poetic novel—belles lettres—as the genre by which religious traditions and religious-philosophical ideas might reach into and transform the world.

NOTES

1. Boris Pasternak, *Doktor Zhivago*, vol. 3 of *Sobranie sochinenii v piati tomakh* (Moscow: Khudozhestvennaia literatura, 1990), 360, 362, 370.

2. For an account of this set of events, see Lazar Fleishman, "The Nobel Scandal," in *Boris Pasternak: The Poet and His Politics* (Cambridge, MA: Harvard University Press, 1990), 273–300.

3. Fleishman, *Boris Pasternak*, 278–79.

4. In a letter of 1950 Pasternak speaks of Tolstoy's "perception of the world and of life activity" as being the "basis of my existence, my whole manner of living and seeing." Lev Tolstoi, *Polnoe sobranie sochinenii* (Moscow: Khudozhestvennaia literatura, 1953), 62:269, cited in Per-Arne Bodin, *Eternity and Time: Studies in Russian Literature and the*

Orthodox Tradition (Stockholm: Stockholm University Press, 2007), 192. As I will show, however, Pasternak objects to certain aspects of Tolstoy's later teachings, especially as evinced in "What Is Art?" and in his late novel *Resurrection*.

5. Lev Tolstoi, "Chto takoe isskustvo?," in *Polnoe sobranie sochinenii* (Moscow-Leningrad: Khudozhestvennaia literatura, 1951), 30:27–203.

6. Here I speak of the figural in reference to Erich Auerbach's discussion of figurae. See his essay "Figura," in *Scenes from the Drama of European Literature* (Minneapolis: University of Minnesota Press, 1984), 11–78.

7. Ronald Hingley recounts this in his biography of Pasternak. Ronald Hingley, *Pasternak: A Biography* (London: Weidenfeld and Nicolson, 1983), 16.

8. Fleishman, *Boris Pasternak*, 286.

9. Judith Deutsch Kornblatt, "The Truth of the Word: Solovyov's 'Three Conversations' Speaks on Tolstoy's *Resurrection*," *Slavic and East European Journal* 45, no. 2 (2001): 301–21.

10. Lev Tolstoi, *Voskresenie*, vol. 32 of *Polnoe sobranie sochinenii* (Moscow-Leningrad: Khudozhestvennaia literatura, 1933–35).

11. I use the term "liturgy" in its broader sense, meaning the cycle of Church services, including their texts and connected rites.

12. In "Chto takoe isskustvo?" Tolstoy states his intention to move away from a discussion of beauty per se in order to focus on what defines art more fundamentally—that is, art's capacity to draw many people together by conveying a common feeling. For Tolstoy a concern with beauty in art manifests merely a concern with pleasure and with being overwhelmed by artistic effects. His particular concern over abundant depictions of sexuality in contemporary works of art exemplifies his argument that bad art uses beauty to seduce its reader, debilitating his moral capacity and his sense of responsibility for others. Therefore I use the term "beauty" polemically when describing Tolstoy's views, meaning overpowering artistic effects, since it is precisely art's seductive power that Tolstoy avers and Pasternak prefers.

13. Tolstoi, *Voskresenie*, 134–35. In this passage I have drawn mainly on Anthony Briggs's translation, though I have made adjustments where more precision seemed necessary (Lev Tolstoy, *Resurrection*, trans. Anthony Briggs [London: Penguin Classics, 2009], 154–55).

14. Tolstoi, *Voskresenie*, 139.

15. Tolstoy developed an increasingly high regard for the Gospels as Christian art with a deeply moral sensibility—that is, art that fostered in form and content a sense of universal brotherhood ("Chto takoe iskusstvo?," 156). For a discussion of Tolstoy's views on and editing of the Gospels, see Rosamund Bartlett, *Tolstoy: A Russian Life* (New York: Houghton Mifflin Harcourt, 2011), 285–87.

16. Tolstoi, *Voskresenie*, 249.

17. As we see in "What Is Art?," Tolstoy does not reject poetry outright, but he associates it much more strongly than simple story forms with the dangers of artistic obfuscation. See especially the tenth and eleventh chapters ("Chto takoe iskusstvo?," 89–121).

18. Tolstoi, *Voskresenie*, 443.

19. Tolstoi, "Chto takoe isskustvo?," 156.

20. Tolstoi, *Voskresenie*, 372.

21. The relationship between the novel's prose and its cycle of poems is a well-studied topic. See, for instance, Henrik Birnbaum, "On the Poetry of Prose: Land- and Cityscape 'Defamiliarized' in *Doctor Zhivago*," in *Fiction and Drama in Eastern and Southeastern Europe*, ed. Henrik Birnbaum and Thomas Eekman (Columbus, OH: Slavica, 1980), 27–60; Dina Magomedova, "The Relationship of Lyrical and Narrative 'Plot' in *Doctor Zhivago*," in *Doctor Zhivago: A Critical Companion*, ed. Edith W. Clowes (Evanston, IL: Northwestern University Press, 1995), 115–24.

22. Edith Clowes has noted Lara's association with Mary Magdalene. See Edith Clowes, "Characterization in *Doctor Zhivago*: Lara and Tonya," in Clowes, *Doctor Zhivago*, 62–75, here 70–71.

23. Tolstoi, "Chto takoe isskustvo?," 178. Tolstoy writes, "The art of our time and our circle has turned into a whore.... It is just as garish, just as for sale, just as deceptive and ruinous."

24. Pasternak, *Doktor Zhivago*, 401, 404, 409. Here and throughout this essay I draw from, but make adjustments to, Max Hayward and Manya Harari's translation (Boris Pasternak, *Doctor Zhivago* [New York: Pantheon Books, 1991]).

25. Pasternak, *Doktor Zhivago*, 67.

26. Ibid., 43.

27. Ibid., 40.

28. Ibid., 44.

29. Ibid., 407–8.

30. Ibid.

31. Ibid.

32. Dmitrii Merezhkovskii, "Gogol' i o. Matvei"—first published serially as "Sud'ba Gogol'ia" in the first three issues of *Novyi put'* (A New Way) (Dmitrii Merezhkovskii, "Sud'ba Gogol'ia. Chast' I: Tvorchestvo," *Novyi put'*, January 1903, 37–81; "Sud'ba Gogol'ia. Chast' II. Zhizn' i religiia," *Novyi put'*, February 1903, 1–41; and "Sud'ba Gogol'ia. Chast' II. Zhizn' i religiia," *Novyi put'*, March 1903, 123–61). Prefacing his paper, Merezhkovskii characterizes the divide he perceives between the Church's ideal and the intelligentsia's ideal. In the transcription of the general discussion in the first meeting, Merezhkovskii delineates, "The earth has its own ideal, just as 'Flesh' has an independent significance, not subordinated to its relationship to Spirit. It is absolutely essential to define the relation of these two ideals; will the content of the heavenly ideal be identical with the content of the earthly ideal? I think there might be a great differentiation here. To clarify that is the task for our subsequent meetings." "Zapiski religiozno-filosofskikh sobranii," *Novyi put'*, January 1903, 32.

33. "Zapiski religiozno-filosofskikh sobranii. 3-e zasedanie," *Novyi put'*, February 1903, 87.

34. V. V. Uspenskii, a professor at the Saint Petersburg Spiritual Academy, makes a comment along these lines in the tenth meeting. "Zapiski religiozno-filosofskikh sobranii. 10-oe Religiozno-filosofskoe sobranie. 18-go aprelia," *Novyi put'*, May 1903, 281.

35. Olga Matich, "Religious-Philosophical Meetings: Celibacy contra Marriage," in *Erotic Utopia: The Decadent Imagination in Russia's Fin de Siècle* (Madison: University of Wisconsin Press, 2005), 212–35.

36. The paper read in a meeting by Archimandrite Mikhail Semenov, "On Marriage: The Psychology of a Sacrament ("O brake [psikhologiia tainstva]: 12-e Religiozno-filosofskoe Sobranie," *Novyi put'*, June 1903, 248–56), offers a representative articulation

of a pro-marriage stance. Father Mikhail contrasts his own views with those represented by Tolstoy in *The Kreutzer Sonata*. The cleric argues that a relationship of love and involving sex between two people can help instill in them a greater, sacrificial capacity for love for all people. Nevertheless he warns against sex driven by a desire for pleasure rather than for offspring.

37. Solov'ev, "Smysl liubvi," in *Sobranie sochinenii V. S. Solov'eva* (Brussels, 1966), 7:3-60, here 59. In my quotes of Solov'ev I am using the translation of Vladimir Wozniuk (Vladimir Solovyov, "The Meaning of Love," in *The Heart of Reality: Essays on Beauty, Love, and Ethics*, ed. and trans. Vladimir Wozniuk [Notre Dame, IN: University of Notre Dame Press, 2003]), here 132.

38. Solov'ev, "Smysl liubvi," 10, 60; Solovyov, "The Meaning of Love," 89, 133.

39. Solov'ev, "Smysl liubvi," 15; Solovyov, "The Meaning of Love," 94.

40. Solov'ev, "Smysl liubvi," 25; Solovyov, "The Meaning of Love," 103.

41. Solov'ev, "Smysl liubvi," 44; Solovyov, "The Meaning of Love," 119-20.

42. For a focused discussion of Solov'ev's response on sexuality to Tolstoy's *Kreutzer Sonata*, see Peter Ulf Møller, *Postlude to the Kreutzer Sonata: Tolstoj and the Debate on Sexual Morality in Russian Literature in the 1890s* (New York: E. J. Brill, 1988), 281-96.

43. Solov'ev, "Smysl liubvi," 22; Solovyov, "The Meaning of Love," 100.

44. Solov'ev, "Smysl liubvi," 31; Solovyov, "The Meaning of Love," 108.

45. Solov'ev, "Smysl liubvi," 59; Solovyov, "The Meaning of Love," 132.

46. Kornblatt, "The Truth of the Word," 305.

47. Ibid., 314.

48. Steven Cassedy, "P. A. Florensky and the Celebration of Matter," in *Russian Religious Thought*, ed. Judith Deutsch Kornblatt and Richard F. Gustafson (Madison: University of Wisconsin Press, 1996), 95-111.

49. Pavel Florenskii, *Stolp i utverzhdenie istiny: Opyt pravoslavnoi teoditsei v dvenadtsati pis'makh* (Moscow: Lepta, 2002). All translations of this text are my own. For a relatively recent translation into English, see P. A. Florenskii, *The Pillar and Ground of the Truth: An Essay in Orthodox Theodicy in Twelve Letters*, trans. Boris Jakim (Princeton, NJ: Princeton University Press, 2004). For more on this work, see Ruth Coates's chapter in this volume. For a discussion of Pasternak's study of philosophy and his exploration of the problem of philosophy in his literary work, see Edith Clowes, "'Sheer Philosophy' and 'Vegetative Thinking': Pasternak's Suspension and Preservation of Philosophy," in *Fiction's Overcoat: Russian Literary Culture and the Question of Philosophy*, ed. Edith W. Clowes (Ithaca, NY: Cornell University Press, 2004), 258-81.

50. See Avril Pyman, *Pavel Florensky: A Quiet Genius* (New York: Continuum, 2010), 286n.

51. Witt points out a reference in *Doctor Zhivago* to the institution where Florenskii was lecturing at the time he was writing *Iconostasis*, which coincides with the years during which Zhivago was to have written his poetry cycle. A lecture Florenskii gave in this period (in a different setting from his teaching institution) circulated widely in samizdat form. Susanna Witt, *Creating Creation: Readings of Pasternak's "Doktor Živago"* (Stockholm: Almqvist och Wiksell International, 2000), 45-46.

52. Pavel Florenskii, *Ikonostas*, in *Sochineniia v chetyrekh tomakh*, vol. 2 (Moscow: Mysl', 1996), 419-526. In my quotes from *Iconostasis* I am using Sheehan and Andrejev's translation (Pavel Florenskii, *Iconostasis*, trans. Donald Sheehan and Olga Andrejev [Crestwood, NY: St. Vladimir's Seminary Press, 1996]).

53. Florenskii, *Ikonostas*, 487; Florenskii, *Iconostasis*, 117.
54. Florenskii, *Ikonostas*, 488; Florenskii, *Iconostasis*, 118.
55. Pasternak, *Doktor Zhivago*, 282, 181.
56. Ibid., 293.
57. Ibid., 362–63.
58. Solov'ev, "Smysl liubvi," 44; Solovyov, "The Meaning of Love," 119–20.
59. Pasternak, *Doktor Zhivago*, 363.
60. Martha M. F. Kelly, "Cultural Transformation as Transdisfiguration in Pasternak's *Doctor Zhivago*," *Russian History* 40, no. 1 (2013): 1:68–89.
61. Clowes, "Characterization in *Doctor Zhivago*," 72.
62. Pasternak, *Doktor Zhivago*, 7.
63. Ibid., 8.
64. See the following poems in Pasternak, *Doktor Zhivago*: "Holy Week" ("Na Strastnoi"), 512–13; "Winter Night" ("Zimniaia noch'"), 526–27; "Encounter" ("Svidanie"), 528–79; "Star of the Nativity" ("Rozhdestvenskaia zvezda"), 530–32.
65. Pasternak, *Doktor Zhivago*, 278.
66. Ibid., 537.
67. "But three days will go by, / Encountering such emptiness / That over this terrible interval / I will grow into Resurrection." Ibid., 538.
68. Ibid., 206.
69. See, for instance, Per-Arne Bodin, *Nine Poems from "Doktor Živago": A Study of Christian Motifs in Boris Pasternak's Poetry* (Stockholm: Almqvist & Wiksell International, 1976). In this study Bodin points to and describes many references in *Doctor Zhivago* to Christian and especially Orthodox liturgical tradition. This work offers more a study of motifs and allusions than something that could be called a poetics. In another work, *Eternity and Time*, Bodin offers something closer to a poetics, along with a discussion of Christian themes across Pasternak's oeuvre. He describes in particular Pasternak's poetic principle of *stseplenie* or interconnection. Bodin, "Boris Pasternak and the Christian Tradition," in *Eternity and Time*, 182–204.

Afterword

PAUL VALLIERE

The scholarly study of Russian religious thought did not begin in the English-speaking world before the middle of the twentieth century. If a starting point is wanted, the best choice would be the publication of George L. Kline's translation of V. V. Zen'kovskii's *History of Russian Philosophy*, which appeared in 1953.[1] Although the title makes no reference to religion, *A History of Russian Philosophy* is a classic of Russian religious thought. Zen'kovskii was a Russian Orthodox priest whose commitment to the religious-philosophical tradition led him to devote large sections of his book to religious thinkers.

In 1965, a team of Kline's younger contemporaries produced a second landmark work in the field with the publication of the first sizable English-language anthology of primary sources of Russian philosophy.[2] While the editors devoted considerable space to secular, especially revolutionary Russian thinkers, they also incorporated many seminal texts by religious philosophers. Given that the 1950s and 1960s was a time of massive expansion in American higher education and in Slavic studies in particular, one might have predicted a bright future for Russian religious-philosophical studies in North America. For a number of reasons, however, this future did not materialize. To begin with, a seismic shift was underway in academic philosophy at the time. The traditional schools of American philosophy, idealism and pragmatism, were giving way to the analytic school, which was less hospitable to religious thought than the traditions it displaced. The hegemony of Marxist ideology in Soviet Russia was a second disincentive to the study of religious philosophy. Most North American specialists on Russia had difficulty imagining that Russian religious thought was anything but a dead letter. The idea that this tradition might reconstitute itself seemed as far-fetched as Andrei Amal'rik's musings on whether the Soviet Union would survive until 1984.[3]

The 1950s and 1960s were also the high point of modernization theory, which involved the view that religion was becoming an increasingly marginal factor in the social, political, and economic development of contemporary civilization. The inevitable decline of religion seemed all but certain in the case of Orthodox Christianity, which even many Western Christians, not to speak of non-Christians and the non-religious, regarded as a primitive form of Christianity. This assessment was not based on firsthand knowledge. Even among professional Slavists, exposure to Orthodoxy was relatively rare. The Orthodox population in North America was small, unevenly distributed, mostly working-class and poorly represented in the academy. Contact with the Orthodox community in the Soviet Union was tightly controlled.

Ironically, even scholars of religion failed to take up the study of modern Orthodoxy. The academic study of religion expanded rapidly in America during the 1960s and 1970s, not least because of the opening of religion programs in state universities, an unprecedented development in American higher education. The new departments insisted that their approach to the study of religion was secular, an affirmation that many scholars of religion in private institutions also began to profess. But deeply ingrained religious attitudes, often in secularized form, exercise far more influence over appointments and other investments made by academic religion departments than most putatively secular religion scholars would care to admit. The disregard of Orthodoxy as a subject worthy of sustained attention is a good example. Only after the demise of the Soviet Union, when the rebuilding of Russian Orthodoxy became an obvious fact, did a few American religion departments make appointments in the field. Even today, the number of such positions is miniscule compared with the dimensions of the subject.

So how did the study of Russian religious thought take root in the English-speaking world? For scholars who came of age in the 1960s and 1970s, by far the most important stimulus was the study of Russian literature. Gogol', Dostoevsky, and Tolstoy led perspicacious readers to discover Russian Orthodoxy and, in turn, its religious thinkers. This was certainly the order of things for Richard Gustafson and Judith Deutsch Kornblatt, the coeditors of *Russian Religious Thought* (1996), predecessor of the present volume. In the twenty-first century, opportunities for engagement with Russian Orthodoxy are vastly more numerous than they were in the 1960s and 1970s. But I suspect that classical Russian literature still remains the most powerful generator of interest in Russian religious thought among people who were not raised in the Orthodox tradition, and even some who were.

If this is the case, it shines a particular light on Martha Kelly's contribution to the present volume. Her mapping of the connections between Pasternak's *Doctor Zhivago* and the religious philosophy of the Russian Silver Age recapitulates the kind of journey that brought many of us into the field in the first place. While Kelly's essay comes last in the present collection, it could easily have been placed first as a portrait of the gateway to our subject.

To create a field of study, scholars captivated by the religious culture embedded in Russian literature had to find each other. In North America, they did so chiefly in the American Association for the Advancement of Slavic Studies, now the Association for Slavic, East European, and Eurasian Studies. While the number of AAASS members who thought about religion was small compared with the Marxologists and Kremlinologists who dominated the organization during the Cold War decades, they were sustained by intellectual enthusiasm and by the sense that they were engaged in what a theologian would call a prophetic vocation. A few historians who came of age in the 1960s and 1970s also took up the challenge of thinking about Russian Orthodoxy, as if responding to Hugh Seton-Watson's call for "pioneers" to explore the subject.[4] The most notable pioneer was Gregory L. Freeze, whose monographs on the imperial church set a standard that has not been surpassed.[5] By the mid-1970s, this small flock of literary scholars, historians, and bibliographers collaborated regularly at AAASS meetings, helping to create what Rowan Williams has called "the exceptionally lively climate of North American Slavonic studies."[6]

Also in the 1970s, a new kind of personal contact with the Russian intelligentsia became possible thanks to the arrival in the West of a new wave of Soviet émigrés, a product of the détente era. North American Slavists benefited enormously from this development, not just because some of the newcomers were expert scholars but because they were in a position to introduce the Americans to colleagues and friends in the Soviet Union. As these relationships grew, Western Slavists discovered something they had not known before or had greatly underestimated: that a significant revival of religious faith was taking place in Russia, especially in the intelligentsia. Visiting Russian intellectuals in their homes in those days, one would often be shown nineteenth- and early twentieth-century editions of Russian religious philosophers, items that one's hosts counted as treasured possessions. Discerning visitors could see that Russian religious philosophy was not just a thing of the past but a thing of the present, a renewed tradition.

By the time the third generation of American Slavists was completing its education in the late 1980s and 1990s, the Russian world had changed completely. The ferment of the *glasnost'* years, the spectacular celebration of the millennium of the Russian Orthodox Church in 1988 and the dissolution of the Soviet Union in 1991 stimulated the study of Orthodoxy and cognate subjects as never before. What had been a marginal tributary became mainstream. In graduate schools and scholarly meetings, Russian Orthodoxy and everything connected with it began receiving attention, and with good reason, since the rebuilding of the Russian Church ranks as one of the most remarkable religious developments in modern times. The fruits of the third generation's labors are what we see on display in the present volume.

What are the characteristics of this body of work when we compare it with the contributions of the first two generations? The most striking feature is the dominance of attention to the historical context of Russian religious thought, something that the editors of this volume point out in the introduction. The majority of the contributors to this book are historians, and they bring to our subject the care that professional historians show for the concrete, the particular, the situational. They have also "broadened [our] conceptualization of what constitutes 'thought,'" as Vera Shevzov puts it in her essay. Religious thought no longer means systematic reasoning alone, but the whole complex of ideas and feelings that motivate the practitioners of a religion, whether they were academically trained or not, educated or not, officially sanctioned or not. Without drowning us in a mass of unconnected details, our contributors make it possible for us to hear a remarkably wide range of Russian religious voices speaking in many different registers.

Besides introducing us to new interlocutors, expert contextual scholarship also enables us to hear familiar voices and interpret familiar events in a new way. Scott Kenworthy's essay on the *Imiaslavie* controversy is a case in point. By demonstrating that one of the supposedly "scholastic," "bureaucratic," and "rationalist" opponents of the *Imiaslavtsy* was in fact a leading promoter of hesychastic piety in the Russian Orthodox monastic world, Kenworthy explodes the stereotypical interpretation of this sad episode, making plain the need for a fresh start, and though he does not say so, the need for a fresh start on how the concept of Hesychasm as such should be applied with respect to the imperial period.

Several of the papers in this volume present voices from the Russian Orthodox Church's theological schools or from influential episcopal sees. This marks a change from the approach taken in *Russian Religious Thought* (1996), where the focus was on lay religious philosophers, with the exception of Pavel Florenskii, who could scarcely be considered a typical representative of the theological schools of his time (or of any other).[7] The attention to what theological professors were teaching future priests and to what leading clerics were preaching from the ambo is a natural concomitant of the third generation's commitment to contextualizing Russian religious thought. It should be noted, however, that the inclusion of church theologians in the panorama of Russian religious thought actually represents a return to the inclusive approach of an earlier generation. In *A History of Russian Philosophy* (1948), Zen'kovskii devoted considerable space to thinkers from the theological schools. A remarkably diverse mix of lay religious thinkers, church theologians, and literary artists is also a prominent feature of Florovsky's *Paths of Russian Theology* (1937). Going back even further, we should note that the first book ever published on the thought of Vladimir Solov'ev, that quintessential lay religious philosopher, was written by a professor in one of the Orthodox Church's provincial theological schools.[8]

Closer to home, two successive deans of Saint Vladimir's Orthodox Theological Seminary, Father Alexander Schmemann and Father John Meyendorff, were incalculably important mentors to many North Americans working on Russian religious thought from the 1960s and to the 1990s. Schmemann and Meyendorff were Renaissance men who distinguished themselves in a number of fields, but they saw themselves first and foremost as theologians of the Orthodox Church; and it was as inspiring models of theological intellectuality that they exercised such a formative influence on their protégés, most of whom were not Orthodox.

The contextual approach to Russian Orthodoxy is elevating our knowledge of Russian religious thought to a level far beyond any achieved before. Clearly, there cannot be too much of this good thing. One may, however, ask whether other approaches to our subject are receiving sufficient attention at the present time. The question is especially pressing with respect to systematic philosophy. The chapters by Randall Poole and Vanessa Rampton on the Russian Kantian tradition deal with an important stream of philosophizing in late imperial Russia, but otherwise there is not much attention to systematic philosophy in this volume. Our editors rightly observe that Poole's essay bears the closest resemblance to the kind of work that predominated in *Russian Religious Thought* (1996), but they do not comment on what has become of this kind of work more recently. Has systematic philosophy yielded to "context and contingency," to use our editors' words, or does it still have an important place in the field? The question is a serious one to the extent that "thought," if one thinks about it, implies some sort of limit to context and contingency. How could it not? Thought is impossible without general ideas, and as soon as one admits general ideas, one admits the *possibility* of a system of ideas. Lest the aspiration to philosophical system-building seem old fashioned in our day, one should consider that the best contextual scholarship demonstrates the need for it in very practical terms. Consider, for example, Vera Shevzov's observation on nineteenth- and early twentieth-century Orthodox apologists for belief in miracles: "Orthodox thinkers argued that those who embrace the notion of divine revelation 'know that they do not lose freedom but discover it.'" This arresting statement serves as a fitting conclusion to Shevzov's historical essay, but it could stand equally well at the head of a religious-philosophical essay as the proposition to be demonstrated. If Solov'ev had written such an essay, he would have called it something like "The Justification of Revelation." Berdiaev would have written it up as a paean to "meonic" freedom with a title such as "The Revelation of Freedom." The task of showing how the revelation given in the Bible and Church dogma grounds rather than negates freedom is a task for a philosopher or theologian, and not an easy task. Most of the apologists whom Shevzov canvasses would probably not have been up to it.

As soon as the prospect of a religious-philosophical project arises, however, a longstanding deficiency in our field must give us pause: the absence of professionally trained philosophers among us. Philosophers have been rarities in English-speaking Slavic studies from the beginning. In America, the impact of this deficiency was reduced for a long time by George L. Kline and James P. Scanlan, whose intellectual leadership and personal example inspired two generations of Slavists. Philip T. Grier is another notable exception. But the fact remains that Russian religious philosophy has not captured the broad attention of American or British philosophers, not just because of the linguistic barrier (always a factor) but because most Anglo-American philosophers do not consider the kind of material we work on to be philosophy. Does this unhappy fact mean that the study of Russian religious philosophy must do without the collaboration of philosophers for the foreseeable future?

Actually, it does not. There are at least two ways forward. The first is to engage more intentionally with scholars of the history of philosophy. History of philosophy is a discipline where the traditional concerns of Western philosophy, including religious questions, are still cultivated. If English-speaking scholars of Russian religious thought have been relatively slow to draw upon this resource, the recent publication of two well-conceived volumes on the history of Russian philosophy is a sign of movement in the right direction.[9] Contemporary scholarship on the history of philosophy, especially in the Continental tradition, offers tremendous opportunities to enliven and deepen our work on Russian thought. The renaissance of Schelling studies in the last twenty years is a case in point. Long regarded as the most aberrant of the German idealists, Schelling is receiving fresh attention today because of features of his thought that anticipated postmodern sensibility, albeit within a framework that was still grounded in the classical traditions of Western philosophy.[10] Needless to say, a Schelling renaissance is no small matter for scholars of Russian religious thought. Russian religious philosophy was created by the Russian Schellingians of the Society for the Love of Wisdom (Obshchestvo liubomudriia) in the 1820s and 1830s, and some of the greatest figures of Russian religious thought, such as Kireevskii, Solov'ev, and Bulgakov, cannot be rightly appreciated if their connection with the Schellingian stream of idealism is not recognized.

A second way of compensating for the relative absence of Anglo-American philosophers in our field is to forge relationships with philosophers in Russia, Ukraine, and Belarus, where philosophy, religious thought, and theology are usually perceived as cognate disciplines. In the older generation Sergei Khoruzhii, whose "synergistic anthropology" rests upon a synthesis of modern Continental philosophy and Byzantine Hesychasm, has set a remarkable example.[11] The reconstruction of academic philosophy in the post-Soviet East has also produced a generation of younger philosophers who are congenial to discussing religious issues.

A good example of religious-philosophical collaboration in the post-Soviet East can be seen in the Kiev Summer Theological Institute, an annual two-week symposium on Orthodox thought and culture organized by the Kiev publisher Konstantin Sigov in collaboration with Archimandrite Filaret (Egorov). Since its inception in 2003, professional philosophers have never been absent from the Institute's rostrum. Specialists on Aquinas, Descartes, Bergson, Levinas, and other philosophers work side by side with Orthodox theologians, liturgists, and ethicists to explore the religious and cultural dynamics not just of Orthodoxy but of contemporary global civilization. The same team also organizes the Uspenskii Lectures, an annual scholarly conference at the Kievan Caves Monastery that brings together Church theologians, scholars from secular institutions, cultural figures, and clergy.[12]

There is no aspect of the study of Russian religious thought or Russian Orthodoxy in the English-speaking world today that would not benefit from more regular collaboration with scholars in Russia and the other post-Soviet lands. The benefits would flow in both directions, for the new generation in the

East hungers for closer relations with Western scholars just as much as the late-Soviet generation did. Even though the ideological barriers are gone, the obstacles presented by distance and money still greatly limit contact. The community of North American Slavists should give serious attention to how ways and means might be found to promote more sustained collaboration.

The number of potential institutional partners in such an enterprise is greater than ever before thanks to the rise of a new breed of Orthodox academic institutions in the post-Soviet East. The new schools are neither state universities nor theological schools of the Russian Orthodox Church but independent institutions that have a religious foundation but serve a diverse clientele. Examples of this phenomenon in Russian higher education include the Russian Christian Humanities Academy (www.rhga.ru) in Saint Petersburg and, in Moscow, Saint Tikhon's Orthodox Humanities University (www.pstgu.ru), Saint Filaret's Orthodox Christian Institute (www.sfi.ru), and Saint Andrew's Biblical Theological Institute (www.standrews.ru). These new institutions are especially attractive venues for collaboration because of their commitment to lay theology, the enterprise that gave birth to Russian religious thought in the first place.

The older centers of religious and philosophical studies in the Russian Orthodox world are also doing new things. An example is afforded by the graduate school of religion recently opened by the Moscow Patriarchate—the Saints Cyril and Methodius General Ecclesiastical Graduate and Doctoral Program.[13] An entity of this kind, namely a program for advanced religious and theological studies operated by the Church but independent of the theological academies, is unprecedented in the history of Orthodoxy. Scholars at state universities are also engaged in fresh initiatives. An example is the Florovsky Center at Odessa National University, successor to the Imperial University of New Russia, Florovsky's alma mater. Researchers at the center, utilizing unpublished or previously unavailable materials on Florovsky's early intellectual formation, are deepening our perspective on the great neo-Patristic theologian.[14] In short, throughout the Russian Orthodox world today, a new generation of scholars is breaking fresh ground, defying stereotypes, and building interdisciplinary bridges linking theology, philosophy, and the humanities.

The conclusion to be drawn from this proliferation and diversification of institutions is that Russian religious philosophy is a living tradition in our day. It has escaped the temporal confines of the modernizing and modernist era during which it arose, and it has acquired contemporary resonance. Thinkers who are supposed to have fallen silent have not. I recall a moment at the concluding banquet of a theological conference in Moscow not so long ago when I mentioned to my dinner companion, a lay theologian I had not met before, that I worked on Sergei Bulgakov. "How nice," she replied, "he is my favorite theologian."

In encounters such as this one, we see the twofold vocation of scholars of religious thought. On the one hand, we are called to practice historicism by taking seriously the temporal context of thinking. At the same time, we are called by the material we study to interrogate, indeed to challenge, historicism. All religious thinkers claim in one way or another to have caught a glimpse of *svet nevechernii*, "the unfading light," and to have said something meaningful about it. However problematic or paradoxical their claim may be, we cannot ignore it. Like Jacob at the ford of the Jabbok, we have an angel to wrestle with.

NOTES

1. V. V. Zenkovsky, *A History of Russian Philosophy*, trans. George L. Kline, 2 vols. (New York: Columbia University Press, 1953). The original Russian edition was published in Paris by YMCA-Press in 1948.

2. James M. Edie, James P. Scanlan, and Mary-Barbara Zeldin, eds., with the collaboration of George L. Kline, *Russian Philosophy*, 3 vols. (Chicago: Quadrangle Books, 1965).

3. Andrei Amal'rik, *Will the Soviet Union Survive until 1984?*, preface by Henry Kamm, commentary by Sidney Monas (New York: Harper & Row, 1970).

4. In the preface to his volume on imperial Russia for *The Oxford History of Modern Europe*, Seton-Watson wrote: "The history of the [Russian Orthodox] Church and of religious ideas remains virtually untouched. This is a field of immense importance, of which with deep regret I confess my ignorance, while expressing the hope that pioneers will soon appear." Hugh Seton-Watson, *The Russian Empire, 1801–1917*, The Oxford History of Modern Europe (Oxford: Clarendon Press, 1967), xi.

5. Gregory L. Freeze, *The Russian Levites: Parish Clergy in the Eighteenth Century* (Cambridge, MA: Harvard University Press, 1977); Gregory L. Freeze, *The Parish Clergy in Nineteenth-Century Russia: Crisis, Reform, Counter-Reform* (Princeton, NJ: Princeton University Press, 1983). Other pioneering historical studies during the 1960s and 1970s include James H. Billington's widely read survey history, *The Icon and the Axe: An Interpretive History of Russian Culture* (New York: Alfred A. Knopf, 1968), which emphasized the centrality of Orthodox Christianity in Russian civilization; James Cracraft, *The Church Reform of Peter the Great* (Stanford, CA: Stanford University Press, 1971); Robert L. Nichols and Theofanis G. Stavrou, eds., *Russian Orthodoxy under the Old Regime* (Minneapolis: University of Minnesota Press, 1978).

6. Rowan Williams, *Dostoevsky: Language, Faith, and Fiction* (Waco, TX: Baylor University Press, 2008), 4. It should be noted that one of the editors of the present volume, Judith Deutsch Kornblatt, is a past president (2012) of the Association for Slavic, East European, and Eurasian Studies. Among the bibliographers who contributed significantly to the study of Russian Orthodoxy, Edward Kasinec deserves special mention.

7. The essays on Bulgakov in *Russian Religious Thought* (1996) deal largely, albeit not entirely, with his thought in the years before his ordination to the priesthood in 1918.

8. A. A. Nikol'skii, *Russkii Origen XIX veka Vl. S. Solov'ev* (St. Petersburg: Nauka, 2000). The book first appeared serially in *Vera i razum* (Faith and Reason) in 1902.

9. G. M. Hamburg and Randall A. Poole, eds., *A History of Russian Philosophy, 1830–1930: Faith, Reason, and the Defense of Human Dignity* (Cambridge: Cambridge University Press, 2010); William Leatherbarrow and Derek Offord, eds., *A History of Russian Thought* (Cambridge: Cambridge University Press, 2013).

10. See Andrew Bowie, *Schelling and Modern European Philosophy: An Introduction* (New York: Routledge, 1993); Judith Norman and Alistair Welchman, eds., *The New Schelling* (New York: Continuum, 2004); Jason M. Wirth, ed., *Schelling Now: Contemporary Readings* (Bloomington: Indiana University Press, 2005).

11. See S. S. Khoruzhii, ed., *Sinergiia: Problemy asketiki i mistiki pravoslaviia* (Moscow: Di-Dik, 1995); *K fenomenologii askezy* (Moscow: Izdatel'stvo gumanitarnoi literatury, 1998); *Ocherki sinergiinoi antropologii* (Moscow: Institut filosofii, teologii i istorii sv. Fomy, 2005); *Fonar' Diogena: Kriticheskaia retrospektiva evropeiskoi antropologii* (Moscow: Institut filosofii, teologii i istorii sv. Fomy, 2010). See also the website of the Institute of Synergistic Anthropology in Moscow, http:synergia-isa.ru.

12. For information on the Kiev Summer Theological Institute and the Uspenskii Lectures, see the website of Saint Clement's Center in Kiev, http://clement.kiev.ua. Sigov's publishing house in Kiev, Dukh i Litera (The Spirit and the Letter), brings out books on religion, philosophy, social sciences, and Judaica in Russian and Ukrainian. Their website is at http://duh-i-litera.com.

13. Obshchetserkovnaia aspirantura i doktorantura im. sviatykh ravnoapostol'nykh Kirilla i Mefodiia, http://www.doctorantura.ru.

14. See, for example, Anna Golubitskaia, "Genezis filosofskoi refleksii Georgiia Florovskogo (po materialam retsenzii 'odesskogo perioda')," *Sententiae* 25, no. 2 (2011): 194–208.

Contributors

RUTH COATES is a senior lecturer in Russian studies at the University of Bristol, UK. She is the author of *Christianity in Bakhtin: God and the Exiled Author* (1998), as well as numerous articles on the Russian intellectual tradition, and is coeditor of *Landmarks Revisited: The Vekhi Symposium 100 Years On* (2013). She is currently working on the reception of the doctrine of deification in Russian culture, with an emphasis on the late imperial period.

HEATHER J. COLEMAN is Canada Research Chair in Imperial Russian History and an associate professor in the Department of History and Classics at the University of Alberta. She is the author of *Russian Baptists and Spiritual Revolution, 1905–1929* (2005), editor (with Mark D. Steinberg) of *Sacred Stories: Religion and Spirituality in Modern Russia* (2007), and editor of *Orthodox Christianity in Imperial Russia: A Sourcebook on Lived Religion* (2014). She serves as editor of *Canadian Slavonic Papers/Revue canadienne des slavistes*.

SEAN GILLEN received his PhD in history at the University of Wisconsin–Madison in May 2012. His dissertation is titled "'A Foggy Youth': Faith, Reason, and Social Thought in the Young Vladimir Sergeevich Solov'ev, 1853–1881." He presently works as an analyst for a defense contractor in Tampa, Florida.

MARTHA M. F. KELLY is an assistant professor of Russian studies at the University of Missouri. Much of her work centers on how writers adapt religious traditions in a modern setting. Along these lines, she is increasingly interested in various models of religion's role in the public sphere. Her current book project, titled "Unorthodox Beauty: Russian Modernism and Its New Religious Aesthetic," focuses on the intersection of religion and poetry. She also writes on religious discourse in literary journalism, and on the poetry and essays of Olga Sedakova.

SCOTT M. KENWORTHY is an associate professor of comparative religion at Miami University (Ohio). His first book, *The Heart of Russia: Trinity-Sergius, Monasticism and Society After 1825* (2010), won the American Society of Church History's Brewer Prize. He is currently writing a book on Patriarch Tikhon Bellavin and the Orthodox Church during the Russian Revolution as well as a monograph on the Name-Glorifiers controversy.

NADIESZDA KIZENKO is an associate professor of history at the University at Albany. Her first book, *A Prodigal Saint: Father John of Kronstadt and the Russian People* (2000), won the Heldt Prize. She is currently completing the book project "A History of Confession in Russia, 1666–Present."

JUDITH DEUTSCH KORNBLATT is a professor emerita of Slavic languages and literature at the University of Wisconsin–Madison. She is the coeditor with Richard F. Gustafson of *Russian Religious Thought* (1996), as well as the author of *The Cossack Hero in Russian Literature: A Study in Cultural Mythology* (1992), *Doubly Chosen: Jewish Identity, the Soviet Intelligentsia, and the Russian Orthodox Church* (2004), and *Divine Sophia: The Wisdom Writings of Vladimir Solovyov* (2009).

PATRICK LALLY MICHELSON is an assistant professor of religious studies at Indiana University. His current book project examines the idea of asceticism in Russian Orthodox thought in the late imperial period.

RANDALL A. POOLE is a professor of history at the College of St. Scholastica in Duluth, Minnesota. He has translated and edited *Problems of Idealism: Essays in Russian Social Philosophy* (2003) and edited (with G. M. Hamburg) *A History of Russian Philosophy, 1830–1930: Faith, Reason, and the Defense of Human Dignity* (2010). In addition, he has written numerous articles and book chapters on Russian intellectual history and philosophy. During the spring semester of 2012, he was Visiting Professor of Russian Intellectual History at the University of Toronto.

VANESSA RAMPTON recently completed a PhD on Russian liberalism at King's College, University of Cambridge. She is the coeditor of a special edition of *Studies in East European Thought* on contemporary Russian culture and has published articles on Russian nationalism, liberalism, and on Dostoevsky. Vanessa works as a translator for the English version of the president of Russia's official website, eng.kremlin.ru.

VERA SHEVZOV is a professor of religion at Smith College. Author of *Russian Orthodoxy on the Eve of Revolution* (2004), she has since published articles on various aspects of Russian Orthodoxy in modern Russia, including "The Burdens of Tradition: Orthodox Constructions of the West in Russia (late 19th–early 20th cc.)," in *Orthodox Constructions of the West*, edited by George Demacopolous and Aristotle Papanikolaou (2013), and "Mary and Women in Late Imperial Russian Orthodoxy," in *Women in Nineteenth-Century Russia: Culture and Lives*, edited by Wendy Rosslyn and Alessandra Tosi (2012). She is currently completing a book on the image of Mary in late imperial and contemporary Russia.

At the time this chapter was written, OLIVER SMITH (1979–2013) was a lecturer in Russian at the University of St. Andrews. His publications include the monograph *Vladimir Soloviev and the Spiritualization of Matter* (2011) and numerous articles on the Russian theological and philosophical traditions, as well as on Russian environmental thought.

PAUL VALLIERE is McGregor Professor in the Humanities in the Department of Philosophy and Religion at Butler University. He writes on Russian religious philosophy, Orthodox theology, modern Russian Orthodoxy, and church councils in the Christian tradition. His most notable books are *Modern Russian Theology: Bukharev, Soloviev, Bulgakov* (2000) and *Conciliarism: A History of Decision-Making in the Church* (2012).

ELISE KIMERLING WIRTSCHAFTER is a professor of history at California State Polytechnic University in Pomona. Her recent publications include *Religion and Enlightenment in Catherinian Russia: The Teachings of Metropolitan Platon* (2013), *Russia's Age of Serfdom 1649–1861* (2008), and *The Play of Ideas in Russian Enlightenment Theater* (2003).

Index

absolution, 178, 180, 182, 186–87, 192n19
Admonition to the Schismatics
  [(*Uveshchanie k raskol'nikam*) Platon],
  199
Aivazov, Ivan G., 79
Aksakov, I. S., 72, 113
Alexander II (Emperor), 113, 135
Alfeev, Ilarion, 89, 90, 91, 94, 101
allegory, use of, 196–97, 199, 210n3
All-Russian Church Council, 18
Amal'rik, Andrei, 276
Amvrosii (Serebrennikov), 45, 157
anagogy: ascent in, 197–204, 212n29;
  icons, 16, 131, 144–45, 197, 266, 268,
  273n51; Scripture and, 200–202,
  203–5
Anna Karenina (Tolstoy), 265
Annenkov, P. V., 114
anthropology, 112, 114–15, 221, 281
anti-sectarian missionary work, 65,
  67–68
anti-Semitism, 18
Antonii (Khrapovitskii), Archbishop, 10,
  17, 87, 88, 91, 97, 101
Antonii (Vadkovskii), Metropolitan, 18,
  79
apologetics (*osnovnoe bogoslovie*), 14, 118
*Apology of Faith in the Name of God and
  in the Name of Jesus* (Bulatovich,
  Antonii), 87, 88
Aquinas, 199, 211n16

art, 197, 254–55, 257–58, 263, 271n12
ascent, 197–205, 212n29
asceticism, 156, 157, 261–62, 263
Askol'dov, Sergei, 136
atheism, 11, 57, 119, 134, 163–64,
  213n51
Aufhebung (Hegel), 199
Aufklärung (Enlightenment), 45, 167n1,
  168n5
Augustine of Dacia, 210n3

Bakhtin, Mikhail, 172n53
Bakunin, Mikhail, 114, 208
Baptists, 64, 73, 74, 76
Basil the Great, 201
Bayle, Pierre, 115
Bazhanov, Vasilii, Archpriest, 179–80
beauty: in art, 197, 254–55, 257–58,
  271n12; and Church ritual, 256–57;
  and the erotic, 255, 262, 268–69; in life
  of the Spirit, 166; and love, 264–65;
  Mary Magdalene, 255; passion, 264,
  265; Pasternak on, 253, 254, 261, 268;
  Tolstoy on, 254, 256–57, 271n12
Belinskii, Vissarion, 12, 25; Bakunin's
  conflict with, 208; on Goethe, 207–8;
  his model of criticism, 208–10; on
  pathos, 209–10; on Pushkin, 196,
  205, 206–7, 213n46; on rhetoric, 206;
  secularism and, 113, 213n49, 213n50;
  Sochineniia Aleksandra Pushkina, 205

289

The Bell (*Kolokol*), 68
Belyi, Andrei, 12, 266
Berdiaev, Nikolai, 7, 11, 12, 88, 239
Berlin, Isaiah, 213n49
Beseda circle of reformers, 76
Bible: anagogy as means of interpretation, 197, 203, 210n4; in confessional writing, 187–88; in discussion of miracles, 136; first Slavonic Bible, 13; and *kardia* (heart), 158–59; lay knowledge of, 186, 187; modern biblical criticism, 136
Biblical references: Genesis: *1:26*, 122; *50:20*, 55; Exodus: *20:5*, 56; 2 Samuel: *3:1*, 55; 6, 203–4; Psalms: *36:6 [35:7]*, 62n36; *84:6*, 212n29; *118 [117]:15*, 49; *119 [118]:45*, 51; *139:8*, 186; Matthew: *5:48*, 226; *7:14*, 49; *11*, 162–63; *15:24*, 55; *17:2*, 153; John: *1:4–5*, 9, 152–53; *4*, 267; *14:6*, 154; Acts, Book of: *14:22*, 49; Romans: *1:21–22*, 164; *1:25*, 183; *11:11*, 17; 1 Corinthians: *1:18*, 199; *9:27*, 53; 2 Corinthians: *3*, 203; *4:16*, 53; Galatians: *4:6*, 204; Ephesians: *6:13*, 53; Colossians: *1:24*, 51; *2:8*, 119; 1 Peter: *2:21*, 54
Biel, Anna, 193n24
Bilinkoff, Jodi, 188
Blok, A. A., 12
Bobrishchev-Pushkin, Pavel, 187, 194n54
Bodin, Per-Arne, 270, 274n69
body imagery, 93, 264, 265, 266, 267–68
Bogoliubov, Dmitrii I., 17; apologia of, 22; communal consciousness (*sobornoe soznanie*), 73, 74, 82n43; conservative nationalism, 69; criticism of, 78–79; Danilevskii's influence on, 73; education of, 71–72; on freedom of conscience, 76–78; missionary activities of, 21–22, 29, 65–66, 69–70, 73–74; narratives by, 69–70; nations as historical constructs, 75–76; populism of, 69; religious toleration, 77; renaissance of the parish, 76; on sectarianism, 72–73; service in Tambov, 66, 68, 70; Slavophilism, 69

Botkin, Vasilii, 209
bride of Christ, 184
Bulatovich, Antonii, 87, 88, 99, 101
Bulgakov, Sergei, 5, 6, 12, 78, 88, 99, 239, 281

Caputo, John, 210
Cassedy, Steven, 266
Cassian, John, 196, 197
Catherine II (Catherine the Great), 15, 201
Celestial Hierarchy (Dionysius), 198
Chaadaev, P. Ia., 9, 35n28
Chalcedonian Christology, 172n48, 222–23
Chaldean Oracles, 196
Charcot, Jean-Martin, 23, 136
Chernyshevskii, Nikolai, 113, 114, 115, 120
Chicherin, Boris, 229, 239
Christian Reading (*Khristianskoe chtenie*), 16, 135
Christ, the Word of God, 153, 168n9
Church News (*Tserkovnye vedomosti*), 135
Clay, Eugene, 75
clergy: authority of, 17, 18; education of, 3, 10, 12, 16, 17, 90, 236; emigration of, 19; on the miraculous, 132–33; portrayals of, 12, 206, 213n54, 257; relationship with laity, 82n43, 132, 262–63; on sexuality, 264; social status of, 9, 71, 90. *See also* confessors; Hesychasm; missionary movement; monasticism
Clowes, Edith, 268
communal consciousness (*sobornoe soznanie*), 73, 74, 82n43
Conference on Russian Religious Thought, 5
confession: authorial voice in, 188–89; clerical guides to, 180; as communal action, 178–79; confessor-penitent relationships, 185; Filaret-Novosil'tseva correspondence, 177, 189–90; goals of, 188, 189–90; instructional texts for, 180–81, 183;

language of, 177–78; preparation for, 178, 179–80; purpose of, 178–79; in Roman Catholicism, 178, 179, 192n19; in Russian literature, 191, 257–58; secrecy of, 15, 188, 189; secular, 182; spatial arrangements for, 179; spiritual growth as goal of, 188, 189
confessional writing: as autobiographical narratives, 188–89; hagiographic elements in, 183–84, 189; as life confession, 182–83, 184, 185; prayer and, 183; redemption in, 186–87; religious reading reflected in, 186, 187–88, 189; responses to, 189; style of, 183–84, 187–88
confessors: confessional writings of noblewomen, 182; influence on penitents, 184; instructional texts for, 180–81, 183; obligations of, 190; as penitents, 185–86; relations with penitent, 184, 189–90; spiritual direction offered by, 189–90
Constitutional Democratic (Kadet) Party (Konstitutsionno-demokraticheskaia partiia). See Kadet Party
The Contemporary (Sovremennik), 114
Cor ardens (Ivanov), 205
Corpus Areopagaticum (Pseudo-Dionysius), 198
Council of Ministers, 68
Crisis of Contemporary Legal Consciousness [(Krizis sovremennogo pravosoznaniia) Novgorodtsev], 244
Critique of Abstract Principles [(Kritika otvlechennykh nachal) Solov'ev], 216, 219, 220, 221–22, 223, 227, 231n20
Critique of Judgment (Kant), 117, 154
cross of Christ, 199–200
Cudworth, Ralph, 112, 121, 122

Damaskin (Semenov-Rudnev), 45
Danilevskii, Nikolai, 69, 73, 74
David (Biblical figure), 203–4
"The Death of Ivan Il'ich" (Tolstoy), 265
Decembrists, 24, 181

de Circourt, Anastasie (née Khliustina), 178
deification, 153, 165, 202, 217–18
deism, 117, 119, 123, 220
de Lubac, Henri, 198–99, 210n3
de Segur, Madame (née Rostopchina), 178
Desert Fathers, 156, 157, 165
D'iachenko, Grigorii, 135, 139
dianoia, 158, 164
Dimitrii (Tuptalo) of Rostov, Archbishop, 181, 197
Dimitrii of Uglich, Tsarevich, 47, 48–52, 54–55, 56, 57, 518
Dionysius, 198, 211n24
Dobroliubov, Nikolai, 114
Dobronravov, Nikolai, 23, 135
Dobrotoliubie (translation of Philokalia), 15, 16, 157
Doctor Zhivago [(Doktor Zhivago) Pasternak], 27, 253; beauty, 254, 261; Christological imagery in, 268, 269; criticism of Marxist ideology, 254; death of Zhivago's mother, 269; erotic line of the fabric in, 264, 265, 266, 268, 269, 271; female figure in, 264, 267, 268–69; interpretations of Christianity in, 260; Mary Magdalene in, 27, 255, 259, 261, 262, 269; poetry in, 259, 263–64, 269, 274n69; pokrov images in, 268; radicalism of, 254; revision of Tolstoyan narrative in, 261; Sima Tuntseva, 259, 260, 261–62; Solov'ev's influence on, 360; Vedeniapin's encounter with Vyvolochnov, 360
Dostoevsky, F. M., 3, 7, 12, 24, 25, 69, 73, 74
Dunn, John, 113

Eastern Christian mystical ascetism. See Hesychasm
edict (ukaz) of 1764, 15
elders and eldership (startsy/starchestvo), 3, 24, 91, 152, 156–57, 162, 164, 170n23
Emancipation Manifesto (1861), 3

Encyclical of the Eastern Patriarchs (1848), 92
Encyclopedic Dictionary Composed by Russian Scholars and Writers, 115–16
Encyklopädie und Methodologie der theologischen Wissenschaften (Hagenbach), 118, 119
Engelstein, Laura, 155
Enlightenment: Church responses to, 21; interpretations of, 152–55, 168n5; *lumière/lumières*, 152–53, 168n5; moral development of the human person, 58; Orthodox enlightenment (*liubomudrie*), 25, 48, 152, 224; philosophical modernity, 61n17; *The Pillar and Ground of the Truth* [(*Stolp i utverzhdenie istiny*) Florenskii], 20, 159–67, 266; *prosveshchenie* (enlightenment), 151, 153, 167n1; Radical Enlightenment, 61n17; rationalism, 45–46, 58, 88, 89, 93, 102, 159–61; reason in, 154–55; secular (*filosofiia*) v. Orthodox enlightenment (*liubomudrie*), 25; theodicy question, 47; use of term, 151–52. *See also* Florenskii, Pavel; Kireevskii, Ivan; *Philokalia*; Platon (Levshin), Metropolitan
Epstein, Mikhail, 213n51
Ern, Vladimir, 88
eroticism, 205, 253, 262, 269
Esiukov, Al'bert, 212n27
"The Essence of the Russian Orthodox Consciousness" [("Sushchestvo russkogo pravoslavnogo soznaniia") Novgorodtsev], 246
Eunomius, 164
Evagrius, 95, 202
Evlogii (Georgievskii), Metropolitan, 64–65
Extended Catechism [Filaret (Drozdov)], 183

Father Zosima (in Dostoevsky's *Brothers Karamazov*), 16
feast day of Tsarevich Dimitrii of Uglich (May 15), 47, 48, 50
Feast of the *Pokrov*, 269
Feast of the Transfiguration, 153–54, 166, 169n10
feat of virtue (*podvig dobrodeteli*), 53
Fedor Ivanovich, 47–48
fellowship (*sobornost'*), 22, 39n66, 76, 82n43, 238, 246
Feodor (Bukharev), Archimandrite, 6, 10
Feofan (Govorov) the Recluse, 15–16, 91, 98–99, 156, 188
Feofan (Prokopovich), 43, 44
Feofan (Tuliakov), 23, 134, 135
Feofan, bishop of Kronstadt, 140, 142
Festugière, Andrè-Jean, 158
Fichte, I. H., 136
Fichte, Johann Gottlieb, 23, 121
Filaret (Drozdov), Metropolitan, 16, 17, 156, 183, 187, 189–90
Filaret (Egorov), Archimandrite, 281
Filaret-Novosil'tseva correspondence, 177, 189–90
Filosofiia kul'ta [(*Philosophy of Cult*) Florenskii], 204
First State Duma (April 1906), 18, 251n39
Fleishman, Lazar, 254
flesh: beauty, 27, 266; in Scripture, 203–4; sex identified with sin, 173n58, 184, 185, 262, 263, 272n32; spirituality in contrast with, 141, 142, 143
Florenskii, Pavel: on beauty, 266–67, 268; on the common people, 161–62, 163; criticism of, 161, 166–67; education of, 24; on God's attributes, 99–103, 172n48; on Hegelian dialectical reason, 161, 172n45; on Hesychasm, 173n62; on intellectual preparation, 95; Isidor of the Gethsemane Skete as mentor of, 161–62; Kant's influence on, 161; on knowledge, 164–65; on light, 168n9; on the meaning of symbols, 103; on miracles, 143–44; Name-Glorifiers supported by, 88, 89–90, 92–93; Nikon challenged by, 92–94; and Philokalic discourse, 173n60, 173n62; on prayer, 95–96,

97–98, 102; rationalism challenged by, 159, 161, 163–64, 166–67; scientific world view, 144; sophiological movement, 204; on spirituality, 94, 95–96, 163–66; works: "About Superstition and Miracle," 143; *Filosofiia kul'ta* (*Philosophy of Cult*), 20, 159–67, 204, 266; *Iconostasis*, 266, 273n51; "The Light of the Truth," 164–66; *The Pillar and Ground of the Truth* (*Stolp i utverzhdenie istiny*), 20, 159–67, 266; "Two Worlds," 162–63

Florovsky, Georges, Father, 7, 34n20, 43, 45, 57, 89, 156, 161, 166, 279

Fonvizina, Natal'ia, confessional writings of: background of, 181–85; hagiographic elements in, 183–84, 189; as life confession, 182–83; prayers of, 183; redemption in, 186–87; religious reading reflected in, 186, 187–88, 189; sexual impropriety of, 182, 183, 184, 185; style of, 183–84, 187–88

Fourth State Duma (October 1917), 18

Frank, Semen, 5, 222, 239, 243, 244

freedom, 76–78, 240–41, 244–45, 280

free will, 56, 139–40

Freeze, Gregory L., 44, 277

Fundamental Laws of April 1906, 243

Giliarov-Platonov, N. P., 10

Gillen, Sean, 154

Gippius, Z. N., 12, 79

Glagolev, Sergei S., 17, 23, 135–36, 138, 141–42, 144

God: agency of, 24; anthropomorphization of, 124; closeness to, 158; conception of, 117; divine-human union, 62n37, 159, 164–66, 217–18; divine names of, 102–3; essence and operations of, 98, 99–100; in the historical development of religion, 122–24; human link with, 240; immanence of, 119–22, 140; and the kingdom of ends, 223–24; *lumière* as referring to, 152–53; manifestations of, 100; Providence (*Promysl*), 3, 52,

54–55, 121–23, 140; theodicy question, 46–47; *theoprepes*, 122; *theotis*, 99–100; transcendence of, 119–22, 120, 121, 140. *See also* deism; miracles; theism; theosis

Godmanhood (Solov'ev), 215, 216, 217–18, 221–22, 231n20

Godunov, Boris, 47–48

Goethe, Johann Wolfgang von, 207–8

Gogol', Nikolai, 3, 12, 263, 276

Golovina, Varvara, Countess, 178

Golubinskii, E. E., 18

Golubinskii, Fedor, Archpriest, 7, 10

Gorskii, A. V., 118

Gospels: divine light in, 152–53, 159, 166; on knowledge, 162–63; miracles in, 136, 137, 140; personal experience of, 204; and salvation, 200, 203; in Tolstoy's works, 257, 258, 271n15

Great Lent, 99, 179, 180, 189

The Great Menologion (Macarius), 198

Greek Desert Fathers, 156, 157, 165

Gregory of Nazianzus, 201

Grier, Philip T., 280

Groundwork of the Metaphysics of Morals (Kant), 219, 224, 232n26

Gustafson, Richard, 173n67, 222–23, 276

Hagenbach, K. R., 118–19, 120

Halki (Greek theological school), 87

happiness, 48–52

heart imagery, 158, 199–200, 203, 204, 205

Hegel, G. W. F., 23, 121, 136, 160, 199, 208–10

Heilbrun, Carolyn, 188

Herzen, Alexander, 12, 36n35, 113–14

Hesychasm: asceticism, 261–62, 263; communion with God, 98, 165–66; Jesus Prayer, 16, 87, 91, 97, 170n22; light of Tabor, 153–54, 166, 173n62; Mount Athos monks and, 22, 24, 85–87, 91–92; mystical union as goal of, 159, 164; Paisii Velichkovskii and the founding of, 15, 98–99, 157; piety, 3, 12; on prayer, 156, 158–59;

Hesychasm (continued)
    relationship of intellect and heart in, 158–59; spiritual elders and eldership (startsy/starchestvo), 3, 24, 91, 152, 156–57, 162, 164, 170n23; synergistic anthropology, 281. See also Name-Glorifiers (Imiaslavie); Philokalia
Historical and Critical Dictionary (Bayle), 115
historical-critical method, 17
"The Historical Tasks of Philosophy" [("Istoricheskie dela filosofii") Solov'ev], 221–22
History of Russian Philosophy (Zen'kovskii), 275, 279
Hitchcock, Edward, 136
holiness: and human perfectibility, 216, 224–26, 227
Holy Synod, 9, 10, 12, 15, 18, 68–69, 85–88
Homer, 122
"the human I" (Solov'ev), 218–19
human perfectibility, 216, 218, 220, 223–26, 232n29
Hume, David, 23, 112, 121, 134

Iamblichus, 196
Iconostasis (Florenskii), 266, 273n51
icons, 16, 131, 144–45, 197, 266, 268, 273n51
Ignatii (Brianchaninov), 23, 136–37, 141–45, 149n26, 156
Ilarion (Athonite schemamonk), 86, 87, 101
Il'in, I. A., 246
Imiaslavie (Name-Glorifiers). See Name-Glorifiers (Imiaslavie)
Imperial Moscow University, 24
Imperial Orthodox Missionary Society, 67
incarnation, 200, 204, 218, 223
Inquiry into the Sectarian Faith of Brynsk [(Rozysk o raskol'nicheskoi Brynskoi vere) Dimitrii (Tuptalo) of Rostov], 197
intellect (nous), 158–59, 163

In the Caucasus Mountains [(Na gorakh Kavkaza) Ilarion], 86, 87
Ioann (Sergiev) of Kronstadt, Father, 188
Isidor of the Gethsemane Skete, 161–62
Israel, Jonathan, 61n17
Iurkevich, P. I., 171n42
Ivanov, Viacheslav, 205
Ivantsov-Platonov, A. M., 10

Jacobi, F. H., 117, 119, 123–24
James, William, 23, 136
Jesus Christ: Chalcedonian Christology, 172n48, 222–23; cross of, 199–200; doctrine of consubstantiality, 161, 164, 165, 172n48; as ideal humanity, 225–26; imagery in Doctor Zhivago, 268, 269; incarnation of, 200, 204, 218, 223; kenosis of, 223; mandylion, 268; Mary Magdalene and, 27, 255, 257–59, 261, 262, 269; and the path to true knowledge, 161; resurrection of, 136, 137, 223; theosis attained by, 222–23
Jesus Prayer, 16, 87, 91, 96, 97, 170n22
John Chrysostom, 201
"The Joy of All Who Sorrow" (icon), 131, 144–45
Justification of the Good [(Opravdanie dobra) Solov'ev], 216, 223, 224, 225, 231n21, 232n29

Kadet Party, 236, 238, 243, 251n38
Kalitin, Petr, 198
Kant, Immanuel: on autonomy as self-determination, 219, 221, 239; on Christ as ideal humanity, 225–26; on Christianity, 227–28; dualism in thought of, 240; on the ethical community, 216–17, 226–27; on holiness, 216, 224–25; on human perfectibility, 216, 218, 220, 224–25; on the kingdom of ends, 216–17, 223–25, 226; on the kingdom of God, 216, 226–27; on miracles, 226, 233n55; morality of, 117–18, 120–21, 123, 216, 218–19, 224–25; on practical reason, 219; on pure religious faith, 154, 227;

on salvation, 228; on selfhood and human dignity, 239–41; on the supernatural, 123–24; on theism, 112, 118, 239; on the visible Church, 226–27; works: *Critique of Judgment*, 117, 154; *Groundwork of the Metaphysics of Morals*, 219, 224, 232n26; *Religion within the Limits of Reason Alone*, 112, 117, 118, 120, 121, 226. See also Solov'ev, Vladimir
Kareev, A. A., 18
Kareev, Nikolai I., 74
Katkov, M. N., 116
Kelly, Martha, 277
kenosis, 223
Kenworthy, Scott, 278
Khomiakov, Aleksei, 7, 9, 72, 78, 82n43, 113
Khomiakov, D. A., 18
Khoruzhii, Sergei, 105n18, 161, 172n45, 281
Kievan Caves Monastery (*Lavra*), 182, 281
Kiev-Mohyla Collegium, 14
Kiev Spiritual Academy, 8, 14, 68
Kiev Summer Theological Institute, 281
kingdom of God, 226–27, 244, 247. See also Godmanhood
Kireevskaia, Natal'ia, 188, 194n54
Kireevskii, Ivan: "believing reason" concept, 215; critique of Orthodoxy, 11–12, 72; German metaphysical idealism, 160–61; integral knowledge (*tselostnoe znanie*), 160; Makarii as mentor of, 171n44; patristic roots of philosophical practice in Russia, 160; secular enlightenment (*filosofiia*) v. Christian enlightenment (*liubomudrie*), 160; Slavophilism, 72, 113, 114; works: "On the Necessity and Possibility of New Principles in Philosophy" ("O neobkhodimosti i vozmozhnosti novykh nachal dlia filosofii"), 160–61
Kline, George L., 275, 280

Kliuchevskii, Vasilii, 75, 83n47
Koialovich, I. O., Archpriest, 18
Kollyvades movement, 157
Kornblatt, Judith, 256, 265, 276
Kotliarevskii, Sergei, 155, 239, 243
Kreutzer Sonata [(*Kreitserova sonata*) Tolstoy], 256, 260, 265, 273n36
Kubarikha (folk healer in *Doctor Zhivago*), 253, 268
Kudriavtsev-Platonov, V. D.: apologetics (*osnovnoe bogoslovie*), 118; chiliastic vision of, 116; education of, 111; on *Encyclopedic Dictionary Composed by Russian Scholars and Writers*, 116; on God's relationship with man, 122–23; on the historical development of religion, 120–23; on history of the development (*razvitie*) of religious consciousness, 117, 121; on immanence v. transcendence, 119–22; influence on Solov'ev, 23; Kant's influence on, 117–18, 119, 123; religious sense (*religioznoe chuvstvo*), 123; on secularization, 114, 119, 121; theism of, 23, 112, 113, 116, 117, 119–20, 121; works: *Lectures in the Philosophy of Religion*, 117, 120, 121, 124; "Religion: Its Essence and Provenance," 118

Ladouceur, Paul, 89
landowners, 243, 251n38
Lara (in *Doctor Zhivago*), 253, 259, 261, 262, 267–69
Lavrov, Petr, 113, 114, 115, 120
League of the Militant Godless (Soiuz voinstvuiushchikh bezbozhnikov), 19
Lectures in the Philosophy of Religion (Kudriavtsev), 117, 120, 121, 124
Lectures on Godmanhood [(*Chteniia o bogochelovechestve*) Solov'ev], 215, 216, 217–18, 219, 222
Leibniz, Gottfried Wilhelm, 46, 168n5
Lenin, Vladimir, 125, 205
Leskin, Dimitrii, 89

Lessing, Gotthold Ephraim, 134
Lev (elder of the Optina Pustyn' hermitage), 157
Liberation Movement (*Osvoboditel'noe dvizhenie*), 12, 236, 242–43, 244, 251n39
light imagery, 152–54, 159, 164–66, 168n5, 173n62
Linitskii, Petr, 145
liturgy: and beauty, 255; Great Lent, 99, 179, 180, 189; as illusionism, 257–58; influence of Pseudo-Dionysius the Areopagite on, 198; Mary Magdalene in Holy Wednesday liturgy, 262; Pasternak's characters, 255; revisions in, 14; Tolstoy's use of, 255, 257
Lomonosov, Mikhail, 206
Lossky, Vladimir, 89
Lotman, Iurii, 151, 153
Louth, Andrew, 158, 167n2, 172n52
love, 220, 260, 264–65, 268
Loviagin, Evgraf, 23, 135
lumière/lumières (use of terms), 152–53, 168n5

Macarius, Metropolitan, 198
"Magdalene" (Zhivago poem), 269
Magdalene, Mary, 27, 255, 257–59, 261, 262, 269
Makarii (elder of the Optina Pustyn' hermitage), 157, 194n54
Makarii (Glukharev), Hieromonk, 187
Manchester, Laurie, 66, 72
marriage, 263, 272n36
martyrdom, 47, 48–52, 181
Mary of Egypt, Saint, 189
Mary the Mother of God (*Bogomater'*), 269
Maslova, Katia (in *Resurrection* [(*Voskresenie*) Tolstoy]), 256, 258
Massillon, Jean Baptiste, 45
Matich, Olga, 263
Maximus the Confessor, 222–23
"The Meaning of Love" [("Smysl liubvi") Solov'ev], 220, 260, 264–65, 268
Mendelssohn, Moses, 117, 119

Merezhkovskii, Dmitrii S., 12, 78, 171n43, 265, 272n32
Meyendorff, John, Father, 89, 279
Michel, Alphonse, 178
Michelson, Patrick Lally, 233n51
Mill, John Stuart, 113
miracles: apologists on, 134, 141, 280; divine agency, 24, 137–38, 139–40; and the exercise of free will, 139–40; Gospel texts, 136, 137; icons, 16, 131, 144–45, 197, 266, 268, 273n51; laws of nature and, 138–40; modern views of, 133–34; perception and discernment of, 140–43; and personal agency, 139–40; in relation to science (*nauka*) of theology, 24; superstition, 143–44, 145; Western attitudes toward, 135–36
Missionary Digest (*Missionerskii sbornik*), 66
missionary movement: anti-sectarian missionary work in villages, 22, 65, 66, 69–70, 72; congresses, 70, 76, 78, 91; defining the Russian soul, 73–76, 78–79; education as goal of, 76; freedom of conscience, 76–77; internal mission, 14, 29, 64–65, 67–68; missionary training, 70; narratives of, 65–66; to Old Believers, 64, 67–68; publications of, 66, 68, 77, 79; renaissance of the parish, 76
Missionary Review (*Missionerskoe obozrenie*), 66, 68, 77, 79
Modest, Igumen (Strel'bitskii), 99
Mohyla, Petro, Metropolitan, 14, 180
monasticism: challenges to Synodal Church, 16; edict (*ukaz*) of 1764, 15; elders and eldership (*startsy/starchestvo*), 3, 24, 91, 152, 156–57, 162, 164, 170n23; Kievan Caves Monastery (*Lavra*), 182, 281; Optina Pustyn' hermitage, 15, 91, 157, 171n44, 194n54; secularization of monastic property, 15; Trinity-Sergius Monastery (*Lavra*), 13, 90, 91, 161, 184. *See also* Hesychasm; Name-Glorifiers (*Imiaslavie*)

moral law: on autonomy, 216, 242; on God, 117; on human dignity and personhood, 216; human perfectibility, 216, 218, 220, 223-27, 232n29; influences of, 26-27, 117-18, 123, 161, 215-16; Kantian, 117-18, 120-21, 123, 216, 218-19, 224-25; on miracles, 136; on the Pantheism Controversy, 119; rational ethics of, 216; reason in Enlightenment thought, 154-55; religion and, 120, 123-24, 154-55; theism of, 118

Moscow Psychological Society (Moskovskoe psikhologicheskoe obshchestvo), 10, 236, 239

Moscow Spiritual Academy (Moskovskaia dukhovnaia akademiia), 10, 14, 21, 65, 72, 138

Mount Athos monks, 22, 24, 85-87, 91-92

Müller, Max, 116

mystical experience. *See* Hesychasm

Name-Glorifiers (*Imiaslavie*): appeal to mysticism, 94; criticism of, 85-88, 92-93; Halki (Greek theological school), 87; Hesychasm controversy compared with, 98; Mount Athos monks as, 22, 24, 85-87, 91-92; "the Name of God is God Himself" (*Imia Bozhie est' Sam Bog*), 87, 91-92, 93; on the operations of God, 98; Palamite theology, 98, 99-100, 101; spiritual life v. academic theology, 89, 94-95; *theotis*, 99-100; and use of term "dogma," 92. *See also* Florenskii, Pavel; Nikon (Rozhdestvenskii), Archbishop

"the Name of God is God Himself" (*Imia Bozhie est' Sam Bog*), 87, 91-92, 93

Negrov, Alexander, 210n4

Nekhliudov (in *Resurrection* [(*Voskresenie*) Tolstoy]), 256, 258

Neptic Fathers, 163

A New Way (*Novyi put'*), 263

Nicene Creed, 172n48

Nicholas II, Tsar, 18, 77, 114

Nikol'skii, Iakov, 201

Nikon (Rozhdestvenskii), Archbishop: on the attributes of God, 96, 99-102; as bishop of Vologda, 90-91; character of, 90; on Church authority, 92; on dogma, 89, 91-92, 93, 94; on the essence of God, 102; fullness of the Church, 92; his philosophy of language, 91, 92, 93, 94; importance of theological education, 95; on the Jesus Prayer, 96, 97; on language, 93; monastic life of, 90, 91; on Name-Glorifiers (*Imiaslavie*), 22-23, 86, 87, 88, 89, 91-92; "the Name of God is God Himself" (*Imia Bozhie est' Sam Bog*), 91-92; on prayer, 96, 97-98, 101-2; on the spiritual life, 94-95; *Trinity Leaflets* (*Troitskie listki*) published by, 90; *The Way of a Pilgrim* (*Otkrovennye rasskazy strannika dukhovnomy svoemu ottsu*), 16, 91

nous (intellect), 158-59, 163

Novgorodtsev, Pavel: anti-utopian social philosophy, 237, 244-45, 246; engagement with religion, 238; on the existence of a transcendental absolute, 240; on freedom, 240-42, 244-45; on idealism, 27, 228-29, 238-39; individual self-perfection, 244; intellectuals associated with, 239; Kant's influence on, 239-41; kingdom of God, 247; liberal social philosophy of, 237; link between religion and politics, 245-46; Moscow Psychological Society, 10, 236, 239; natural law, 242; participation in Liberation Movement, 243-44, 251n39; on personhood, 239-41; policy platform of, 245; on religious belief, 237; on religious consciousness, 245-46; on Russian Orthodoxy, 155, 246-47; on self-determination, 241; social Christianity, 241; Solov'ev's influence on, 240-41; works: *Crisis of Contemporary Legal Consciousness* (*Krizis sovremennogo pravosoznaniia*), 244; "equality as a starting point"

Novgorodtsev, Pavel (*continued*) (*ravenstvo iskhodnogo punkta*), 245, 246; "The Essence of the Russian Orthodox Consciousness" ("Sushchestvo russkogo pravoslavnogo soznaniia"), 246; *Problems of Idealism* (*Problemy idealizma*), 27, 228–29; *On the Social Ideal* (*Ob obshchestvennom ideale*), 244, 245

Novoselov, Mikhail, 88

Novosil'tseva, Ekaterina (née Countess Orlova), 177, 189

obrazovannoe obshchestvo (educated society), 3–4

occultism, 143, 185

Old Believers, 14, 29, 64, 67–68, 72, 197, 199, 210n4

Olshausen, Hermann, 136

"On Counterfeits" [("O poddelkakh") Solov'ev], 228

"One Hundred and Fifty Chapters" (Palamas), 98–99

"On the Reasons for the Collapse of the Medieval Worldview" [("O prichinakh upadka srednevekovogo mirosozertsania") Solov'ev], 228

"On the Necessity and Possibility of New Principles in Philosophy" [("O neobkhodimosti i vozmozhnosti novykh nachal dlia filosofii") Kireevskii], 160–61

On the Social Ideal [(*Ob obshchestvennom ideale*) Novgorodtsev], 244, 245

Optina Pustyn' hermitage, 15, 91, 157, 171n44, 194n54

Orfanitskii, Ioann, 23, 135, 139

Orthodox Church. *See* Russian Orthodoxy

"The Orthodox Church and its Relationship to the Spiritual Life of New Russia" [("Pravoslavnaia tserkov' v ee otnoshenii k dukhovnoi zhizni novoi Rossii") Novgorodtsev], 246

Orthodox Interlocutor (*Pravoslavnyi sobesednik*), 17

Orthodox Review (*Pravoslavnoe obozrenie*), 10

Ostroumov, Stefan, 23, 134, 135, 138, 141

Paert, Irina, 157, 170n23

Palamas, Gregory: defense of Hesychasm, 157, 173n62; on the mystical union, 159; *Philokalia*, 15, 24, 89, 98–99; relationship of intellect and heart, 159; theology of, 99, 100. *See also* Hesychasm

pantheism, 117, 119, 123, 220

Pasternak, Boris: art's effects on society, 254; ascetic self-restraint rejected by, 261–62; beauty, 254, 261, 268; characters' responses to liturgy, 255; the erotic in works of, 255, 262; fabric imagery, 264, 265, 266, 268; knowledge of Florenskii's work, 266; materiality in *Doctor Zhivago*, 263–64, 265, 266, 268, 269; Nobel Prize awarded to, 254; Orthodox Church criticized by, 261–62; poetry of, 259, 263–64, 269, 274n69; Religious-Philosophical Meetings, 262–63, 266; Solov'ev's influence on, 255, 260–61, 264, 265, 360; Tolstoy's influence on, 254–55, 259, 270n4. *See also Doctor Zhivago* [(*Doktor Zhivago*) Pasternak]

pathos, 209–10

Paths of Russian Theology (Florovsky), 279

Paul the Apostle, 50–51, 53, 55

penitents: confessor-penitent relationships, 185; instructional texts for, 180–81; noblewomen as, 177–78; reconciliation of, 180, 192n19

perfectibility, human, 216, 218, 220, 223–27, 232n29

personalist theory, 239–40

personhood: dignity, 216, 225, 245; divine element in, 240; foundations of, 240; freedom, 241–42, 245; practical reason, 220; rational autonomy, 220; sanctity, 239–40; self-determination, 216, 217, 218–26, 232n29, 241

Peter I, Tsar, 15, 16, 43, 44, 132
Philokalia, 15, 24, 89, 152; as experiential philosophy, 158; intellect (*nous*) in, 158–59, 163; Kollyvades movement, 157; mystical ascetic practice, 157; noetic reception of, 167n2, 172n52; personal moral perfection, 158; relationship of intellect and heart in, 158–59; revival of, 89, 98–99, 157–58; translation of, 201; union with God, 165–66
philosophy of similarity (*homoiousian* philosophy), 165, 172n48
The Pillar and Ground of the Truth [(*Stolp i utverzhdenie istiny*) Florenskii], 20, 159–67, 266
Pisarev, Dmitrii, 114
Plato, 88, 121, 122
Platon (Fiveiskii), Archbishop, 190
Platon (Levshin), Metropolitan: on anagogical ascent, 26, 198, 200–202, 212n29; Christianity of the heart, 199; criticism of, 56–57; on the cross of Christ, 199–200; on Dimitrii of Uglich, 47, 48–50; enlightened orientation of, 26, 45, 57–58; historicist sensibility of, 57–58; on Holy Scripture, 196, 203; impact of Enlightenment on, 26, 57, 200–201; on the movement to the spiritual, 202; on the natural knowledge of God, 199; pan-European religious Enlightenment, 21; on the relationship between revealed and natural theology, 199; relations with imperial family, 179–80; on the righteous sufferer, 55–57; self-witnessing of the human heart, 199–200; on sensory perception, 200–201; theodicy question, 47; on union of body and soul, 202. *See also* sermons of Platon (Levshin)
Pobedonostsev, Konstantin P., 10, 12, 64, 71
pochvenniki (enthusiasts of the soil), 69
poetry, Russian, 206–7, 259, 263–64, 269, 274n69
pokrov (Mary's protective veil), 268

polytheism, 123–24
Ponticus, Evagrius, 85
Poole, Randall, 24, 154, 240, 279
Pope, Alexander, 46
Popov, I. V., 18
Porfirii, Bishop (Uspenskii), 99
post-Soviet Orthodox academic institutions, 282
Powell, Bladen, 136
prayer: communion with God, 96–98; as confession, 183; grace, 97–98; Hesychasm on, 156, 158–59; Jesus Prayer, 16, 87, 91, 96, 97; at mass, 257; Name-Glorifiers (*Imiaslavie*) on, 89–90; name of God in, 94, 97–98; subjectivity in, 96–97
Predtechenskii, Andrei, 23, 24, 138–39, 148n21
priests: celibacy, 29, 263; hierarchy of, 28–29; in lay religious thought, 12; punitive actions against, 19. *See also* confession; missionary movement; penitents
Principles of Integral Knowledge [*Filosofskie nachala tsel'nogo znaniia* (Solov'ev)], 215, 216
Problems of Idealism [(*Problemy idealizma*) Novgorodtsev,], 27, 228–29
Problems of Idealism [(*Problemy idealizma*) seminar 1902], 77, 239
Protestantism, 75, 113, 117–18, 119, 120–21, 133
Providence (*Promysl*), 3, 52, 54–55, 121–23, 140
Provisional Government (March 1917), 18–19
Pseudo-Dionysius the Areopagite. *See* Dionysius
Pushkin, Alexander S.: Belinskii's criticism of, 196, 205, 206–7, 213n46; Goethe compared with, 207; mystery in works of, 208; nature in works of, 207; his painting in poetry, 207; realism of, 207–8; and Russian poetry, 206–7; secular scriptures of, 196, 205
Pyman, Avril, 161

Questions of Philosophy and Psychology
   (*Voprosy filosofii i psikhologii*), 10

radical Enlightenment, 46, 61n17
Rampton, Vanessa, 24, 279
rationalism, 45–46, 58, 88, 89, 93, 102, 159–61
realism, 88, 207–8, 254
Reimarus, Hermann Samuel, 23, 136
"Religion: Its Essence and Provenance" (Kudriavtsev), 118
Religion within the Boundaries of Mere Reason (Kant). See *Religion within the Limits of Reason Alone* (Kant)
Religion within the Limits of Reason Alone (Kant), 112, 117, 118, 120, 121, 226
Religious-Philosophical Meetings, 12, 77, 79, 262–63, 266
Religious-Philosophical Society, 65, 68, 77–78
Renan, Ernest, 23, 136
resurrection, 133–34, 136, 137, 153
Resurrection [(*Voskresenie*) Tolstoy]: beauty in, 254–55, 258–59, 261, 271n12; Church service described in, 257–58; female body in, 258; Mary Magdalene in, 257, 258; Pasternak's relationship with, 254–55, 256; religious conversion in, 258; Solov'ev on, 265–66
revealed theology, 211n16
Revolution of 1905, 11, 17–18, 243, 244, 245
Roger, Jacques, 152, 153
Roman Catholicism, 178, 179, 192n19
Rothe, Richard, 118, 119
Rousseau, Jean-Jacques, 112, 182, 184
Rozanov, Vasilii, 78, 263, 266
Russian Christian Humanities Academy, 282
Russian Civil War (1918–20), 19
Russian Orthodoxy: authority in, 9, 14; development of, 3, 13–18; feast days, 30, 47, 48, 50, 62n36, 153–54, 166, 167n1, 169n10, 269; individualism, 246–47; light in, 152–54, 159, 164–66, 168n5, 173n62; in the modern era, 275–83; Old Believers, 14, 29, 64, 67–68, 72, 197, 199, 210n4; Petrine reforms in, 16, 18, 43, 44, 58; publications of, 16–17; Russian literature and engagement with, 276–77; Soviet Russia, 19, 191, 277, 278; spiritual academies, 10, 14, 21, 65, 72, 138; *Spiritual Regulation* (*Dukhovnyi reglament*), 15. See also Hesychasm; Jesus Christ; missionary movement; monasticism; Name-Glorifiers (*Imiaslavie*)
Russian religious-philosophical studies, development of, 275–76
Russian Religious Thought (1996), 5, 276, 278–79
Russian religious thought in the English-speaking world, 276–77

Sack, August Friedrich Wilhelm, 45
Saint Andrew's Biblical Theological Institute, 282
Saint Filaret's Orthodox Christian Institute, 282
Saint Petersburg, 8, 16–18, 65, 68, 77–78, 138, 282
Saint Tikhon's Orthodox Humanities University, 282
Saint Vasilii Brotherhood of Riazan' diocese, 66
Saint Vladimir's Orthodox Theological Seminary, 279
Samarin, F. D., 18
Samarin, Iurii, 18, 113
Savior as Bridegroom, 184
Schelling, Friedrich Wilhelm Joseph von, 23, 121, 136, 160, 220, 223, 281
Schmemann, Alexander, Father, 279
Scripture. *See* Bible
self-determination, 216, 217, 218–26, 232n29, 241
sensuality, 264, 265, 266, 268, 269, 271
Serafim of Sarov, Saint, 15, 91, 157, 162, 166
Sergii (Shein), Archmandrite, 19

Sergii (Stragorodskii), Archbishop, 87
Sergius of Radonezh, Saint, 13, 168n9
Sermon on the Mount, 49
sermons of Platon (Levshin): on Dimitrii
    of Uglich, 48–50, 51, 54–55, 56, 57;
    divine providence in, 52; everyday
    life in, 52–53; human free will, 56,
    62n37; human happiness in, 48–52;
    the righteous sufferer, 47; scholarly
    investigation of historical events v.
    moral lessons of events, 57–58;
    scriptural sources of, 49, 51, 196, 203;
    spiritual courage, 53–54
Seton-Watson, Hugh, 277
sexuality, 182, 183, 184, 185, 263
Shaposhnikov, L. E., 6
Shevzov, Vera, 66, 72, 82n43, 278, 280
Short History of the Russian Church
    (Platon [Levshin], Metropolitan),
    57
Shpet, Gustav, 197, 210n3
shtundism, 68, 73
Sidorova, Marina, 193n24
Sigov, Konstantin, 281
Silver Age, 12, 72, 77, 78, 238–39, 277
Sima Tuntseva (*Doctor Zhivago*), 259,
    260, 261–62
sin: anagogical ascent, 197–204, 212n29;
    in confessional writings of noble-
    women, 182; sexuality, 263
skepticism, 141
Skvortsov, Vasilii M., 68, 77, 79
Slavic studies, development of, 275
Slavonic-Greek-Latin Academy
    (Moscow), 14, 45
Slavophilism, 69, 73–76, 82n43, 114
Smirnov, Petr, 23, 139
Smith, Oliver, 24, 182, 223, 229n1
sobornost', 238
Society for the Love of Wisdom
    (Obshchestvo liubomudriia), 281
Solov'ev, Vladimir: art and realization of
    humanity's full potential, 255; author-
    ship of works on, 279; on beauty,
    254, 255, 261, 264–65; Bogoliubov
    influenced by, 78; Christology of,
    172n48, 222–23; divine principle as
    the eternal all-one, 217–18; free
    theocracy, 217, 226; Godmanhood,
    215, 216, 217–18, 221, 231n20; on
    human perfectibility, 216, 218–21,
    223, 225, 232n29; Kantian philosophy
    of, 25, 215–17, 220–21, 224, 226;
    the kingdom of ends, 224, 226; on
    the kingdom of God, 216, 223;
    Kudriavtsev-Platonov's influence on,
    23; Maximus the Confessor's influence
    on, 222–23; on miracles, 136, 226,
    233n55; on moral religion, 215–16,
    217, 219, 228, 231n21; on the mystical
    experience, 217, 231n17; Novgorod-
    tsev on, 240–41; Pasternak influenced
    by, 260–61; on reason and faith, 26,
    215, 217, 219, 229n1; on revelation,
    219, 280; on self-determination,
    218–21, 222, 232n29, 241; on Tolstoy,
    265–66; use of fiction by, 265–66;
    works: *Critique of Abstract Principles*
    (*Kritika otvlechennykh nachal*), 216,
    219, 220, 221–22, 223, 227, 231n20;
    Justification of the Good (*Opravdanie
    dobra*), 216, 223, 224, 225, 231n21,
    232n29; *Lectures on Godmanhood*
    (*Chteniia o bogochelovechestve*), 215,
    216, 217–18, 219, 222; "The Meaning
    of Love" ("Smysl liubvi"), 220, 260,
    264–65, 268; "On Counterfeits"
    ("O poddelkakh"), 228; *Principles of
    Integral Knowledge* (*Filosofskie nachala
    tsel'nogo znaniia*), 215, 216
Sophia Ivanova [*Iconostasis* (Florenskii)],
    266
sophiological movement, 204–5
Soviet Russia, 19, 191, 277, 278
Spalding, Johann Joachim, 45
Spencer, Herbert, 23, 116, 136
Spinoza, Baruch, 23, 135
spiritual academies, 8, 10, 14, 17, 21, 45,
    65, 68, 72, 138
spiritual elders and eldership
    (*startsy/starchestvo*), 3, 24, 91, 152,
    156–57, 162, 164, 170n23

Spiritual Regulation (*Dukhovnyi reglament*), 15
Stakhovich, Mikhail, 76–77
startsy/starchestvo (spiritual elders/eldership), 3, 24, 91, 152, 156–57, 162, 164, 170n23
Strauss, David, 136
Struve, Petr, 12, 77, 239, 243, 244, 248
Stuke, Horst, 168n5
Subbotin, Nikolai, 72
sud'ba (God's judgment), 56, 62n36
Sukhova, Nataliia, 137
Sumarokov, Aleksandr P., 49
Svetchina, Sofia, 178
Svetlov, Pavel, 18, 23, 135, 140, 144
Symeon the New Theologian, Saint, 159
Synodal Church, 4, 6, 10–13, 15–16
Systematic Theology (Hagenbach), 118–19

Tareev, Mikhail, 137, 205
Taylor, A. E., 113
theism: Church Fathers as source of, 120; dipolar theism, 119; Enlightenment, 154; and the future of the Russian Empire, 117; humanization of God, 119; Kant on, 112, 118, 227; of Kudriavtsev, 23, 112–13, 116, 117, 119, 121; moral law, 216; pantheism, 117, 119, 123, 220; providential God in, 122–23; as reasonable faith, 154; Systematic Theology (Hagenbach), 118–19
theodicy, 46–56
Theological Herald, 16
theoprepes, 122
theosis (deification/divinization): anagogical ascent, 197–204, 212n29; Chalcedonian Christology, 222; of Christ, 222–23; Godmanhood (Solov'ev), 215, 216, 217–18, 221–22, 231n20; human perfectibility, 202, 216, 218, 220, 223–27, 232n29; incarnation, 200, 204, 218, 223; mystical union, 159; resurrection, 136, 137, 153. *See also* deification

theotis, 99–100
Tikhon (Bellavin), Patriarch of Moscow and All Russia, 18, 19
Tikhon of Zadonsk, Saint, 181, 190, 192n21, 212n27
Tillotson, John, 45
Time of Troubles (1598–1613), 47, 55
Toland, John, 134
Tolstoy, Lev, 9, 12, 93; on art, 254, 256, 259, 271n12; beauty identified with art, 254, 256–57, 271n12; on Church liturgy, 255, 257; the erotic in works of, 255; excommunication of, 12, 256; Gospels in works of, 257, 258, 271n15; parable of the fallen woman, 258; self-restraint advocated by, 261; Solov'ev on, 265–66; use of fiction by, 265–66; works: *Anna Karenina*, 265; "The Death of Ivan Il'ich," 265; *Kreutzer Sonata* (*Kreitserova sonata*), 256, 260, 265, 273n36; *Resurrection* (*Voskresenie*), 254–59, 261, 265–66; "What Is Art?" ("Chto takoe iskusstvo"), 254, 256, 258, 271n12
Tonia (wife of Zhivago), 269
"transfigured Eros" (Vysheslavtsev), 205
Trench, Richard, 136
Trinity Leaflets (*Troitskie listki*), 90
Trinity-Sergius Monastery (*Lavra*), 13, 90, 91, 161, 184
Troitskii, S. V., 87
tropology, 196, 197, 198, 199
Trubetskoi, E. N., 18, 220, 229, 232n29, 239
Trubetskoi, Sergei, 136, 239
truth (*istina*), 151, 154, 163, 208
Tuliakov, Vasilii Stepanovich. *See* Feofan, bishop of Kronstadt
"Turmoil" ["Smiatenie" (Zhivago poem)], 269
"Two Worlds" (Florenskii), 162–63
Tylor, E. B., 116

Uspenski, Boris, 151, 281
utopianism, 220, 228–29, 237, 244–45, 246

Valliere, Paul, 6, 235
Vasilii Shuiskii, Tsar, 47
Vedeniapin, Nikolai (*Doctor Zhivago*), 259–61, 267
Velichkovskii, Paisii, 15, 98–99, 157
Veniamin (Kazanskii), Metropolitan of Petrograd and Gdov, 19
Vielogorskii, Iosif, 178
Vissarion (Nechaev), bishop of Kostroma, 140
Vladimir (Bogoiavlenskii), Metropolitan, 79
Vladimir (Aliavdin) of Tobol'sk, Archbishop, 187
Voltaire, 46–47
Vyborg appeal (1906), 251n39
Vysheslavtsev, Boris, 205
Vyvolochnov (*Doctor Zhivago*), 262, 360, 361

Wagner, William, 66
The Way of a Pilgrim (*Otkrovennye rasskazy strannika dukhovnomy svoemu ottsu*), 16, 91

Weber, Max, 170n23
"What Is Art?" [("Chto takoe iskusstvo") Tolstoy], 254, 256, 258, 271n12
Williams, Rowan, 277
Wirtschafter, Elise, 154
Witt, Susanna, 266, 273n51
Wolf, F. A., 120
Wolff, Christian, 45
Works of the Holy Fathers in Russian Translation, 16

Xenophanes, 122

zakonomernnost', 114
Zen'kovskii, V. V., 275, 279
Zernov, Nicolas, 6
Zhivago, Iurii (*Doctor Zhivago*, Pasternak), 259, 267–68